# LANDSCAPE ARCHITECT'S

*Portable*
*Handbook*

# LANDSCAPE ARCHITECT'S
## *Portable Handbook*

Nicholas T. Dines *&* Kyle D. Brown

Jeffrey D. Blankenship
ASSISTANT EDITOR

**McGraw-Hill**

New York • San Francisco • Washington, D.C. • Auckland • Bogatá • Caracas • Lisbon
London • Madrid • Mexico City • Milan • Montreal • New Delhi • San Juan
Singapore • Sydney • Tokyo • Toronto

Cataloging-in-Publication Data on file with the Library of Congress

# *McGraw-Hill*

A Division of The *McGraw·Hill* Companies

13 14 15 16 17 18 19 20  QDB QDB  14 13 12

ISBN 978-0-07-134422-7
MHID 0-07-134422-5

*The sponsoring editor for this book was Wendy Lochner and the production supervisor was Pamela A. Pelton. Design: Jeff Potter / Potter Publishing Studio; Susan Gierman / Suzani Design. Production: Jeff Potter (chief), Soren Johnson, Ben Shippee.*

*Printed and bound by Quad/Graphics.*

McGraw-Hill books are available at special quantity discounts to use as premiums and sales promotions, or for use in corporate training programs. For more information, please write to the Director of Special Sales, Professional Publishing, McGraw-Hill, Two Penn Plaza, New York, NY 10121-2298. Or contact your local bookstore.

For Susan, Betsy, and Kirin.

# CONTENTS

## 2  Techniques

**3** **Devices**

## 4 Administration

# ACKNOWLEDGEMENTS

THE COMPLETION OF THIS BOOK would not have been possible without the assistance of a significant group of individuals. We are grateful for their combined efforts on behalf of this project and acknowledge our appreciation of their fine work.

Jeffrey Blankenship served as assistant editor and was an essential participant in establishing editorial policy, as well as the authoring of many important chapters. We truly thank him for his diligence, important contributions, and his critical perspective. This book could not have been conceived or completed without his ideas.

A number of students at the University of Massachusetts and California State Polytechnic University, Pomona contributed to this effort. We thank Michael Schreiber for his proofreading and graphics assistance; Amy Schulenberg for her work on graphics; Betsy Brown and Kirin Joya Makker for their assistance with proofreading; and the staff from the second edition of *Time-Saver Standards for Landscape Architecture,* who contributed a number of graphics included in this book.

The Department of Landscape Architecture and Regional Planning at the University of Massachusetts in Amherst generously provided the research office for this book. Special thanks go to Dale Morrow for her clerical assistance. In addition, we acknowledge the support of the California State Polytechnic University, Pomona, in particular Linda Sanders, FAIA, Dean of the College of Environmental Design. Special thanks also go to the firm of Lewis Scully Gionet, Inc. for their support and invaluable input.

We wish to also acknowledge the outstanding work of Potter Publishing Studio in final design and layout of the book. Jeff Potter's attention to detail and dedication to this project were unsurpassed. We also thank his staff, in particular Soren Johnson and Ben Shippee, for their excellent work. Finally, we wish to acknowledge McGraw-Hill for sponsoring this project, and the leadership, trust, and support offered by our editor, Wendy Lochner.

# INTRODUCTION

# *A Framework for Design*

# 1

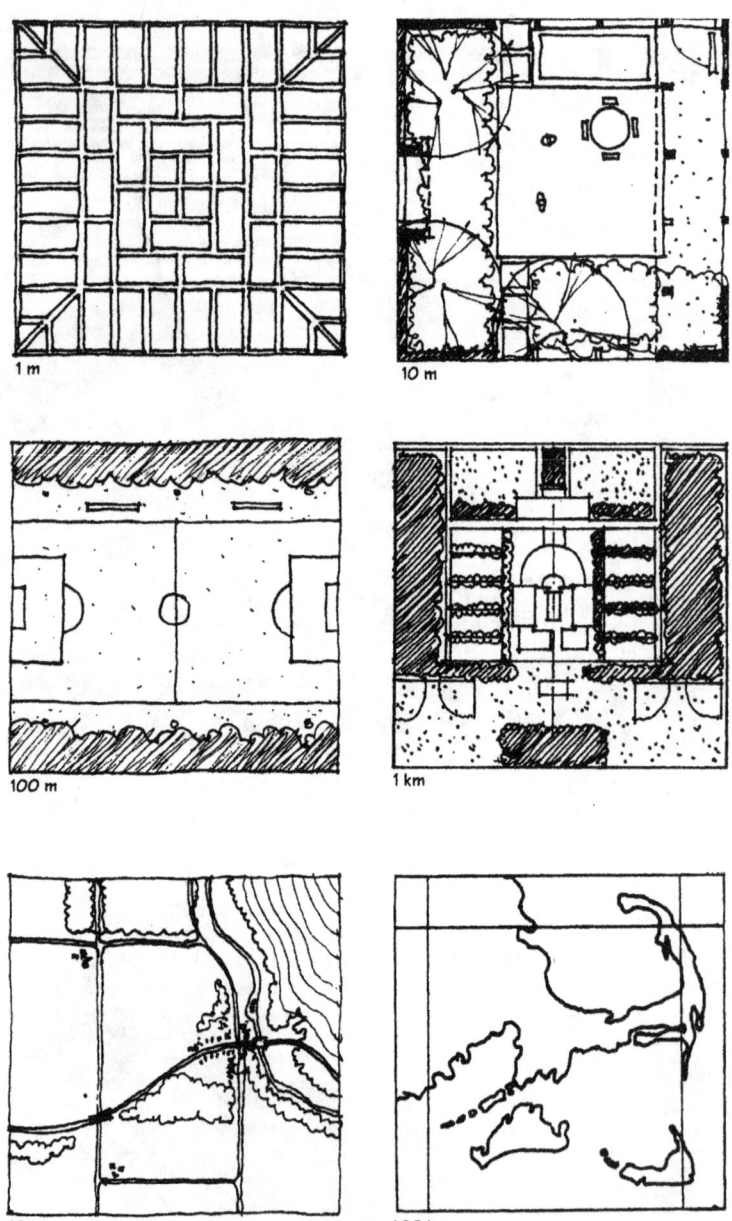

1 m

10 m

100 m

1 km

10 km

100 km

## DETAIL AND SPATIAL SCALES

These scales encompass detail construction and garden design. They reveal the detailed artistic expression of the designer and the craft of the builder. The user is aware of the degree of enclosure, color, light quality, odors, and pattern of arranged detail features (benches, tables, artwork, signs, etc.). Spatial depth is focused on foreground elements. Any Landscape Architectural project that results in a built work, regardless of its overall size, is inherently concerned with these scales.

## PLACE AND NEIGHBORHOOD SCALES

These scales are associated with most land use and design development projects. Design standards for specific land use types (housing, athletic fields, parking lots, etc.), pedestrian, and vehicular circulation are central concerns. A serial sequence of pedestrian or vehicular movement is typically required to comprehend the neighborhood scale.

## COMMUNITY AND REGIONAL SCALES

These scales focus on land use and landscape planning, ecological habitat and stormwater management, transportation, and infrastructure planning which may transcend local political boundaries. The "sense of the region," which is often perceived through important nodes, landmarks, paths, and edges that define spatial boundaries, as well as natural features such as topography, vegetation and climate. Maps are typically required to perceive the region as a whole, and citizen participation is particularly influential at these scales of concern.

IN 1968, THE OFFICE OF Charles and Ray Eames produced a ten-minute documentary film entitled *Powers of Ten*, illustrating what the universe looks like at different scales. The film (and book of the same name) provides a series of framed views centered on a picnic spot along the lake front in Chicago. Each framed view is ten times the size of the previous smaller frame. The intent of the filmmakers was to illustrate the extent of our scientific knowledge, and illustrate the interrelationship of patterns that are revealed at varying scales.

The notion of scale articulated in this film is immensely important to Landscape Architecture. Our work tends to focus on only a few of the scales illustrated by the film: Primarily between 1 meter resolution ($10^0$), and 100 kilometer resolution ($10^5$). But the Landscape Architect must consider the interrelationship between these scales, as well as larger and smaller scales. John Tillman Lyle stressed this point eloquently in his book *Design for Human Ecosystems* when he wrote:

> Landscapes, like people, rarely stand alone. Every landscape is joined with all other landscapes in a network of interdependence that extends over the entire earth. Everything, as the saying goes, is indeed related, at some level, to everything else. So when we shape a landscape of any size, we need to place it in a larger perspective, to see the web of relationships and avoid breaking critical strands, and sometimes perhaps to create new ones. (p. 24).

This web of relationships that joins landscapes at various scales is comprised of a wide spectrum of ecological, cultural, and economic processes. In order to avoid "breaking critical strands" Landscape Architects have proposed a number of methods or frameworks to structure analysis and design in response to these processes at multiple scales (consult references at the end of this chapter). These frameworks may articulate differences in terms of epistemology or terminology, but most reflect that Landscape Architecture is principally concerned with 1) diagnosing or analyzing situations influenced by ecological, cultural and economic factors at multiple scales, a process we call *interpretation;* 2) proposing solutions, a process we call *conceptualization;* 3) assessing both intended and unintended consequences of design decisions, a process known as *evaluation;* and 4) presenting ideas through verbal and graphic *communication.* These actions constitute a design process that is typically iterative in nature, often requiring the conceptualization and evaluation of several solutions before determining the most appropriate course of action.

# DESIGN FRAMEWORK

In this chapter we propose a framework for interpretation, conceptualization, evaluation, and communication at multiple scales, regardless of the type of planning or design project. The framework articulates a series of axioms that guide the work of Landscape Architects related to each action at various scales of concern, and is based on the exponential "frames" of reference outlined in the film, *Powers of Ten*, beginning with a landscape 1 meter by 1 meter in size ($10^0$) up to a landscape 100 km by 100 km in size ($10^5$). Figures 1.2 through 1.7 describe these axioms as they pertain to each of the particular scales of inquiry.

This framework is not intended to supplant or suggest one appropriate design approach or method. Rather its intent is to emphasize the importance of addressing multiple scales in design. A fundamental premise is that the concept of a "site," representing the boundaries of our work, must be re-conceptualized as a "place," representing the confluence of seen and unseen environmental, cultural, and economic processes operating at larger and smaller scales. Design of a particular place must account for the effects of larger patterns from these processes not perceptible at the human sensory scale. Conversely, planning policies and concepts affecting large land areas require a heightened awareness of implications for the human experience "on the ground."

The remaining chapters of this book provide information useful to a wide variety of common project types pursued by Landscape Architects and other designers. Where appropriate, the issue of scale is presented through opening triptych graphics and captions designed to provide general information about design strategies in varying contexts. In addition, general diagnostic questions are provided in each chapter, intended to prompt the designer to consider important issues in developing appropriate design solutions.

## Defining Parameters

Historically, the work of landscape architecture encompasses a wide variety of contexts and scales. Work may include greenway or landscape planning over vast landscapes, institutional master planning, arboretum planning, urban design, housing, recreation, or public garden design. *The type of project dictates the primary scales of concern for the Landscape Architect.* For example, forest management, campus planning and garden design detailing require very different types, scales, and resolution of data. However, any project directly resulting in construction drawings and a built work inherently requires scales of concern down to the detail scale, regardless of the size of the overall project. Figure 1.1 illustrates the primary scales of concern for common project types.

## Interpretation

Interpretation requires analysis and assessment of various data, including ecological, cultural, and economic processes. These analyses and assessments result in a diagnosis of existing conditions that indicate appropriate responses to be explored during conceptualization.

### Axiom 1: Landscape Architects must have general knowledge of ecological, cultural, and economic processes operating at all scales, regardless of the project.

Landscape architecture operates at the confluence of economics, culture, and the natural environment. The processes that characterize these three realms operate at multiple scales, often larger and smaller than the designer's primary scales of concern (e.g. the global economy, microscopic pathogens, etc.). While specific knowledge of all processes influencing a project is impossible, the Landscape Architect must be cognizant of general trends and phenomena that may have unforeseen consequences on the viability of their proposed solution.

### Axiom 2: Landscape Architects must have particular knowledge of ecological, cultural, and economic processes operating at the primary scales of concern.

While general knowledge of ecological, cultural and economic processes operating at all scales is important, more specific knowledge of these processes related to the primary scales of concern (Figure 1.1) is imperative (e.g. user characteristics, critical natural resources, etc.). Data related to these systems should be compiled, analyzed and assessed to determine appropriate design responses to the given problem. This data must characterize the functioning of these processes at a particular time and place in order to adequately assess existing conditions. Precise data required is a function of the project's intent and the environmental context of the proposal.

### Axiom 3: Resolution of required data increases as one moves towards the detail scale.

Detailed design requires specific spatial and dimensional choices, which in turn require more precise base data. Conversely, landscape planning of large areas addresses gross patterns and processes characterizing the regional landscape. Data used in interpretation must be appropriate to the scale of inquiry, to avoid information overload and excessive cost stemming from data that is too precise, or false assumptions stemming from data that is too general. To illustrate these differences in data needs, Table 1.1 lists common data for just a few factors that may be appropriate at different scales of inquiry.

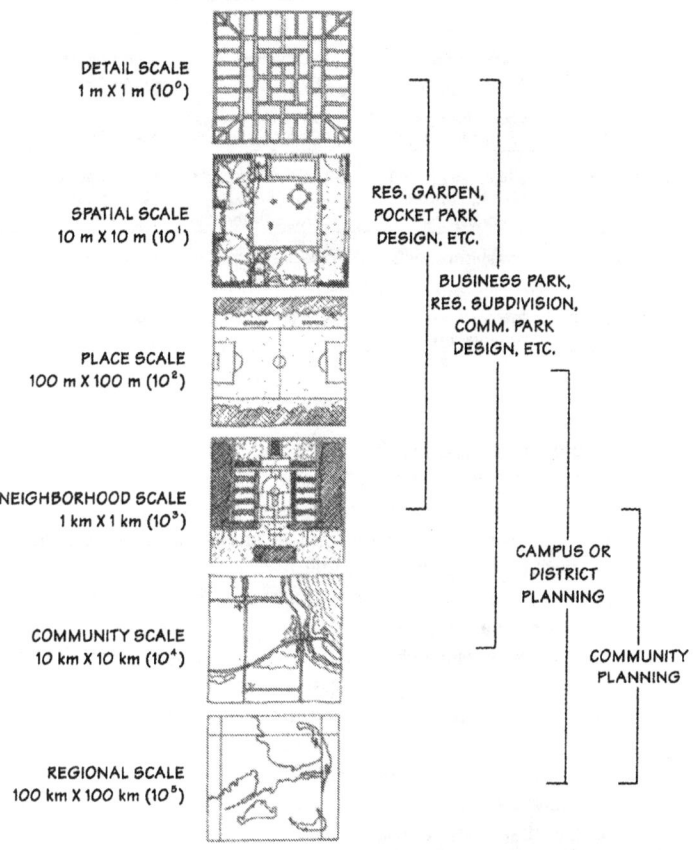

DETAIL SCALE
1 m X 1 m ($10^0$)

SPATIAL SCALE
10 m X 10 m ($10^1$)

PLACE SCALE
100 m X 100 m ($10^2$)

NEIGHBORHOOD SCALE
1 km X 1 km ($10^3$)

COMMUNITY SCALE
10 km X 10 km ($10^4$)

REGIONAL SCALE
100 km X 100 km ($10^5$)

RES. GARDEN,
POCKET PARK
DESIGN, ETC.

BUSINESS PARK,
RES. SUBDIVISION,
COMM. PARK
DESIGN, ETC.

CAMPUS OR
DISTRICT
PLANNING

COMMUNITY
PLANNING

**Figure 1.1. Typical primary scales of concern for common project types. Scales of concern for specific projects will depend on design objectives and project size, as well as ecological, cultural and economic context.**

*A Framework for Design* • 7

**TABLE 1.1. Examples of common data appropriate at various scales of inquiry.**

| Factors | Detail and Spatial Scales | Place and Neighborhood Scales | Community and Regional Scales |
|---------|---------------------------|-------------------------------|-------------------------------|
| *Soils* | Laboratory soil tests of on-site samples | Soil types from NRCS Soil Surveys | Soil associations from NRCS Soil Surveys |
| *Topography* | Site survey [1.5-1 m (1-2 ft) contour intervals] | USGS quadrangle maps (5-20 ft contour intervals) | USGS digital elevation models (10-30 m resolution) |
| *Biodiversity* | Organism counts | Species counts | Plant community or biome counts |
| *Socio-economic* | Interviews and observations | Observations and surveys | Community surveys and Census data |

## Axiom 4: Relevant questions that diagnose the situation and indicate appropriate actions shift from scale to scale.

Diagnostic questions are related to the general aim of a given project, as well as the desire to respect and respond to ecological, cultural, and economic processes. Examples may include:

- What are the expected stormwater runoff volumes and peak discharge rates in a given watershed?
- What are the physical characteristics of the human form that influence decisions about required spatial dimensions?

Appropriate design strategies are determined by examining these fundamental questions in the context of a particular landscape. As the scale of inquiry shifts, the nature and specificity of the diagnostic questions and the data used to answer them also change. The following chapters in this book provide general diagnostic questions, intended to prompt the designer to consider key issues related to various aspects of Landscape Architecture. Designers are expected to develop more specific questions based on the context of a given project.

## Conceptualization

Conceptualization represents a synthesis of ideas inspired by the process of interpretation, the objectives of the project, and philosophical perspectives. Conceptualization results in a proposed solution to the given problem, primarily in response to the diagnosis obtained during interpretation.

### Axiom 5: Scales of concern shift during the conceptualization process.

Conceptualization tends to result in design occurring at multiple scales, perhaps even simultaneously. As a result, emphasis on particular scales of concern may change during the design process. For example, a community park design may initially focus on spatial organization of elements (e.g. ball fields, rest rooms, parking, etc), their interrelationship as well as the relationship with the surrounding neighborhood. Ultimately however, the emphasis must shift to spatial and detail scales in order to develop specific designs for particular areas of the park and the accompanying construction documents.

**Axiom 6: The rigidity of proposed solutions increases as one moves towards the detail scale.**

Conceptualization at the detail design scale typically translates into built works, requiring great precision, manifested in construction documents. These documents offer little flexibility in terms of materials, techniques, or layout, except perhaps to accommodate discrepancies between data and actual conditions. Conversely, conceptualization at the regional scale typically emphasizes flexibility, offering broader policies that may result in a variety of solutions applied at finer scales that achieve a common set of objectives.

## Evaluation

Evaluation serves to assess the impact of the proposed solution(s) developed during conceptualization, and perhaps to choose among a set of alternatives being considered. This process requires the measurement of intended as well as unintended consequences of proposed solutions, particularly in terms of changes to ecological, cultural, and economic structure and function.

**Axiom 7: Relevant questions that evaluate the intended and unintended consequences from the proposed solution shift from scale to scale.**

Just as appropriate diagnostic questions shift from scale to scale during interpretation, relevant evaluation questions will also change depending on the scale of concern. These questions seek to measure the effectiveness of solutions in terms of meeting defined objectives, as well as assess the "hidden" or unforeseen impacts (both positive and negative) on ecology, culture, and the economy. In many respects, these questions should resemble diagnostic questions used to assess existing conditions, with the inclusion of the proposed design solution within the evaluative model. Examples may include:

- What are the impacts of the proposal on stormwater runoff volumes and peak discharge rates in a given watershed?
- Is the proposed design conducive to physical human comfort and accommodating of a wide spectrum of potential users with varying physical abilities?

**Axiom 8: Appropriate methods for measuring consequences shift from scale to scale.**

Techniques for evaluating the impacts of a proposed solution will vary depending on the scale of concern and the nature of the impact. For example, measures of biotic diversity may be obtained from field counts of individual organisms at the detail scale, while measuring the range of ecological communities or associations from aerial photographs may be more appropriate at coarser scales. Similarly, measures of user satisfaction may be determined through observations or interviews at the spatial scale, while quantitative surveys or raw counts of total users may be more effective at coarser scales.

## Communication

Communication transforms concepts into visual, graphic, verbal, and numerical presentations and information exchanges with clients, consultants, and the general public. Various forms of communication will occur throughout the design process, depending on the number of parties involved in the project, the sensitivity of issues revealed during interpretation, and the clarity with which goals and objectives are articulated by the client or community.

**Axiom 9: Appropriate forms of graphic presentation shift from scale to scale.**

As the scale of conceptual content changes, the techniques and forms of communication also shift (See Figures 1.2 through 1.7 illustrating plan, section, and perspective views). In addition, the resolution of the graphic presentations also changes appropriately. Generally, graphics should simplify in terms of content and technique as you move towards the regional scale. Table 1.2 illustrates drawing scales commonly used for design documents.

**Axiom 10: The number of participants involved in communication decreases as you move towards the detail scale.**

As projects increase in size, the number of clients and consultants as well as affected community residents and property owners also increases. These projects require significant investments in communication between professionals, regulators, clients, and the community. In contrast, smaller projects typically result in simplified communications between Landscape Architects, their clients, and occasionally other consultants or concerned citizens.

**TABLE 1.2. Drawing scales used in common practice.**

| Drawing Type | Metric Ratio | U. S. Customary Scale |
|---|---|---|
| **DETAIL SCALE: 1 m × 1 m** | | |
| Construction Details | 1:5 | 3" = 1'0" |
| | 1:10 | 1" = 1'0" |
| | 1:20 | ¾" = 1'0"; ½"=1'0" |
| **SPATIAL SCALE: 10 m × 10 m** | | |
| Design Layout | 1:50 | ¼" = 1'0" |
| | 1:100 | ⅛" = 1'0" |
| | 1:200 | 1/16" = 1'0" ; 1' = 20" |
| **PLACE SCALE: 100 m × 100 m** | | |
| Site Engineering Layout | 1:500 | 1" = 40' ; 1" = 50' |
| **NEIGHBORHOOD SCALE: 1 km × 1 km** | | |
| Schematic Master Plan | 1:1000 | 1" = 100' |
| | 1:2000 | 1" = 200' |
| Contextual Master Plan | 1:5000 | 1" = 400' |
| **COMMUNITY SCALE: 10 km × 10 km** | | |
| Landscape Planning | 1:10 000 | 1" = 1000' |
| Landscape (USGS) | 1:25 000 | 1" = 2000' |
| **REGIONAL SCALE: 100 km × 100 km** | | |
| Regional Plan | 1:50 000 | 1" = 1 mile |
| | 1:100 000 | ½" = 1 mile |

# SUGGESTED REFERENCES

Lyle, John Tillman, *Design for Human Ecosystems*, Island Press, Washington D.C., 1999.

Lynch, Kevin, *Managing the Sense of a Region*, MIT Press, Cambridge, 1976.

Lynch, Kevin, *The Image of the City*, MIT Press, Cambridge, 1960.

Lynch, Kevin and Gary Hack, *Site Planning*, 3rd Edition, MIT Press, Cambridge, 1984.

Morrison, Philip and Phylis Morrison and the Office of Charles and Ray Eames, *Powers of Ten*, Scientific American Library, Redding, 1982.

Steiner, Frederick, *The Living Landscape*, McGraw-Hill, New York, 1991.

Steinitz, Carl, "A Framework for Theory Applicable to the Education of Landscape Architects (and Other Design Professionals)," *Landscape Journal*, vol. 9, no. 2, 1990.

Steinitz, Carl, "Design is a Verb; Design is a Noun," *Landscape Journal*, vol. 14, no. 2, 1995.

Figure 1.2. DETAIL SCALE: 1 m × 1 m (10⁰)

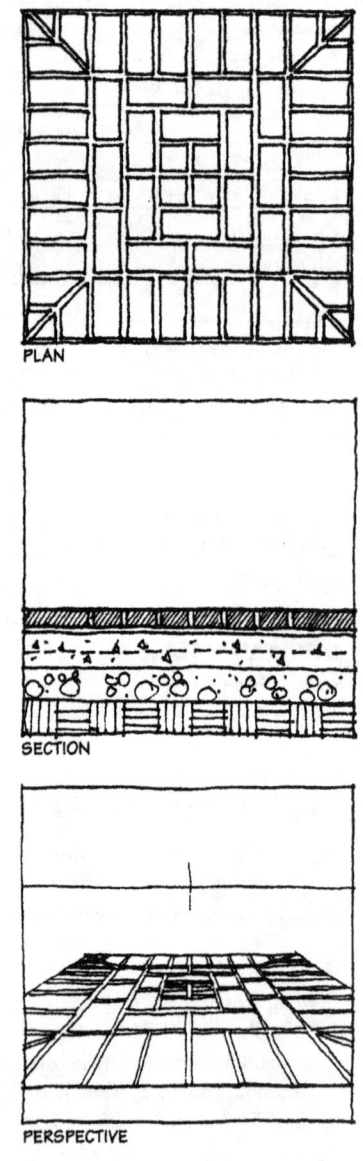

PLAN

SECTION

PERSPECTIVE

I ndividual plant and animal organisms, materials, assembly, joinery, finishes, color, and texture characterize the detail scale. It reveals the detailed artistic expression of the designer and the craft of the builder. Design elements are significantly apparent to the user. Any Landscape Architectural project that results in a built work, regardless of its overall size, is inherently concerned with this scale.

## Interpretation

- *Actions at this scale rely on understanding soil/subgrade conditions, microclimate conditions, existing land cover characteristics, cultural styles, etc.*
- *The resolution of data must be quite fine. Field surveys and soil sample testing characterize the data sources commonly relied upon to yield meaningful results.*
- *Diagnostic questions are principally concerned with understanding how conditions influence construction techniques and selection of materials.*

## Conceptualization

- *This scale is typically addressed in the later stages of conceptualization, after decisions have been made concerning the overall site organization and programming. However it is often at this scale where the designer's expression of their concept is revealed through material choices and design detailing.*
- *Conceptualization typically translates into built works, requiring construction documents. These documents offer little flexibility in terms of materials, techniques, or layout.*

## Evaluation

- *Evaluative questions are primarily concerned with assessing the sustainability of materials and construction techniques, including unintended impacts from material extraction, manufacturing, transport and installation.*

## Communication

- *Construction details are the most common form of graphic presentation. Plan, section and axonometric drawings are the most effective techniques.*
- *Communication is typically required with clients and contractors for selection of materials and finishes. In addition, building inspectors or other regulators concerned with construction methods often require consultation.*

Figure 1.3. SPATIAL SCALE: 10 m × 10 m (10¹)

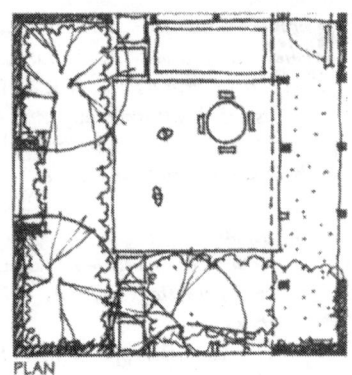

PLAN

SECTION

PERSPECTIVE

**T**his is the scale of garden or small plaza design and the focus is on the spatial arrangement of detail elements to create a specialized environment for a particular group of people in a particular setting. Floor, wall, and canopy combine with human activity to create a sense of space. The user is aware of degree of enclosure, color, light quality, odors, and pattern of arranged detail features (benches, tables, artwork, signs, etc.).

### Interpretation

- *Actions rely on an understanding of microclimate conditions, land cover characteristics, and anticipated qualities of human activities. Ergonomics and cultural characteristics related to spatial preferences must also be considered.*
- *The resolution of data must be quite fine and specific to the situation. Field surveys and observational studies characterize data sources commonly relied upon to yield meaningful results.*
- *Diagnostic questions are principally concerned with human comfort, and understanding how spatial characteristics of the site influence the intended use.*

### Conceptualization

- *In larger projects, this scale is typically addressed in the later stages of conceptualization, after decisions have been made concerning the overall site organization and programming. However the human experience within the landscape occurs primarily at this scale, and as such it is arguably the most critical stage of conceptualization for the designer.*
- *Solutions proposed are generally rigid with regard to spatial definition and characteristics related to floor, wall, and canopy. But designs may offer great flexibility in terms of selection and arrangement of furnishings, to allow for a variety of uses and changes in cultural behavior over time.*

### Evaluation

- *Evaluative questions are primarily concerned with assessing human comfort within the design in terms of microclimate, spatial preferences, and other factors such as auditory or visual stimulation.*

### Communication

- *The purpose of graphic presentation is typically to illustrate characteristics of the design in terms of human function. Plan, section-elevation and perspective drawings are all effective techniques.*
- *Communication is typically required with clients and other design and building consultants to convey design intent.*

Figure 1.4. PLACE SCALE: 100 m × 100 m (10?)

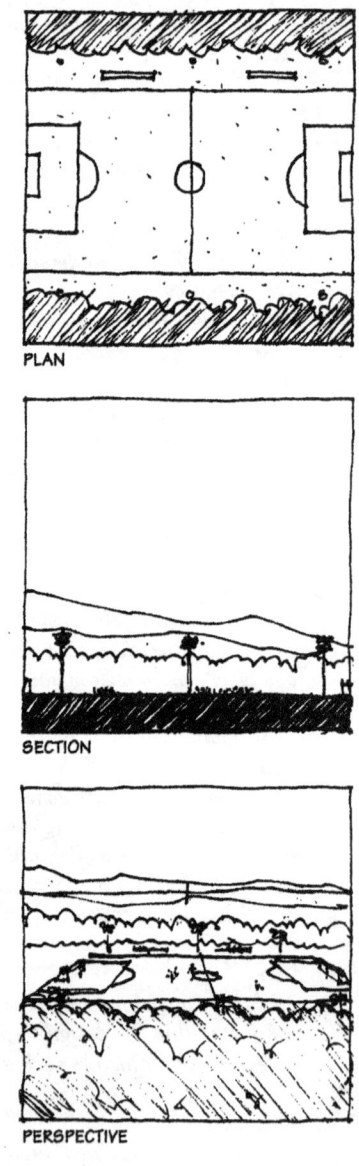

PLAN

SECTION

PERSPECTIVE

**T**his scale focuses on creating distinct places through organization of design components. For a wide variety of projects, this scale often corresponds to the limits of development parcels. Design standards for specific land use types (housing, athletic fields, parking lots, etc.), pedestrian and vehicular circulation are central concerns. Although culturally variable, this scale also marks the outer threshold of perceived human-scaled space.

### Interpretation

- *Actions rely on an understanding of conditions that will influence the location of design components in the landscape, including critical natural resources, areas with development limitations for proposed uses, and characteristics of the program.*
- *Field surveys, spatial standards and observational studies characterize the types of data sources commonly relied upon to yield meaningful results.*
- *Diagnostic questions are principally concerned with the successful functioning of the place, and understanding how conditions influence the spatial characteristics of the proposed solution.*

### Conceptualization

- *For many projects resulting in built works, this scale often represents the initial stages of conceptualization, requiring decisions concerning overall site organization and programming.*
- *Solutions proposed are generally rigid with regard to the spatial organization of design components, but typically allow significant flexibility in terms of detail design of these components.*

### Evaluation

- *Evaluative questions are primarily concerned with assessing effectiveness in terms of intended uses, vehicular and/or pedestrian circulation. Unintended consequences of design decisions must also be considered, including impacts on regional water resources, operational and maintenance costs.*

### Communication

- *The purpose of graphic presentation is typically to illustrate the layout of proposed elements. Plan, section-elevation, perspective and birds-eye perspective or axonometric drawings are all effective techniques.*
- *Communication is typically required with clients and other design consultants to convey design intent. Review by local regulatory agencies may also require communication. In addition, citizen participation may also be an integral part of the design process in public projects.*

Figure 1.5. NEIGHBORHOOD SCALE: 1 km × 1 km (10?)

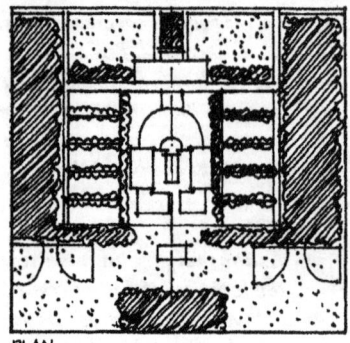

PLAN

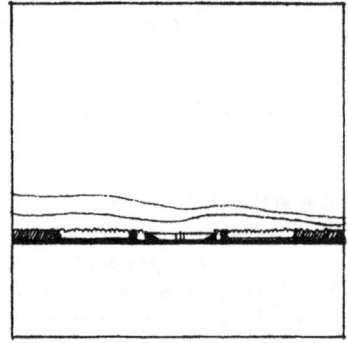

SECTION

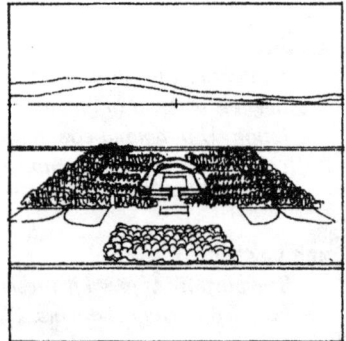

PERSPECTIVE

**T**his is typically a conceptual planning and design scale, aimed at establishing land development feasibility, overall landscape pattern, and various strategies for integrating proposed projects with the neighborhood. Aerial views or a sequence of pedestrian views are typically required to comprehend this scale.

### Interpretation

- *Actions at this scale rely on understanding neighborhood conditions that will influence design at finer scales, including integration with surrounding land uses, cultural character, circulation systems, economic conditions and ecological processes that are effectively addressed at coarser scales, such as stormwater management.*
- *Field surveys, high-resolution aerial photography, and generalized mapping characterize the data sources commonly relied upon to yield meaningful results.*
- *Diagnostic questions are principally concerned with understanding the neighborhood, and conditions that allow for successful integration of design at finer scales.*

### Conceptualization

- *For larger conceptual projects, this scale may represent one of the final stages of conceptualization, culminating in proposed land use classifications, zoning districts, or ecological communities. For smaller projects it may represent the initial stage of conceptualization focusing on integration of the project with its context.*
- *Solutions are generally flexible in terms of physical design, but establish fixed parameters for future development or restoration.*

### Evaluation

- *Evaluative questions are primarily concerned with assessing the solution in terms of impacts on processes operating at the neighborhood scale (e.g. hydrology, property values, public service costs vs. anticipated tax revenues, wayfinding, etc.).*

### Communication

- *The purpose of graphic presentation is typically to illustrate the layout of proposed elements. Plan, birds-eye perspective or axonometric drawings are all effective techniques. Section-elevation graphics may only be useful to illustrate dramatic changes in elevation across the landscape.*
- *Citizen participation is particularly important at this scale, as proposed solutions may have significant impacts on local populations. In addition, design review by local planning agencies will also require significant communication.*

Figure 1.6. COMMUNITY SCALE: 10 km × 10 km (10⁵

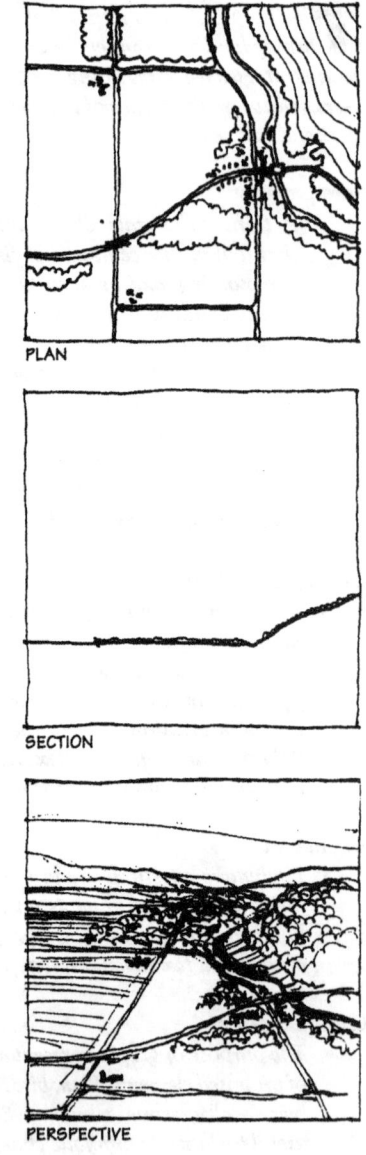

PLAN

SECTION

PERSPECTIVE

**T**his scale focuses on community land use planning, ecological habitat, stormwater management, transportation and infrastructure planning. The "sense of community" is often perceived through important nodes, landmarks, paths, and edges that define spatial boundaries, and discrete districts that reflect neighborhood character at finer scales.

### Interpretation

- *Actions rely on an understanding of community conditions that will influence land use/land cover decisions, including topoclimatic effects, ecological patterns and processes, cognitive mapping by residents and community visioning techniques.*
- *The resolution of data must be fine enough to support the interpretation process, but coarse enough to avoid information overload. High-resolution aerial photography, community surveys, and generalized mapping characterize data sources commonly relied upon to yield meaningful results.*
- *Diagnostic questions are principally concerned with understanding the community, and conditions that will allow for preservation or even enhancement of ecological, economic, and cultural processes.*

### Conceptualization

- *This scale is typically addressed in the early stages of conceptualization, culminating in proposed land use classifications, zoning districts, or ecological communities and/or network plans.*
- *Solutions proposed are generally flexible in terms of physical design and perhaps even for specific uses for individual development parcels, but establish fixed policies for future development in terms of pattern and process.*

### Evaluation

- *Evaluative questions are primarily concerned with assessing impacts on cultural, economic and ecological processes operating at the community scale (e.g. biodiversity, transportation efficiency, environmental justice, etc.).*

### Communication

- *The purpose of graphic presentation is typically to illustrate community patterns. Plan drawings and maps are the primary techniques, but birds-eye perspectives may also be effective techniques.*
- *Citizen participation is particularly important at this scale, as proposed solutions may have significant impacts on local populations. In addition, development proposals at this scale often require federal and/or state environmental impact review.*

**Figure 1.7. REGIONAL SCALE:** 100 km × 100 km (10⁵)

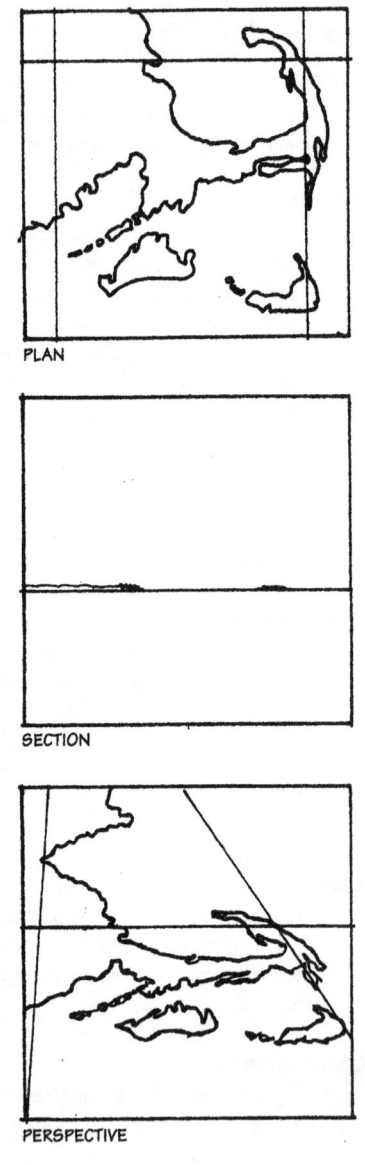

PLAN

SECTION

PERSPECTIVE

**T**his scale focuses on regional land use planning, ecological habitat and stormwater management, transportation and infrastructure planning that tends to transcend local political boundaries. The "sense of a region" is often perceived at this scale via transportation systems and prominent vistas.

### Interpretation
- *Actions rely on an understanding of regional conditions that influence land use/land cover decisions, including large watershed systems, geological and climatological phenomena, regional economies and development trends.*
- *The resolution of data is generally coarse to avoid information overload. Aerial photography and other remotely-sensed data, community surveys, and generalized mapping characterize the data sources commonly relied upon to yield meaningful results.*
- *Diagnostic questions are principally concerned with understanding the region, and conditions that will allow for maintenance or even enhancement of ecological, economic, and cultural processes.*

### Conceptualization
- *This scale is typically addressed in the early stages of conceptualization, culminating in proposed land use classifications, zoning districts, or ecological communities and/or network plans.*
- *Solutions proposed are generally quite flexible in terms of physical design and specific uses for individual development parcels. Emphasis is on establishing policies for future development consistent with desired objectives.*

### Evaluation
- *Evaluative questions are primarily concerned with impacts on cultural, economic and ecological processes operating at the regional scale (e.g. biodiversity, transportation efficiency, environmental justice, etc.).*

### Communication
- *The purpose of graphic presentation at this scale is to illustrate regional patterns. Plan drawings and maps are the primary techniques for representation.*
- *Citizen participation is important at this scale and projects typically involve multiple political entities requiring considerable communication and coordination. In addition, development proposals at this scale often require federal and/or state environmental impact review.*

STANDARDS

TECHNIQUES

DEVICES

ADMINISTRATION

STANDARDS

# Pedestrian
# Standards

2

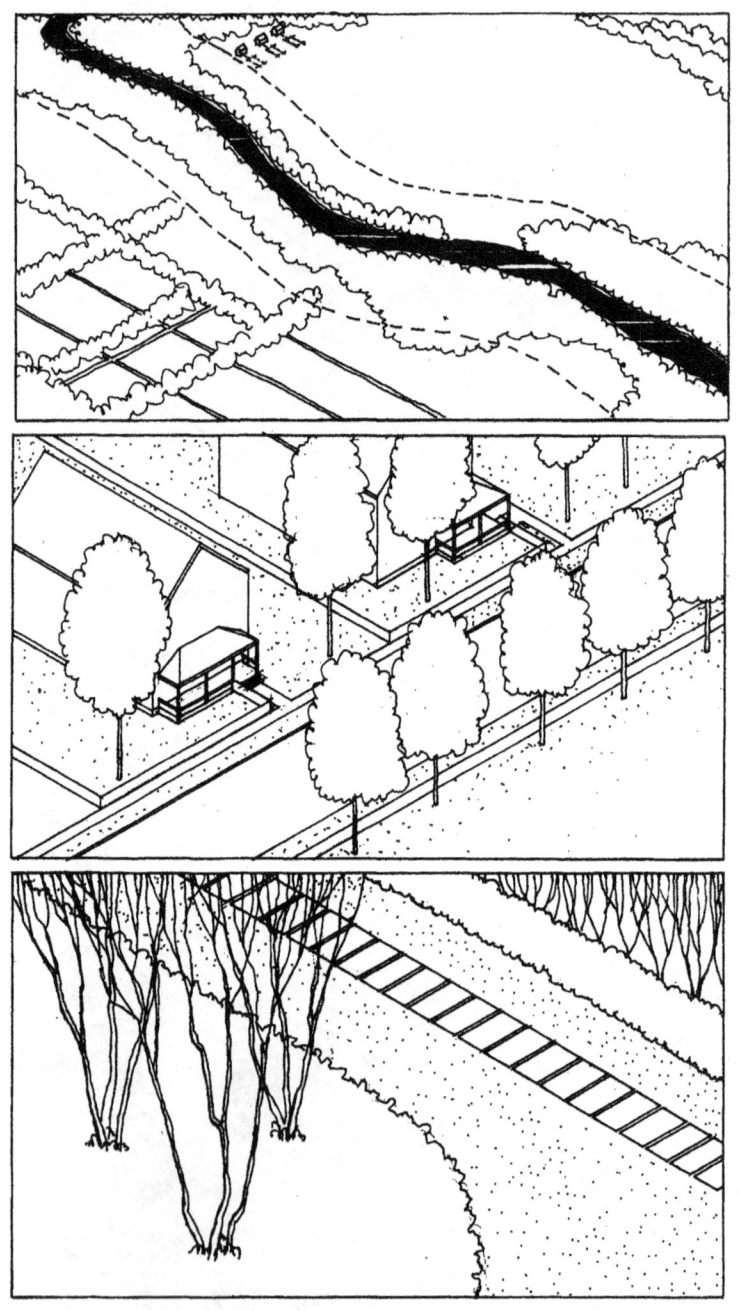

# REGIONAL PEDESTRIAN SYSTEMS

Regional pedestrian systems, including urban networks and recreational greenway linkages, require a hierarchy of support elements, which ensures the safety and utility of both the system and its local components. System widths, slope, and materials vary by the intended carrying capacity and by local climate and maintenance practices.

**STANDARDS**

# LOCAL PEDESTRIAN NETWORKS

Local pedestrian networks connect important recreational, residential, commercial, and institutional resources. They typically are constrained by local climate and topographic characteristics. Regionally appropriate materials, dimensional standards, and associated signage and lighting contribute to local identity and character of the pedestrian experience.

# SITE SCALE PEDESTRIAN WAYS

Site scale pedestrian walkways require careful integration of vehicular and architectural transition zones, multiple user needs, spatial and visual clearances (for reasons of safety and aesthetic experience), and a degree of finish appropriate to the urban, suburban, or rural contexts. Microclimate and temperature extremes are important factors in pavement detailing and configuration choices.

**P**EDESTRIAN CIRCULATION is an integral part of any design scheme. The pedestrian's experience of place is never from a completely fixed point of view. Nodes that serve as gathering spaces or destination points must also be concerned with modes of access and egress. How people move through and experience space (kinesthetics) is an area of inquiry that should not be limited to the standards presented in this chapter, but explored throughout a career of research and observation.

## DIAGNOSTIC ASSESSMENT

*What are the functional and aesthetic factors affecting the pedestrian experience?*

The primary goal of pedestrian planning and design is to integrate the functional requirements of circulation with the aesthetic preferences of the pedestrian. In addition to connecting origin and destination points, circulation routes should be convenient, establish relationships to natural and cultural amenities, provide a range of human sensory stimuli, and reflect the climatic and cultural constraints, which influence physical design standards and material choices.

*What are the physical characteristics of the human form that influence decisions about required spatial dimensions?*

Physical and spatial design standards are derived from the study of human ergonomics and the influence of cultural modifiers, which influence how individuals and groups move and behave in various spatial and cultural settings. Knowledge of human dimensions, movement preferences, and thresholds of visual perception are required for the design of adequate pedestrian circulation systems.

*What spatial and dimensional relationships are essential for all pedestrian circulation systems?*

Each system should reflect its scale context and the intended use volume. Walkway width, slope, and canopy height determine both its potential capacity and its ambiance. Most standards are aimed at achieving minimal levels of adequacy and therefore should be tempered by local conditions.

*What provisions for universal design will create a variety of accessible and safe pedestrian spaces?*

Universal design is a philosophical approach seeking to eliminate barriers in the pedestrian environment, while providing access and usability to the broadest possible range of people. Passage of the Americans with Disabilities Act (ADA) in 1990 has produced both published legal guidelines and recommendations for access. For more information, see the Uniform

Federal Accessibility Standards (UFAS) and the Americans with Disabilities Act Accessibility Guidelines (ADAAG).

# PEDESTRIAN EXPERIENCE

## Convenience

"Convenience" is a measure of the functional quality offered by a pedestrian system. The two most important factors in assessing the convenience of a system are orientation and negotiation.

### Orientation

Visual cues in the landscape (including signage) aid in way-finding within a larger environmental context. This is especially important in complex environments. Landmark features and visual cues within a hierarchically ordered system can suggest purpose and expected behavior to the pedestrian.

### Negotiation

Negotiation refers to the relative ease of moving from one destination to another. Factors affecting negotiation include pedestrian density, the presence of physical obstructions, the condition of the walking surface, and climate conditions.

## Amenities

One of the purposes of any pedestrian circulation system is the connection it offers between various natural or cultural amenities, including the attraction of human activity. Social interaction, both passive and active, is extremely important and requires spaces to gather with opportunities to sit and watch other pedestrians.

## Sensory Stimuli

Pedestrians typically perceive and utilize most urban circulation systems as a functional device more than as media for aesthetic experience, a characteristic often reserved for park systems, and other recreational open spaces. A purely utilitarian circulation path may successfully function as a convenient access route while spatially and aesthetically providing a negative experience. Designers should remain aware of the many environmental factors that contribute to the enjoyment of outdoor places by pedestrians, providing for a myriad of sensory and intellectual experiences. Table 2.1 is a checklist of various sensory stimuli, some of which relate to pleasant experiences and others, which are unpleasant and require mitigation.

**TABLE 2.1. Common sensory stimuli in pedestrian environments.**

**Tactile**

Temperature
Humidity
Wind and breezes
Precipitation
Benches and seatwalls
Sittable ground surfaces
Bars, knobs, and handles
Handrailings and armrests
Telephones, vending and
    banking machines
Textures under foot
Vegetation within reach
Water
Architectural facades
Food and drink
Human contact

**Auditory**

Normal traffic noise
Excessive truck traffic
Underground rumblings
Air traffic
Distant highway noise
Echo
Conversation
Play activity
Music and song
Professional and amateur entertainment
Wind
Water
Wildlife
Bells, chimes, and whistles
Wind-blown flags and fabrics
Movable furniture
Vendors
Machinery
Heating, ventilation, and
cooling systems
Foot traffic on various pavements

**Visual**

Spatial perception (form, scale, etc.)
Form of objects
Proportion and scale of objects
Social activity

**Visual (continued)**

Vehicular activity
Prominent landforms
Vegetation
Water features
Miscellaneous natural features
Sun and shadow
Rain, snow, fog, mist
Smoke
Litter
Signage
Storefront advertisements
Window displays
Posted bills
Billboards
Walls and fences
Street furniture and features
Overhead wires and cables
Architecture
Vegetation
Wildlife
Overall character of a place
Sites under construction
Surface textures
Color compositions
Tonal contrasts
Diurnal change
Seasonal change
Moonlight
Night-lighting
Glare and albedo
Viewsheds from important
vantage points
General order
Overall congruencies

**Olfactory**

Vehicular emissions
Odorous smoke
Fresh air
Fragrant vegetation
Restaurant doorways
Outdoor cafes
Odorous litter and debris
Refuse areas
Exhaust fans

# PHYSICAL CHARACTERISTICS

## Dimensional Criteria

Figure 2.1 illustrates approximate dimensions of human figures in various activity positions. Spatial requirements differ in various regions and between different cultures as a function of accustomed densities of people, heritage, social and environmental values.

Forward spatial bubbles, as illustrated in Figure 2.2, refer to the extent of unobstructed forward vision held to be psychologically comfortable for the average pedestrian under various circumstances.

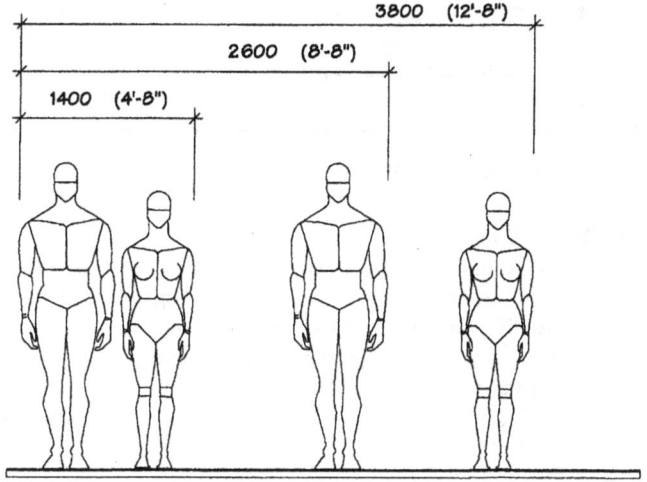

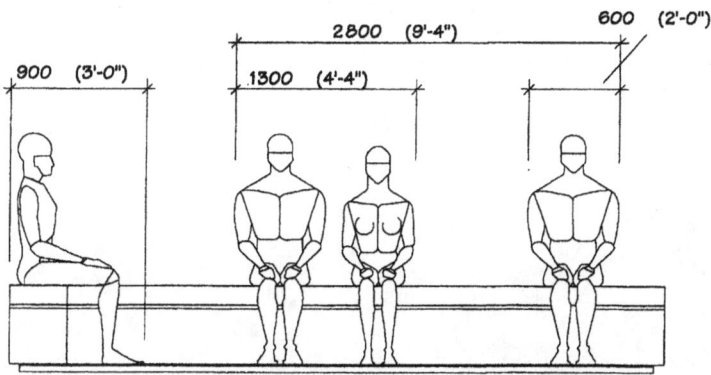

**Figure 2.1. Human dimensions in various activity positions. These dimensions are approximate average spatial requirements that are used primarily as an aid to professional judgment, rather than as standard criteria.**

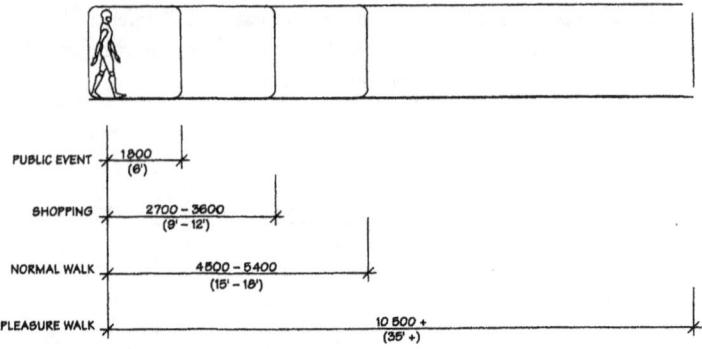

**Figure 2.2. Forward spatial bubbles.**

## Movement Criteria

The average walking distance that people in the United States are typically willing to walk between activities or from parking areas are subject to variation depending on the purpose of the trip, climatic conditions, or cultural differences. As shown in Figure 2.3, most people are not willing to walk distances greater than about 220 m (700 ft).

Figures 2.4 and 2.5 show pedestrian flow volume, speed, and density for walkways and stairways.

## Visual Criteria

Cones of vision and eye levels are important in terms of placement and orientation of pedestrian signage. The human cone of vision has approximately a 30-degree vertical range and a 60-degree horizontal range (Figure 2.6). The eye level of an average adult is 1525 mm (5'-2") standing and 1125 mm (3'-9") sitting (Figure 2.7).

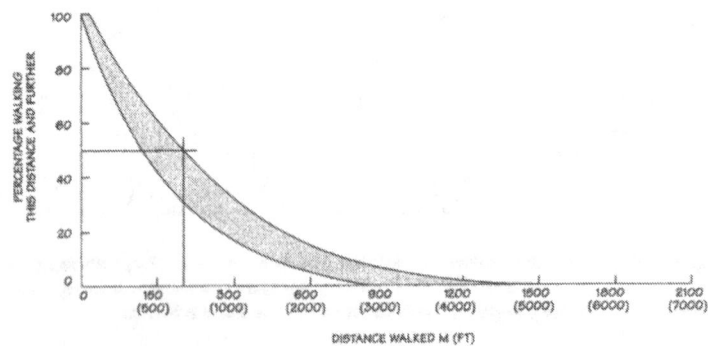

**Figure 2.3. Range of acceptable walking distances (U.S. cities). Most people are not willing to walk distances greater than about 220 m (700 ft).**

It is helpful to possess a general understanding of the capabilities and limitations of normal human vision in terms of social communication. Figure 2.8 illustrates several examples.

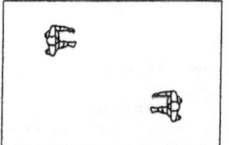

Average Flow Volume:  23 PMM* or less (7 PFM or less)
Average Speed:  79 m/min (260 ft/min)
Average Pedestrian Area Occupancy:  3.3 m²/person or greater
                                     (36 ft²/person or greater)
Description: Virtually unrestricted choice of speed; minimum maneuvering to pass; crossing and reverse movements unrestricted; flow approximately 25% of maximum capacity.

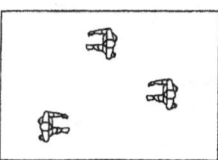

Average Flow Volume: 23-33 PMM (7-10 PFM)
Average Speed: 76-79 m/min (250-260 ft/min)
Average Pedestrian Area Occupancy: 2.3-3.2 m²/person
                                   (25-35 ft²/person)
Description: Normal walking speeds only occasionally restricted; some occasional interference in passing; crossing and reverse movements possible with occasional conflict; flow approximately 35% of maximum capacity.

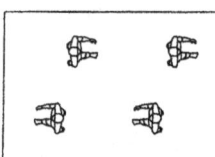

Average Flow Volume:  33-49 PMM (10-15 PFM)
Average Speed:  70-76 m/min (230-250 ft/min)
Average Pedestrian Area Occupancy:  1.4-2.3 m²/person
                                    (15-25 ft²/person)
Description: Walking speeds partially restricted; passing restricted but possible with maneuvering; crossing and reverse movements restricted and require significant maneuvering to avoid conflict; flow reasonably fluid and about 40-65% of maximum capacity.

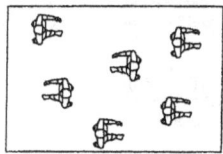

Average Flow Volume:  49-66 PMM (15-20 PFM)
Average Speed:  61-70 m/min (200-230 ft/min)
Average Pedestrian Area Occupancy: .9-1.4 m²/person
                                    (10-15 ft²/person)
Description:  Walking speeds restricted and reduced; passing rarely possible without conflict; crossing and reverse movements severely restricted with multiple conflicts; some probability of momentary flow stoppages when critical densities might be intermittently reached; flow approximately 65-80% of maximum capacity.

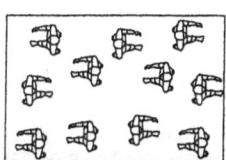

Average Flow Volume:  66-82 PMM (20-25 PFM)
Average Speed:  34-61 m/min (110-200 ft/min)
Average Pedestrian Area Occupancy: .5-.9 m²/person
                                    (5-10 ft²/person)
Description:  Walking speeds restricted and frequently reduced to shuffling; frequent adjustment of gait required; passing impossible without conflict; crossings and reverse movements severely restricted with unavoidable conflicts; flows attain maximum capacity under pressure, but with frequent stoppages and interruptions of flow.

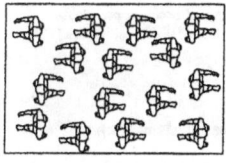

Average Flow Volume: 82 PMM or more (25 PFM or more)
Average Speed:  0-34 m/min (0-110 ft/min)
Average Pedestrian Area Occupancy: .5 m²/person or less
                                    (5 ft²/person or less)
Description: Walking speed reduced to shuffling; passing impossible; crossing and reverse movements impossible; physical contact frequent and unavoidable; flow sporadic and on the verge of complete breakdown and stoppage.

*PMM=pedestrians per meter width of walkway, per minute.
 (PFM=pedestrians per foot width of walkway, per minute.)

**Figure 2.4. Average flow volume, speed, and density (walkways).**

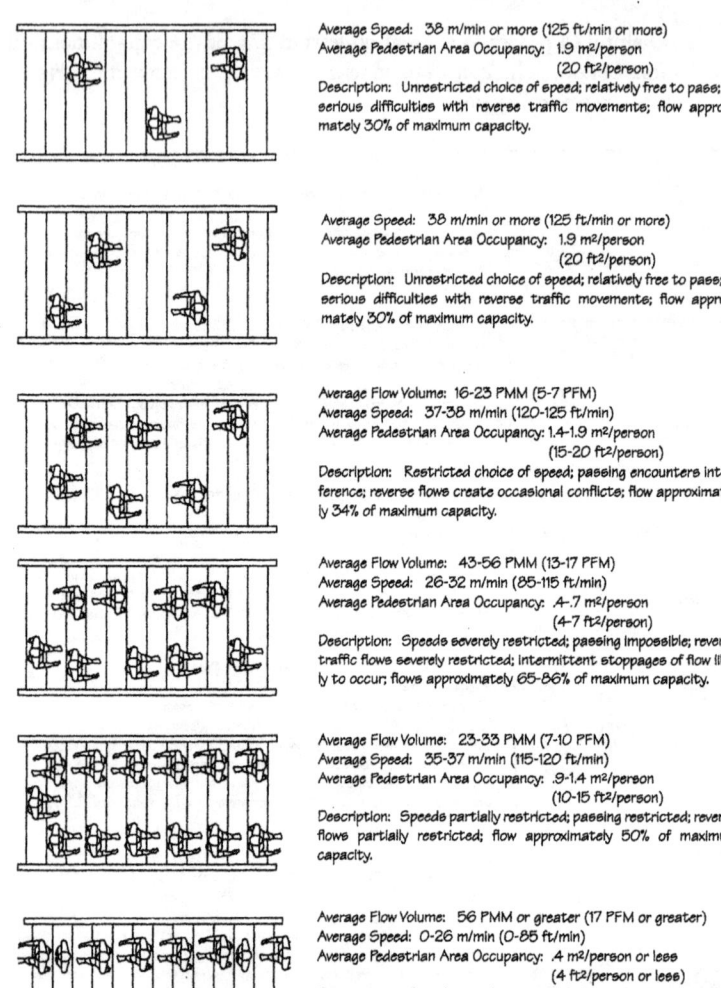

Average Speed: 38 m/min or more (125 ft/min or more)
Average Pedestrian Area Occupancy: 1.9 m²/person
(20 ft²/person)
Description: Unrestricted choice of speed; relatively free to pass; no serious difficulties with reverse traffic movements; flow approximately 30% of maximum capacity.

Average Speed: 38 m/min or more (125 ft/min or more)
Average Pedestrian Area Occupancy: 1.9 m²/person
(20 ft²/person)
Description: Unrestricted choice of speed; relatively free to pass; no serious difficulties with reverse traffic movements; flow approximately 30% of maximum capacity.

Average Flow Volume: 16-23 PMM (5-7 PFM)
Average Speed: 37-38 m/min (120-125 ft/min)
Average Pedestrian Area Occupancy: 1.4-1.9 m²/person
(15-20 ft²/person)
Description: Restricted choice of speed; passing encounters interference; reverse flows create occasional conflicts; flow approximately 34% of maximum capacity.

Average Flow Volume: 43-56 PMM (13-17 PFM)
Average Speed: 26-32 m/min (85-115 ft/min)
Average Pedestrian Area Occupancy: .4-.7 m²/person
(4-7 ft²/person)
Description: Speeds severely restricted; passing impossible; reverse traffic flows severely restricted; intermittent stoppages of flow likely to occur; flows approximately 65-86% of maximum capacity.

Average Flow Volume: 23-33 PMM (7-10 PFM)
Average Speed: 35-37 m/min (115-120 ft/min)
Average Pedestrian Area Occupancy: .9-1.4 m²/person
(10-15 ft²/person)
Description: Speeds partially restricted; passing restricted; reverse flows partially restricted; flow approximately 50% of maximum capacity.

Average Flow Volume: 56 PMM or greater (17 PFM or greater)
Average Speed: 0-26 m/min (0-85 ft/min)
Average Pedestrian Area Occupancy: .4 m²/person or less
(4 ft²/person or less)
Description: Speed severely restricted; flow subject to complete breakdown with many stoppages; passing as well as reverse flows impossible.

*PMM=pedestrians per meter width of stairway, per minute.
(PFM=pedestrians per foot width of stairway, per minute.)

**Figure 2.5. Average flow volume, speed, and density (stairways).**

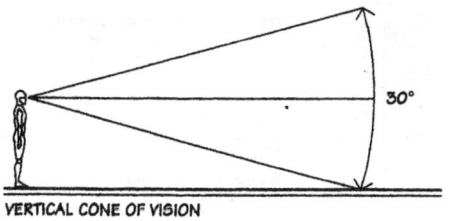

VERTICAL CONE OF VISION

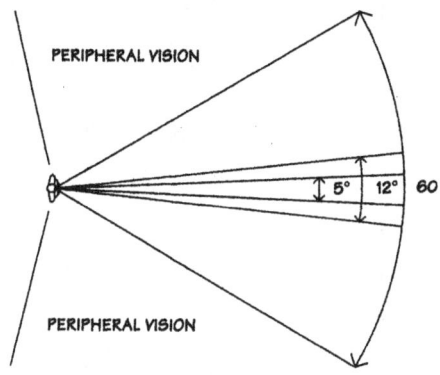

PERIPHERAL VISION

5°   12°   60

PERIPHERAL VISION

HORIZONTAL CONE OF VISION:

ANGLE OF MOST ACUTE VISION: 3 – 5°
ANGLE OF LESS ACUTE VISION: 5 – 12°
ANGLE OF COMFORTABLE, LESS DETAILED VISION: 12 – 60°

**Figure 2.6. Normal cone of vision.**

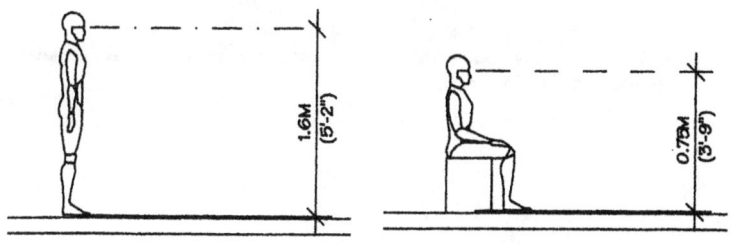

1.6M (5'-2")

0.75M (3'-9")

**Figure 2.7. Eye levels of an average adult.**

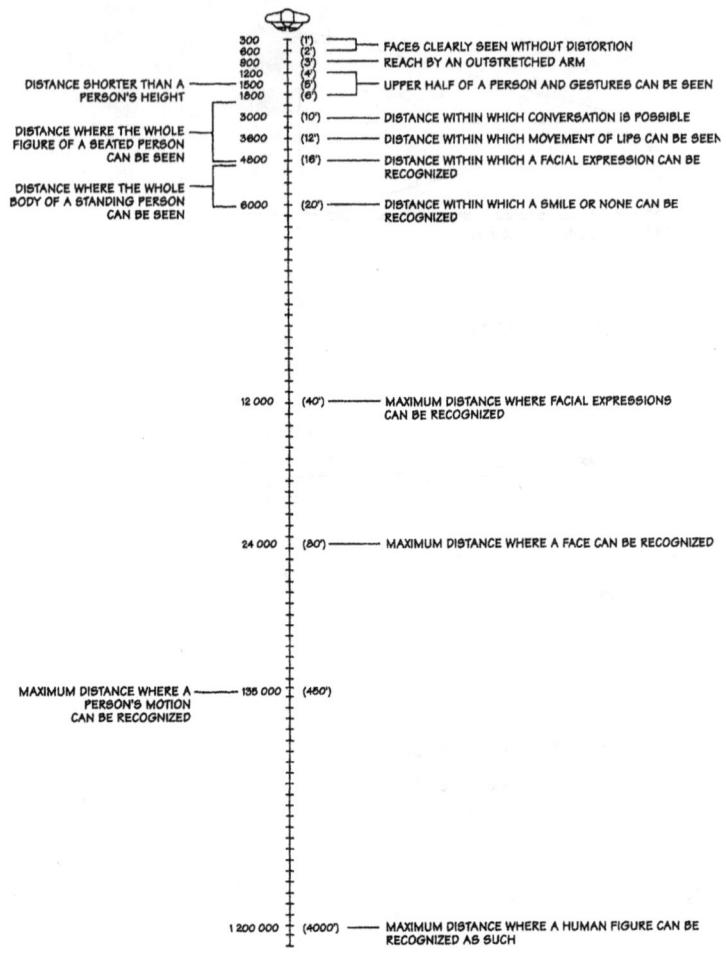

| | | |
|---|---|---|
| | 300 | (1') — FACES CLEARLY SEEN WITHOUT DISTORTION |
| | 600 | (2') — REACH BY AN OUTSTRETCHED ARM |
| | 900 | (3') |
| | 1200 | (4') |
| DISTANCE SHORTER THAN A PERSON'S HEIGHT | 1500 | (5') — UPPER HALF OF A PERSON AND GESTURES CAN BE SEEN |
| | 1800 | (6') |
| | 3000 | (10') — DISTANCE WITHIN WHICH CONVERSATION IS POSSIBLE |
| DISTANCE WHERE THE WHOLE FIGURE OF A SEATED PERSON CAN BE SEEN | 3600 | (12') — DISTANCE WITHIN WHICH MOVEMENT OF LIPS CAN BE SEEN |
| | 4800 | (16') — DISTANCE WITHIN WHICH A FACIAL EXPRESSION CAN BE RECOGNIZED |
| DISTANCE WHERE THE WHOLE BODY OF A STANDING PERSON CAN BE SEEN | 6000 | (20') — DISTANCE WITHIN WHICH A SMILE OR NONE CAN BE RECOGNIZED |
| | 12 000 | (40') — MAXIMUM DISTANCE WHERE FACIAL EXPRESSIONS CAN BE RECOGNIZED |
| | 24 000 | (80') — MAXIMUM DISTANCE WHERE A FACE CAN BE RECOGNIZED |
| MAXIMUM DISTANCE WHERE A PERSON'S MOTION CAN BE RECOGNIZED | 135 000 | (450') |
| | 1 200 000 | (4000') — MAXIMUM DISTANCE WHERE A HUMAN FIGURE CAN BE RECOGNIZED AS SUCH |

**Figure 2.8. Inherent capabilities of human vision in terms of social communication (not to scale).**

# SPATIAL STANDARDS

## Pathways

In general, a 600 mm (24 in) width is necessary for each pedestrian, which suggests a minimum pathway width of 1200 mm (4 ft) for public walkways. When more precision is required, calculate minimum acceptable widths of a pathway using the following formula:

$$\text{Pathway Width} = \frac{V(M)}{S}$$

where
$V$ = volume, pedestrians/minute
$M$ = space module, m² (ft²)/pedestrian
$S$ = walking speed, m (ft)/minute

**EXAMPLE (SI UNITS)**

$V$ = 200 pedestrians/minute
$M$ = 1.67 m²/pedestrian
$S$ = 79.25 m/minute

$$\frac{200 \times 1.67}{79.25} = \frac{334}{79.25} = 4.22 \ m$$

*(minimum width to accommodate pedestrian flow)*

User abilities and design objectives determine longitudinal slope criteria, while the need for positive drainage suggests cross-slope criteria, depending on paving material. Figure 2.9 provides longitudinal and cross-slope criteria for walkways under various circumstances.

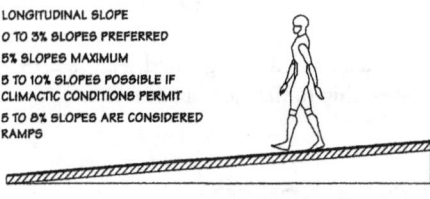

LONGITUDINAL SLOPE
0 TO 3% SLOPES PREFERRED
5% SLOPES MAXIMUM
5 TO 10% SLOPES POSSIBLE IF CLIMACTIC CONDITIONS PERMIT
5 TO 8% SLOPES ARE CONSIDERED RAMPS

**Figure 2.9. Walkway slope criteria.**

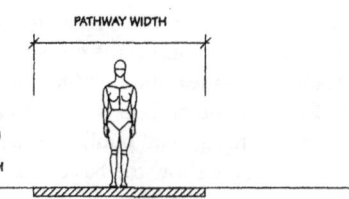

PATHWAY WIDTH

CROSS-SLOPE
1% CROSS-SLOPE MINIMUM (DEPENDING ON MATERIAL)
2% CROSS-SLOPE TYPICAL
3% CROSS-SLOPE MAXIMUM

## Stairways

Minimum width for stairways should be 1500 mm (60 in) for public spaces and 1050 mm (42 in) for private spaces.

Recommended tread-riser ratios for outdoor stairways can be calculated using the formula 2R(riser) + T (tread) = 650 to 675 mm (26 to 27 in). Risers for outdoor stairways should be a minimum of 115 mm (4.5 in) and a maximum of 150 mm (6 in). Under utilitarian circumstances, a maximum 175 mm (7 in) riser may be considered. Figure 2.10 is a quick reference chart of typical tread/riser ratios for outdoor stairways. Heights between stair landings should be a maximum of 1500 (5 ft) to allow an average adult standing on one landing to see the ground plane of the next higher landing.

## Ramps

Figure 2.11 shows the dimensional criteria for a two-way accessible ramp. Landings should be provided every 9 m (30 ft) or less of ramp length. Ramp slopes should be no greater than 1:12 or 8.33%. Ramps may be 1:8 or 12% for a maximum rise of 75 mm (3 in).

## Seating

Seatwalls are typically 400 to 450 mm (16 to 18 in) wide and between 350 and 450 mm (14 and 18 in) in height. Figure 2.12 illustrates preferred height and seating angle for outdoor benches.

## Handrailings

Handrailing heights for outdoor stairway and ramps typically range from 750 to 850 mm (30 to 34 in). The railing ends should extend beyond the top and bottom step by 300 to 450 mm (12 to 18 in). Figure 2.13 shows preferred handrailing profiles.

## Signage

Design and placement of signs for use by pedestrians involves consideration of visual field, scale of letters, proportion of letters, and contrast between letters and background. Figure 2.14 addresses the scale of letters in relationship to the viewing distance.

# ACCESSIBILITY

Providing an accessible route is the most important way to ensure universal access. It connects the primary elements and spaces of a site, parking, entrances, facilities, and buildings. An accessible route must be continuous and free from obstructions. This route must also coincide with the route planned for the general public to the maximum extent feasible. Figure 2.15 and Figure 2.16 show the basic considerations of an accessible route.

| RISER | TREAD |
|---|---|
| 100 | 450 – 475 |
| (4") | (18 – 19") |
| 106.25 | 437.5 –462.5 |
| (4.25") | (17.5 – 18.5") |
| 112.5 | 425 – 450 |
| (4.5") | (17 – 18") |
| 118.75 | 412.5 – 437.5 |
| (4.75") | (16.5 – 17.5") |
| 125 | 400 – 425 |
| (5") | (16 – 17") |
| 131.25 | 387.5 – 412.5 |
| (5.25") | (15.5 – 16.5") |
| 137.5 | 375 –400 |
| (5.5") | (15 – 16") |
| 143.75 | 362.5 –387.5 |
| (5.75") | (14.5 – 15.5") |
| 150 | 350 – 375 |
| (6") | (14 – 15") |
| 156.25 | 337.5 –362.5 |
| (6.25") | (13.5 – 14.5") |
| 162.5 | 325 – 350 |
| (6.5") | (13 – 14") |
| 168.75 | 312.5 – 337.5 |
| (6.75") | (12.5 – 13.5") |
| 175 | 330 – 325 |
| (7") | (12 – 13") |
| 181.25 | 287.5-312.5 |
| (7.25") | (11.5"-12.5") |
| 187.5 | 275-300 |
| (7.5") | (11-12") |

**Figure 2.10. Quick reference chart of typical tread-risers ratios for outdoor stairways in mm (ft). Check state codes where applicable.**

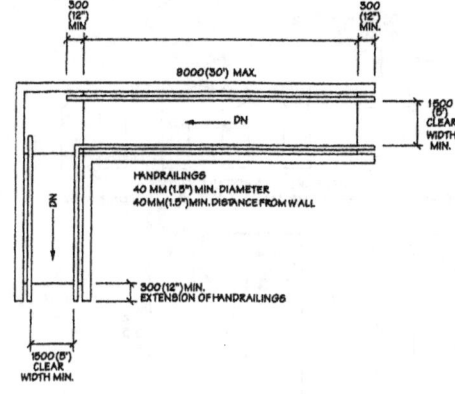

**Figure 2.11. Dimensional criteria for two-way handicap ramp. Minimum clear width for one-way travel is 900 mm (36 in.) Check state codes where applicable.**

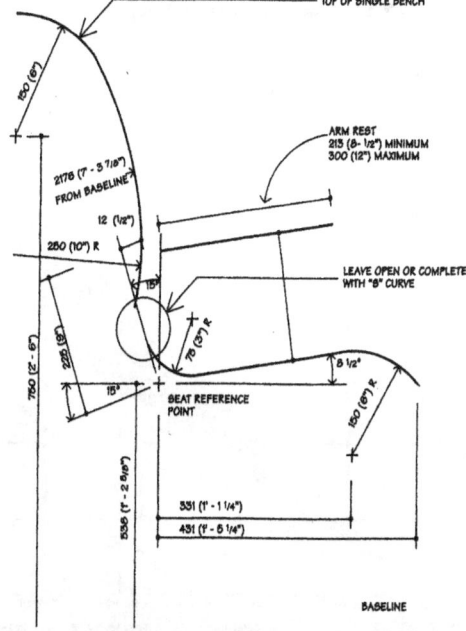

**Figure 2.12. Preferred height and seating angle for outdoor benches. Dimensions shown are for optional double- and single-bench contour.**

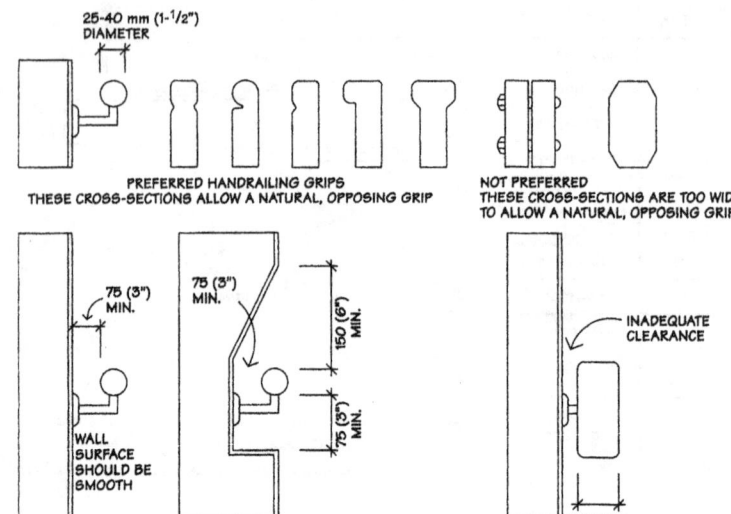

25-40 mm (1-1/2") DIAMETER

PREFERRED HANDRAILING GRIPS
THESE CROSS-SECTIONS ALLOW A NATURAL, OPPOSING GRIP

NOT PREFERRED
THESE CROSS-SECTIONS ARE TOO WIDE
TO ALLOW A NATURAL, OPPOSING GRIP

75 (3") MIN.

75 (3") MIN.

150 (6") MIN.

75 (3") MIN.

WALL SURFACE SHOULD BE SMOOTH

INADEQUATE CLEARANCE

TOO WIDE

**Figure 2.13. Preferred handrailing profiles.**

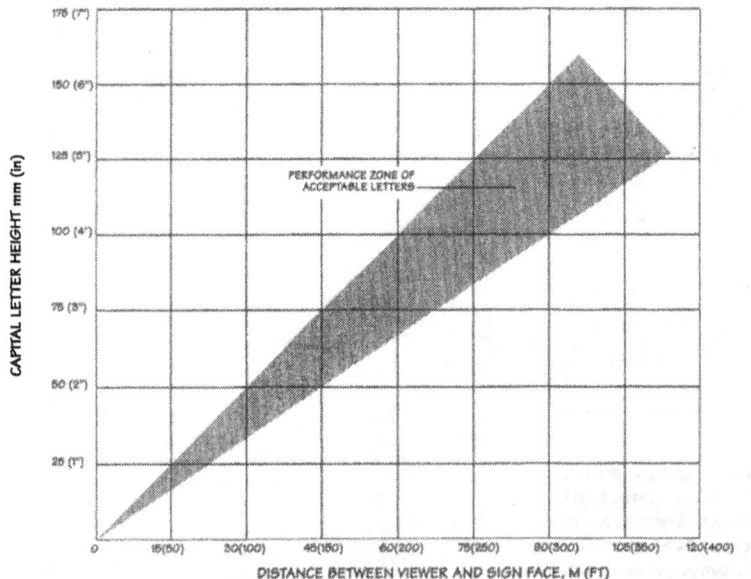

CAPITAL LETTER HEIGHT mm (in)

175 (7")
150 (6")
125 (5")
100 (4")
75 (3")
50 (2")
25 (1")

PERFORMANCE ZONE OF ACCEPTABLE LETTERS

0   15(50)   30(100)   45(150)   60(200)   75(250)   90(300)   105(350)   120(400)

DISTANCE BETWEEN VIEWER AND SIGN FACE, M (FT)

**Figure 2.14. Minimum legibility for capital letter height for pedestrian signage. Under normal daylight conditions with an angular distortion of 0 degrees, approximately 15m/25mm of capital letter height can be taken as a guideline for minimal legibility.**

1. Parking areas should be related directly to the buildings which they serve. 'Handicapped' parking stalls should be no more than 30 000mm (100') from building entries.

2. Drop-off zones should be located as close as possible to primary entryways. No grade changes should exist between road surfaces and adjacent walkways. Vehicular connections to drop-offs, site entrance and parking areas should be direct.

3. Site entrances should be well identified with obvious relationship to the buildings and sites they serve.

4. Clear and legible signage should be provided to direct pedestrians to various destinations.

5. Building entries should be clearly identified; combined means of entry should be provided for handicapped individuals (i.e. both ramps and stairs); public facilities should be located near accessible entryways (lavatories, phones, drinking fountains, etc.); no grade changes should exist between entryways and these facilities.

6. Waiting areas preferably should be located within 90 000 mm (300') of building entry; avoid traffic congestion; and overhead shelter should be provided for protection from weather; adequate seating and lighting should also be provided.

7. Rest areas should be provided where pedestrians must walk long distances; keep rest areas off walkway throughfares.

8. Walkways should provide clear and direct routes throughout sites; surfaces should be firm and level; curb cuts and ramps should be provided where necessary; accessible walkways should consist of closed loops rather than dead ends.

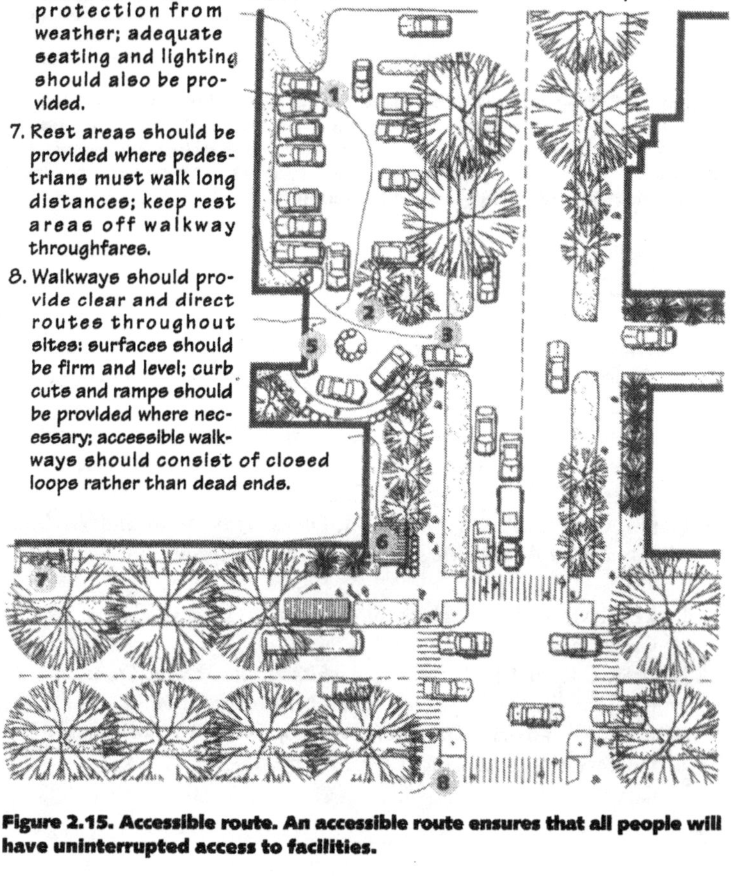

**Figure 2.15. Accessible route. An accessible route ensures that all people will have uninterrupted access to facilities.**

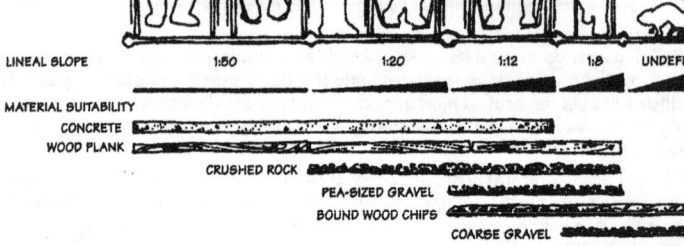

**Figure 2.16. Trail classification system. This recreation trail classification system was developed by the Minnesota Department of Natural Resources as part of a comprehensive scheme to accommodate all types of people in a statewide recreation model. The five trail classifications represent "graduated difficulty" in terms of accessibility.**

# SUGGESTED REFERENCES

*Americans with Disabilities Act Handbook,* U.S. Equal Employment Opportunity Commission : U.S. Dept. of Justice, Washington, DC, 1992.

*Americans with Disabilities Act Accessibility Guidelines for Buildings and Facilities,* Transportation Facilities, Transportation Vehicles, U.S. Access Board, Washington, DC, 1994.

Harris, Charles W. and Nicholas T. Dines, *Time-Saver Standards for Landscape Architecture, 2nd Edition,* McGraw-Hill, New York, 1998.

Lynch, Kevin and Gary Hack, *Site Planning,* 3rd ed., The MIT Press, Cambridge, 1984.

Ramsey, C.G. and H.R. Sleeper, *Architectural Graphic Standards,* 10 ed., John Ray Hoke Jr., ed., Wiley, New York, 2000.

Whyte, William H., *The Social Life of Small Urban Places,* The Conservation Foundation, Washington, D.C., 1980.

# Vehicular Standards

3

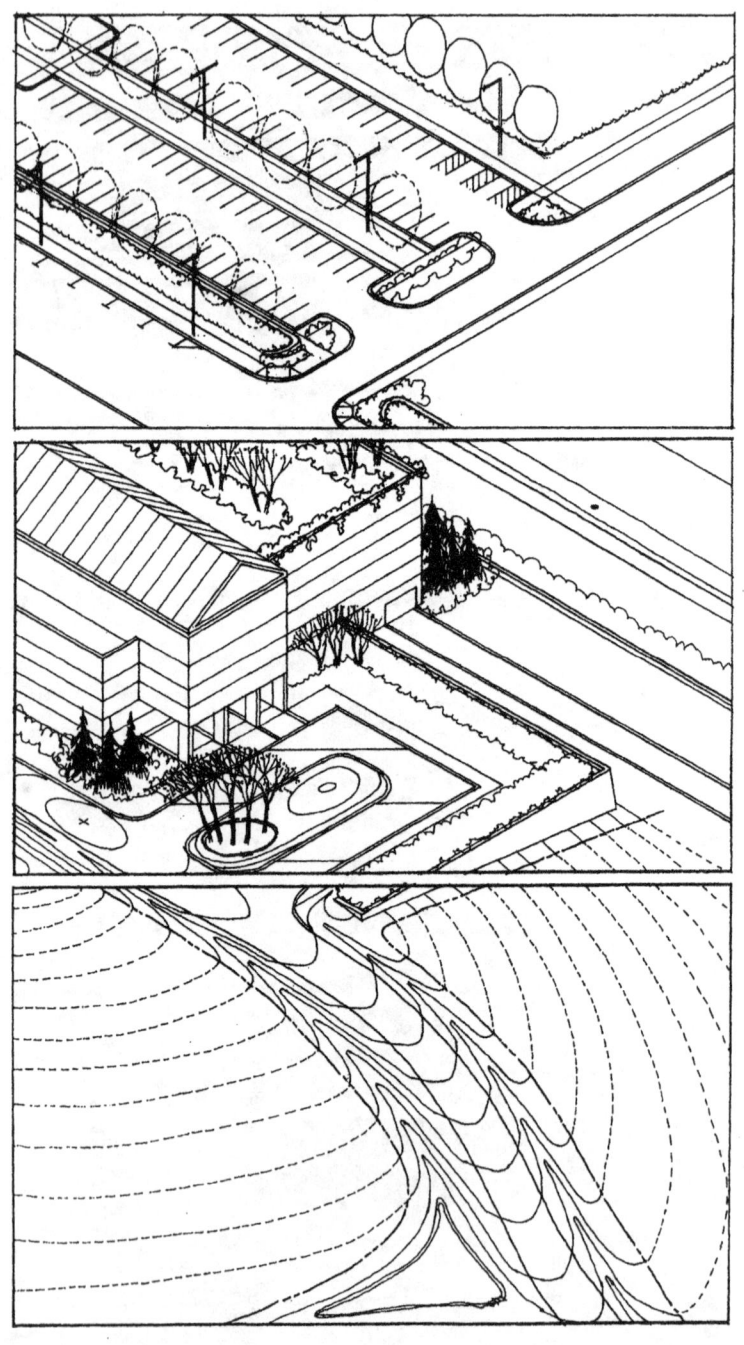

LARGE SCALE PARKING LOTS AND ACCESS ROADS

## LARGE SCALE PARKING LOTS AND ACCESS ROADS

Large scale parking and access roads typically require heavy duty lighting, stormwater management systems, curbs, screens and barriers, planting, and signage to increase safety and legibility, while mitigating negative environmental impacts due to run-off, glare, noise, and visual intrusion. Careful use of existing topography and vegetative cover are two key strategic factors which serve to lessen such impacts.

## SITE ACCESS ROADS AND BUILDING ARRIVAL AND DROP-OFF AREAS

Site access roads should be aligned to conform to favorable site features, such as unique views, mature vegetative stands, wetlands, rock outcrops, and cultural artifacts. The corridor should result in a serial sequence, which culminates at the designated arrival area, commonly at a building drop-off turn-a-round configuration. These nodal points require careful dimensional precision and supportive amenities (plantings, lighting, etc.), to allow for safe and aesthetically pleasing pedestrian transfer activity.

## SMALL SCALE DRIVEWAYS AND SERVICE ROADS

Driveways and service roads and their associated parking areas are typically controlled by local curb-cut ordinances. Careful planning is required on small lots to prevent the driveway from dominating views from critical use areas. Proper alignment, grading, and the use of plant and fence screens are common design elements used to mitigate negative visual effects. Planting setbacks and turning radii should allow for safe and efficient movement.

UNDERSTANDING THE ROLE of the automobile in the land development process is essential for designers concerned with the livability of communities and the continued health of regional ecosystems. Often vehicular circulation patterns set the scale and form of future development; however, a responsible approach to site planning requires balancing the needs of the automobile with the comfort and safety of the pedestrian and the continued health of ecological systems. The design requirements, circulation patterns, and spatial and dimensional standards of the automobile inform the mitigation of vehicular impacts on the pedestrian and natural landscape.

## DIAGNOSTIC ASSESSMENT

*What are the environmental, social, and economic impacts of the proposed vehicular circulation system?*

The proliferation of roadways and parking lots in the landscape can produce many negative environmental and social impacts if careful consideration is not given to the existing patterns of the hydrologic cycle, species migration, and human habitation. In addition, road construction has associated impacts on local and regional economies, whether in the form of public expenditure for road construction or impacts on future or existing business in the area.

*What critical spatial and dimensional standards must guide the design of the proposed vehicular system?*

Vehicular and spatial dimensional requirements vary by vehicle type, land-use setting, and movement pattern. Spatial standards must accommodate the intermingling of both large vehicles and pedestrians. Safe setbacks and clearances must be provided to protect pedestrians, plantings, structures, lights, and other elements of the designed environment, while providing adequate maneuvering room for various types of vehicles.

*How can the vertical and horizontal alignment of the proposed roadway be coordinated to ecologically and aesthetically fit into the landscape.*

Due to cost factors, roadways tend to be laid out using the most efficient and direct route. However, the design of vehicular circulation systems involves both sound engineering practice and aesthetic judgment. A roadway should be so aligned and constructed as to preserve and accentuate the best qualities of the landscape, providing for a variety of visual experiences.

# DESIGN IMPACTS

## Environmental

The ecological impact of a proposed road depends on the existing flora, fauna, and hydrological patterns, the width of the road, and the expected density of traffic. There is a wide range of possible environmental consequences to roads that should be examined during the design process. Table 3.1 lists some common environmental impacts of roads.

**TABLE 3.1. Possible environmental effects from road corridors.**

| Increased | Decreased |
|---|---|
| • Access for human activity<br>• Invasion by roadside edge, weed, exotic and pest species<br>• Hydrological effects on wetlands, water table, and vegetation<br>• Salt damage to pines and cedar in farmland<br>• Lead, salt, etc. effects in aquatic systems<br>• Silt, sand, nutrients from dust | • Stream habitat and fish by sediment eroded from roadside and road<br>• Grassland birds<br>• Large mammals in woodland<br>• Interior species due to predominance of edge and generalist species |

Adapted From: Forman, Richard T.T., *Land Mosaics: The Ecology of Landscapes and Regions*, Cambridge University Press, Cambridge, 1997.

## Social

Roads and their adjacent land uses can be places where people feel safe and comfortable and where communities come together. For instance, traditional Main Streets in the United States have often served as places for farmers markets, parades, and other informal meetings between people. However, some roads are barriers between people and communities. These barriers create privacy, division, or isolation depending on your point of view. Much the same way that large, high traffic roads serve as barriers to species migration, they also can sever the contacts between neighborhoods and people.

## Economic

The economic model that perpetuates urban sprawl often indicates that new roads and parking lots will pay for themselves by connecting people to businesses and new neighborhoods. It should be noted, however, that there are tremendous infrastructure costs to the type of extensive development that follows roads further away from cities. The cost of maintaining roads

# TABLE 3.2. Summary of minimum design standards for urban streets.

**PRINCIPAL ARTERIAL**

| Design Elements | Freeways and Expressways | Other | Minor Arterials |
|---|---|---|---|
| Design Speed, km/h (mph) | 95 (60) | 65 (40) | 50 (30) |
| Number of Traffic Lanes | 4 up | 4 up | 4-6 |
| Width of Traffic Lanes, mm (ft) | 3660 (12') | 3660 (12') | 3660 (12') |
| Width of Curb Parking Lane or Shoulder, mm (ft) | 3660 (12') | 3050 (10') | 3050 (10') |
| Width of Right-of-way, mm (ft) | 36 575 up (120' up) | 36 575 up (120' up) | 30 480 - 36 575 (100-120') |

**COLLECTOR STREETS**

| Design Elements | Single-Family Residential Areas | Other |
|---|---|---|
| Design Speed, km/h (mph) | 50 (30) | 50 (30) |
| Number of Traffic Lanes | 2 | 4 |
| Width of Traffic Lanes, mm (ft) | 3660 (12') | 3660 (12') |
| Width of Curb Parking Lane or Shoulder, mm (ft) | 3050 (10') | 3050 (10') |
| Width of Right-of-way, mm (ft) | 18 290 (60') | 24 385 (80') |

**LOCAL STREETS**

| Design Elements | Single-Family Residential Areas | Other |
|---|---|---|
| Design Speed, km/h (mph) | 30 (20) | 50 (30) |
| Number of Traffic Lanes | 2 | 2-4 |
| Width of Traffic Lanes, mm (ft) | 3050 (10') | 3355 (11') |
| Width of Curb Parking Lane or Shoulder, mm (ft) | 2440 (8') | 3050 (10') |
| Width of Right-of-way, mm (ft) | 15 240 - 18 290 (50-60') | 18 290 - 24 385 (60-80') |

should be considered along with initial costs. Initial road construction costs can be reduced by:

1. minimizing the length of road frontage per property by creating a continuous and dense series of narrow-fronted developments on both sides of the road,
2. establishing a hierarchy of minor streets and arterials to allow cheaper road construction in less dense areas, and
3. avoiding steep grades and sharp curves that require more intensive, and therefore expensive, earthwork and drainage strategies.

**TABLE 3.3. Collector street design standards.**

| | Level Terrain | Rolling Terrain | Hilly Terrain |
|---|---|---|---|
| Right-of-way Width, mm (ft) | 21 335 (70') | 21 335 (70') | 21 335 (70') |
| Pavement Width, mm (ft) | 10 975 - 12 190 (36' to 40') | 10 975 - 12 190 (36' to 40') | 10 975 - 12 190 (36' to 40') |
| Type of Curb | Vertical Face | Vertical Face | Vertical Face |
| Sidewalk Width, mm (ft) | 1525 (5') | 1525 (5') | 1525 (5') |
| Sidewalk Distance From Curb Face, mm (ft) | 3050 (10') | 3050 (10') | 3050 (10') |
| Minimum Sight Distance, mm (ft) | 76 200 (250') | 60 960 (200') | 45 720 (150') |
| Maximum Grade | 4% | 8% | 12% |
| Minimum Spacing Along Major Traffic Route, mm (ft) | 396 240 (1300') | 396 240 (1300') | 396 240 (1300') |
| Design Speed, km/h (mph) | 55 (35) | 50 (30) | 40 (25) |
| Minimum Centerline Radius, mm (ft) | 106 680 (350') | 70 105 (230') | 45 720 (150') |

# SPATIAL STANDARDS

## General Roadway Standards
### Classification of Vehicular Circulation Systems

*Local or Minor Streets* allow local traffic movement and direct access to abutting properties.

*Collector Streets* allow traffic movement between major arterials and local streets with direct access to abutting properties.

*Arterial Streets* allow through-traffic movement between and across urban areas with access to abutting properties controlled but not excluded.

*Freeway or Distributor Systems* (including expressways and parkways) allow rapid movement of large volumes of through-traffic between and across urban areas with limited access allowed with grade-separated interchanges (see Figure 3.1. Vehicle circulation systems).

### Roadway Dimensions and Design Speed

Table 3.2 is a comparative summary of design standards for arterial, collector, and local streets. Tables 3.3 and 3.4 give standards for collector and local streets based on terrain and development density.

## Maneuvering Patterns

Figure 3.2 illustrates dimensional requirements of common vehicular access maneuvers at a facility drop-off. Figure 3.3 illustrates minimum turning radii for some large vehicles.

## Parking Dimensions

Pedestrians move from vehicles to pathways within parking lot settings. Figure 3.4 illustrates the typical design elements and spatial standards that may be employed in parking area design. Figure 3.5 illustrates basic parking lot dimensions required of perpendicular and angle parking.

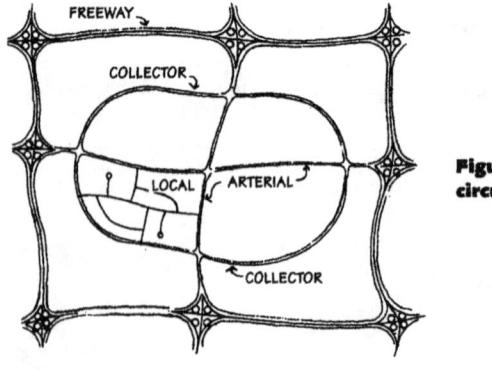

**Figure 3.1. Vehicular circulation systems.**

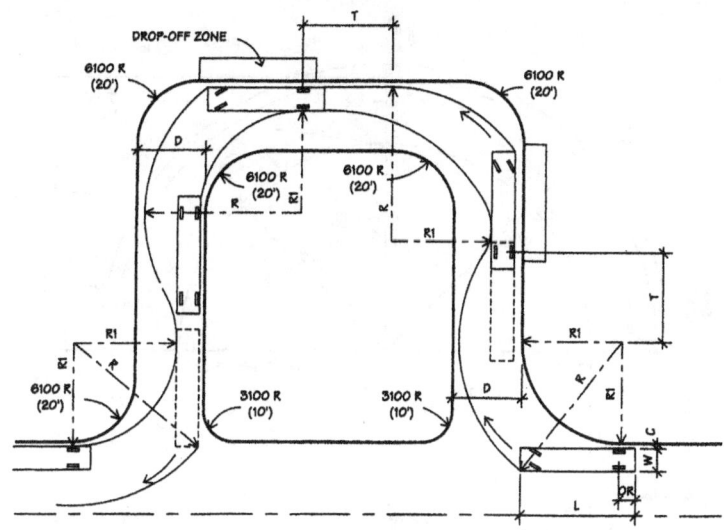

**Figure 3.2. Dimensions and turning radii for arrival and drop-off facilities.**

## TABLE 3-4. Local street design standards.

|  | Level Terrain | Rolling Terrain | Hilly Terrain |
|---|---|---|---|
| Right-of-way Width, mm (ft) | 18 290 (60') | 18 290 (60') | 15 240 - 18 290 (50' to 60') |
| Pavement Width, mm (ft) | 6705 - 10 975 (22' to 36') | 6705 - 10 975 (22' to 36') | 8230 - 10 975 (27' to 36') |
| Type of Curb | Vertical Face | Vertical Face | Vertical Face |
| Sidewalk Width, mm (ft) | 0 - 1525 (0' to 5') | 0 - 1525 (0' to 5') | 0 - 1525 (0' to 5') |
| Sidewalk Distance From Curb Face, mm (ft) | 0 - 1830 (0' to 6') | 0 - 1830 (0' to 6') | 0 - 1830 (0' to 6') |
| Minimum Sight Distance, mm (ft) | 60 960 (200') | 45 720 (150') | 33 530 (110') |
| Maximum Grade | 4% | 8% | 15% |
| Minimum Spacing Along Major Traffic Route, mm (ft) | 152 400 - 304 800 (500' to 1000') | 152 400 - 304 800 (500' to 1000') | 152 400 - 304 800 (500' to 1000') |
| Design Speed, km/h (mph) | 50 (30) | 40 (25) | 30 (20) |
| Minimum Centerline Radius, mm (ft) | 76 200 (250') | 53 340 (175') | 33 530 (110') |

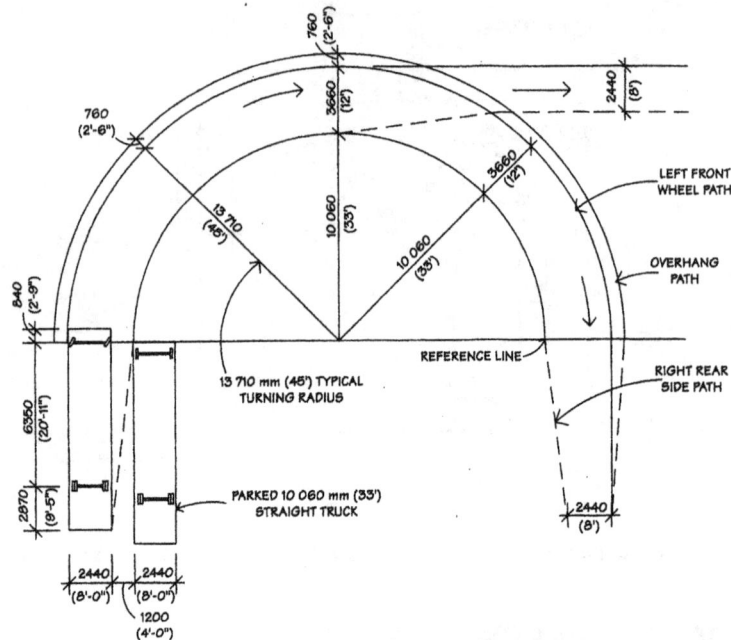

760
(2'-6")

2440
(8')

760
(2'-6")

3660
(12")

LEFT FRONT
WHEEL PATH

13 710
(45')

OVERHANG
PATH

10 060
(33')

3660
(12")

840
(2'-9")

10 060
(33')

REFERENCE LINE

RIGHT REAR
SIDE PATH

6350
(20'-11")

13 710 mm (45') TYPICAL
TURNING RADIUS

2970
(9'-5")

PARKED 10 060 mm (33')
STRAIGHT TRUCK

2440
(8')

2440
(8'-0")

2440
(8'-0")

2440
(8')

1200
(4'-0")

**Figure 3.3. Turning radii for
buses and semi trailers.**

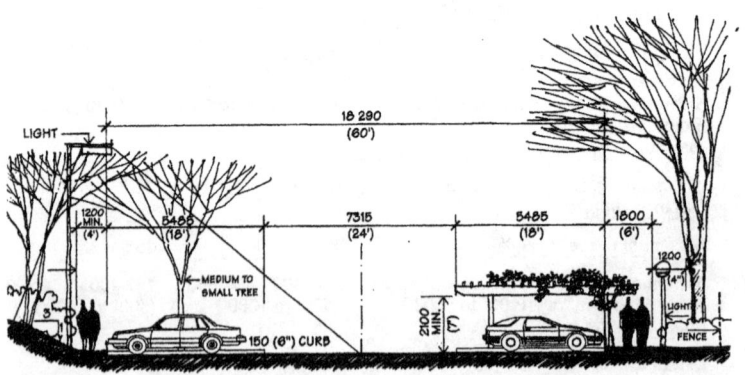

18 290
(60')

LIGHT

1200
MIN.
(4')

5485
(18')

7315
(24')

5485
(18')

1800
(6')

MEDIUM TO
SMALL TREE

2100
MIN.
(7')

1200
(4')

LIGHT

150 (6") CURB

FENCE

**Figure 3.4. Auto parking elements and typical spatial dimensions. Typical
plantings, landform, screens, and structures are used to create a more
hospitable transition from auto to pedestrian path.**

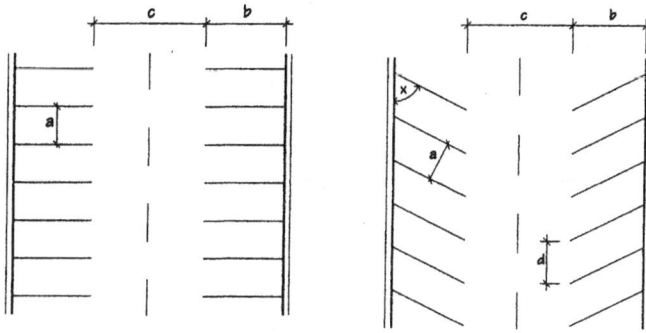

| x° | Stall Width a | Stall Depth b | Aisle Width c | Skew Width d |
|---|---|---|---|---|
| 90° | 2440 (8'-0") | 5485 (18'-0") | 8530 - 9750 (28' to 32') | |
| | 2590 (8'-6") | 5485 (18'-0") | 7620 - 8840 (25' to 29') | |
| | 2740 (9'-0") | 5485 (18'-0") | 7010 - 8230 (23' to 27') | |
| 60° | 2440 (8'-0") | 5970 (19'-7") | 5790 (19'-0") | 2820 (9'-3") |
| | 2590 (8'-6") | 5485 (18'-0") | 5485 (18'-0") | 2995 (9'-10") |
| | 2740 (9'-0") | 5180 (17'-0") | 5180 (17'-0") | 3175 (10'-5") |
| 45° | 2440 (8'-0") | 5610 (18'-5") | 3660 (12'-0") | 3450 (11'-4") |
| | 2590 (8'-6") | 5690 (18'-8") | 3350 (11'-0") | 3660 (12'-0") |
| | 2740 (9'-0") | 5815 (19'-1") | 3350 (11'-0") | 3885 (12'-9") |
| 30° | 2440 (8'-0") | 4850 (15'-11") | 3350 (11'-0") | 4875 (16'-0") |
| | 2590 (8'-6") | 5000 (16'-5") | 3040 (10'-0") | 5180 (17'-0") |
| | 2740 (9'-0") | 5130 (16'-10") | 2740 (9'-0") | 5485 (18'-0") |
| 0° | 2440 (8'-0") | 6700 (22'-0") | 3350 (11'-0") | |
| | 2590 (8'-6") | 6700 (22'-0") | 3505 (11'-6") | |
| | 2740 (9'-0") | 7010 (23'-0") | 3660 (12'-0") | |

**Figure 3.5. Parking lot dimensions for various stall widths and angles.**
(Adaptation courtesy of Vollmer Associates).

# ROADWAY DESIGN ELEMENTS

## Horizontal Alignment
### General Design Criteria of Horizontal Alignments
- Alignment should be as direct as possible, but respectful of topography and other critical natural or cultural features.
- Longer curves are preferred to those that satisfy minimum radii.
- Abrupt changes from straight lines to sharp curves should be avoided.
- Abrupt reversal in alignment (i.e., S curves) without transitional tangents should be avoided.

## Components of Horizontal Alignment

Horizontal alignment is generally composed of two geometric components: straight lines (tangents) and circular curves (arcs). Figure 3.6 illustrates the geometric components of a circular curve. Formulas necessary to calculate the components of circular curves are as follows:

$$D = \frac{5729.58}{R} \text{ or } D = \frac{100a}{L}$$

$$L = \frac{100a}{D} \text{ or } L = \frac{(\pi)(R)a}{180}$$

$$R = \frac{5729.58}{D}$$

$$T = R\tan\frac{a}{2}$$

$$C = 2R\sin\frac{a}{2}$$

$$E = T\tan\frac{a}{4}$$

$$M = R\left(1 - \cos\frac{a}{2}\right)$$

where a = angle and $\pi$ = 3.14

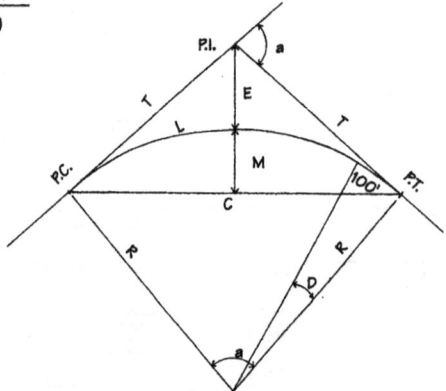

**Figure 3.6. Geometric components of a circular curve** (horizontal alignment).

P.C. (point of curvature): the beginning of the curve in the direction of stationing

P.T. (point of tangency): the end of the curve in the direction of stationing

P.I. (point of intersection): point where the tangents, if extended, will intersect

a (delta, intersection angle, central angle): the angle deflection between the tangents, also equal to the angle between radii

T (tangent distance): horizontal distance between P.C. to P.I. and P.T. to P.I. (They are always equal.)

R (radius): radius of curve

L (length of curve): computed (actual) length of curve (arc) from P.C. to P.T.

C (long chord): distance measured along a straight line (shortest distance) between P.C. and P.T.

E (external distance): distance from the P.I. to the center of the curve

M (middle ordinate): distance form the center of the curve to the center of the long chord

D (degree of curvature): the angle at the center subtended by an arc of 100 ft which corresponds to a radius of 5729.58 ft for a central angle of 1 degree

## Superelevation

Superelevation refers to the cross slope of a road from the outside edge to the inside edge. Superelevation is necessary on higher speed curves to counter-act centrifugal force and provide a safe coefficient of friction between tires and roadway surface.

## Vertical Alignment
### Components of Vertical Alignment

The vertical plane or profile of a road or drive is essentially made up of two geometric components: inclined straight lines (i.e., tangent grades) and vertical curves.

*Grades:* Maximum grades for roads vary considerably, depending on terrain, speed, capacity, and use of the road. Table 3.5 shows the relationship between maximum grades and design speeds for major roadways. Maximum grades for secondary roads can generally be increased by 2%.

*Vertical Curves:* Vertical curves are constructed from parts of parabolas rather than circles, and connect two different grades or tangents. Figure 3.7 illustrates the geometry of a vertical curve.

*Note: For further information on calculating horizontal and vertical curves see the References at the end of this chapter.*

**TABLE 3.5. Relation of maximum grades to design speed (main highways), (% slope).**

| Type of topography | Design speed, km/h (mph) | | | | | |
|---|---|---|---|---|---|---|
| | 48 (30) | 64 (40) | 80 (50) | 96 (60) | 104 (65) | 112 (70) |
| Flat | 6 | 5 | 4 | 3 | 3 | 3 |
| Rolling | 7 | 6 | 5 | 4 | 4 | 4 |

Source: AASHTO, *A Policy on Geometric Design of Rural Highways,* 1965.

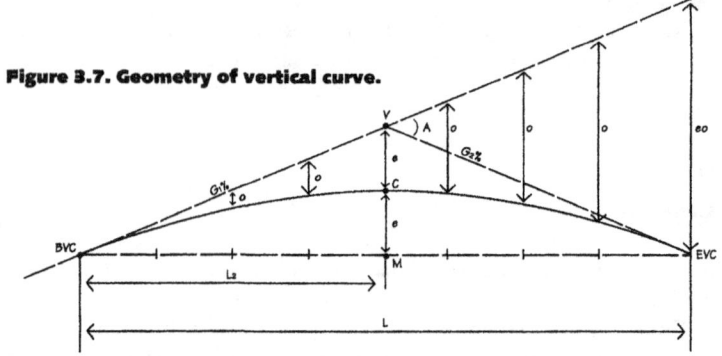

**Figure 3.7. Geometry of vertical curve.**

V = vertex or intersection of two grads

A = algebraic difference in grades (percent) of the grade tangents = $G_2 - G_1$

BVC = beginning of the vertical curve (in relation to stationing)

EVC = end of the vertical curve (in relation to stationing)

C = middle point on the parabolic curve between BVC-EVC and middle point between M-V

$G_1\%$ = percentage of slope on the entering grade tangent

$G_2\%$ = percentage of slope on the leaving grade tangent

M = middle point or distance halfway on chord between BVC-EVC

e = middle ordinate (offset) between C-V and C-M

L = length (horizontally) of the vertical curve

o = ordinates or station offsets

eo = end ordinate or station offset at EVC

## SUGGESTED REFERENCES

American Association of State Highway and Transportation Officials (AASHTO). *A Policy on Design Standards — Interstate System*, Washington, DC, 1989.

American Association of State Highway and Transportation Officials (AASHTO). *A Policy on Geometric Design of Highways and Streets*, Washington, DC, 1990.

Forman, Richard T.T., *Land Mosaics: The Ecology of Landscapes and Regions*, Cambridge University Press, Cambridge, 1997.

Harris, Charles W. and Nicholas T. Dines, *Time-Saver Standards for Landscape Architecture, 2nd Edition*, McGraw-Hill, New York, 1998.

Lay, M.G. *Handbook of Road Technology*. 2nd ed. Gordon and Breach, 1990.

Lynch, Kevin, and Gary Hack. *Site Planning*. 3rd ed., MIT Press, Cambridge, MA, 1984.

Wright, Paul H. *Highway Engineering*. 6th ed. Wiley, New York, 1996.

# STANDARDS

# *Recreation Standards*

4

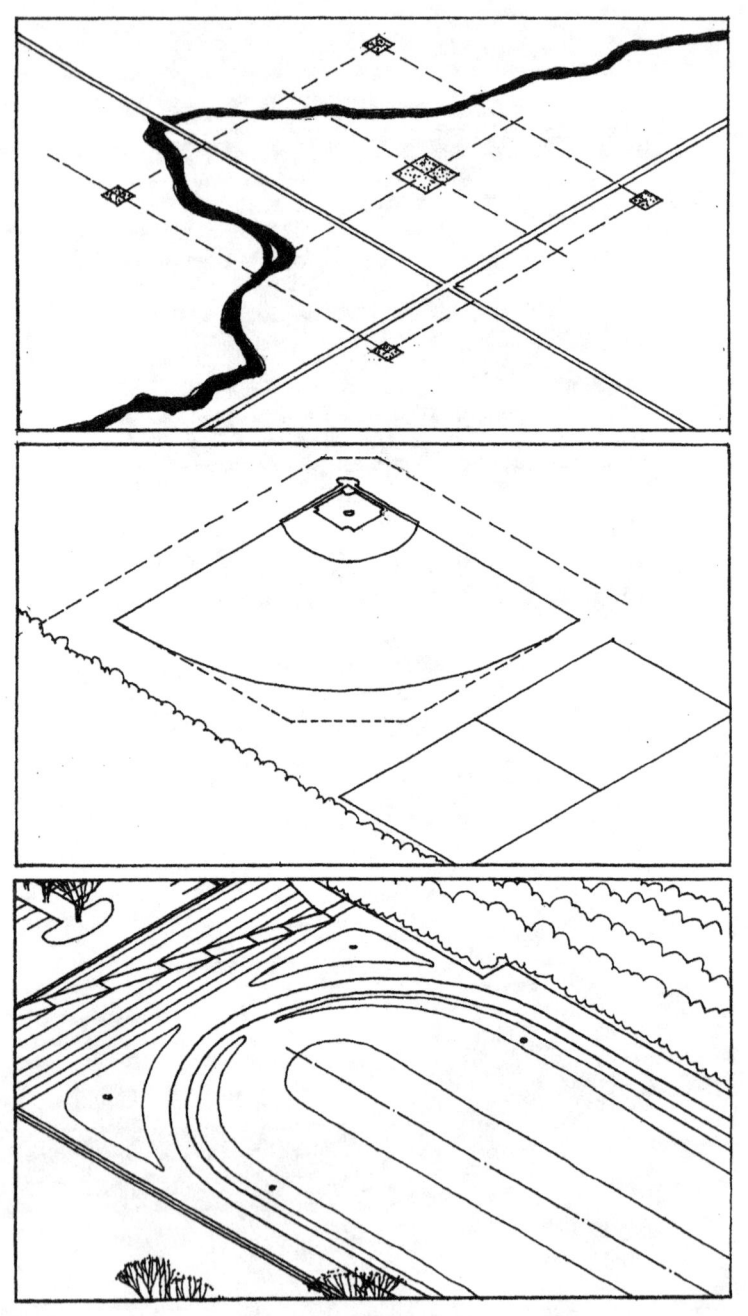

## COMMUNITY SCALE RECREATION STANDARDS

Local population and environmental characteristics commonly serve as a basis for determining spatial allocation standards at the community scale of planning. It is recommended that existing or proposed greenway systems be used to organize various types of facilities along a natural or cultural corridor. Recreation facilities are more commonly distributed according to neighborhood density and vehicular and pedestrian access corridors.

## RECREATION FACILITIES DESIGN STANDARDS

Recreation facilities are typically organized around specific athletic or cultural uses. Design standards are derived from specific spatial and dimensional requirements of field and court games and their associated infrastructure requirements. Local terrain, surrounding land uses, and vegetative patterns often require design adaptation to appropriately integrate the facility with the surrounding community and landscape setting.

## FIELD AND SURFACE STANDARDS

Field and surface standards are commonly determined by local, national, or international dimensional requirements. Use intensity, loading characteristics, and local climate and soils determine construction standards required to properly install the facilities. The long-term maintenance requirements and the infrastructure support requirements are important cost factors to consider.

**P**ARTICIPATION IN RECREATIONAL AND ATHLETIC activities involves virtually every age group and segment of society from children to senior citizens and goes beyond exercise and athletic programs to embrace every interest, physical stature, and level of skill. The standards for recreational and athletic facilities are compiled from numerous sources and range from rigid dimensions required for regulation play to suggestions derived from experience. This chapter covers the spatial requirements of various recreational activities, as well as functional issues such as orientation, drainage, and surfacing requirements.

## DIAGNOSTIC ASSESSMENT

*What are the recreational needs of the population?*

Designers planning for the park and recreational needs of a community have access to a variety of standards and data that recommend the quantity, spatial pattern, and maximum distance of various recreation facilities. The recreational needs of any community are subject to great regional variability; therefore, these standards should be considered the first step in the planning process.

*What are the layout requirements of specific recreational and athletic facilities?*

For most athletic and recreational facilities, adherence to standards assures continuity of experience, regardless of location. The requirements of any athletic organization that may use the recreation facilities often dictate dimensional standards. It is a challenge for a designer to effectively integrate these organizational requirements with the local conditions in order to enhance and preserve local character. However, non-competitive facilities may allow for variability based on local conditions, budget, and client needs.

*What are the surfacing requirements for various courts and fields?*

Athletic and game surfaces typically include general field play, sanctioned games such as baseball, field hockey, softball, and soccer, as well as specialized games such as lawn bowling, tennis, and croquet. Local climate and soils are key determinates of specific construction methods required to install various surfaces to achieve the desired level of performance.

# NEEDS ASSESSMENT

## Community Parks and Recreation Planning Data

Table 4.1 lists recommendations for open space and recreation areas ranging from small neighborhood parks to large regional recreation centers. The table lists area requirements, maximum travel distances, and the size of the population served.

**TABLE 4.1. Standards for open space and recreation areas**

| Type of Facility | Area Requirements | Service Distance | Hectares (Acres) per 1000 Population |
|---|---|---|---|
| Neighborhood Park | 2-4 hectare (5-10 acres) | 0.80 km (½ mile) | .80-1.20 (2-3) |
| District Park | 4-12 hectare (10-30 acres) | 1.60 km (1 mile) | .60-1.20 (1.5-3) |
| Community Park | 60-80 hectare (150-200 acres) | 4.80-8 km (3-5 miles) | 2-2.60 (5-6.5) |
| Regional Park | 200-400 hectare (500-1000 acres) | 16-32 km (10-20 miles) | 4-12 (10-30) |

## Facilities Planning Data

Tables 4.2 and 4.3 are a compilation of planning data for specific recreational facilities. Table 4.2 lists the number of required facilities per 1000 population and the maximum radius or travel distance served. Table 4.3 lists area requirements and capacities for various play equipment and activity areas.

**TABLE 4.2. Area space standards for outdoor sport facilities**

| AREA SPACE STANDARDS (BASED UPON POPULATION) | | |
|---|---|---|
| Sport | Facilities per 1,000 population | Notes |
| Multicourt | Minimum 1 + 1/2,000–light 25-50% | 1.5 mile maximum radius |
| Handball " | Minimum 1 + 1/5,000-10,000 1/10,000 | |
| Volleyball | 1/2,000 to 1/3000-4,000 | communities 10,000+ |
| Shuffleboard | Minimum 1-2 + 1/2,000–light 25% | communities over 500 |
| Basketball " " | 1 goal/500 1 goal/1,000 + one full court 1 acre/5,000 persons | communities under 3,000 communities over 3,000 |

➤ continued on next page

# TABLE 4.2. Area space standards for outdoor sport facilities (continued).

**AREA SPACE STANDARDS (BASED UPON POPULATION)**

| Sport | Facilities per 1,000 population | Notes |
|---|---|---|
| Croquet | 1/2,000–light 25% | |
| Horsehoe | Minimum 2 + 1/2,000–light 25-50% | community over 500 |
| Softball | Minimum 1 + 1/3,000–light 50% | community over 1,000 |
| Little League | 1/10,000<br>Minimum 1 + 1/4,000–light 25% | |
| Baseball<br>"<br>" | 1/3,000<br>Minimum 1 + 1/6,000–light 50%<br>1/30,,000<br>1/6,000 | community over 1500<br><br>community 1 mile<br>maximum radius |
| Football, soccer<br>"<br>" | Minimum 1 + 1/5-15,000<br>Minimum 1 + 1/8,000 for football<br>2 acres/1000<br>1/80,000 | |
| Tennis<br>"<br>"<br>" | Minimum 1 + 1/2,000–light 50-76%<br>1/1,0000<br>1/2,000<br>1500 S.F./player<br>1 acre/5,000 | community 0.67 miles<br>radius |
| Athletic field | Approximate 20 acres<br>1/50,000–lighted<br>accommodate 200 people/acre | 1-2 miles or 20 minutes |

# TABLE 4.3. Area requirements for playgrounds and sports areas

| Type of equipment or area | Area per unit m² (f²) | Capacity in numbers of users | Suggested number to be included |
|---|---|---|---|
| **APPARATUS** | | | |
| Slide | 42 (450) | 6 | 1** |
| Horizontal bars | 17 (180) | 4 | 3** |
| Horizontal ladders | 35 (375) | 8 | 2** |
| Traveling rings | 58 (625) | 6 | 1 |
| Giant stride | 114 (1,225) | 6 | 1 |
| Small junglegym | 17 (180) | 10 | 1 |
| Low swing | 14 (150) | 1 | 4* |
| High swing | 23 (250) | 1 | 6* |
| Balance beam | 9 (100) | 4 | 1 |
| See-saw | 9 (100) | 2 | 4 |
| Medium junglegym | 46 (500) | 20 | 1 |

## TABLE 4.3. Area requirements for playgrounds and sports areas (continued).

| Type of equipment or area | Area per unit m2 (f2) | Capacity in numbers of users | Suggested number to be included |
|---|---|---|---|
| **MISCELLANEOUS EQUIPMENT AND AREAS** | | | |
| Open space for games (ages 6-10) | 929 (10,000) | 80 | 1* |
| Wading pool | 279 (3,000) | 40 | 1* |
| Handcraft, quiet games | 149 (1,600) | 30 | 1* |
| Outdoor theater | 186 (2,000) | 30 | 1 |
| Sand box | 28 (300) | 15 | 2 |
| Shelter house | 232 (2,500) | 30 | 1† |
| **SPECIAL SPORTS AREAS** | | | |
| Soccer field | 3344 (36,000) | 22 | 1 |
| Playground baseball | 1858 (20,000) | 20 | 2 |
| Volleyball court | 260 (2,800) | 20 | 1 |
| Basketball court | 348 (3,750) | 16 | 1 |
| Jumping pits | 111 (1,200) | 12 | 1 |
| Paddle tennis courts | 167 (1,800) | 4 | 2‡ |
| Handball courts | 98 (1,050) | 4 | 2 |
| Tether tennis courts | 37 (400) | 2 | 2‡ |
| Horseshoe courts | 56 (600) | 4 | 2 |
| Tennis courts | 669 (7,200) | 4 | 2‡ |
| Straightaway track | 669 (7,200) | 10 | 1‡ |
| Landscaping | 557 (6,000) | | |
| Paths, circulation, etc. | 650 (7,000) | | |

\* Minimum desirable.

\*\* One or all of these units may be omitted if playground is not used in conjunction with a school.

† May be omitted it sanitary facilities are supplied elsewhere.

‡ May be omitted if space if limited.

Source: From Architectural Systems Community Planning.

# LAYOUT REQUIREMENTS

## Court Games

Court games are sports played primarily on hard surfaces rather than on turf. The standards for courts vary depending on whether competition is under the auspices of international, national, collegiate, or high school societies. Major regulating organizations are listed at the end of this chapter.

- Table 4.4 is a summary of the area requirements, dimensions, orientation, and surfacing of various court sports.
- Figures 4.1 through 4.3 illustrate court layout for basketball, volleyball, and tennis.

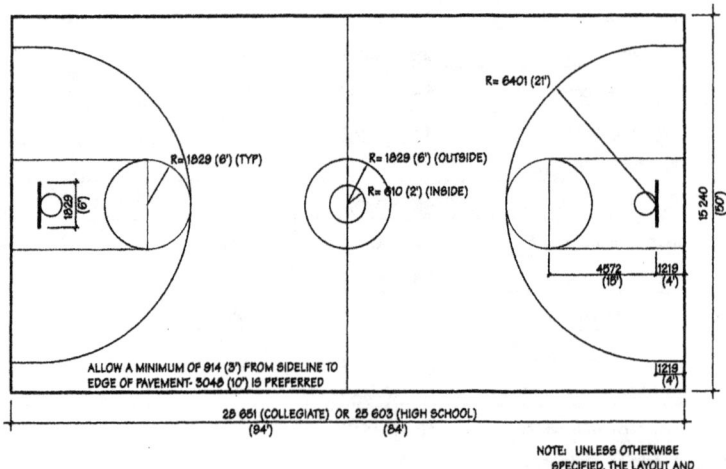

**Figure 4.1. Basketball.**

NOTE: UNLESS OTHERWISE
SPECIFIED, THE LAYOUT AND
DIMENSIONS OF ALL COURTS
ARE SYMMETRICAL AROUND
THE CENTER LINES.

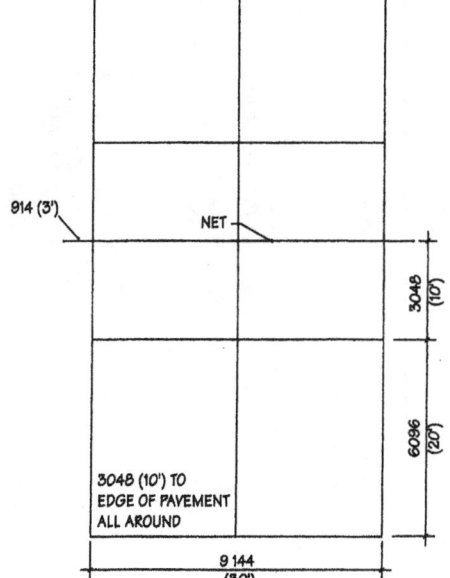

914 (3')

NET

3048 (10')

6096 (20')

3048 (10') TO
EDGE OF PAVEMENT
ALL AROUND

9 144
(30')

**Figure 4.2. Volleyball.**

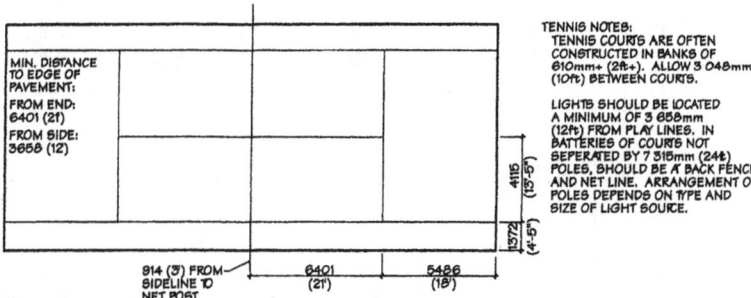

MIN. DISTANCE
TO EDGE OF
PAVEMENT:
FROM END:
6401 (21)
FROM SIDE:
3658 (12)

4115
(13'-5")

1372
(4'-5")

914 (3') FROM
SIDELINE TO
NET POST

6401
(21')

5486
(18')

TENNIS

TENNIS NOTES:
TENNIS COURTS ARE OFTEN
CONSTRUCTED IN BANKS OF
610mm+ (2ft+). ALLOW 3 048mm
(10ft) BETWEEN COURTS.

LIGHTS SHOULD BE LOCATED
A MINIMUM OF 3 658mm
(12ft) FROM PLAY LINES. IN
BATTERIES OF COURTS NOT
SEPERATED BY 7 315mm (24t)
POLES, SHOULD BE A BACK FENCE
AND NET LINE. ARRANGEMENT OF
POLES DEPENDS ON TYPE AND
SIZE OF LIGHT SOURCE.

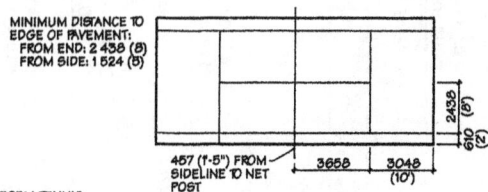

MINIMUM DISTANCE TO
EDGE OF PAVEMENT:
FROM END: 2 438 (8)
FROM SIDE: 1 524 (5)

2438
(8')

610
(2')

457 (1'-5") FROM
SIDELINE TO NET
POST

3658
(12')

3048
(10')

PLATFORM TENNIS

**Figure 4.3. Tennis.**

# TABLE 4.4. Court Games

| Sport | Use area required including clear zones | Court dimensions* | Orientation | Surface |
|---|---|---|---|---|
| **BADMINTON** | | | | |
| Doubles | 1500 mm (5 ft) clear zones between courts and at end | 6096 × 13 411.2 mm (20 × 44 ft) | Competition play is usually indoors. Outdoor courts long axis north-south. | Any hard surface or turf, drain as in tennis. |
| Singles | Same as doubles | 5181.6 × 13 411.2 mm (17 × 44 ft) | (Same) | (Same) |
| **BASKETBALL** | | | | |
| High school | 34 200 × 21 000 mm (114 × 70 ft) | 25 603.2 × 15 240 mm (84 × 50 ft) | North-south | Concrete, drain end to end at 25 mm per 3 m (1 in per 10 ft) |
| College | | 28 651.2 × 15 240 mm (94 × 50 ft) | (Same) | (Same) |
| International | 18 m × 30 m | 14 000 × 26 000 mm | (Same) | (Same) |
| Goal-hi | 18 000 × 18 000 mm to 24 000 × 24 000 mm (60 X 60 ft to 80 X 80 ft) | Circle—12 000 to 18 000 mm (40 to 60 ft) in diameter | Optional | Asphalt or synthetic; drain to edges. |
| **HANDBALL** | | | | |
| One wall | 10 200 × 6000 × 4800 mm (34 × 20 × 16 ft) high | 10 363.2 × 6096 × 4876.8 (34 × 20 × 16 ft) high | Can be added to exteriors of gym or may be free standing | Any hard surface; drain from front to rear. |
| Three or four walls | 12 000 × 6000 × 6000 mm (40 × 20 × 20 ft) high | 12 192 × 6096 × 6096 mm (40 × 20 × 20 ft) high | Competition play normally indoors | (Same) |

**TABLE 4.4. Court Games (continued).**

| Sport | Use area required including clear zones | Court dimensions* | Orientation | Surface |
|---|---|---|---|---|
| **RACQUETBALL** | Same as handball | | | |
| **SHUFFLEBOARD** | 15 600 × 3000 mm (52 × 10 ft), including 1 200 mm (4 ft) between courts | 15 849.6 × 1828.8 mm (52 × 6 ft) | Long axis north-south | Hard/smooth concrete without expansion joints. Alley depressed and drained with catch basins. |
| **TENNIS** | 18 000 × 36 000 mm (60 × 120 ft) for one doubles court. Multiples can be designed with 3000 to 3600 mm (10 to 12 ft) between courts. | 10 972.8 × 23 774.4 mm (36 × 78 ft) | Long axis north-south is OK, long axis 22 degrees west of north and east of south is better in southern latitudes. | Many, including concrete, clay, asphalt, and turf. Drain side to side (preferred) or end to end at 0.8 to 1% (nonporous) or 0.003 to 0.004% (porous). Never allow high point at net. |
| Deck | 7800 × 15 000 mm (26 × 50 ft) (doubles) [needs a 3000 mm (10 ft) fence] | 5486.4 × 12 192 mm (18 × 40 ft) | Long axis north-south. | Asphalt or concrete; drain side to side at 25 mm per 3 m (1 in per 10 ft) |
| Paddle | 11 100 × 24 000 mm (37 × 80 ft) [needs an 2400 mm (8 ft) fence] | 6096 × 15 240 mm (20 × 50 ft) | Long axis north-south. | Same as deck tennis |
| Platform | 9000 × 18 000 mm (30 × 60 ft) [needs a 3600 mm (12 ft) fence] | 6096 × 13 411.2 mm (20 × 44 ft) | Long axis north-south. | Raised level wood or aluminum platform; 5 mm (1/4 in) spacing between 150 mm (6 in) decking. |
| **VOLLEYBALL** | 15 000 × 24 000 mm (50 × 80 ft) preferred; (42 × 72 ft) OK | 9144 × 18 288 mm (30 × 60 ft) | Long axis north-south. | Asphalt, sand, clay mix, turf (ropes are used for marking sand and turf); drain at 25 mm per 3 m (1 in per 10 ft) |

* All conversions to metric are exact.

STANDARDS

## Field Sports

Field sports include any activities played, preferably, on soft turf surfaces. Where temporary bleachers are used, allow a width of 20-30 m (60-90 ft) between the sidelines and the playing fields.

- Figure 4.4 illustrates four drainage alternatives for fields (see Chapter 10: Grading for more information).
- Table 4.5 is a summary of the area requirements, dimensions, orientation, and drainage strategies for various field sports.

A
HP
"HOGBACK"
A
HP
"TURTLEBACK"
B
HP
1% TYP
C
HP

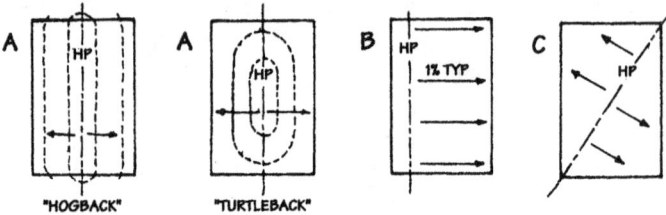

**Figure 4.4. Drainage alternatives for fields.**

'POCKET'
DARK BACKGROUND
DARK BACKGROUND
SCOREBOARD AND FLAG
LIGHTING LOCATION TYP. 70' HIGH 1500 W LAMPS
300-400' (HOME PLATE TO POCKET)
A WARNING TRACK IS RECOMMENDED IN FRONT OF THE OUTFIELD FENCE, BACKSTOP AND DUGOUTS. THE TRACK SHOULD BE 15-20' WIDE AND SURFACED IN A MATERIAL CONTRASTING TO TURF UNDERFOOT (E.G. CRUSHED STONE)
FOUL POLE
FOUL POLE ABOUT 20' HIGH METAL SCREEN EXTENDS ABOUT 12" TOWARD CENTER FIELD ALONG ENTIRE HEIGHT
FOUL POLE
TURF
GRASS LINE
FENCE 4-6' HIGH NOT REQUIRED IN SOME LEAGUES
SKINNED
90'
95'
250-350'
18' DIA. RAISED 10"
ORIENTATION A LINE RUNNING FROM HOME PLATE TO 2ND BASE SHOULD POINT EAST-NORTHEAST
26' DIA.
60'-6"
GRADING DRAIN AWAY FROM HOME PLATE. BASE LINES SHOULD BE LEVEL
PROTECTIVE FENCE 6' HIGH
'ON DECK' CIRCLE, 3-5' DIAMETER
BENCH, ABOUT 20' LONG
THESE ELEMENTS MAY BE COMBINED INTO A DUGOUT
60'
NOTE: THIS DIAGRAM IS GENERALIZED FOR ADULT COMPETITION AND MAY NOT REFLECT SPECIFIC REQUIREMENTS OF EACH LEAGUE.
MINIMUM SLOPE OF OUTFIELD TURF IS 1% WITH ADEQUATE SUBSURFACE DRAINAGE. MAXIMUM SLOPE IS 2.5 %
BASIC GRADING

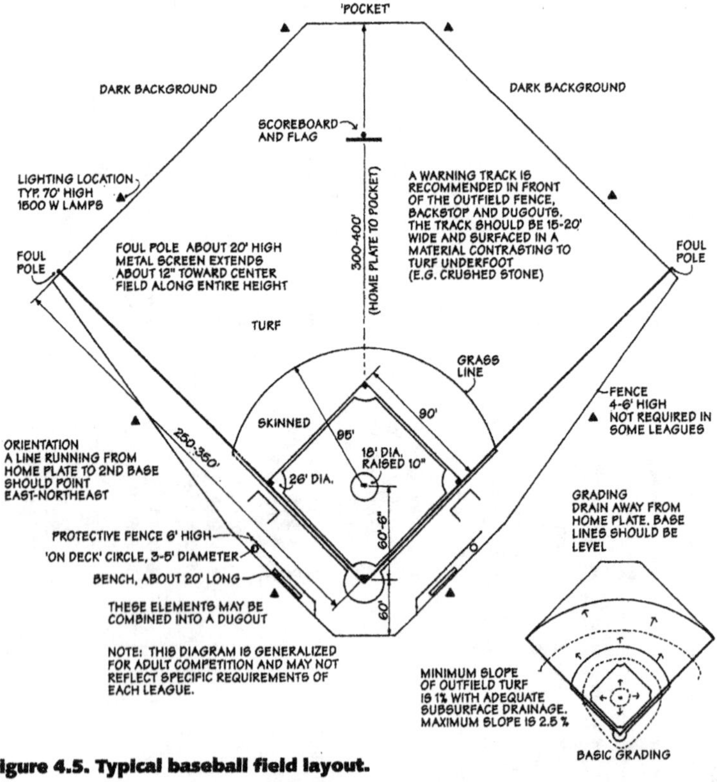

**Figure 4.5. Typical baseball field layout.**

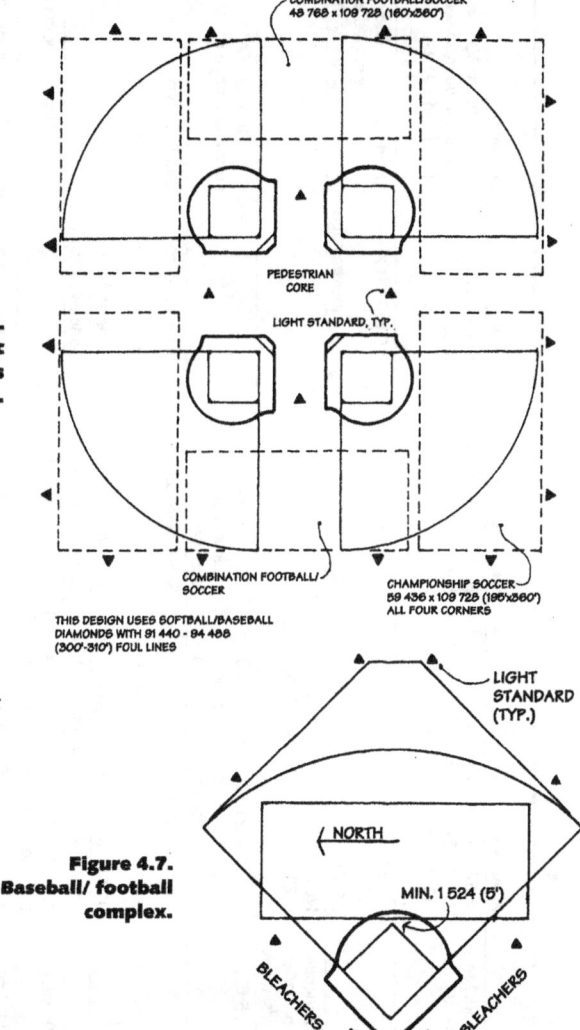

COMBINATION FOOTBALL/SOCCER
48 768 x 109 728 (160'x360')

**Figure 4.6. Schematic sports complex.**

PEDESTRIAN CORE

LIGHT STANDARD, TYP.

COMBINATION FOOTBALL/ SOCCER

CHAMPIONSHIP SOCCER
59 436 x 109 728 (195'x360')
ALL FOUR CORNERS

THIS DESIGN USES SOFTBALL/BASEBALL DIAMONDS WITH 91 440 - 94 488 (300'-310') FOUL LINES

LIGHT STANDARD (TYP.)

NORTH

MIN. 1 524 (5')

**Figure 4.7. Baseball/ football complex.**

BLEACHERS

BLEACHERS

- Figures 4.5 through 4.7 show the layout requirements for softball and baseball fields and how they can be combined with football and soccer fields to create multipurpose sports complexes. Multipurpose complexes have many advantages associated with reducing the total land required to accommodate many activities. Advantages include the common use of parking, support facilities, irrigation, and lighting systems. Disadvantages include possible scheduling conflicts, the need for portable outfield fences and goals, and the increased traffic, noise, and glare associated with high-density recreation.

*Recreation Standards* • 71

**TABLE 4.5. Field Sports**

| Sport | Use area required | Playing area*** | Orientation | Drainage | Comments |
|---|---|---|---|---|---|
| Bocce | 5.7 to 7.7 m × 24.6-30.3 m (19 to 25 ft 6 in × 82-101 ft) | 3962.4 to 5791.2 mm × 23 400-27 600 mm (13 to 19 ft 6 in × 78-92 ft) | North-south preferred but not critical | Drain in any direction at 1% | 250 to 300 mm wooden boards used at end and side as backstops |
| Bowling (lawn) | | 39 × 39 m (130 × 130 ft) 36 576 mm | 5791.2 to 6400.8 mm × 120 ft) alleys | (19 to 21 ft X use underdrainage | Dead level— Alleys grouped in banks of six |
| Cricket | Size varies, but area generally oval with no part of boundary closer than 70 m (75 yds) to pitch | No official size for field, but pitch is 20 116.8 × 3048 mm (66 × 10 ft) | | | |
| Croquet | 3.5 × 22.5 m (45 × 75 ft) | 12 192 × 21 336 mm (40 × 70 ft) (smaller size is appropriate for nonregulation play) | Orient so that bleachers do not face sun | | Drain as in A** at a maximum slope of 2% |
| Fieldball | Same as soccer | Same as soccer | Same as soccer | Same as soccer | Same as soccer |
| Field hockey Women | * | 91 440 × 45 720 mm (300 × 150 ft) | Same as football | Same as football | |
| Men | * | 91 440 × 54 864 mm (300 × 180 ft) | Same as football | Same as football | |
| Flag or touch football | 40 × 95 m (44 × 104 yds) | 12 192 × 30 480 mm (40 × 100 yds) [includes two 9 m (10 yd) end zones] | Same as football | | Same as football |
| Football | Minimum 51.6 × 111.6 m (172 × 372 ft) | 48 768 × 109 728 mm (160 × 360 ft) [including two 9 m (10 yd) end zones] | Long axis, northwest to southeast, or north-south for longer season | Drain as in A; B or C** are permitted but not preferred; provide adequate underdrainage | |
| Horseshoes | 6 × 21 m (20 × 70 ft) | 3048 × 15 240 mm (10 × 50 ft) | Long axis, north-south | | Drain as in "A"; two end pegs must have identical elevation |

**TABLE 4.5. Field Sports (continued)**

| Sport | Use area required | Playing area*** | Orientation | Drainage | Comments |
|---|---|---|---|---|---|
| *Lacrosse*<br>Women | | Boundaries set by referee; minimum width 45 720 mm (150 ft), length 109 728-124 968 mm (360-410 ft) | Same as football | Same as football | |
| Men | 60 × 105 m (200 × 350 ft) with fence; 66 × 111 m (220 × 370 ft) without fence | Prefer 54 864 × 100 584mm (180 × 330 ft), but can be played on football field | Same as football | Same as football | |
| Polo | Play area includes safety area | 91 440 × 48 768 mm (300 × 160 yds) if boarded; 91 440 × 60 960 mm (300 × 200 yds) if not | | | |
| Quoits | Allow 1500-3000 mm (5-10 ft) at side and back boundaries | 16 459.2-21 945.6 mm × ~3000 mm (54-72 ft × ~10 ft) | Same as horseshoes | Same as horseshoes | |
| Rogue | 120 × 210 m (40 × 70 ft) | 9144 × 18 288 mm (30 × 60 ft) | Same as croquet | Dead level; use underground drainage | Surface is packed earth |
| *Rugby*<br>(League-<br>professional) * | | 100.6 × 54.9 m (110 × 60 yds) plus 5.5-11 m (6-12 yds) at each end for ingoal | Same as football | Same as football | |
| (union-<br>amateur) * | | 100.6 × 54.9 m (110 × 60 yds) plus 22.8 m (25 yds) at each end for ingoal | Same as football | Same as football | |
| Soccer | 9 m (10 yds) on all sides free of obstructions | 50-70 m × 90-110 m × 100-120 yds) 68.58 × 109.73 m (75 × 120 yds) for championship | North-south, except south of 38th parallel where long axis may approach 20 degrees west of north | Same as football | There are no official standards for soccer size varies even among Olympic sites |
| *Speedball*<br>Women | * | 54.86 × 91.44 m (60 × 100 yds) | Same as football | Same as football | |
| Men | * | 48.77 × 109.73 m (53⅓ X 120 yds) | Same as football | Same as football | |

*When not specified, no standard exists; 9 m (10 yds) is recommended on all sides.

** See Figure 4.4.     *** All conversions to metric are exact.

## Track and Field

- According to standards published in the United States by the NCAA, a championship track shall be at least 400 m (440 yd) in length with six to eight lanes at 900-1200 mm (36-48 in) in width.
- Longitudinal slopes for tracks, runways, and landing areas for field events should not exceed a maximum of 0.1 percent (1:1000). Cross slopes should be no more than 1 percent (1:100) or, for high school, 2 percent (2:100).
- Both the NCAA and the IAFF require a curb 50 mm (2 in) high along the inner edge of an oval track. American and world records will not be accepted without the inside curb.
- Figure 4.8 illustrates the layout requirements of a 400-meter track.

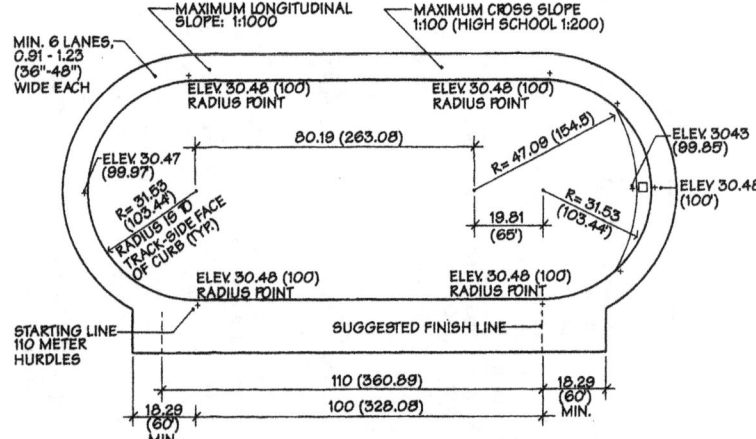

**Figure 4.8. Basic layout: 400-meter track.**

## Golf and Driving Ranges

Golf course design is too complex to be fully covered in this section, however some of the major area requirements are listed below.

- Regulation 18 hole courses have pars ranging from 68 to 72. Courses can be laid out in one of five basic configurations, their required areas ranging from 60 to 75 ha (140 to 175 acres) as shown in Figure 4.9
- The configuration of the holes will depend on upon the character of the site, the design program, and adjacent land use. Figure 4.10 shows the layout requirements of a typical golf hole without hazards.
- Driving ranges should include multiple tee areas to hit into and across the wind. Figure 4.11 shows the layout requirements of a typical driving range.

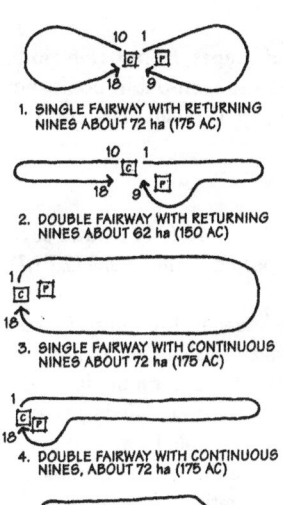

1. SINGLE FAIRWAY WITH RETURNING NINES ABOUT 72 ha (175 AC)

2. DOUBLE FAIRWAY WITH RETURNING NINES ABOUT 62 ha (150 AC)

3. SINGLE FAIRWAY WITH CONTINUOUS NINES ABOUT 72 ha (175 AC)

4. DOUBLE FAIRWAY WITH CONTINUOUS NINES, ABOUT 72 ha (175 AC)

5. CORE, ABOUT 57 ha (140 AC) BUT PROVIDES THE LEAST HOUSING FRONTAGE

C CLUBHOUSE
P PUTTING GREEN
DR DRIVING RANGE

**Figure 4. 9. Typical golf course arrangements.**

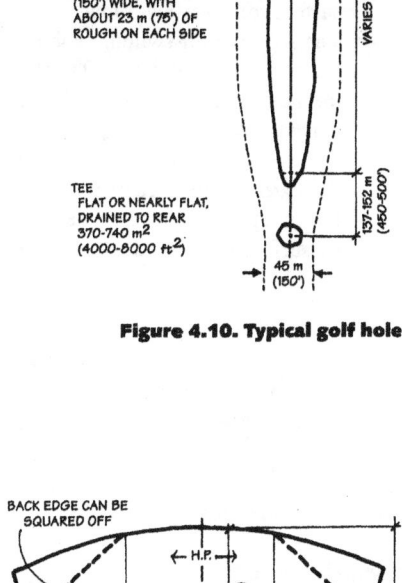

GREEN
GENTLY UNDULATING SLOPES, 1-3% IN PIN-SET AREA. 418-790 m² (4500-8500 ft²)

EDGE OF BUILDING LINE

FAIRWAY
GENERALLY ABOUT 45 m (150') WIDE, WITH ABOUT 23 m (75') OF ROUGH ON EACH SIDE

TEE
FLAT OR NEARLY FLAT, DRAINED TO REAR 370-740 m² (4000-8000 ft²)

45 m (150') | 45 m (150')

VARIES WITH PAR OF HOLE

137-152 m (450-500')

45 m (150')

**Figure 4.10. Typical golf hole.**

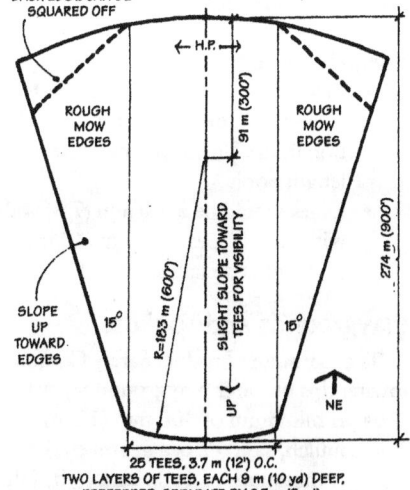

BACK EDGE CAN BE SQUARED OFF

H.P.

ROUGH MOW EDGES

ROUGH MOW EDGES

91 m (300')

274 m (900')

SLOPE UP TOWARD EDGES

R=183 m (600')

SLIGHT SLOPE TOWARD TEES FOR VISIBILITY

UP

15°    15°

NE

25 TEES, 3.7 m (12') O.C.
TWO LAYERS OF TEES, EACH 9 m (10 yd) DEEP, PREFERRED. SEPARATE BY 2.7 m (3 yd).

**Figure 4.11. Driving range.**

*Recreation Standards* ▪ 75

# Swimming

Swimming pools are made in a variety of shapes, from free-form to T or L shapes, but the basic design of all public and semi-public pools should be checked against local codes (Refer to Chapter 17: Water Features for information on pool construction and design).

## Recreational Pools

- Recreational pools are sized to allow 1 m² (10 ft²) of water surface for every wader or non-swimmer expected, and 2.5 m² (27 ft²) of surface for every swimmer.
- The area for non-swimmers should be less than 1500 mm (5 ft) deep.
- Many public pools have 80% of the water area devoted to non-swimmers as shown in the typical schematic pool section in Figure 4.12.
- An extra 28 m² (300 ft²) should be added for each diving board.
- The deck space around recreational pools should be at least equal to the water surface because generally only one-third of the swimmers will be in the pool at any one time. A 3:1 to 4:1 ratio between deck and water surface provides the most functional arrangement.

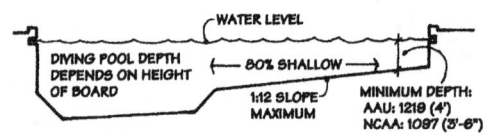

**Figure 4.12. Schematic pool section.**

## Competition Pools

- Twenty-five yards (75 ft 1½ in to accommodate timing equipment) is the minimum length for interscholastic or intercollegiate competition in the United States. International competition requires a 50 m length pool.
- Lanes should be 2100 mm (7 ft) wide between the centerlines, marked with lane stripes 250 mm (10 in) wide. Add 450 mm (18 in) to each of the outside lanes.

# Playgrounds and Tot Lots

The Consumer Product Safety Commission (CPSC) recommends the following tips on safer playground layout.

- A minimum of 300 mm (12 in) of protective surfacing (wood chips, mulch, sand or pea gravel etc.).
- A minimum of 1800 mm (6 ft) fall zone (shock absorbing material) in all directions from stationary pieces of play equipment. In front

of and behind swings, the material should extend a distance equal to twice the height of the suspension bar.

- Play structures should be spaced at least 3600 mm (12 ft) apart.
- Openings in play equipment should measure less than 90 mm (3.5 in) or more than 225 mm (9 in) to prevent children from being trapped.
- There should be no exposed concrete footings, abrupt changes in surface elevations, tree roots, stumps, or rocks that can trip children.
- Elevated surfaces such as platforms, ramps, and bridge ways should have guardrails to prevent falls.

## Camping and Picnicking

- Although camps vary in size and configuration based on terrain, vegetation, etc., a camp for 75 to 100 campers averages approximately 14 to 17 ha (35 to 40 acres) in size.
- Family size campsites should be approximately 4 m × 5 m (14 ft ×16 ft).
- Picnic areas are generally designed in clusters of 10 to 100 units with 10 m (35 ft) between units. 50 units/ha (20 units/acre) is desired.
- Figure 4.13 shows three alternative motor camping layouts.

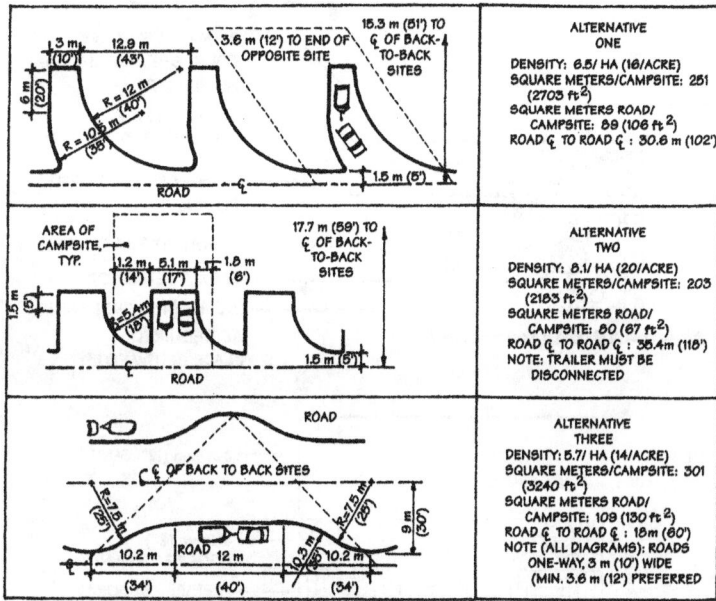

**Figure 4.13. Sample motor camping layouts.**

# SURFACING REQUIREMENTS

The goal of these details is to provide a smooth uniform playing surface capable of supporting light service vehicle loading. It is common practice to carefully screen and amend soil to secure the best combination of structural bearing, infiltration, and capillarity (Refer to Chapter 14: Paving for more information on pavement design).

## Court Surfaces

Figure 4.14 to 4.16 show details for the construction of various game courts that occur on asphalt, clay, and sand.

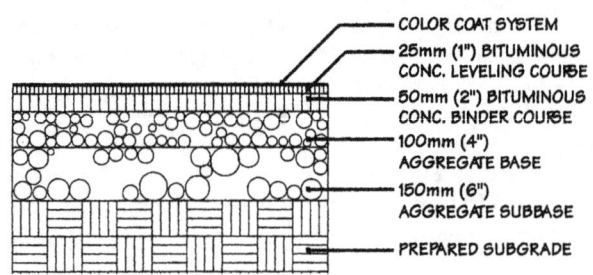

COLOR COAT SYSTEM

25mm (1") BITUMINOUS CONC. LEVELING COURSE

50mm (2") BITUMINOUS CONC. BINDER COURSE

100mm (4") AGGREGATE BASE

150mm (6") AGGREGATE SUBBASE

PREPARED SUBGRADE

**Figure 4.14. Asphalt tennis court on aggregate base.**

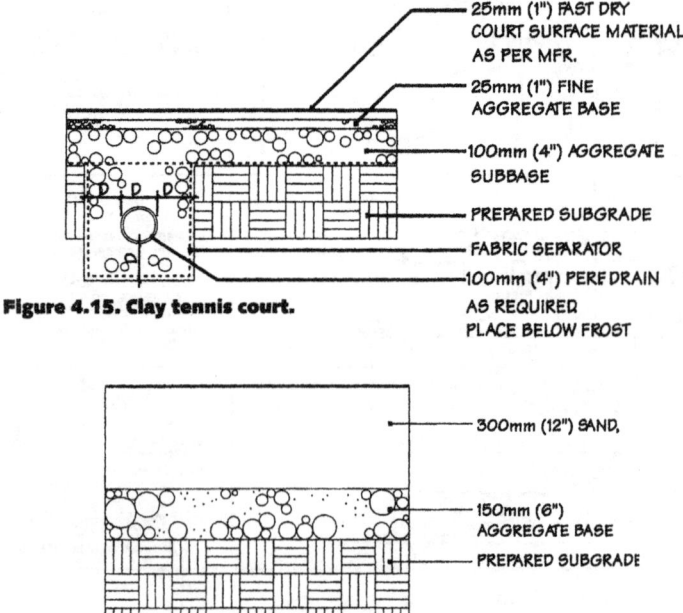

25mm (1") FAST DRY COURT SURFACE MATERIAL AS PER MFR.

25mm (1") FINE AGGREGATE BASE

100mm (4") AGGREGATE SUBBASE

PREPARED SUBGRADE

FABRIC SEPARATOR

100mm (4") PERF DRAIN AS REQUIRED PLACE BELOW FROST

**Figure 4.15. Clay tennis court.**

300mm (12") SAND.

150mm (6") AGGREGATE BASE

PREPARED SUBGRADE

**Figure 4.16. Sand volleyball court on aggregate base.**

## Field Surfaces

All natural turf requires irrigation, and may be heated in cold climates for professional or collegiate play (see Figures 4.17 to 4.20).

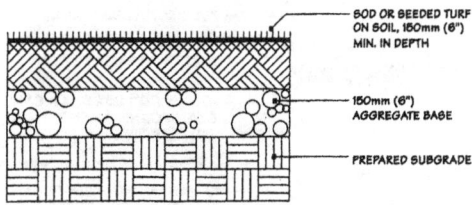

**Figure 4.17. Game lawn on aggregate base.**

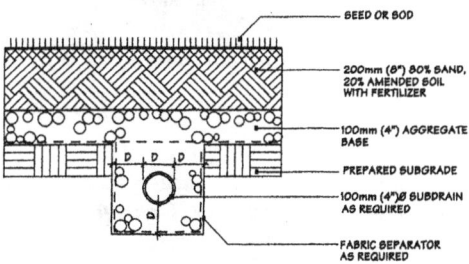

**Figure 4.18. Natural turf athletic field.**

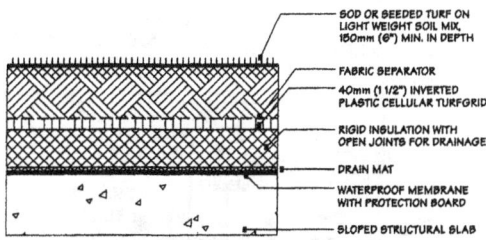

**Figure 4.19. Game lawn with inverted cellular turfgrid on structure.**

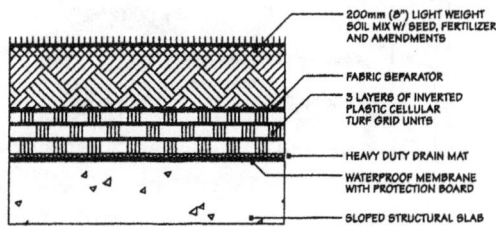

**Figure 4.20. Natural turf athletic field on structure.**

Synthetic turf consists of a monolithic resilient porous pad under the synthetic surface to absorb impacts for greater player protection and better internal drainage (see Figure 4.21).

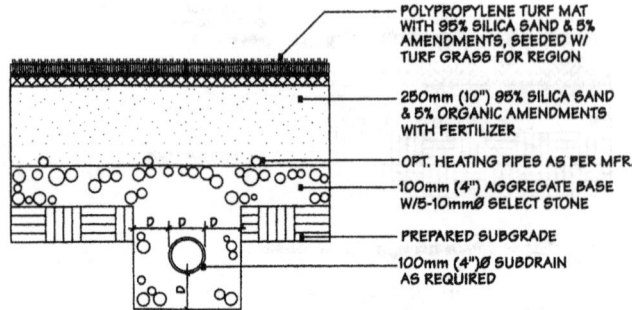

**Figure 4.21. Polypropylene reinforced athletic field.**

## Track Surfaces

Tracks should be constructed of materials that will create a uniform, smooth, safe, and comfortable running surface. Figure 4.22 shows typical cinder and synthetic track sections.

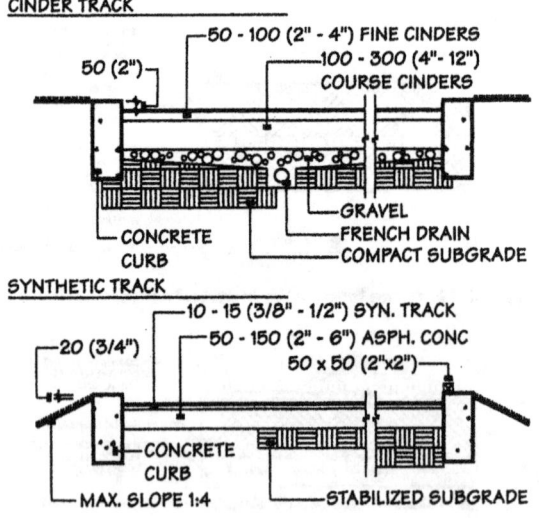

**Figure 4.22. Typical track sections.**

## Play Surfaces

Resilient and soft play surfaces are generally rated to provide for a fall from an 18 000 mm (6 ft) height. Figures 4.23 to 4.25 illustrate common resilient play surface details.

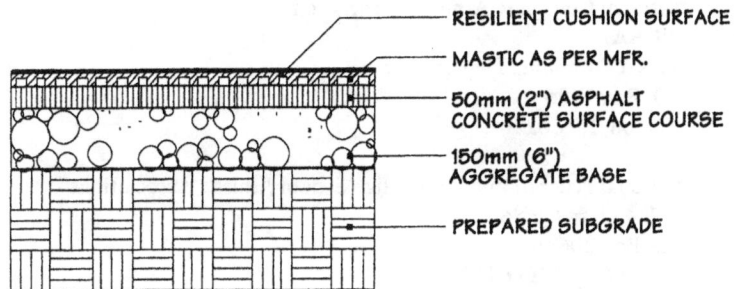

RESILIENT CUSHION SURFACE

MASTIC AS PER MFR.

50mm (2") ASPHALT CONCRETE SURFACE COURSE

150mm (6") AGGREGATE BASE

PREPARED SUBGRADE

**Figure 4.23. Resilient play surface on bituminous base.**

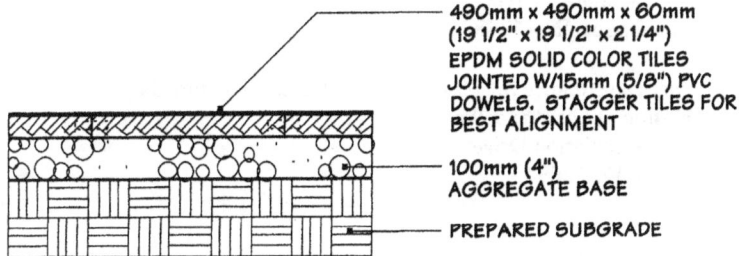

490mm x 490mm x 60mm (19 1/2" x 19 1/2" x 2 1/4") EPDM SOLID COLOR TILES JOINTED W/15mm (5/8") PVC DOWELS. STAGGER TILES FOR BEST ALIGNMENT

100mm (4") AGGREGATE BASE

PREPARED SUBGRADE

**Figure 4.24. Resilient play surface on aggregate base.**

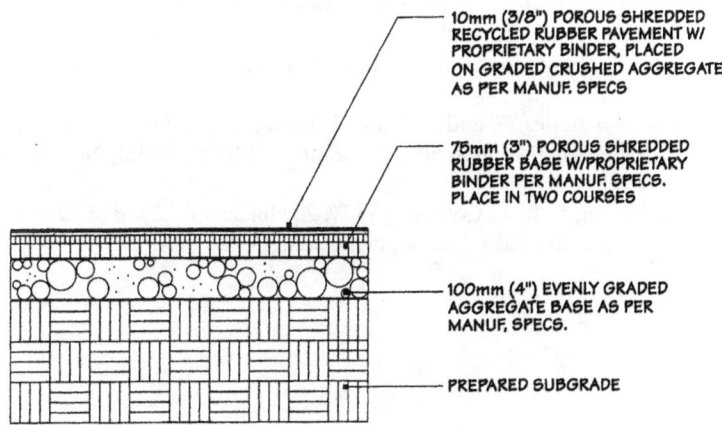

10mm (3/8") POROUS SHREDDED RECYCLED RUBBER PAVEMENT W/ PROPRIETARY BINDER, PLACED ON GRADED CRUSHED AGGREGATE AS PER MANUF. SPECS

75mm (3") POROUS SHREDDED RUBBER BASE W/PROPRIETARY BINDER PER MANUF. SPECS. PLACE IN TWO COURSES

100mm (4") EVENLY GRADED AGGREGATE BASE AS PER MANUF. SPECS.

PREPARED SUBGRADE

**Figure 4.25. Porous play surface on aggregate base.**

# GENERAL RESOURCES

International Amateur Athletic Federation (IAAF)
162 Upper Richmond Road
Putney, London SW152SL, England

National Collegiate Athletic Association
(NCAA)
NCAA Publishing Department
P.O. Box 1906
Mission, KS 66226

National Federation of State High School Athletic Associations
11724 Plaza Circle
P.O. Box 20626
Kansas City, MO 64195

Amateur Athletic Union of The U.S.
3400 West 86th Street
Indianapolis, IN 46268

American Alliance for Health, Physical Education and Dance
Division of Girls' and Women's Sports
1900 Association Drive
Reston, VA 22091

# SUGGESTED REFERENCES

Cordell, K., *Outdoor Recreation In American Life*, Sagamore Publishing, Champaign, IL, 1999.

Bell, S., *Design for Outdoor Recreation*, E&FN Spon., London, UK, 1997.

Harris, Charles W. and Nicholas T. Dines, *Time-Saver Standards for Landscape Architecture, 2nd Edition*, McGraw-Hill, New York, 1998.

Hultsman, J., R. L. Cottrell, and W. Z. Hultsman, *Planning Parks for People* (2nd Ed.). Venture Press, State College, PA, 1998.

STANDARDS

# *Conservation Standards*

5

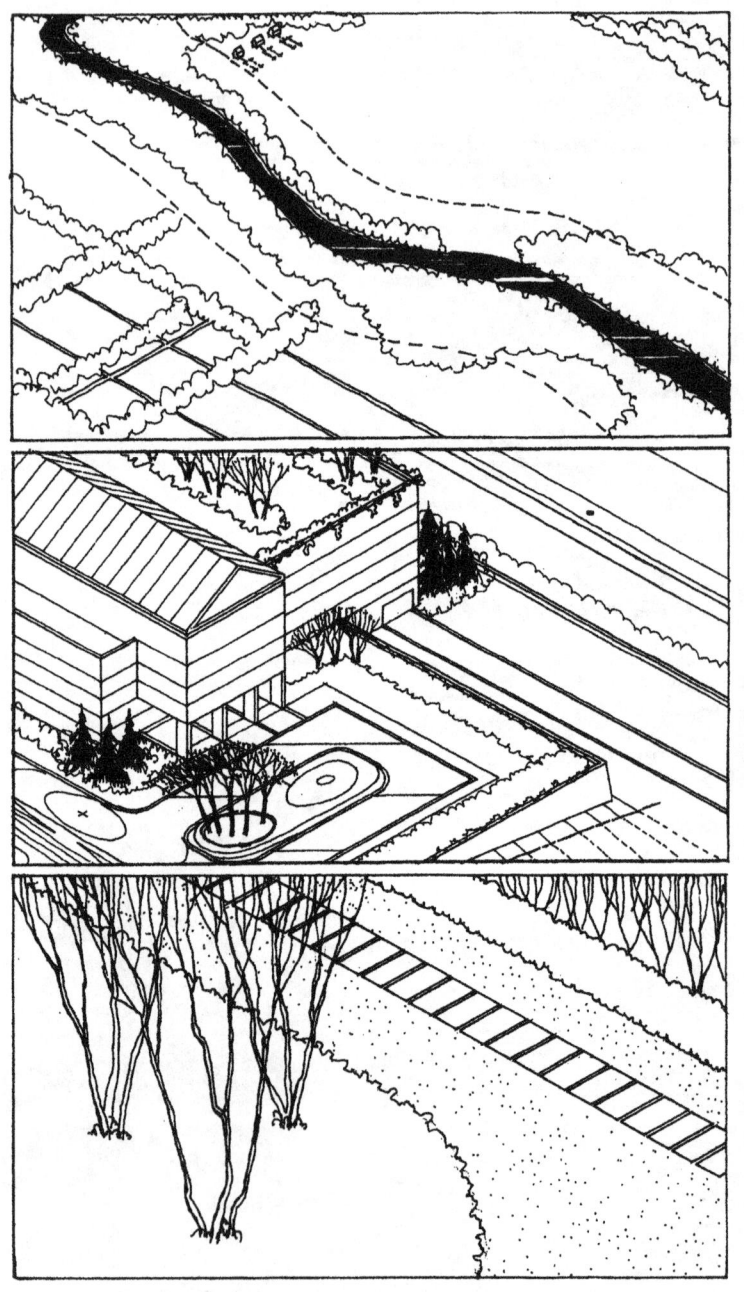

## REGIONAL OR LANDSCAPE PLANNING

Regional and landscape planning strategies should focus on concentrating urban land uses and minimizing sprawl to prevent landscape fragmentation and reduce infrastructure and transportation costs. Critical natural resources, particularly natural drainageways should be protected from urbanization, and efforts should be made to sustain native plant and animal habitat in the region, through application of state-of-the-art scientific knowledge.

## SITE PLANNING

Site planning strategies should seek to minimize site disruption during construction and preserve critical on-site natural processes after project completion. Attention should be paid to larger scales in the site planning process to assess impacts of proposed site plan on issues of hydrology, species habitat and migration, and energy demands resulting from infrastructure and transportation needs. Grading schemes should take advantage of natural drainageways wherever possible. Buildings should be designed and sited for passive heating and cooling, which typically suggests a SSE to SSW orientation in northern latitudes.

## DETAILED SITE DESIGN

Local climate should be considered in the selection of materials, and the design of spaces to minimize long-term maintenance costs, ensure human comfort, and reduce energy costs. Materials should be locally available and recycled whenever possible. Plant material should be native or water-conserving, and efforts should be made to minimize inputs such as fertilizers, and maximize plant biomass.

ONSERVATION OF ENERGY and natural resources requires sound planning at multiple scales. This chapter describes strategies for the protection and enhancement of natural processes in large-scale landscape planning as well as site planning and detail design. Effective strategies minimize the consumption of non-renewable resources, and respond to natural flows of water, nutrients, species and energy to regenerate the landscape in a self-sustaining manner.

## DIAGNOSTIC ASSESSMENT

*How can natural processes be effectively preserved or enhanced in the context of urbanization?*

Conservation of natural processes must be addressed at multiple scales of design, including the landscape and regional scales. A number of landscape planning strategies have been developed at these scales to concentrate urbanization, protect critical natural resources from development, and minimize adverse impacts on natural processes.

*What site planning strategies are conducive to minimizing energy costs and adverse impacts of development?*

Efforts should be made to select sites for proposed activities that minimize disruption of natural areas, extension of services, and transportation needs. Site design should minimize site disruption, protect natural drainageways and other critical natural resources, respond to local climatic conditions, and minimize embodied energy of materials. Planting design strategies should minimize water, fertilizer, and maintenance needs, as well as add significant biomass to the landscape.

*How can waste be used as a resource?*

To the extent feasible, landscapes should be regenerative in their use of energy, nutrients, and water in order to maximize their efficiency and minimize the wasting of these resources. Efforts should be made to utilize greenwaste and human sewage resources in the landscape, through the development of safe and innovative composting and wastewater treatment methods.

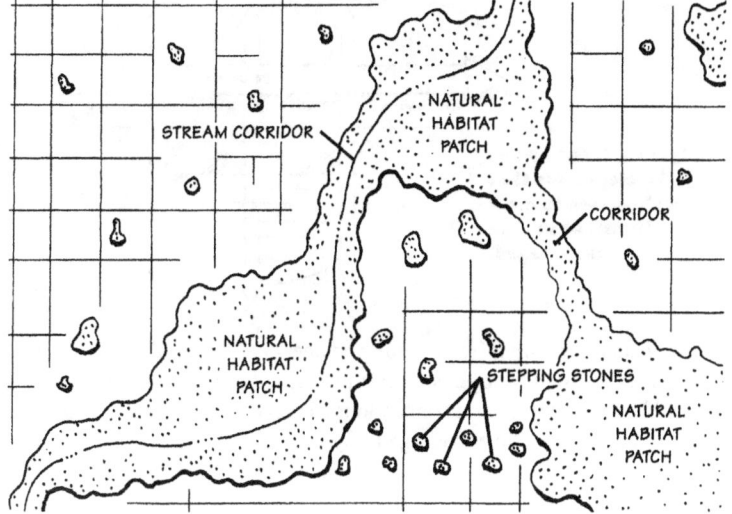

**Figure 5.1. Urban landscape framework suggested by Forman (1997).**

# LANDSCAPE PLANNING STRATEGIES

- In general, urban land uses should be concentrated around urban centers, with staged growth occurring in a progressively outward manner in order to minimize landscape fragmentation and infrastructure costs. The allocation of sanitary sewer and public water service is often used as a strategy for controlling regional growth.

- Critical natural resources, including plant and animal habitat, surface water resources, groundwater recharge areas, mining resources and prime farmland should be inventoried and adequately protected from urbanization. In addition, urban development should be protected from natural hazards such as floods, fires, and areas susceptible to landslides or other geologic hazards.

- Efforts to preserve native plants and animals should identify critical patches of habitat to be protected, as well as habitat corridors that facilitate species movement and genetic exchange across the landscape. Forman (1997) suggests at a minimum, a framework that preserves major stream or river corridors, a few large patches connected by corridors or stepping stones (small patches), and numerous smaller patches of nature spread across the urban landscape (Figure 5.1).

- The preservation of natural drainageways often provides opportunities to achieve multiple conservation objectives, including habitat connectivity, protection of water resources, and protection from flood hazards.

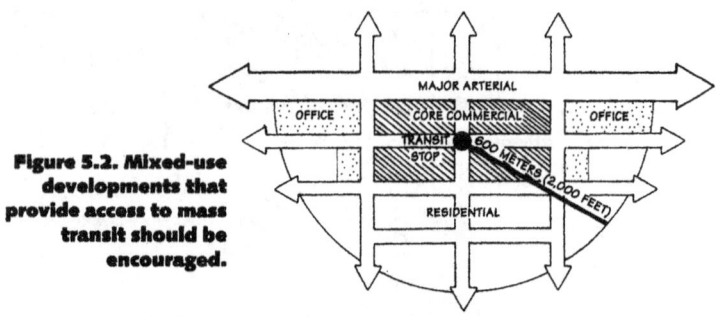

Figure 5.2. Mixed-use developments that provide access to mass transit should be encouraged.

- Transportation infrastructure and energy costs should be minimized. Mixed-use developments that integrate opportunities for housing, shopping, work, and connections to mass transit within walking distances should be encouraged (Figure 5.2).

# SITE PLANNING STRATEGIES

## Site Selection

The site selection process for urban land use projects should consider the feasibility of the following alternatives (in order):

1. Previously disturbed sites, such as abandoned commercial and industrial sites. Redevelopment of these "Brownfield" sites typically requires minimal disruption of natural systems, and may provide significant social benefits to the surrounding neighborhood. Testing for contamination on commercial and industrial sites is needed, and appropriate clean-up strategies should be incorporated into the overall redevelopment plan. Governmental assistance for clean up may be available.
2. Previously undisturbed sites surrounded by urban land uses (patches). Generally, small patches with low habitat value that are isolated from other natural areas should be given priority for development.
3. Previously undisturbed sites adjacent to existing urban development. Development of these "Greenfield" sites should only be considered if no other viable alternative exists. Site selection should preserve the integrity of habitat areas, prime farmland, and other critical resources.

## Layout and Design Considerations

- Natural drainageways should be preserved to protect water resources and accommodate site drainage. Urban streams should be protected by a vegetated buffer strip or other water quality management technique (Figure 5.3).

- Minimize road length, building footprint, and total area disrupted by site improvements, to reduce infrastructure costs and site impacts. Common utility, pedestrian, and vehicular corridors should be utilized wherever possible.
- In situations where the site impacts the edge of a natural habitat, a curvilinear or interdigitated edge may increase species diversity and wildlife usage, and should be considered where appropriate (Figure 5.4).
- Table 5.1 lists specific strategies for energy and resource conservation in four broad climate zones. Figures 5.5 through 5.7 illustrate these strategies.

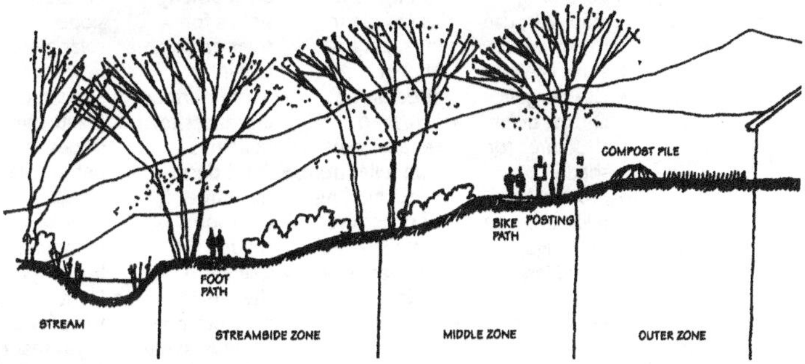

| CHARACTERISTICS | STREAMSIDE ZONE | MIDDLE ZONE | OUTER ZONE |
|---|---|---|---|
| FUNCTION | Protect the physical integrity of the stream ecosystem | Provide distance between upland development and streamside zone | Prevent encroachment and filter backyard runoff |
| WIDTH | Min. 8 m (25'), plus wetland and critical habitats | 15 to 30 m (50'-100') depending on stream order, slope, and 100 year floodplain | 8m (25') minimum setback to structures |
| VEGETATIVE TARGET | Undisturbed mature forest. Reforest if grass | Managed forest, some clearing allowable | Forest encouraged, but usually turfgrass |
| ALLOWABLE USES | VERY RESTRICTED (e.g., flood control, utility right of ways, footpaths, etc.) | RESTRICTED (e.g., some recreational uses, some stormwater BMPs, bike paths, tree removal by permit) | UNRESTRICTED (e.g., residential uses including lawn, garden, compost, yard wastes, most stormwater BMPs) |

**Figure 5.3. Recommended buffer for urban streams.**

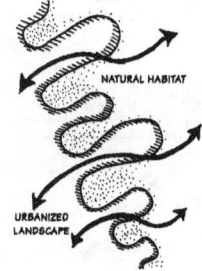

**Figure 5.4. Edges of natural habitat areas should be curvilinear or interdigitated to increase species diversity.**

## TABLE 5.1. Regional conservation strategies.

| Factors Modified by Landform, Vegetation, and Structures | Hot Arid *Hot, dry summers [>20°C (70°F)] and mild to cool winters [>0°C (32°F)] (Figure 5.5)* | Hot Humid *Hot, humid summers [>20°C (70°F)] and mild to cool winters [>0°C (32°F)] (Figure 5.6)* | Temperate *Hot, often humid summers [>20°C (70°F)] and cold winters [<0°C (32°F)] (Figure 5.7)* | Cold *Mild summer temps [>10°C (50°F)] and very cold winters [<-10°C (15°F)] (Figure 5.7)* |
|---|---|---|---|---|
| *Sun* | • Avoid heat-absorbing materials; use thick walls or earth shelters<br>• Use pergola and/or trellis structures for shade<br>• Provide large overhangs on buildings<br>• Avoid large areas of exposed glass | • Maximize shade through the use of plantings, pergolas, and/or trellis structures<br>• Screened terraces provide relief from direct heating of structures<br>• Provide large overhangs on buildings<br>• Use high ceilings and vent all roof systems | • Site structures on southerly slopes for solar gain in winter<br>• Avoid northern entrances to buildings<br>• Plant deciduous trees for afternoon shade<br>• Use earth shelters to protect from summer sun | • Site structures on southerly slopes for solar gain in winter<br>• Site structures on steeper slopes for better solar access<br>• Avoid northern entrances to buildings<br>• Plant deciduous trees for afternoon shade<br>• Use earth shelters to protect from summer sun and harsh winters |
| *Wind* | • Site structures at toe of slopes for exposure to cold air flows at night<br>• Use plant material, screens, or structures to block dessicating winds | • Site structures at top of slope for exposure to breezes<br>• Avoid excessive earth mounding or landforms that trap moist air<br>• Maximize breezes through use of high canopy trees<br>• Avoid tall solid walls that block wind | • Site structure on middle to upper slope for access to light winds, but protection from high winds<br>• Use landform, plants, and structures to divert northerly winter winds while permitting cooling summer breezes<br>• Use earth shelters to protect from winter winds | • Site structure on middle to lower slope for wind protection<br>• Plant coniferous shelterbelts to block cold winds<br>• Avoid topographic depressions that collect cold air<br>• Use earth shelters that protect from winter winds |

## TABLE 5.1. Regional conservation strategies (continued).

| Factors Modified by Landform, Vegetation, and Structures | Hot Arid<br>*Hot, dry summers [>20°C (70°F)] and mild to cool winters [>0°C (32°F)] (Figure 5.5)* | Hot Humid<br>*Hot, humid summers [>20°C (70°F)] and mild to cool winters [>0°C (32°F)] (Figure 5.6)* | Temperate<br>*Hot, often humid summers [>20°C (70°F)] and cold winters [<0°C (32°F)] (Figure 5.7)* | Cold<br>*Mild summer temps [>10°C (50°F)] and very cold winters [<-10°C (15°F)] (Figure 5.7)* |
|---|---|---|---|---|
| *Water* | • Use moisture-conserving, native plants<br>• Limit impervious surface to minimize runoff<br>• Limit surface water features to minimize evaporation | • Avoid stagnant bodies of water<br>• Maximize infiltration of stormwater runoff | • Use of ponds for stormwater detention also provide evaporative cooling for the site<br>• Foundations for structures and pavement must drain well to prevent damage from frost/thaw action | • Use of ponds for stormwater detention also provide evaporative cooling for the site<br>• Foundations for structures and pavement must drain well to prevent damage from frost/thaw action |

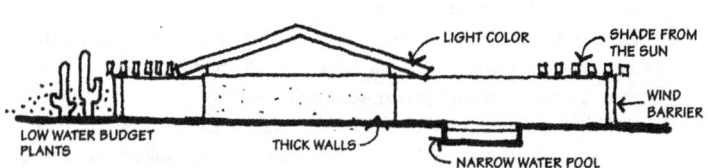

Figure 5.5. Conservation strategies for hot arid regions.

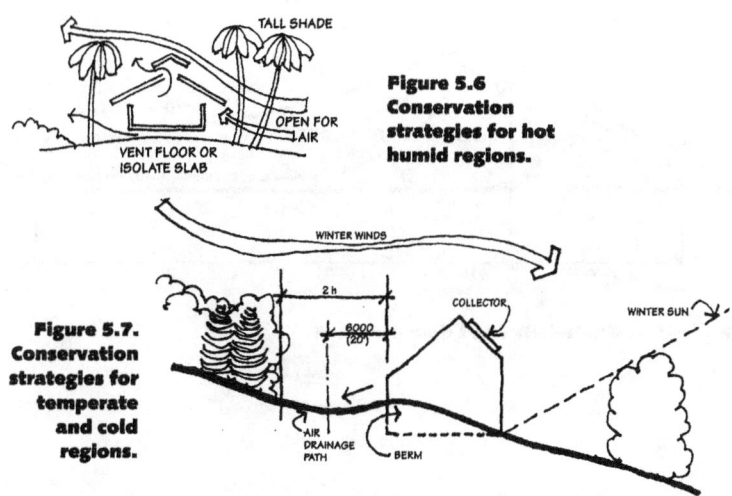

**Figure 5.6 Conservation strategies for hot humid regions.**

**Figure 5.7. Conservation strategies for temperate and cold regions.**

*Conservation Standards* • 91

## Siting of Buildings and Outdoor Use Areas

- Align long buildings, parking areas, and athletic fields with the landscape contours to minimize grading and site disruption during construction. Half-basements and staggered floors may be used in areas of excess slope.
- Orient planted islands in parking lots along north-south axes to maximize shade on pavement during hot summer months.
- Orient buildings to take advantage of passive heating and cooling. Sunlight and wind protection should contribute and conserve heat during winter, while shade and airflows provide passive cooling in summer. Typically, a SSE to SSW structure siting is preferred in northern latitudes.
- Figure 5.8 illustrates potential wind flow dynamics of different shelterbelt designs. Generally speaking, activities requiring the benefits of prevailing cooling breezes should be located sufficient distance away from the windward side of buildings, tree massings or topographic features (>5H). Activities requiring protection from chilling winds should be located close to the leeward side of the feature (<4H) to maximize protection. Activities requiring protection from winter winds as well as access to cooling breezes should be located a distance of 5-6H from the feature.
- Generally, ventilating effects of wind can be promoted by tall thin structures that are one room wide to allow cross flow, or by structures on columns that promote under-venting.
- In cold, temperate, and hot arid climates, earth shelters promote stable interior temperatures. Figure 5.9 illustrates various profile concepts for earth sheltered structures.

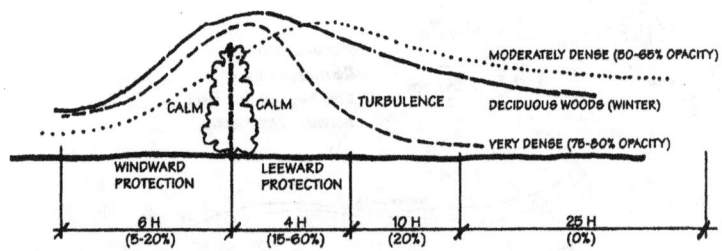

**Figure 5.8. Shelterbelt wind flow dynamics.**

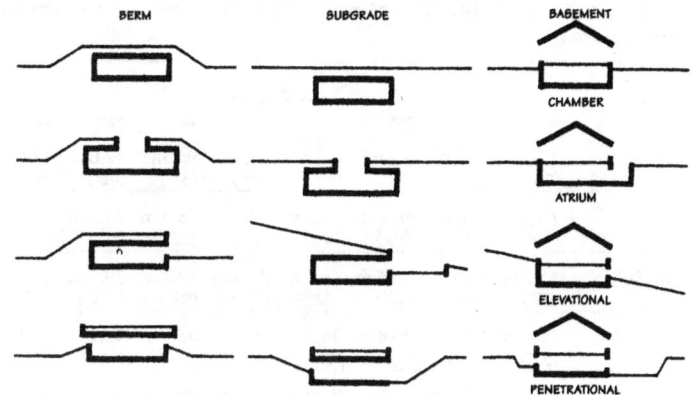

BERM          SUBGRADE          BASEMENT

                                CHAMBER

                                ATRIUM

                                ELEVATIONAL

                                PENETRATIONAL

**Figure 5.9. Profile concepts for earth sheltered structures.**

FIELD NOTE

# Calculating Shadows

Shadow length of trees, structures, or topographic features can be calculated based on the height of the element and the altitude angle of the sun at a given time of day during a given day of the year. Typically, longest shadows in winter, and shortest shadows in summer are used for solar access calculations in northern latitudes. Shadow length is calculated using the formula:

$$\text{shadow length} = \frac{\text{height of element}}{\tan(\text{altitude angle})}$$

As this image illustrates, elevational differences between the structure and the shadow-casting element must be considered in the calculations. This allows taller trees to be planted closer to structures without blocking solar access, if located on a slope.

For quick reference, Tables 5.2 and 5.3 list maximum (winter) and minimum (summer) shadow lengths for elements of different heights, at different latitudes in the northern hemisphere.

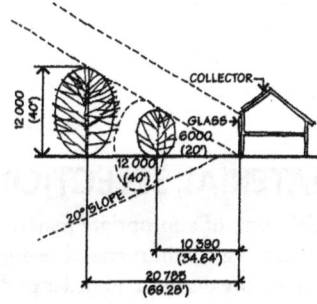

LATITUDE 36°
NOON SUN, DECEMBER 21 = 30°ALTITUDE
SHADOW FOR 12 000 mm (40') TREE:
=12 000/TAN 30°
=20 785 mm (69.28')

**TABLE 5.2. Shadow lengths at noon on December 21 (Northern Hemisphere).**

| Height of Element | Northern Latitude | | | | | | | |
|---|---|---|---|---|---|---|---|---|
| | 28° | 32° | 36° | 40° | 44° | 48° | 52° | 56° |
| 3 m (10') | 3.8 m (13') | 4.4 m (15') | 5.2 m (17') | 6.2 m (21') | 7.4 m (25') | 9.2 m (31') | 12.0 m (40') | 17.0 m (57') |
| 6 m (20') | 7.7 m (26') | 8.9 m (30') | 10.4 m (35') | 12.3 m (41') | 14.9 m (50') | 18.5 m (62') | 24.1 m (80') | 34.0 m (113') |
| 9 m (30') | 11.5 m (38') | 13.3 m (44') | 15.6 m (52') | 18.5 m (62') | 22.3 m (74') | 27.7 m (92') | 36.1 m (120') | 51.0 m (170') |
| 12 m (40') | 15.4 m (51') | 17.8 m (59') | 20.8 m (69') | 24.6 m (82') | 29.7 m (99') | 36.9 m (123') | 48.1 m (160') | 68.1 m (227') |
| 15 m (50') | 19.2 m (64') | 22.2 m (74') | 26.0 m (87') | 30.8 m (103') | 37.1 m (124') | 46.2 m (154') | 60.2 m (200') | 85.1 m (284') |

**TABLE 5.3. Shadow lengths at noon on June 21 (Northern Hemisphere).**

| Height of Element | Northern Latitude | | | | | | | |
|---|---|---|---|---|---|---|---|---|
| | 28° | 32° | 36° | 40° | 44° | 48° | 52° | 56° |
| 3 m (10') | 0.3 m (1') | 0.5 m (2') | 0.7 m (2.5') | 0.9 m (3') | 1.2. m (4') | 1.4 m (5') | 1.7 m (6') | 1.9 m (7') |
| 6 m (20') | 0.6 m (2') | 1.0 m (3') | 1.4 m (5') | 1.8 m (6') | 2.3 m (8') | 2.8 m (9') | 3.3 m (11') | 3.9 m (13') |
| 9 m (30') | 0.8 m (3') | 1.4 m (5') | 2.1 m (7') | 2.8 m (9') | 3.5 m (12') | 4.2 m (14') | 5.0 m (17') | 5.8 m (19') |
| 12 m (40') | 1.0 m (4') | 1.9 m (6') | 2.8 m (9') | 3.7 m (12') | 4.6 m (15') | 5.6 m (19') | 6.7 m (22') | 7.8 m (26') |
| 15 m (50') | 1.3 m (4.5') | 2.4 m (8') | 3.5 m (12') | 4.6 m (15') | 5.8 m (19') | 7.0 m (23') | 8.3 m (28') | 9.7 m (32') |

# MATERIAL SELECTION

Selection of appropriate materials for a design should consider the embodied energy of the material, energy required for installation, maintenance, and ultimate disposal, in order to determine the most energy-conscious alternative from a life-cycle perspective.

## Embodied Energy

Embodied energy is cumulative energy required to extract and/or manufacture, process, and transport a material. Generally, locally available, naturally based materials requiring little processing have the lowest embodied energy, while those involving significant manufacturing processes have the greatest. Reliable data on embodied energy is often difficult to obtain, so values are best used on a comparative basis, to determine consumption levels relative to other alternatives. Table 5.4 lists figures compiled by the National Park Service. The use of recyclable materials can significantly reduce the embodied energy cost of a design.

## Installation

Energy required for installation is a function of materials (formwork, tools, etc) and mechanical energy. Data on installation requirements can be obtained from cost estimating guides (refer to Chapter 22: Cost Estimating for more information). Table 5.5 lists energy embodied in various fuels used by construction machinery.

## Maintenance and Disposal

On-going maintenance of materials must also be considered in comparing energy inputs of different design alternatives. Materials that require mechanical energy, chemical compounds, or additional material for routine maintenance are the most energy intensive. Data on disposal requirements

**TABLE 5.4. Embodied energy of various construction materials.**

| Material | kJ/kg of material | BTUs/lb of material |
|---|---|---|
| Aggregate, crushed | 60 | 26 |
| Aggregate, uncrushed (sand) | 19 | 8 |
| Aluminum | 325 640 | 140,000 |
| Asphalt | 680 | 294 |
| Brass | 156 770 | 67,400 |
| Brick | 8025 | 3,450 |
| Copper | 139 560 | 60,000 |
| Lime | 8723 | 3,750 |
| Plastic, polyethylene | 161 420 | 69,400 |
| Plastic, PVC | 120 020 | 51,600 |
| Portland Cement | 8269 | 3,555 |
| Paperboard | 42 333 | 18,200 |
| Steel | 78 386 | 33,700 |

Adapted from National Capital Region of the National Park Service, "Energy Conservation Concepts in Managing Urban Parks."

**TABLE 5.5. Embodied energy of various fuels used by construction machinery.**

| Fuel | kJ | BTUs |
|---|---|---|
| Diesel Fuel [per liter (gallon)] | 39 000 | 140,000 |
| Gasoline [per liter (gallon)] | 34 500 | 124,000 |
| Natural Gas [per cubic meter (cubic foot)] | 37 250 | 1,000 |

Adapted from National Capital Region of the National Park Service, "Energy Conservation Concepts in Managing Urban Parks."

can be obtained from cost estimating guides (refer to Chapter 22: Cost Estimating for more information).

# PLANTING DESIGN

- Planting design should seek to optimize the relationship between water requirements of plants and local climate. Generally, native plants should be used to minimize energy and resource requirements of irrigation (Refer to Chapter 12: Planting and Chapter 19: Irrigation for further information).
- On-going maintenance of planted areas must also be considered in comparing energy inputs of different design alternatives. Routine mowing, fertilizing and other mechanical maintenance contribute significantly to the energy requirements of a landscape.
- Fertilizers contain significant embodied energy, particularly mixes containing major nitrogen components (Table 5.6) and their use should be minimized. In addition, excess fertilizer can contribute to nutrient loading of streams and water bodies.
- Plant biomass is recognized for its value as carbon storage in mitigating the production of carbon dioxide in the atmosphere from the burning of fossil fuels. Efforts should be made to increase standing levels of biomass in urban environments, through increased density of plantings.
- Adequate buffer zones should be provided around biodiversity or nature reserves, to prevent the invasion of exotic species from adjacent urban or suburban landscapes. Buffer zone width should be based on local landscape conditions and distribution mechanisms of invasive species.

**TABLE 5.6. Embodied energy of fertilizer chemicals.**

| Chemical | kJ/kg | BTUs/lb |
|----------|-------|---------|
| Nitrogen (N) | 77 900 | 33,500 |
| Phosphorus (P$_2$O$_5$) | 7350 | 3,150 |
| Potassium (K$_2$O) | 6850 | 2,950 |

Adapted from National Capital Region of the National Park Service, "Energy Conservation Concepts in Managing Urban Parks."

# WASTE RESOURCES

In regenerative design, waste is a valuable resource that can be used to return nutrients and water consumed by the landscape and humans to the site.

- Greenwaste and other organic refuse should be composted for use on the site as a soil supplement. A number of composting strategies have been developed, and facilities of various scales are commercially available.
- Consideration should be given to use of human sewage resources in the landscape. Sludge compost is commercially available from a number of sanitation districts. Composting toilets or aquatic sewage treatment systems such as aquacultural ponds or constructed wetlands provide opportunities to safely treat wastewater while providing benefits of increased landscape productivity, and potentially wildlife and plant species habitat. Refer to Chapter 6: Water Supply and Wastewater Treatment Standards for information on various alternatives.

# SUGGESTED REFERENCES

Brown, G.Z., *Sun, Wind, and Light: Architectural Design Strategies*, Wiley, New York, 1985.

Dramstad, Wenche E., James D. Olson and Richard T.T. Forman, *Landscape Ecology Principles in Landscape Architecture and Land-Use Planning*, GSD/Island Press/ASLA, Washington D.C., 1997.

Forman, Richard T.T., *Land Mosaics*, Cambridge University Press, Cambridge, 1997.

Givoni, B. *Man, Climate and Architecture,* Van Nostrand Rheinhold, New York, 1981.

Harris, Charles W. and Nicholas T. Dines, *Time-Saver Standards for Landscape Architecture, 2nd Edition*, McGraw-Hill, New York, 1998.

Lyle, John T., *Regenerative Design for Sustainable Development*, Wiley, New York, 1994.

Mazria, Edward. *The Passive Solar Energy Book*, Rodale Press, Emmaus, PA, 1979.

McPherson, Greg, *Site Planning for Energy Conservation*, 1985.

National Capital Region of the National Park Service, "Energy Conservation Concepts in Managing Urban Parks."

Watson, Donald and Kenneth Labs, *Climatic Design*, McGraw-Hill, New York, 1983.

# Water Supply and Wastewater Treatment Standards

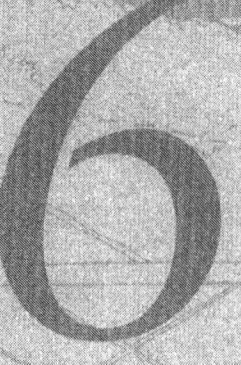

6

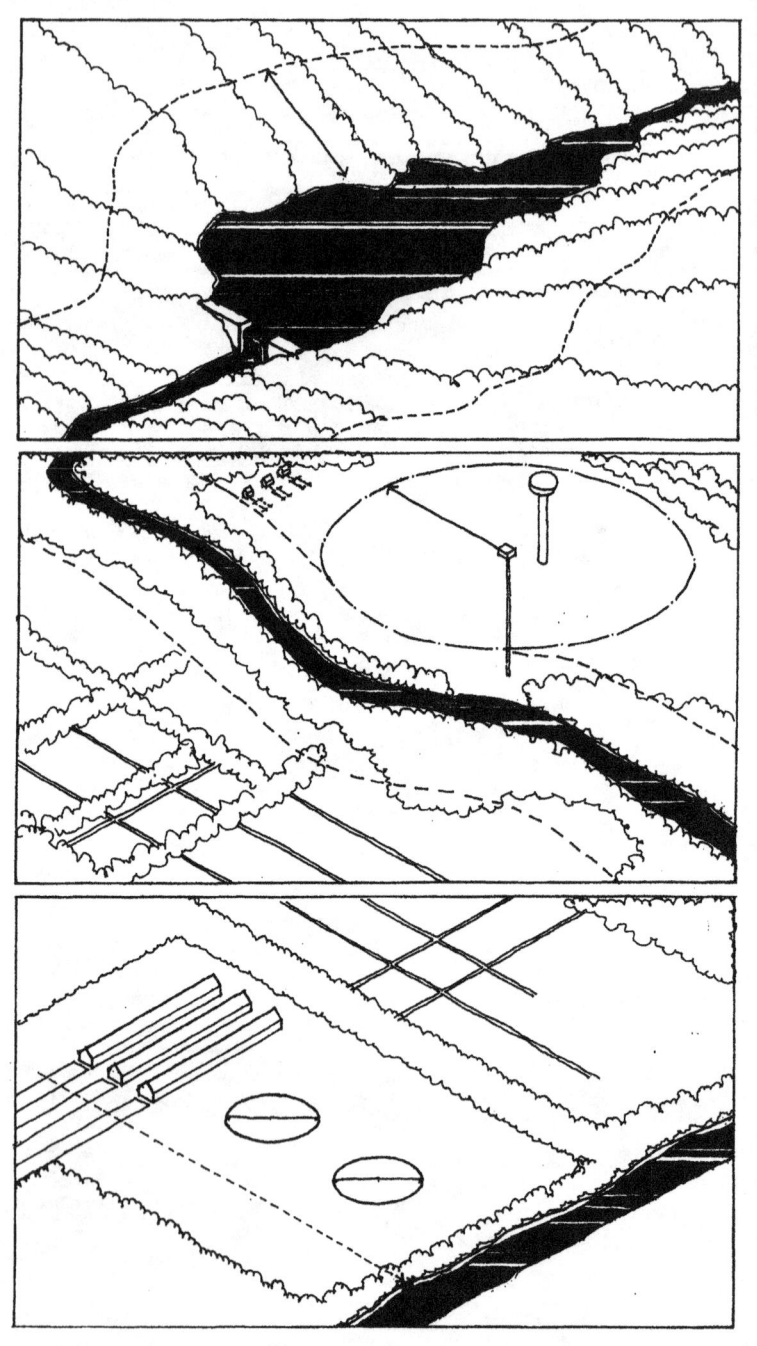

## WATERSHED MANAGEMENT STRATEGIES FOR HEADWATER CONDITIONS

Proper management of water supplies requires regulations, which restrict the land use and transportation patterns adjacent to natural water bodies and constructed reservoirs designated as water sources. Setbacks and forestation are common tools. Typical sources include alpine snowmelt, seasonal precipitation, and groundwater seepage. Hazards include excessive logging or urbanization resulting in silt laden runoff and possible contamination.

## WELLPOINT AND AQUIFER RECHARGE MANAGEMENT DISTRICTS

Public wells require restrictive overlay zoning to protect the aquifer from contamination due to septic field loading, selected agricultural practices, or selected land use activities. In areas adjacent to aquifers recharge areas, residential density standards are commonly determined by septic loading calculations, and the ratio of impervious surface to contiguous open space.

## TREATMENT AND RECYCLING SYSTEMS

Tertiary treatment of septic effluent allows for recycling of wastewater through aeration spraying in naturally sandy soils, by infiltration in well-drained soils, or by solar and biological systems. The amount of water requiring expensive tertiary treatment may be greatly reduced through the reuse of graywater.

WATER SUPPLY AND WASTEWATER TREATMENT standards are designed to protect the public health, safety and welfare by providing adequate supplies of potable drinking water, and protecting from potential exposure to harmful bacteria or other contaminants. In addition, these standards are paramount to the preservation and enhancement of hydrologic and nutrient cycles.

## DIAGNOSTIC ASSESSMENT

*What are the water needs of the project?*

Water demand must be determined for a proposed project, taking into account projected growth within the service area and surrounding region which may utilize the same water source. In addition to everyday human consumption, requirements for fire protection, irrigation, and other uses must be considered.

*What sources of water supply are readily available?*

Drinking water sources include groundwater resources, surface water, and in some circumstances collected rainwater. Selection of an appropriate supply is a function of availability, water quality, and cost. These resources must be adequately preserved and protected to ensure sustained use over the life of the development.

*What is the wastewater treatment need of the project?*

Estimating wastewater flows must take into account projected growth within the service area. In the case of residential development, wastewater flows closely parallel water demands.

*What types of wastewater treatment systems are feasible?*

A wide variety of wastewater treatment techniques are available, ranging from large-scale municipal systems, to a number of on-site strategies. Selection of a system greatly influences the density of development on a site and is often dictated by local regulations.

# WATER DEMAND

Water consumption patterns vary due to cultural, economic and climate factors. Regional data should be obtained when making final design decisions regarding water supply, however Table 6.1 lists average daily consumption for various uses, which may be used for preliminary planning purposes. Systems are typically designed to accommodate maximum daily consumption plus required fire flows, as dictated by local regulations. Table 6.2 lists multipliers for determining maximum daily consumption for residential communities. Table 6.3 lists typical required fire flows for residential communities.

Irrigation may also significantly increase demand. Refer to Chapter 19: Irrigation, for methods on calculating water requirements of different landscapes.

Water pressure is typically provided at 275-400 kPa (40-60 psi) in residential neighborhoods, with 550 kPa (80 psi) as a commonly recommended upper limit. Commercial areas typically require approximately 525 kPa (75 psi) for servicing.

**TABLE 6.1. Average daily water usage and wastewater flows.**

| Type of Use | Liters per person per day (unless otherwise noted) | Gallons per person per day (unless otherwise noted) |
| --- | --- | --- |
| Airports (per passenger) | 20 | 5 |
| Bathhouses and swimming pools | 40 | 10 |
| Camps: | | |
| Construction, semi permanent | 200 | 50 |
| Day (with no meals served) | 60 | 15 |
| Luxury | 400 | 100 |
| Resorts, day and night, with limited plumbing | 200 | 50 |
| Campground with central comfort facilities | 140 | 35 |
| Cottages and small dwellings with seasonal occupancy | 200 | 50 |
| Country clubs (per member) | 100 | 25 |
| Dwellings | 400 | 100 |
| Factories (per person per shift, exclusive of industrial waste) | 140 | 35 |
| Highway rest area (per person) | 20 | 5 |

➤ continued on next page

## TABLE 6.1. Average daily water usage and wastewater flows (continued).

| Type of Use | Liters per person per day (unless otherwise noted) | Gallons per person per day (unless otherwise noted) |
|---|---|---|
| Hotels with private baths (two persons per room) | 240 | 60 |
| Hotels without private baths | 200 | 50 |
| Hospitals (per bed) | 1200 | 300 |
| Institutions other than hospitals | 500 | 125 |
| Laundries, self-serviced (per customer) | 200 | 50 |
| Mobile home parks (per space) | 950 | 250 |
| Motels with bath and kitchen facilities (per bed space) | 200 | 50 |
| Motels (per bed space) | 160 | 40 |
| Picnic parks (toilet wastes only, per picnicker) | 20 | 5 |
| Picnic parks with bathhouses, showers and flush toilets (per picnicker) | 40 | 10 |
| Restaurants | | |
| *With toilet facilities (per patron)* | 40 | 10 |
| *Without toilet facilities (per patron)* | 12 | 3 |
| *With bars and cocktail lounges (additional quantity per patron)* | 8 | 2 |
| Schools: | | |
| *Boarding (per pupil)* | 400 | 100 |
| *Day, with cafeteria, gymnasium and showers (per pupil)* | 100 | 25 |
| *Day, with cafeteria, but no gymnasium and showers (per pupil)* | 80 | 20 |
| *Day, without cafeteria, gymnasium and showers (per pupil)* | 60 | 15 |
| Service Stations (per vehicle) | 40 | 10 |
| Shopping Centers [per 100 m² (1000 ft²) of floor space] | 1200 | 300 |
| Stores (per toilet room) | 1500 | 400 |
| Theaters: | | |
| *Drive-in (per car space)* | 20 | 5 |
| *Movie (per seat)* | 20 | 5 |
| Trailers without individual baths and sewers (per person) | 200 | 50 |

## TABLE 6.2. Estimated peak daily consumption ratios for residential communities.

| Population | Ratio of Maximum Day to Average Daily Use* |
|---|---|
| 0-500 | 3.00 |
| 500-1,000 | 2.75 |
| 1,000-2,000 | 2.50 |
| 2,000-3,000 | 2.25 |
| 3,000-10,000 | 1.90 |
| 10,000-25,000 | 1.80 |
| 25,000-50,000 | 1.80 |
| 50,000-75,000 | 1.75 |
| 75,000-150,000 | 1.65 |
| > 150,000 | 1.50 |

\* Multiply average daily use for community (see Table 6.1) by this ratio to estimate maximum daily consumption. Systems are typically designed to accommodate maximum daily consumption plus required fire flows (see table 6.3).

Adapted from Dewberry and Davis, *Land Development Handbook*, McGraw-Hill, New York, 1996.

## TABLE 6.3. Suggested fire flows for single-family and small two-family dwellings not exceeding two stories in height.

| Distance Between Buildings | Suggested Fire Flow for 2 Hour Duration |
|---|---|
| Over 30 m (> 100 ft) | 2000 LPM (500 GPM) |
| 10-30 m (30-100 ft) | 3000-4000 LPM (750-1,000 GPM) |
| 3-10 m (10-30 ft) | 4000-6000 LPM (1,000-1,500 GPM) |
| Less than 3 m (<10 ft) | 6000-10 000 LPM (1,500-2,500 GPM)* |

\*If buildings are continuous, use a minimum of 10 000 LPM (2,500 GPM). Where wood shingles could contribute to spreading fires, add 2000 (500 GPM).

Adapted from Dewberry and Davis, *Land Development Handbook*, McGraw-Hill, New York, 1996.

# WATER SOURCES

Potable water meets strict physical, chemical and biological standards for human consumption. Sources of potable water are limited and can be costly, particularly in hot arid regions. Wherever feasible, non-potable alternatives should be considered for uses such as irrigation and ornamental water features. Chapter 19: Irrigation describes non-potable sources commonly available.

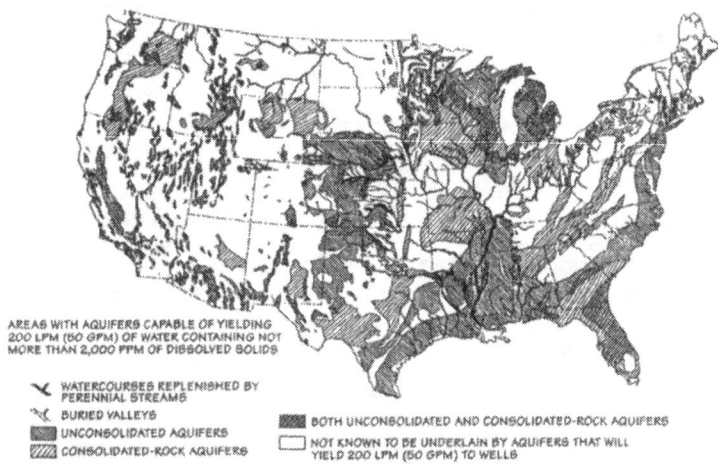

**Figure 6.1. Principal aquifers of the United States.**

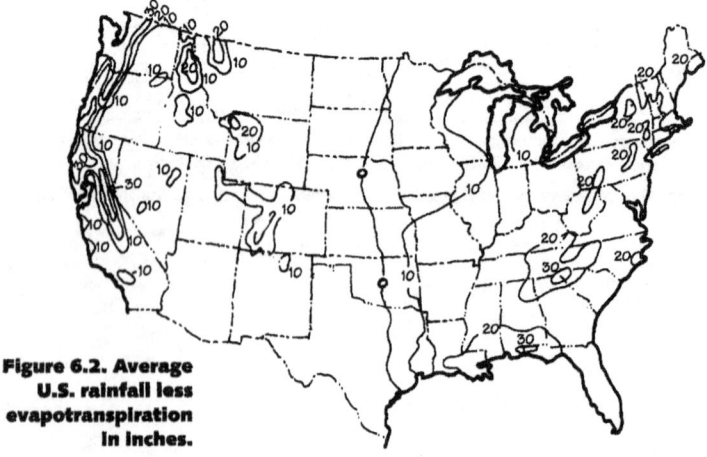

**Figure 6.2. Average U.S. rainfall less evapotranspiration in inches.**

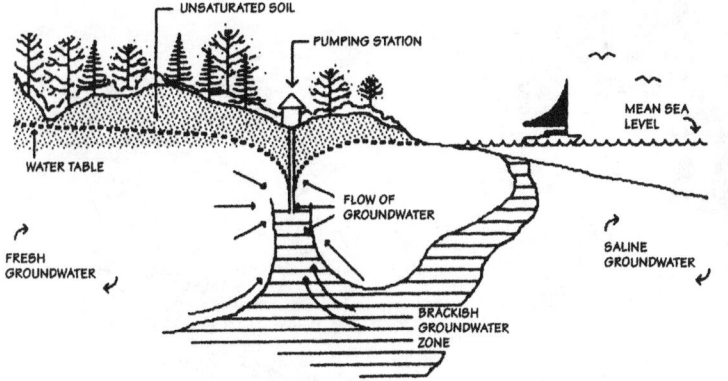

**Figure 6.3. Effect of well drawdown below mean sea level.**

## Groundwater Resources

In many regions, groundwater provides the greatest source of potable water. Landscape planning should adopt proper strategies for extraction, recharge and protection of groundwater resources to sustain continued use.

### Extraction

- High-yield wells are appropriate to serve large populations in regions underlain by major aquifers. Figure 6.1 illustrates principal aquifers of the United States.
- Low-yield on-site wells for small projects are typically feasible in regions where annual rainfall exceeds evapotranspiration rates (Figure 6.2). Site tests are needed to determine viability based on drilling depth required and water quality.
- Wells in coastal environments must sustain adequate water table levels by maintaining extraction rates at or below recharge rates to prevent saltwater intrusion (Figure 6.3).
- The over-pumping of wells — withdrawing groundwater faster than it can be recharged — occurs when established safe yields are regularly exceeded. The resulting aquifer depletion can dry up shallower wells and require the drilling of new wells or the redrilling of existing wells. Over-pumping can also reduce the natural flow of groundwater to surface streams and springs, thus decreasing the potential water availability of these sources. In certain geologic settings, over-pumping can also cause land subsidence.
- Contamination from wastewater is a concern in areas with old or failing cesspools, leaching fields, etc. No well should be developed in areas where its drawdown cone would include wastewater disposal facilities.

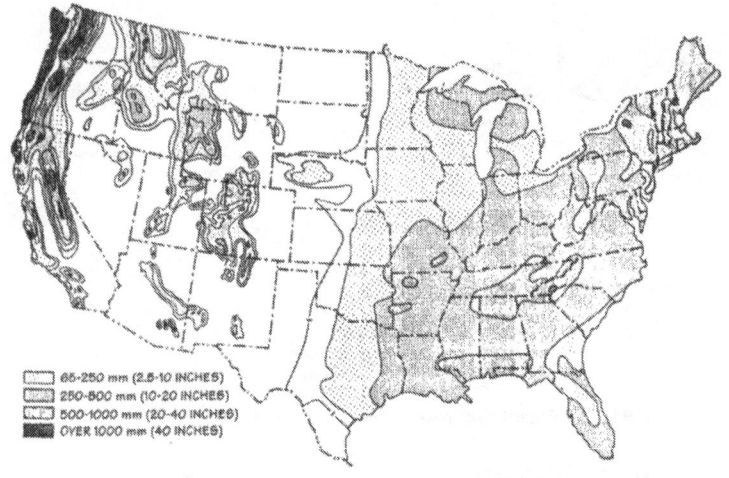

**Figure 6.4. Average annual stormwater runoff in the United States.**

## Groundwater Recharge

- When impervious cover in an aquifer recharge area is increased, higher rates of stormwater runoff and, consequently, lower rates of groundwater recharge result. Aquifer recharge areas should be protected from development that increases impervious cover.
- During storm events, wetlands retain excessive waters, gradually releasing them into the ground or nearby surface waterways. The filling of wetlands reduces ground and surface water recharge and the amounts of water available for use.
- The extension of public sewer system lines into areas with already low groundwater yields can further diminish limited groundwater supplies. This is because public sewers do not replenish area groundwater as do on-lot sewage disposal systems. Where such extension is not accompanied by the provision of public water, inadequate water availability may result.

## Groundwater Protection

- Active or vacant industrial sites, including processing, chemical storage, shipping, or waste disposal, may potentially contaminate groundwater and should not be permitted within aquifer recharge areas.
- Nitrates and other contaminants from on-site wastewater disposal may pollute groundwater if the system is poorly designed or fails, and should not be permitted within aquifer recharge areas, unless analysis demonstrates that contamination problems are not a concern at the proposed densities.

# Surface Water and Collected Water Supplies

## Surface Water Supplies

Surface water supplies include uncontrolled river systems, natural lakes and ponds, multipurpose reservoirs, and reservoirs constructed exclusively for water supply. In the United States, surface waters are typically classified as Class A, suitable for drinking with little or no treatment, Class B, suitable for drinking with treatment, and Class C or lower, not suitable for drinking. Use of surface water systems as a potable supply should consider the following:

- The size of the contributing watershed must yield adequate volumes to meet anticipated consumption. Potential yield is determined by the watershed's annual rainfall less local evapotranspiration rates, as well as the evaporation and leakage rates for the water body.
- The minimum volume of storage should be equal to one year's annual average runoff from its contributing watershed in order to achieve good water quality without extensive treatment (Figure 6.4). Refer to Chapter 11: Stormwater Management for methods of estimating runoff volumes.
- Generally, the deeper the water body, the clearer the water. Depths should be sufficient to provide thermal and chemical stratification and turnover required to settle organic materials.
- Contamination is a primary concern with surface water supplies. The contributing watershed should be free from industrial and waste disposal sites that are potentially harmful, including abandoned facilities. Supplies should also be free from geologic and human sources of phosphorus (such as fertilizers), to prevent algae growth.
- Surface water will likely require some treatment to meet potable standards. This may include chlorination, pH adjustment, fluoridation and/or filtration.

## Collected Water Supplies

In areas with insufficient or inaccessible groundwater or surface water supplies, rainwater collection systems may be a viable alternative. These systems typically employ a cistern or covered reservoir tank to store water collected from rooftops or other relatively clean, impervious surfaces (Figure 6.5). Use of these systems should consider the following:

- Adequate precipitation and catchment area must be provided. Table 6.4 lists minimum catchment areas required to yield 100 Liters (100 gallons) of water per day in regions with different precipitation levels.

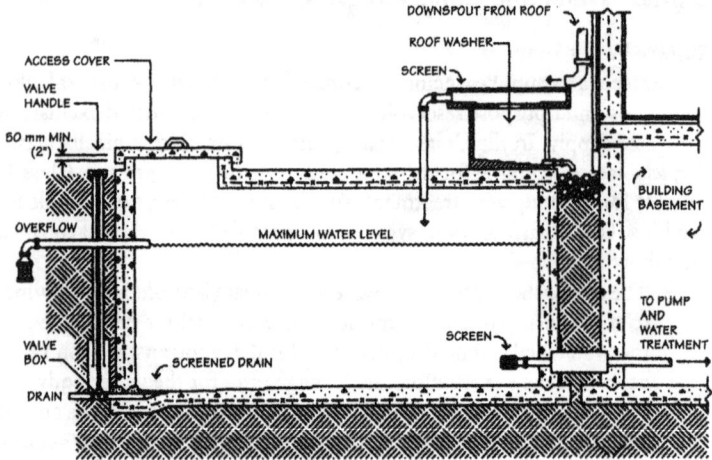

**Figure 6.5. Typical cistern design.**

- Cistern volume is a function of rainfall distribution through the year. In regions with rainfall limited to only one season, approximately 30 000 Liters for 100 LPD of consumption (30,000 gallons for 100 GPD of consumption).
- In regions with adequate rainfall distributed throughout the year, cisterns may only be ¼ as large.

## ESTIMATING WASTEWATER FLOWS

Design standards for quantities of wastewater flows are established by state or local jurisdictions. Wastewater flows closely parallel water demands. Therefore Table 6.1 may be used for preliminary planning purposes.

### TABLE 6.4. Catchment areas for cisterns.

| Annual Precipitation | Catchment area required to yield 100 Liters per day* | Catchment area required to yield 100 gallons per day* |
|---|---|---|
| 500 mm (20″) | 150 m² | 6000 ft² |
| 1000 mm (40″) | 75 m² | 3000 ft² |
| 1500 mm (60″) | 50 m² | 2000 ft² |

*Assumes 75% capture during a dry year.

# TYPES OF WASTEWATER TREATMENT SYSTEMS

Wastewater treatment systems can be broadly classified into three types: Large-scale municipal systems, cluster systems that service local neighborhoods, and individual on-site systems. The type of wastewater treatment system chosen for a project will greatly influence the pattern and density of that development. Generally, on-site treatment requires greater land area and results in lower development densities (Figure 6.6). Clustered or municipal systems allow the greatest density of development, as well as the development of sites incapable of supporting treatment systems due to environmental constraints such as permeable soils or high water tables.

Selection of the appropriate method of treating wastewater is a function of local regulations, cost/benefit ratios of the system and achievable densities, anticipated flows, available space, subgrade characteristics, and concerns over groundwater contamination or other environmental considerations.

## Municipal Sewer Systems

If municipal gravity sewer service is available for a project, its use is often mandated by local regulations, even though it may not be the least costly or the most environmentally desirable alternative. Many municipalities use the extension of municipal sewer service as a strategy for controlling urban growth, by severely restricting densities outside of the service area. As a result, this alternative typically permits the highest density of development and the most intense uses.

## Cluster Treatment Systems

Cluster systems concentrate treatment at one or a few points on a site, servicing a local community. Adequate space must be provided for the large treatment system, so overall gross density may not be significantly higher than that afforded by on-site systems. However, it does provide greater flexibility in the development of sites with environmental constraints for on-site systems, as well as alternative types of development, such as small-lot cluster subdivisions. Figure 6.7 compares minimum site areas required for different cluster treatment systems. Table 6.5 describes typical cluster treatment systems. Regardless of the treatment system selected, efforts should be made to locate the facility in a central location that minimizes the length of pipeline to service each site. Wherever feasible, allow for gravity sewer collection by locating the facility at lower elevations than the sites it services. Consideration should be given to recycling treated water for irrigation or other uses, particularly in regions with stressed potable water supplies.

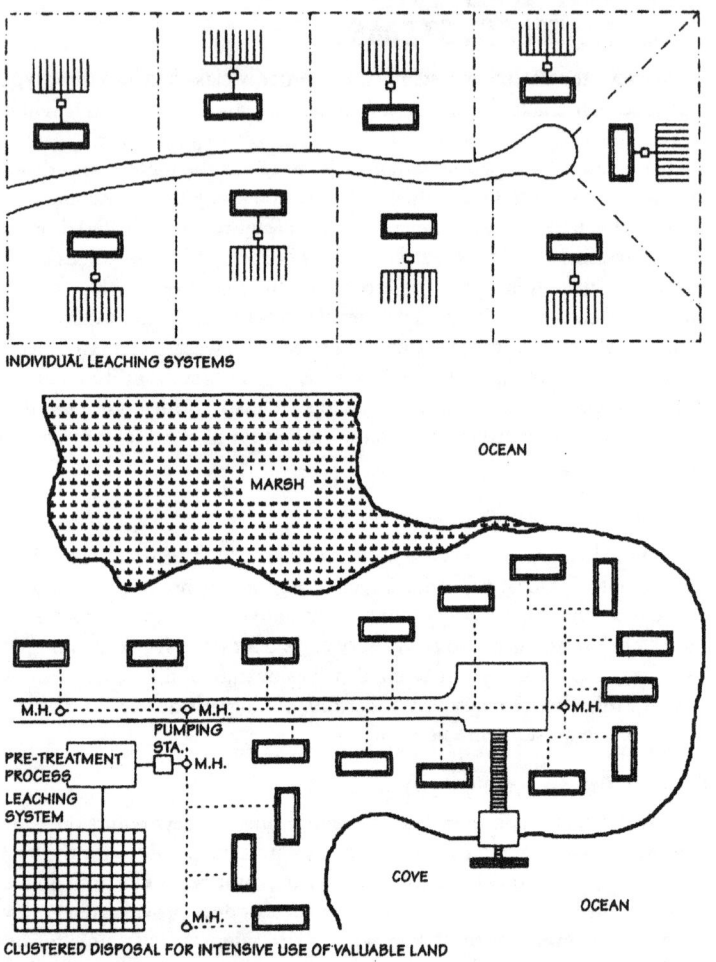

INDIVIDUAL LEACHING SYSTEMS

CLUSTERED DISPOSAL FOR INTENSIVE USE OF VALUABLE LAND

**Figure 6.6. Effect of wastewater treatment strategies on land use patterns.**

## On-Site Treatment Systems

An increasingly wide variety of on-site alternatives are available for wastewater treatment. Table 6.6 describes common on-site treatment systems. In addition to these techniques, jurisdictions are increasingly encouraging the separation of graywater, household wastewater from showers and washbasins, from the treatment stream. This water may be used in subsurface irrigation in regions with stressed water supplies. Refer to Chapter 19: Irrigation for information on the design of these systems.

# SUGGESTED REFERENCES

Biswas, Asit K., *Water Resources : Environmental Planning, Management, and Development*, McGraw-Hill, New York, 1997.

Dewberry and Davis, *Land Development Handbook*, McGraw-Hill, New York, 1996.

Harris, Charles W. and Nicholas T. Dines, *Time-Saver Standards for Landscape Architecture, 2nd Edition*, McGraw-Hill, New York, 1998.

Tchobanoglous, George, et al., *Wastewater Engineering : Treatment, Disposal, and Reuse*, McGraw-Hill, New York, 1991.

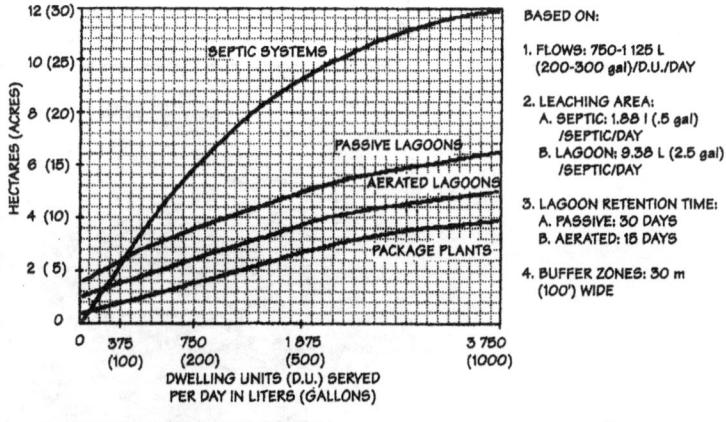

MINIMUM SITE AREA FOR DISPOSAL FACILITIES TREATMENT

1. SEPTIC LEACHING
2. PASSIVE LAGOON AND LEACHING
3. AERATED LAGOON AND LEACHING
4. PACKAGE PLANTS

**Figure 6.7. Site area required for cluster treatment facilities.**

**TABLE 6.5. Cluster wastewater treatment systems.**

| System | Processing of waste | Wastewater Disposal method | Requirements |
|---|---|---|---|
| **Septic Systems –** Most common form of cluster and on-site treatment system in the United States | Anaerobic digestion of solids in tank | Subsurface leaching to control odors via trenches, beds, pits, etc. (Figure 6.8) | Suitable only with sufficient soil permeability [20-25 mm (¾-1") per day]; may be mounded where depth to groundwater is inadequate; requires significant land area for leaching field, which may also be used as open space; must be located at least 15 m (50 ft) from wells or surface waters; requires infrequent draining and cleaning |
| **Package Plants -** Mechanically complex, prefabricated system, enclosed within a building if desired | Aerobic digestion of solids resulting in odor free effluent | Surface infiltration beds on sites with sufficient permeability, applied at rates up to 10 times greater than septic systems; or through plant evapo-transpiration via sub-irrigation, or spray irrigation | Suitable where space and site conditions are constrained; requires frequent pumping to mitigate biomass accumulation |

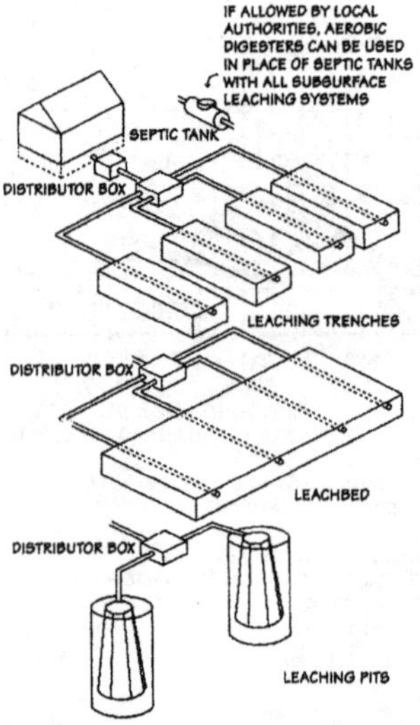

**Figure 6.8. Types of subsurface leaching systems.**

**TABLE 6.5. Cluster wastewater treatment systems (continued).**

| System | Processing of waste | Wastewater Disposal method | Requirements |
|---|---|---|---|
| **Lagoons –** constructed ponds typically 600 to 1500 mm (2-5 ft) deep in warm climates, which rely on natural processes to treat waste. | Anaerobic digestion of solids at bottom of pond; odor is contained by water; nutrients released support algae and/or wetland plant growth and introduce aerobic processes to reduce odor | Surface infiltration sand beds applied at rates up to 0.65 L/m² (1/2 Gal/ft²) per day (figure 6.9) | In cold climates, greater depths and aeration is required to reduce odor during seasonal turnover; infrequent draining and cleaning; alternating and resting of infiltration beds; requires significant land area that cannot be used for other purposes |
| **Constructed Wetlands –** surface or subsurface wetlands. Organic matter and nitrogen are removed by biological mechanisms, while the soil media adsorbs phosphorus; may be combined with lagoons or other techniques to provide tertiary treatment of wastewater | Anaerobic digestion of solids in holding tank | Surface infiltration or subsurface leaching | In cold climates, surface wetland of greater depths are required, to avoid freeze-out and provide continued functioning; infrequent draining and cleaning; alternating and resting of infiltration beds |

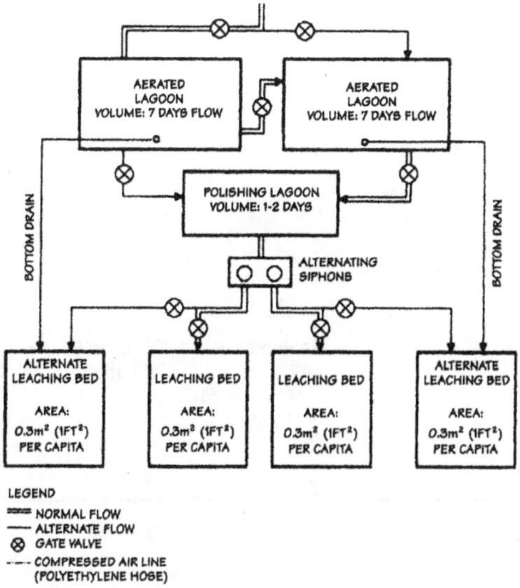

**Figure 6.9. Typical aerated lagoon system.**

**TABLE 6.6. On-site wastewater treatment systems.**

| System | Processing of waste | Wastewater Disposal method | Requirements |
|---|---|---|---|
| **Septic Systems –** Most common form of cluster and on-site treatment system in the United States | Anaerobic digestion of solids in tank | Subsurface leaching to control odors via trenches, beds, pits, etc. (Figure 6.8) | Suitable only with sufficient soil permeability [20-25 mm (³/₄-1") per day]; may be mounded where depth to groundwater is inadequate; Requires large lots for leaching field, which may also be used as open space (Figure 6.10); must be located at least 15 m (50 ft) from wells or surface waters; requires infrequent draining and cleaning |
| **Cesspools –** Infiltration basin (Figure 6.11) | Anaerobic digestion of solids in below-ground pool | Subsurface leaching to control odors around the perimeter of the cesspool | Suitable for small systems up to 575 L (150 Gallons) per day; viable only with sufficient soil permeability [20-25 mm (³/₄-1") per day]; requires very low water table to accommodate pool as well as adequate leaching soil beneath; requires infrequent draining and cleaning |
| **Composting Toilets** – organic treatment system which uses natural, biological decomposition and dehydration to convert toilet waste into a safe fertilizer; combined with separate graywater systems to reduce inflow | Aerobic digestion in manufactured container | Subsurface leaching through separate graywater system (refer to Chapter 22: Irrigation) | Requires significantly less water than other systems; waste material must remain adequately mixed, with the moisture content in an acceptable range. Odors can result from anaerobic conditions if too much moisture accumulates in the unit |
| **Holding Tanks** | Anaerobic digestion of solids in tank or lagoon | Pumping by tank trucks | Suitable for severely constrained sites where infiltration or evapotranspiration is not viable or practical; requires frequent pumping to remove wastewater and solids |

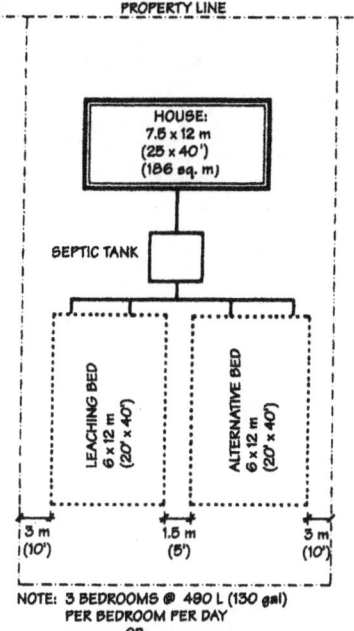

NOTE: 3 BEDROOMS @ 480 L (130 gal) PER BEDROOM PER DAY
OR
6 PEOPLE @ 250 L (66 gal) PER CAPITA PER DAY @ 20.3 L (.5 gal) PER SQUARE METER PER DAY = 74 SQUARE METERS PER LEACHING BED

**Figure 6.10. Typical on-site septic system layout.**

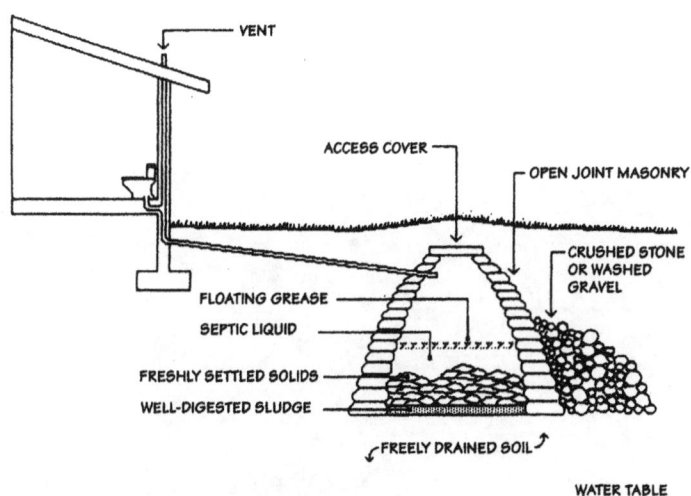

**Figure 6.11. Typical cesspool design.**

# Community
# Standards

7

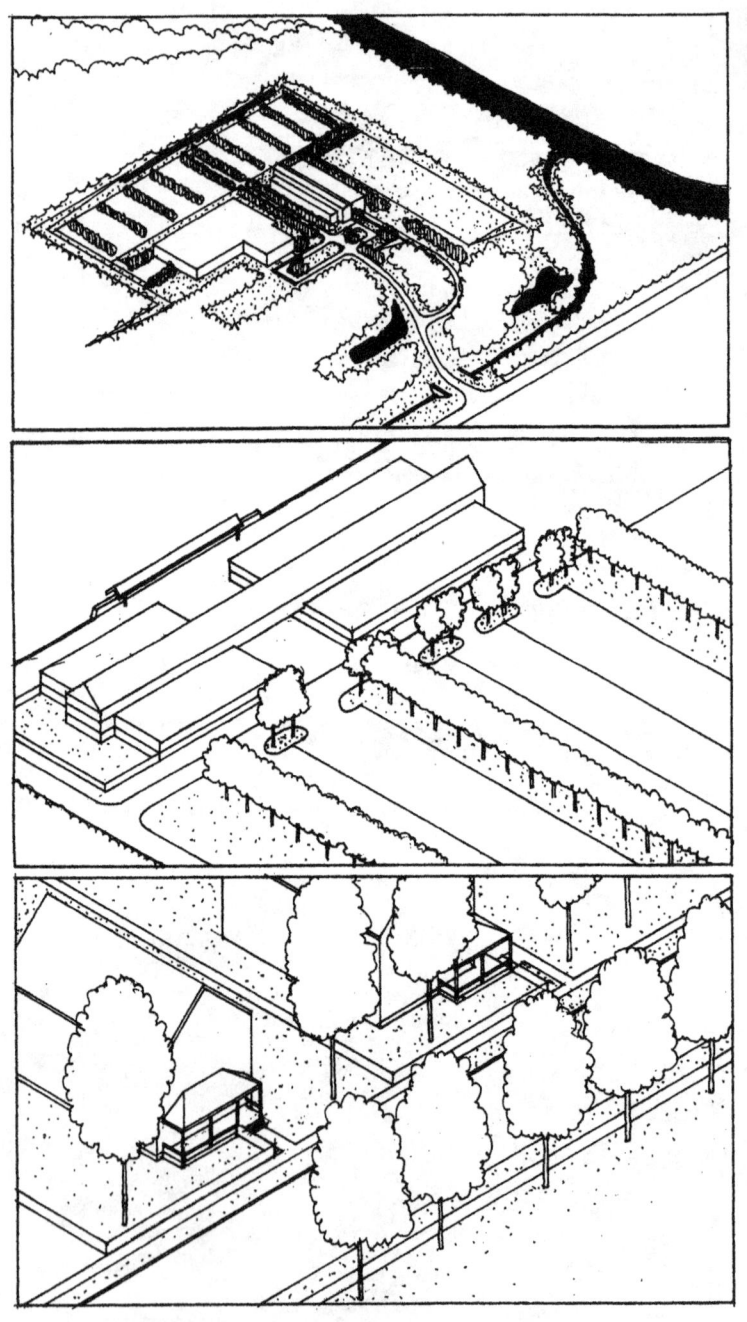

# INDUSTRIAL AND BUSINESS DEVELOPMENT

Current trends in industrial and business development focus on the design of business parks that provide space for offices, research laboratories, light manufacturing, warehousing and supporting uses within a master-planned development. Parks tend to emphasize high quality architectural and environmental design, convenient access, the provision of support services, and high visibility. Planned multiuse developments that integrate employment-based activities, commercial and community services, recreational facilities and housing represent the latest trend in business park design.

# RETAIL COMMERCIAL DEVELOPMENT

Retail commercial facilities are typically categorized as neighborhood, community, or regional in character, each suggesting different design standards. Small neighborhood centers focus on convenience goods and tend to attract customers from within walking distances [up to 1 kilometer (½ mile)]. Community facilities offer neighborhood services as well as more specialized retail services, and will attract customers from local surroundings [3 kilometers (2 miles)]. Regional facilities are much larger in size and include major shopping malls and large-box retailers. They will attract customers from an expanded trade area [greater than 6 kilometers (4 miles)] so parking and vehicular circulation become primary concerns.

# RESIDENTIAL DEVELOPMENT

Residential development occurs at a variety of densities, ranging from single-family detached homes to high-rise multi-family apartment complexes. In addition to density, consideration should be given to the extent of open space and impervious surfaces provided within a development, in order to assess its intensity and potential impact on the community. To this end, cluster-housing arrangements or other alternatives to the conventional single-family detached home typically result in higher public open space ratios and lower impervious surface ratios.

U RBAN LAND USES, INCLUDING RESIDENTIAL, retail commercial, business, industrial, and community services are necessarily interrelated, yet each possesses unique requirements with regard to size, location, arrangement and intensity of development within a community. This chapter provides an overview of various types of development common in today's marketplace, and describes standards for their location, design, and successful operation.

## DIAGNOSTIC ASSESSMENT

*What is the appropriate urban pattern for the community?*

A variety of urban patterns have been adopted for the design of communities. Traditional grid and radial street patterns provide simplicity, directness and even circulation throughout the community. Dendritic patterns work more effectively in hilly terrain, and offer residential cul-de-sac lots that are often viewed as desirable for their reduced traffic levels. Linear networks offer convenient access primarily for commercial uses along major highways.

*What is the range of residential development appropriate for the site and the community?*

Residential development is driven by market demands for a given housing type within a given area. A wide variety of single-family and multi-family housing solutions have been developed to accommodate market demands and site requirements. Generally, a balance of housing alternatives should be provided, to meet the needs of a variety of residential markets (e.g. rental, single-family homes, condominiums), and sustain relatively constant demand for community services (e.g. schools) as the community ages.

*What type of commercial development is appropriate and sustainable for a given site?*

Commercial uses may be classified as neighborhood, community, or regional in character. The size, location, and proximity of other competing commercial centers determine the appropriateness of a given site for commercial development. In addition, the population and demographic characteristics of a community are important in determining the types of commercial uses that are considered to be economically viable.

*What type of business or industrial development is appropriate for the site and the community?*

Business and industrial activities are important employment opportunities for communities. In addition, these activities generate significant tax revenue for local communities, with relatively low service costs. The design of master-planned business parks on undeveloped or redeveloped land represents the most significant trend in business and industrial development. These facilities frequently attempt to attract tenants with high-profile locations, high quality architectural design in a park-like environment, and important amenities such as hotels, restaurants and recreational facilities.

*What are the appropriate size and distribution of public facilities within a community?*

A number of standards have been developed for determining the extent of community facilities, including park and open space necessary within a community, depending on its population. In addition, transportation studies have identified standards for off-street parking for various community activities, including commercial uses.

# CIRCULATION PATTERNS

Table 7.1 identifies common circulation patterns for communities, as well as their advantages and disadvantages. Selection of a particular pattern is often a function of design intent, proposed land uses, and physical characteristics of the site (e.g. topography, presence of wetlands or other limitations for development).

# RESIDENTIAL STANDARDS

## Measures of Intensity

Intensity of residential development can be measured in a variety of ways. Three of the simpler measures are of particular importance: 1) Density; 2) Open Space Ratio; and 3) Impervious Surface Ratio. The combination of all three measures provides a useful picture of a proposed development, and an indication of its potential impact on natural and cultural processes.

## TABLE 7.1. Common circulation patterns.

| Pattern | Advantages | Disadvantages |
|---|---|---|
| Grid Pattern | • Simple and efficient<br>• Ease of design and layout<br>• Convenient access<br>• Good wayfinding<br>• Effective on flat terrain<br>• Suitable for complex distributed flow<br>• Efficient for pedestrian circulation | • Disregard for topography and natural features<br>• Vulnerability to through traffic<br>• Lack of difference between heavily and lightly traveled roads |
| Radial Pattern | • Simple and efficient for most travel<br>• Direct line of travel to key locations in community<br>• Defines community focal point<br>• Good wayfinding<br>• Efficient for pedestrian circulation | • Inefficient for trips where neither origin nor destination are related to the center<br>• Encourages intersections that are not perpendicular<br>• Results in uniquely-shaped parcels/building sites |
| Dendritic Pattern | • Effective in terrain with development limitations from steep slopes or other natural features<br>• Favors specialization of roadways (arterials, collectors and local streets)<br>• Creates cul-de-sac lots and other low-traffic roadways for residential development | • Wayfinding is often diminished<br>• Sensitive to disruptions in traffic flow at a single point<br>• Less efficient for pedestrian circulation |
| Linear Pattern | • Traffic flow is primarily between two points<br>• Effective for development along railroads, rivers, highways and other linear elements | • Lack of community focus<br>• Less efficient for pedestrian circulation<br>• Tends to create significant cross-traffic and intersections along major roadway |

## Density

Density is the most common measure included in community plans and development regulations, and is typically expressed as the number of dwelling units per hectare (acre) of land.

> **EXAMPLE (US UNITS):**
>
> *Assume a proposed development consisting of 39 dwelling units on a 20-acre parcels:*
>
> $$Density = \frac{39\ D.U.}{20\ Ac.}$$
>
> $$Density = 1.95\ Dwelling\ Units\ per\ Acre$$

### Open Space Ratio

Open space ratio is the proportion of a site that is not occupied by private lots or public road right-of-ways. It may include natural areas preserved from development or improved recreational areas. In some situations, more precise definitions of open space may be useful in order to assess the proportion of open space that meets a specific objective (e.g. habitat protection, active recreation, etc.).

**EXAMPLE CONTINUED (US UNITS):**

*Proposed development includes 7 acres of public open space:*

$$Open\ Space\ Ratio = \frac{7\ Ac.}{20\ Ac.}$$

*Open Space Ratio = 0.35*

### Impervious Surface Ratio

Measurement of impervious surfaces (e.g. streets, sidewalks, driveways, buildings, patios, etc.) is important in evaluating impacts of development on stormwater runoff and surface temperatures.

**EXAMPLE CONTINUED (US UNITS):**

*Proposed development includes 5.5 acres of streets, sidewalks, driveways and buildings:*

$$Impervious\ Surface\ Ratio = \frac{5.5\ Ac.}{20\ Ac.}$$

*Impervious Surface Ratio = 0.28*

## Development Types

A wide variety of residential development alternatives are available, ranging from conventional single-family homes, to cluster housing and multi-family complexes. Figures 7.1 through 7.6 illustrate a variety of development alternatives for a single site at a common density of 4.0 du/ha (1.6 du/ac). Table 7.2 summarizes the relative intensity of each development alternative illustrated. Generally speaking, cluster-housing arrangements result in higher open space ratios and lower impervious surface ratios than conventional lots.

**TABLE 7.2. Intensity comparison of residential development types\*.**

| Development Type | Description | Density | Open Space | Impervious Surface |
|---|---|---|---|---|
| Conventional Single-Family Homes (Figure 7.1) | Most common type, characterized by house roughly centered on lot with minimum setback distances from all property lines, as defined by local code. | 4.0 du/ha (1.6 du/ac) | Typically, no open space provided; land is dedicated entirely to private lots or public road right-of-ways. | 0.16 |
| Cluster Homes (Figure 7.2) | Single family homes on smaller lots to provide dedicated open space; shared driveways and trail easements are often employed. | 4.0 du/ha (1.6 du/ac) | 0.72 | 0.13 |
| Zero-Lot-Line Homes (Figure 7.3) | Narrow lots with the house located on a side property line to create a more usable side yard; z-lots are a variation of the lot line approach where side property lines are reconfigured to provide additional useable area. | 4.0 du/ha (1.6 du/ac) | 0.48 | 0.14 |
| Twin Homes (Figure 7.4) | Duplex units connected along a common party wall to similar unit; typically smaller yards than conventional single-family homes. | 4.0 du/ha (1.6 du/ac) | 0.73 | 0.12 |
| Townhomes (Figure 7.5) | Single-family attached units sharing common side walls; typically arranged in rows; private yard areas are small. | 4.0 du/ha (1.6 du/ac) | 0.71 | 0.09 |
| Garden Apts. (Figure 7.6) | Multi-family housing; may be rental or privately owned; common yard areas used for outdoor recreation. | 4.0 du/ha (1.6 du/ac) | 0.88 | 0.10 |

\*Assumes design at a common density on a single site, as illustrated in Figures 7.1 through 7.6).

Source: Example adapted from Bucks County Planning Commission, *Performance Zoning*, 1973

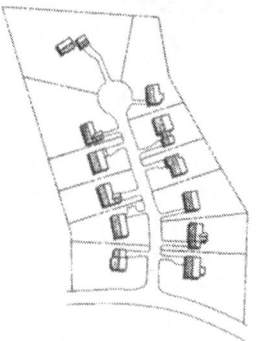

**Figure 7.1. Conventional single-family homes**

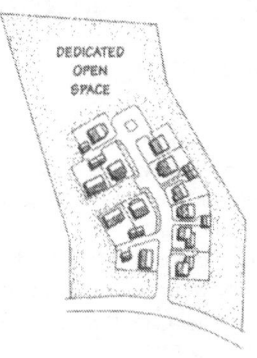

**Figure 7.2. Cluster single-family homes.**

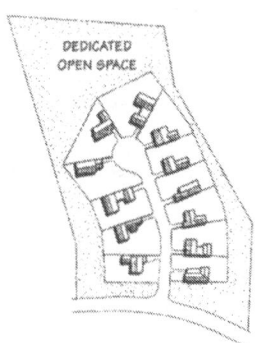

**Figure 7.3. Zero-lot-line homes.**

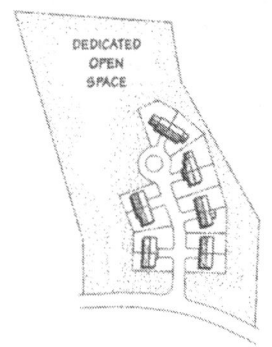

**Figure 7.4. Twin homes.**

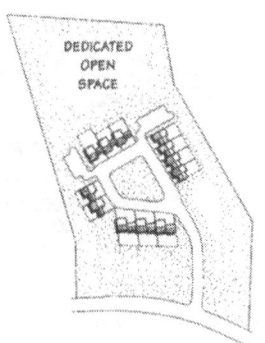

**Figure 7.5. Townhomes.**

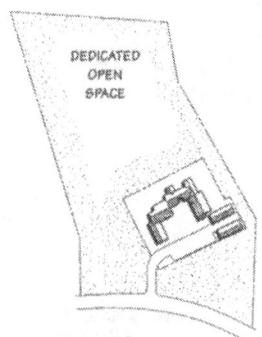

**Figure 7.6. Garden apartments.**

# RETAIL COMMERCIAL STANDARDS

## Measures of Intensity

Floor area ratio (FAR) is a measure of the total building floor area (each story of a multi-story building is included), relative to the total land area. An FAR of 1 allows one square meter (foot) of building floor area for each square meter (foot) of land area. FAR is a common measure of intensity for commercial/industrial uses in zoning ordinances. It may be combined with percentage of lot coverage to dictate lot size and building height requirements. For example, an ordinance permitting an FAR of 1 and 50% lot coverage would result in a two-story building covering half of the lot. In addition, impervious surface ratio, as described in the residential standards section, may be used to further regulate and measure the intensity of hardscape development.

**TABLE 7.3. Comparison of retail commercial types.**

| | Neighborhood | Community | Regional |
|---|---|---|---|
| *Major function* | Convenience goods and personal services | Convenience goods, personal services and shopping goods (books, appliances, etc.) (clothes, furniture, etc.) | Some functions of community commercial types plus general merchandise |
| *Anchor tenants* | Convenience mart; drug store | Variety store; small department store | Major department stores; large discount retailers |
| *Location* | Intersection of collector roads | Intersection of major collectors and arterials | Intersection of arterials; visibility from freeways important |
| *Radius of service** | 1 km (1/2 mile) | 3 km (2 miles) | 6+ km (4+ miles) |
| *Min. population to support center* | 4,000 | 35,000 | 150,000 |
| *Land area required* | 1.5-3 ha (4-8 acres) | 4-12 ha (10-30 acres) | 16-40+ ha (40-100+ acres) |
| *Desirable max. size of center as a percentage of area served* | 1.25% 0.40 ha/1,000 pop. (1 acre/1,000 pop.) | 1.00% 0.30 ha/1,000 pop. (0.75 acres/1,000 pop.) | 0.50% 0.27 ha/1,000 pop. (0.67 acres/1,000 pop.) |
| *Gross floor area* | 2800-7000 m² (30,000-75,000 ft²) | 9000-23 000 m² (100,000-250,000 ft²) | 37 000-93 000 m² (400,000-1,000,000 ft²) |
| *Number of businesses* | 5-20 | 15-40 | 40-80 |

*Radius of service distances are for general planning purposes and vary by density and retail opportunities of the local community.

Source: Adapted from Dechiara, Joseph and Lee Koppelman, *Urban Planning and Design Criteria*, 3rd Edition, Van Nostrand Reinhold, New York, 1982.

## Classification of Retail Commercial Types

Commercial facilities vary from region to region, and may be classified a number of different ways, but they are typically described in terms of their location, function, and radius of service. Table 7.3 describes characteristics of neighborhood, community, and regional commercial facilities.

## Commercial Center Design

A number of basic patterns are used for contemporary commercial center design, with slight variations to accommodate existing development, topographic constraints, or other characteristics of specific sites. Figure 7.7 illustrates these basic patterns. Selection of the appropriate patterns is a function of the size, shape and features of the site, existing circulation systems, and surrounding context.

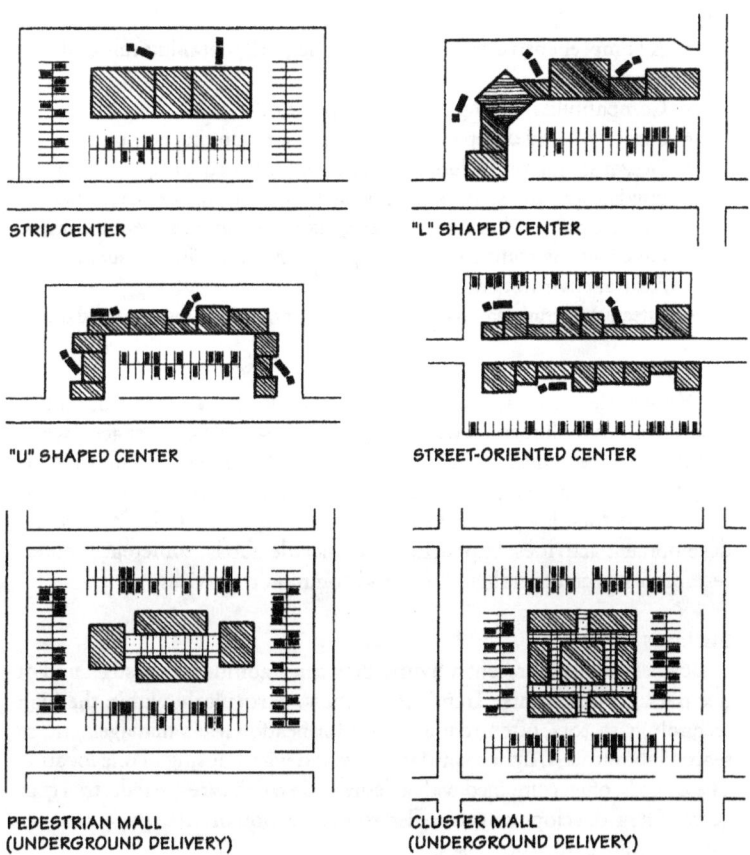

Figure 7.7. Basic commercial center patterns.

# INDUSTRIAL AND BUSINESS DEVELOPMENT STANDARDS

## Industrial and Business Development Types

Industrial zoning districts were the traditional means for accommodating industrial and business activities through much of the 20th century. However, current development trends favor more coordinated developments, in the form of industrial, office and business parks, with increasing attention paid towards multiuse developments.

### Industrial Parks

An industrial park is the assembly of land, under one continuing control, to provide facilities for the production and dissemination of goods and services, consistent with a master plan. Common elements of an industrial park include:

- A comprehensive master plan for the park, detailing full build-out intentions.
- Compatibility among industrial operations.
- Sensitivity and compatibility with the surrounding community.
- Design standards, including street standards adequate for truck traffic, building size and setback requirements, impervious surface restrictions, architectural and landscape design controls, and use requirements.
- Park-like environment, that integrates strongly with the surrounding natural environment.
- Effective operational management to maintain park function and design.

### Office Parks

Office parks are a variation of industrial parks that contain a number of separate office buildings, as well as supporting uses and open spaces, within a master-planned environment. Uses are limited to offices and may include corporate headquarters, back-offices, professional offices for landscape architects, doctors, lawyers, consultants, etc., and compatible research and development activities. Supporting uses include hotels, conference centers, restaurants, recreational facilities, and community services.

### Business Parks

Business parks represent a hybrid between traditional industrial and office park developments. Trends in business, particularly within the high-technology sectors, often require space for headquarters management, research laboratories, light manufacturing and warehousing in one location. These needs, often combined with a desire to de-emphasize the industrial character of new developments have led to the creation of these parks that further integrate compatible uses.

### Planned Multiuse Developments

Planned multiuse developments integrate the array of urban uses, including employment-based office and industrial activities, commercial services, community and recreational facilities and housing. These developments should have the following characteristics.

- A comprehensive plan for the development, detailing full build-out intentions and integration with the surrounding community.
- Serve as a focal point for transportation networks, including mass transit.
- On-site essential services for businesses, employees, and residents, to minimize transportation needs, and encourage a pedestrian-oriented environment.
- A range of housing opportunities.
- Sensitivity and compatibility with the surrounding community.
- Design standards, including architectural and landscape design controls, and use requirements.
- Effective operational management to maintain park function and design.

## Locational Requirements

Because most business parks that are developed today accommodate a mix of light-industrial, office, and research and development facilities, the selection of an appropriate site is dependent on a number of criteria, critical to the successful operation of these diverse facilities. Site selection and design should seek to optimize flexibility in terms of the needs of specific tenants, while ensuring that common fundamental needs are fulfilled. Considerations include:

1. Size of available parcels (should accommodate new development for a 10-15 year period if possible, based on local absorption rates).
2. Convenient access to major highways (often highway frontage is desirable for visibility).
3. Convenient access to airports and harbors, or adjacency to rail lines (depending on types of businesses expected).
4. Proximity of support services, including shopping malls, hotels, restaurants, daycare, and recreational facilities.
5. Availability and quality of local work force.
6. Proximity of university or research centers.
7. High quality of life within community, including affordable housing.
8. Access to utilities (water, sewer, gas, electricity, telecommunications).
9. Access to mass transit.
10. Minimum environmental limitations for building site development (assess suitability based on soils, wetlands, topography, critical natural resources, etc.)
11. Attractive physical landscape that will provide distinction to the proposed development.

# COMMUNITY FACILITY STANDARDS

Table 7.4 lists standards for community facilities, based on residential development types and neighborhood population. Table 7.5 lists parking needs of various land uses.

**TABLE 7.4. Land area requirements for community facilities.**

| Type of development | Neighborhood Population | | | | |
| | 1000 persons 275 families | 2000 persons 550 families | 3000 persons 825 families | 4000 persons 1100 families | 5000 persons 1375 families |
|---|---|---|---|---|---|
| **ONE OR TWO-FAMILY DEVELOPMENTS\*** | | | | | |
| **Area in component uses** | | | | | |
| Acres in school site | 1.20 | 1.20 | 1.50 | 1.80 | 2.20 |
| Acres in playground | 2.75 | 3.25 | 4.00 | 5.00 | 6.00 |
| Acres in park | 1.50 | 2.00 | 2.50 | 3.00 | 3.50 |
| Acres in shopping center | 0.80 | 1.20 | 2.20 | 2.60 | 3.00 |
| Acres in general community facilities† | 0.38 | 0.76 | 1.20 | 1.50 | 1.90 |
| **Aggregate area** | | | | | |
| Acres: total | 6.63 | 8.41 | 11.40 | 13.90 | 16.60 |
| Acres per 1000 persons | 6.63 | 4.20 | 3.80 | 3.47 | 3.32 |
| Square feet per family | 1050 | 670 | 600 | 550 | 530 |
| **MULTIFAMILY DEVELOPMENT‡** | | | | | |
| **Area in component uses** | | | | | |
| Acres in school site | 1.20 | 1.20 | 1.50 | 1.80 | 2.20 |
| Acres in playground | 2.75 | 3.25 | 4.00 | 5.00 | 6.00 |
| Acres in park | 2.00 | 3.00 | 4.00 | 5.00 | 6.00 |
| Acres in shopping center | 0.80 | 1.20 | 2.20 | 2.60 | 3.00 |
| Acres in general community facilities† | 0.38 | 0.76 | 1.20 | 1.50 | 1.90 |

## TABLE 7.4. Land area requirements for community facilities (continued).

| Type of development | Neighborhood Population | | | | |
| --- | --- | --- | --- | --- | --- |
| | 1000 persons 275 families | 2000 persons 550 families | 3000 persons 825 families | 4000 persons 1100 families | 5000 persons 1375 families |
| **Aggregate area** | | | | | |
| Acres: total | 7.13 | 9.41 | 12.90 | 15.90 | 19.10 |
| Acres per 1000 persons | 7.13 | 4.70 | 4.30 | 3.97 | 3.82 |
| Square feet per family | 1130 | 745 | 680 | 630 | 610 |

Note: This table combines the recommended or assumed values.

*With private lot area of less than ¼ acre per family (for private lots of ¼ acre or more park area may be omitted).

†Allowance for indoor social and cultural facilities (church, assembly hall, etc.) or separate health center, nursery school, etc.

‡Or other development predominantly without private yards.

Source: Adapted from *Architectural Systems Community Planning*

## TABLE 7.5. Parking spaces required for various land uses.

| Use of site and/or building | Minimum number of parking spaces required |
| --- | --- |
| **RESIDENTIAL** | |
| Single family homes | 2.0/dwelling unit |
| Multifamily: Efficiency | 1.0/dwelling unit |
| One and two bedrooms | 1.5/dwelling unit |
| Three and more apartments | 2.0/dwelling unit |
| Dormitories, sororities, fraternities | 0.5/units |
| Hotels and motels | 1.0/dwelling unit |
| **COMMERCIAL** | |
| Offices and banks | 3.0/1000 s.f. GFA |
| Business and professional services | 3.3/1000 s.f. GFA |
| Commercial recreational facilities | 8.0/1000 s.f. GFA |
| Bowling alleys | 4.0/lane |
| Regional shopping centers | 4.5/1000 s.f. GFA |

➤ continued on next page

## TABLE 7.5. Parking spaces required for various land uses (continued).

| Use of site and/or building | Minimum number of parking spaces required |
| --- | --- |
| **COMMERCIAL (CONTINUED)** | |
| Community shopping centers | 5.0/1000 s.f. GFA |
| Neighborhood centers | 6.0/1000 s.f. GFH |
| Restaurants | 0.3/seat |
| **EDUCATIONAL** | |
| Elementary and junior high schools | 1.0/teacher and staff |
| High schools and colleges | 1.0/2-5 students |
| **MEDICAL** | |
| Medical and dental offices | 1.0/200 s.f. GFA |
| Hospitals | 1.0/2-3 bed |
| Convalescent & nursing homes | 1.0/3 bed |
| **PUBLIC BUILDING** | |
| Auditoriums, theaters, stadiums | 1.0/4 seats |
| Museums and libraries | 1.0/300 s.f. GFA |
| Public utilities and offices | 1.0/two employees |
| **RECREATION** | |
| Beaches | 1.0/100 s.f. |
| Swimming pools | 1.0/30 s.f. |
| Athletic fields and courts | 1.0/3000 s.f. |
| Golf courses | 1.0/acre |
| **INDUSTRIAL** | |
| Industrial manufacturing | 1.0/2-5 employees |
| **CHURCHES** | |
| Churches | 1.0/4 seats |

* The data was derived from existing conditions in North America. Special conditions including local codes and requirements may be quite different and should be used where appropriate. Study of comparable types of land uses nearby or in other similar situations is recommended. Access to and from the site/building via public transportation will affect significantly the number of parking spaces needed for most types of uses.

# Conventional Colors for Land Use Mapping

Planners, designers and cartographers have established a set of conventions for the mapping of land use categories. While precise color choices vary widely, the hues used to represent the land use categories are generally consistent. Depending on the complexity of the desired map, additional land use categories and hue variations may be added.

| Land Use Category | Recommended Hue |
|---|---|
| *RESIDENTIAL* | |
| Single-Family | Yellow |
| Multi-Family | |
| Moderate Density (duplex, townhouse, etc.) | Ochre to Brown |
| High Density (apartment complex) | Dark Brown |
| *COMMERCIAL* | |
| Local (neighborhood retail) | Pink |
| General Commercial (including shopping centers and offices) | Red |
| *INDUSTRIAL* | |
| Light Industry (including public utilities) | Light Gray or Light Purple |
| Heavy Industry | Dark Gray to Black or Dark Purple |
| *PUBLIC AND SEMI-PUBLIC* | |
| Parks | Olive Green to Dark Green |
| Semi-Public Uses (Schools, Civic Buildings, Churches and Institutions) | Light Green to True Green |
| *Agricultural* | Apple Green |
| *Water Bodies* | Blue |
| *Vacant Land* | No Color |

# SUGGESTED REFERENCES

Arendt, Randall G., *Conservation Design for Subdivisions,* Island Press, Washington, D.C., 1996.

Beyard, Michael D., *Business and Industrial Park Development Handbook,* Urban Land Institute, Washington D.C., 1988.

Bookout, Lloyd W. Jr., *Residential Development Handbook, 2nd Edition,* Urban Land Institute, Washington D.C., 1990.

Bucks County Planning Commission, *Performance Zoning,* 1973

DeChiara, Joseph, *Time-Saver Standards for Residential Development,* McGraw-Hill, New York, 1984.

DeChiara, Joseph and Lee Koppelman, *Urban Planning and Design Criteria,* 3rd Edition, Van Nostrand Reinhold, New York, 1982.

Dewberry and Davis, *Land Development Handbook,* McGraw-Hill, New York, 1996.

Harris, Charles W. and Nicholas T. Dines, *Time-Saver Standards for Landscape Architecture, 2nd Edition,* McGraw-Hill, New York, 1998.

McBee, Susanna., *Downtown Development Handbook, 2nd Edition,* Urban Land Institute, Washington D.C., 1992.

Sanders, Welford, *The Cluster Subdivision: A Cost Effective Approach,* American Planning Association, Chicago, 1980.

Smart, J. Eric, *Recreational Development Handbook,* Urban Land Institute, Washington D.C., 1981.

# STANDARDS

# TECHNIQUES

# DEVICES

# ADMINISTRATION

# TECHNIQUES

# *Layout and Surveying*

8

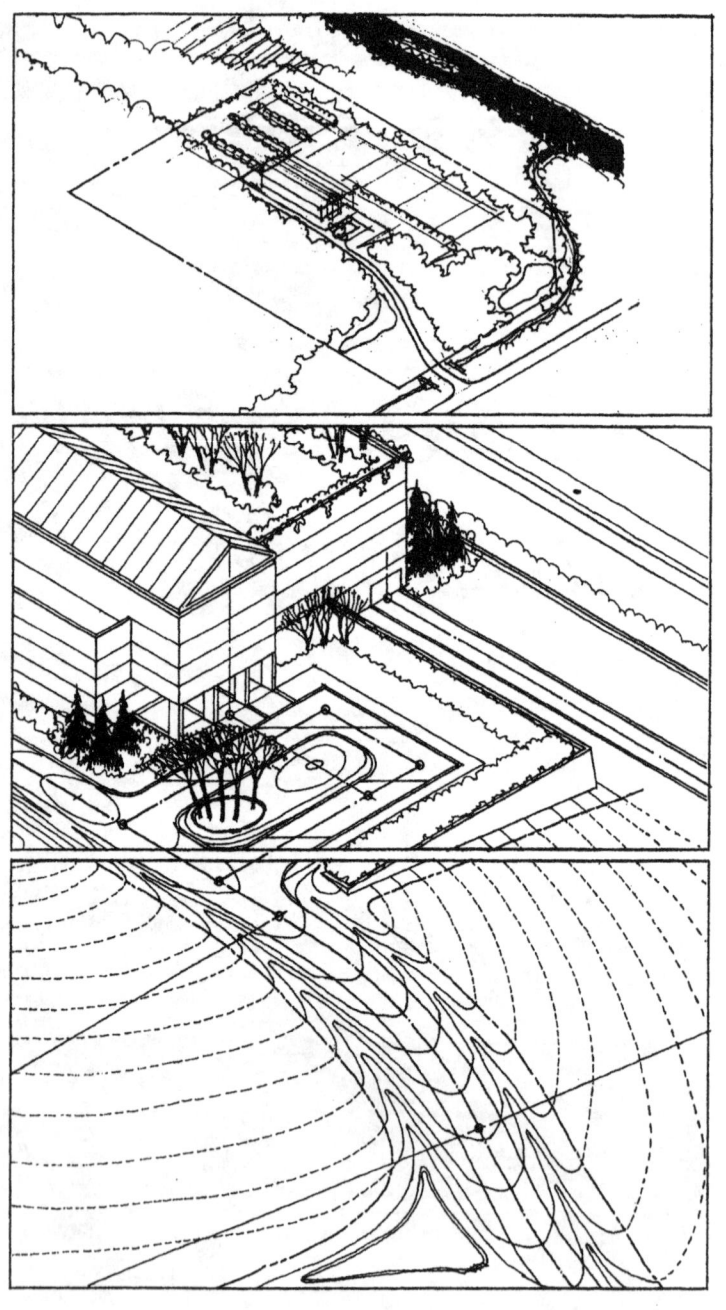

# BOUNDARY AND TOPOGRAPHIC SURVEY

Large scale topographic and parcel boundary surveys are typically tied to a local or regional benchmark, a coordinate grid, and a level-datum. Such surveys are used to indicate township grids, land parcel configuration and ownership, and detailed topographic, biotic, and hydrologic data required for the preparation of landscape planning and design studies and proposals.

# COORDINATE GEOMETRY LOCATION SURVEY

The layout and staking of a site development proposal must accurately transfer the data contained in construction documents to the construction site. Construction is sequential and both the construction drawings and the staking out of new elements in the field should reflect the construction process. Coordinate geometry is used to locate key design benchmarks from which other data may be measured. Coordinates are primary, centerlines are secondary, and dimensions of widths and lengths are tertiary.

# ROUTE ALIGNMENT SURVEY

Road and path alignments are laid out as an open traverse, within which circular and parabolic curves are constructed to negotiate both horizontal and vertical changes in direction respectively. Surveys require a point of origin, points of intersection, and lengths, bearings, and slope of each traverse segment. The path alignment centerline is located on the site by means of station stakes, which are off-set to the roadway edge to avoid construction operations. Together with coordinate data, the route alignment survey serves as the principle means for locating all other site design elements.

A DESIGN PROPOSAL IS DEPENDENT on accurate mapping of existing conditions to insure that the projected plan and grading layout may be properly placed within the property boundary and its site features, as indicated on the development plans. In addition to existing physical features, a survey must document legal easements and a host of regulatory zones, which may pertain to the subject property. The mapping of geographic data is the responsibility of the professional surveyor, who is concerned with documenting the location of existing landscape features, and laying out proposed landscape improvements within accepted norms of mathematical accuracy. Site planning and design require both a general understanding of land surveying, as well as a specific understanding of layout and alignment geometry encountered in professional practice.

## DIAGNOSTIC ASSESSMENT

*What are the basic terms, principles, and methods for recording geographic information?*

A general understanding of the complexities of constructing an accurate survey, and a specific knowledge of the basic principles, will help the designer recognize the source of base information and understand the creation of site surveys.

*What methods are used to layout the proposed design geometry on the land?*

It is the responsibility of the layout engineer to stake out the proposed design geometry according to the construction documents. The dimension and grading plans should reflect the process that the layout engineer uses to stake proposed site improvements on the ground.

*What methods of dimensioning allow for efficient construction layout?*

The design geometry must be mathematically descriptive and arranged in a hierarchy of line weights and values to reduce ambiguity and to promote ease of interpretation by layout surveyors in the field. Standard notation and terms are required for clearly communicating both the spirit and the letter of the design intent.

# SURVEYING

## Terms

*Accuracy* is the degree to which mapped information matches true or accepted values. Accuracy refers to the quality of data and the number of errors contained in a dataset or map. Accuracy, or error, is distinguished from *precision*, which concerns the level of measurement or detail of data in a database.

*Benchmarks* (BM) are permanent markers (usually a bronze disk) at a point of determined location. They are used as a reference point for surveys in their locality. Descriptions of benchmark locations and their elevations are published by government agencies. A temporary benchmark (TBM) is a point of fixed location that is used as a reference for a short-duration project.

*Control points* are fixed points of known coordinates and are determined by high-accuracy surveys.

A *datum* is a fixed starting point of a scale. For example, the datum-level for elevation is typically mean sea level and the datum for latitude is the prime meridian (through the Royal Observatory in Greenwich, England).

*GIS* is the abbreviation for geographic information system. GIS are special-purpose digital databases in which a common spatial coordinate system is the primary means of reference. GIS contain subsystems for: 1) data input; 2) data storage, retrieval, and representation; 3) data management, transformation, and analysis; and 4) data reporting and product generation. A GIS supports data collection, analysis, and decision-making and is far more than a map-making product.

*Magnetic declination* is the horizontal angle between true north (i.e., the geographic meridian) and magnetic north (i.e., the magnetic meridian).

*Map scale* is the relationship between distance on a map and the corresponding distance on the earth's surface. Map scale is often recorded as a representative fraction such as 1:24,000 (1 unit on the map represents 24,000 units on the earth's surface). The terms "large" and "small" refer to the relative magnitude of the representative fraction. Since $\frac{1}{1,000,000}$ is a smaller fraction than $\frac{1}{24,000}$, the former is said to be a smaller scale. Small scales are often used to map large areas because each map unit covers a larger earth distance. Large-scale maps are employed for detailed maps of smaller areas.

*Map projections* are attempts to portray the surface of the earth or a portion of the earth on a flat surface. Some distortions of conformality, distance, direction, scale, and area always result from this process. Some projections minimize distortions in some of these properties at the expense of maximizing errors in others. Other projections are attempts to moderately distort all of these properties. Matching data sets from different map projections is one of the difficult challenges of mapping, particularly within geographic information systems.

*Precision* refers to the level of measurement and exactness of description in a survey that may measure position to a fraction of a unit. It is important to realize, however, that precise data, no matter how carefully measured, may be inaccurate. Surveyors may make mistakes or data may be entered into the database incorrectly. Therefore, a distinction is made between precision and accuracy.

A *traverse* is a series of consecutive line segments whose lengths and directions are determined by field measurements. A closed traverse either closes back upon its starting point, or begins and ends on a known control point. An open traverse does not close on either itself or a known control point and, therefore, does not provide any means to check for errors.

## Types of Surveys
### Plane Survey
Survey where the curvature of the earth is not considered. Usually appropriate for surveys up to 250 km² (100 mi²) where significant discrepancies begin to appear between the area of the horizontal plane and the actual curved area of the earth. In most cases, plane surveys provide the *existing conditions plan* on which the proposed design is overlaid (see Figure 8.1).

### Geodetic Survey
Precise large scale survey taking into account the curvature of the earth and used to locate control points in the landscape from which other surveys are based. Geodetic surveys are usually constructed using Global Positioning Systems (GPS). Developed for the military for navigation and surveying, GPS relies on satellites (and ground stations) for precise determination of location.

### Cadastral or Boundary Survey
Cadastral Survey is the means by which private and public land is defined, divided, traced, and recorded. The term derives from the French cadastre, a register of the survey of lands and is, in effect, the public record of the extent, value, and ownership of land for purposes of taxation. A parcel is a fundamental cadastral unit: land that can be owned, sold, and developed. Parcels have legal descriptions that not only describe their boundaries but also contain information concerning rights and interests.

### Topographic Survey
The mapping of natural and human landscape features and their associated elevations.

### Route Survey
A survey of existing or alignment of proposed linear features in the landscape such as roads, canals, or railroads

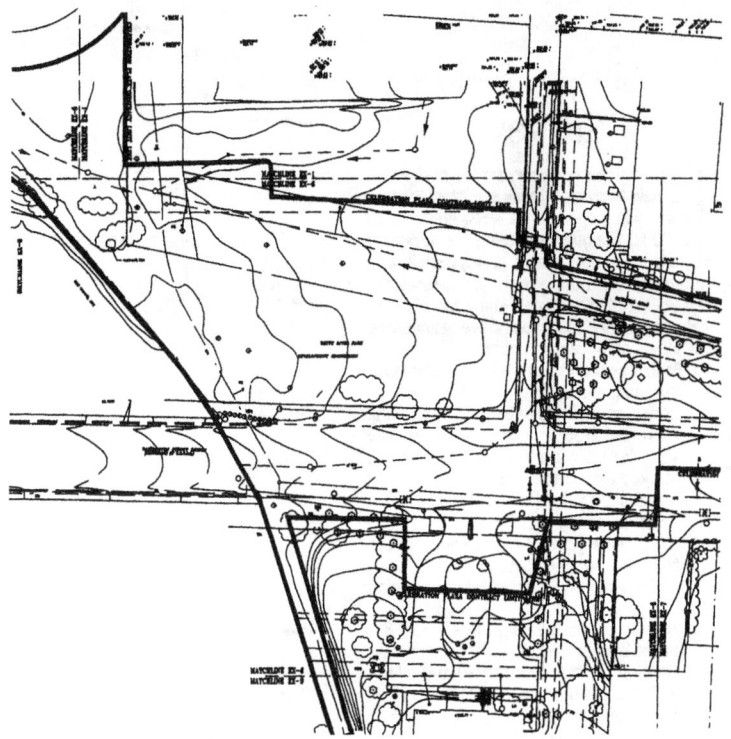

**Figure 8.1. Existing conditions plan.**

## Hydrographic Survey

Survey of lakes, streams, reservoirs, and other bodies of water.

## Aerial Photogrammetry

Photogrammetry uses aerial photographs to produce planimetric and topographic maps of the earth's surface and of features of the built environment. Effective photogrammetry makes use of ground control by which aerial photographs are carefully compared and registered to the locations and characteristics of features identified in ground-level surveys.

## Construction Survey

Survey to layout the location and elevation of proposed landscape features.

# Simple Field Surveys

It is sometimes necessary for the designer in the field to create a quick and simple reconnaissance map. All that is required is a 30 m (100 ft) fiberglass or steel tape, a pocket compass, a hand level, a scale, pencil, and notebook. With these tools, the fieldworker can walk a traverse, establishing the distance between points, the angle between lines, and the elevation of control points.

1. Begin by choosing an easily accessible starting point and designating it Point A.
2. From here, walk along the landscape being traversed stopping wherever there is a sharp turn, or a gradual curve. This point is marked with a stake, chaining pin, or flag and designated as Point B. Then move on determining Point C, D, etc.
3. When all the points are determined, return to Point A, where the azimuth or the bearing is taken on Point B using the pocket compass.
4. The distance between points A and B is paced or measured with the tape (always keeping the tape horizontal) and, along with the azimuth, are recorded in the field notebook.
5. Finally, a hand level is used to determine the difference in height between stations (see Field Note: Using a Hand Level).

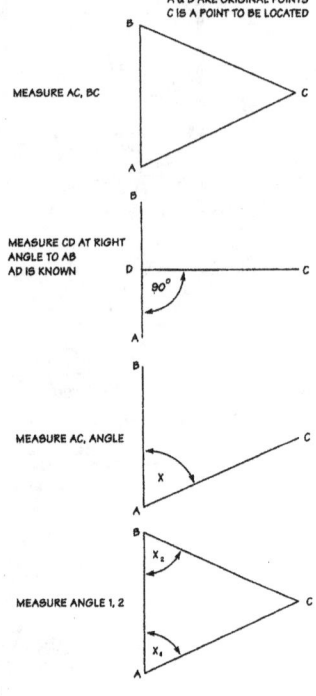

**Figure 8.2. Basic principles of surveying.**

## Basic Principles of Surveying

1. On any area of land it is possible to choose two points and measure the distance between them, creating a base line.
2. Other points can be located relative to the line by taking two other measurements consisting of two distances, one distance and an angle, or two angles.
3. When the whole area to be measured cannot be seen from the base line additional lines are defined using two measurements. The junctions of these lines are called control points and, along with the lines, make up the framework that will serve as the basis for the rest of the survey (see Figure 8.2).

# CONSTRUCTION LAYOUT

## Staking

Staking is the placement of markers on a site to identify certain locations (such as the corners of a building, the right-of-way of a road, the extent of the slope faces of a dam, etc.) with corresponding information (such as cut or fill for earthmoving). Staking is the transferal of information from the plan to the actual site in a manner that the work crews will understand. There are many conventions and methods for staking and marking—the particular practice will depend on the type of job and the type of information to be communicated.

In site layout the two most common tasks are horizontal control, or the staking out of key control points such as road traverse points-of-intersection (PI), proposed building coordinates, parking lots, or other continuous planes; and vertical control, or the establishment of elevations for all proposed elements. The surveyor uses information from the landscape architect's grading plan to establish vertical controls (see Chapter 10: Grading for more information) and information from the landscape architect's layout plan to establish horizontal controls. It is the responsibility of the landscape

FIELD NOTE

# Using a Hand Level

A hand level is a small metal tube with lenses on each end, a leveling bubble, and cross hairs on which items are sighted. The following steps outline the process for measuring the difference in elevation of two points:
1. Determine the height of your eye line above ground level.
2. Stand at a low point of known elevation (a benchmark or datum) and sight a level line through the hand level.
3. The point on the slope at eye height is then noted, usually in reference to a rock, twig, leaf, etc. Walk to that point, stand on it, and repeat the process.
4. The process continues until your eye height is greater than the point whose elevation is being calculated.
5. At this point, the vertical distance between the point where you are standing and the desired point is then estimated. The sum of all the eye heights sighted and the last estimate are added together and then added to the elevation where the process began. Obviously, this procedure can only be used in determining elevations higher than a known point. For determining elevations lower than a known point a second person holding a graduated leveling staff is required.

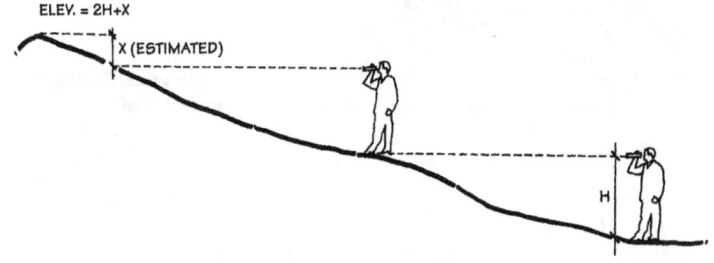

ELEV. = 2H+X

X (ESTIMATED)

H

architect to provide clear and accurate layout and dimensioning plans that can be easily translated by the surveyor into points on the ground.

There are three orders of points that are usually defined on the ground:

1. Primary stations are benchmarks (BM) referenced to the National Grid if necessary. These stations are usually represented on construction documents as the Point-of-Beginning (POB).

2. Secondary stations are established points measured from primary stations. This order is usually where temporary benchmarks (TBM) are established.

3. Detail points locate the corner or center of proposed site features from which the contractor will begin construction.

## Horizontal Layout Methods
### Metes and Bounds

Metes and bounds identify the boundaries of land parcels by describing lengths and directions (or bearings) of lines. Bearings indicate angular orientation with respect to the earth and consist of three components:

- The cardinal direction of the nearest end of the meridian (N or S)
- The angle measured from the nearest end of the meridian (0-90 degrees)
- The cardinal point indicating direction of deflection from the meridian (E or W).

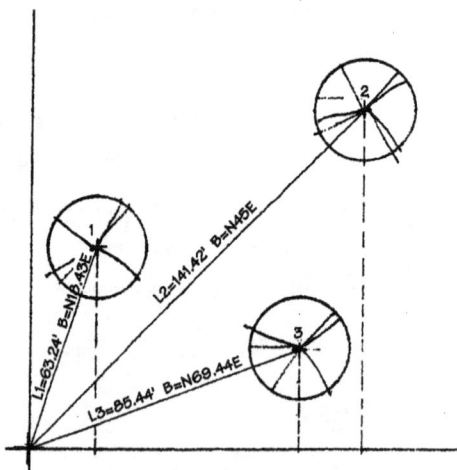

**Figure 8.3. Metes and bounds.**

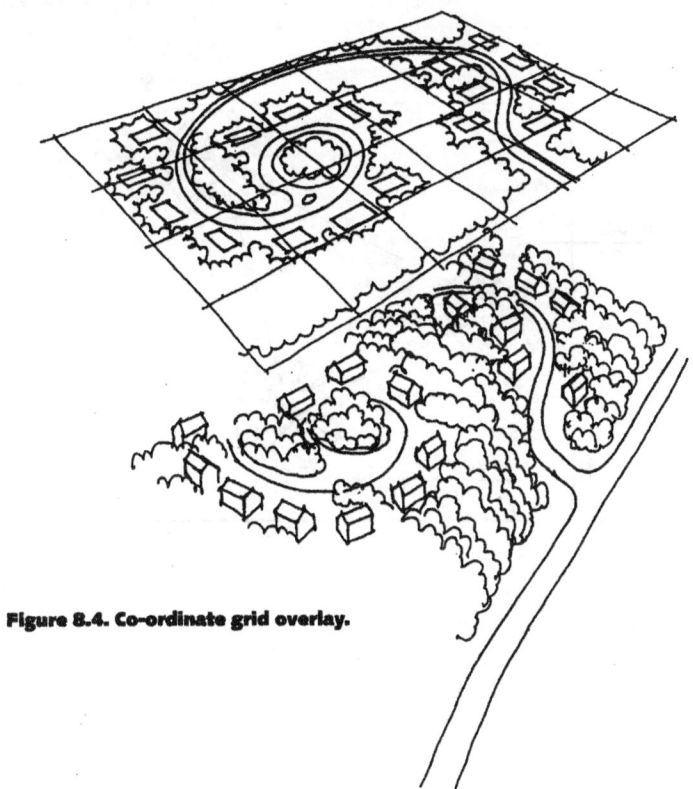

**Figure 8.4. Co-ordinate grid overlay.**

From the primary station, any point can be located by establishing a line with an indicated bearing and distance as shown in Figure 8.3. Property lines are usually defined by metes and bounds.

### Co-ordinates

In this system, a planar rectangular Cartesian co-ordinate grid is used to define points on the land (Figure 8.4). There are many different coordinate systems, based on a variety of geodetic datum, units, projections, and reference systems in use today. Geodetic datum range from flat-earth models used for plane surveying to complex models used for national and international planning applications. Co-ordinate layout systems are usually referenced to a primary station, as shown in Figure 8.5 and read as *eastings* and *northings*. Co-ordinate systems are often used for large sites or dimensionally complex designs.

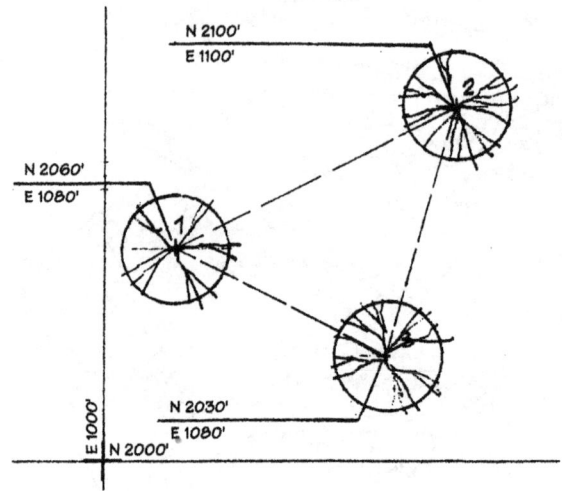

**Figure 8.5. Co-ordinates.**

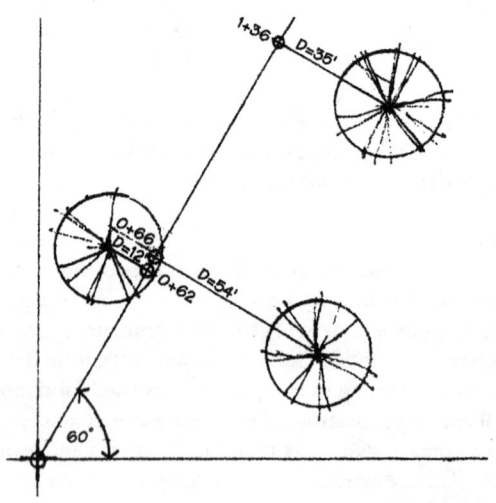

**Figure 8.6. Station offsets.**

## Station Offsets

Station offsetting locates site elements off an established reference line by taking perpendicular measurements from a known station on the line (see figure 8.6). Stationing is most often associated with layout of road centerlines in horizontal alignment (see Chapter 3: Vehicular Standards for more information on horizontal alignment).

## Dimensions

Dimension lines are the most common way of laying out detailed site elements. Figure 8.7 is an example of dimensioning.

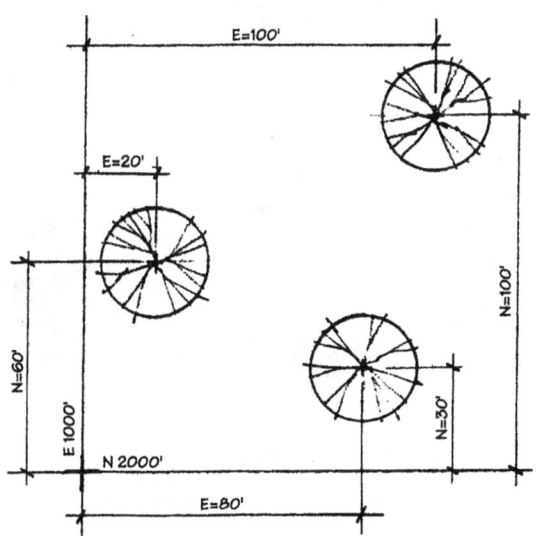

**Figure 8.7. Dimensions.**

# LAYOUT PLANS

## Sequence of Construction

The sequence of how site improvements are constructed will have an impact on how the designer develops the layout plan. With an understanding of how construction operations proceed, the designer can be sure to always dimension from elements that are existing or have already been constructed (see Chapter 9: Construction Operations). Typically, the sequence begins with (1) the construction of the building which is sited from a primary station or point of beginning, then (2) the curbs and gutters of entry roads and

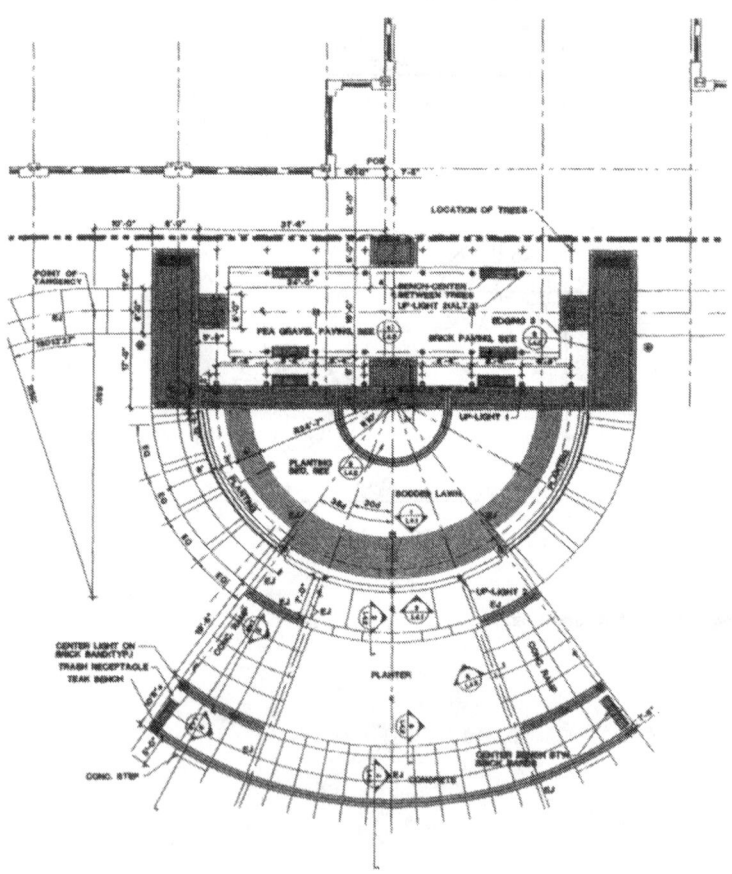

**Figure 8.8. Layout plan.** Courtesy of Lewis Scully Gionet Inc.

drop-off areas which must meet the building at certain points, then (3) parking lots, and finally (4) walks, plazas and site furnishings. Therefore, it would be difficult to layout a curb alignment from a proposed sidewalk that has yet to be built.

## Dimensioning Process

Creating a dimensioning plan for a proposed design involves:

1. Transferring all relevant data from the base survey such as property lines, benchmarks, easements, setbacks, utilities, and existing elements.
2. Selecting a point of beginning (POB) or primary station from which to layout the design. The POB should be permanent with a known elevation.
3. Deciding what dimensions are critical and which are flexible and may be left out without compromising the intent of the design. These *floating dimensions* allow for errors that may accumulate from site irregularities or miscalculations to be distributed without affecting other critical areas.
4. Determine the sequence of construction.
5. Design a clear hierarchy of dimensions. It is recommended that dimension lines are taken from center-points or centerlines whenever possible to avoid over-dimensioning. See Figure 8.8 for an example of a complete layout plan.

# SUGGESTED REFERENCES

Bannister, Arthur, Stanely Raymond and Raymond Baker, *Surveying*, 7th Edition, Longman, Essex, 1998.

Carpenter, Jot D., *Handbook of Landscape Architectural Construction*, LAF, Vienna, VA, 1976.

Harris, Charles W. and Nicholas T. Dines, *Time-Saver Standards for Landscape Architecture*, 2nd Edition, McGraw-Hill, New York, 1998.

Landphair, Harlow C. and John L. Motloch, *Site Reconnaissance and Engineering: An Introduction for Architects, Landscape Architects, and Planners*, Elsevier, New York, 1985.

Lynch, Kevin and Gary Hack, *Site Planning*, The MIT Press, Cambridge, 1984.

# Construction Operations

9

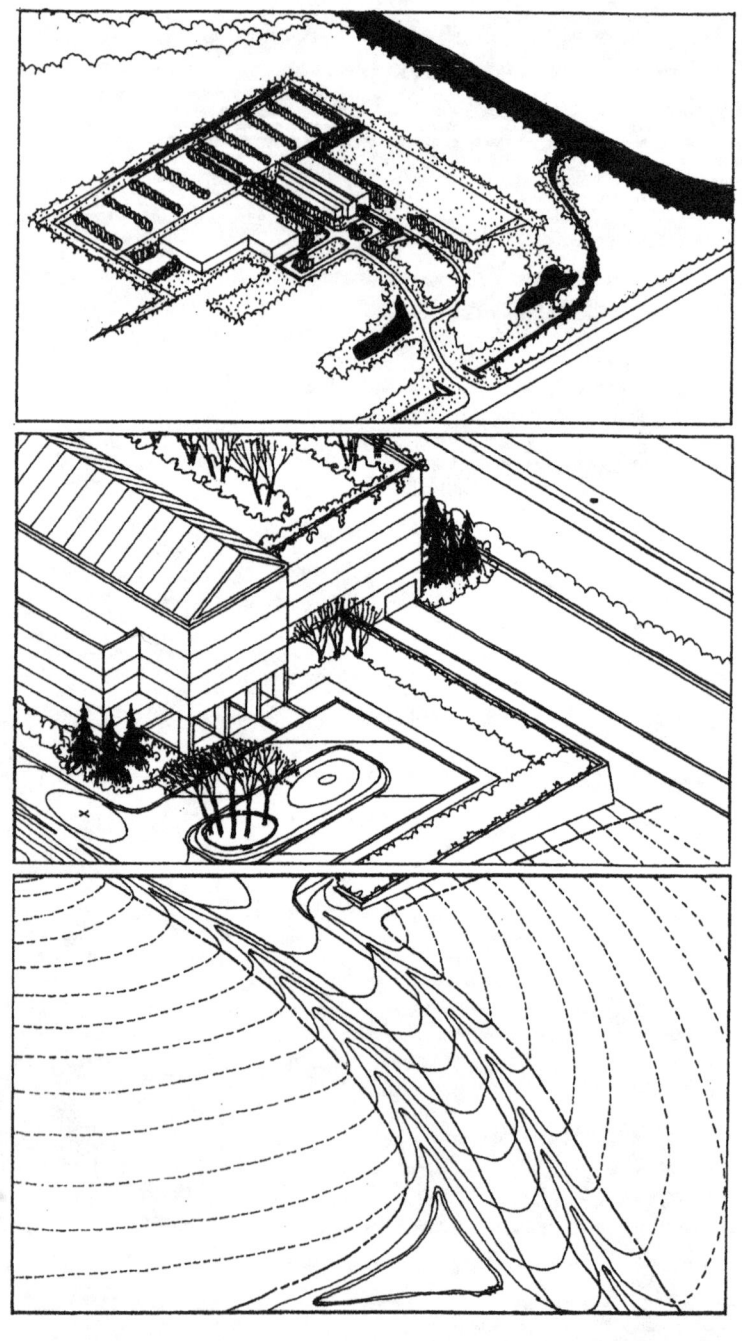

## LARGE SCALE FIELD, PARKING, AND OPEN SPACE CONSTRUCTION OPERATIONS

These operations typically occur on large tracts of open or cleared land, employing heavy equipment for all phases of work. Care is required to manage stormwater runoff during construction to prevent extensive silting of local streams and drainage systems. Existing vegetation tends to be saved as discreet patches providing rather clear working areas for grading or terracing as required. Due to economy of scale, square unit prices are moderate for site preparation, but proprietary surfaces may increase final costs.

## ARCHITECTURE AND RELATED LANDSCAPE CONSTRUCTION OPERATIONS

Operations at this scale and level of detail are complex and require effective coordination among trades and careful logistical planning due to restricted work areas and overlapping regulatory jurisdictions. Costs are higher per square unit due to specialized labor and smaller equipment, especially in urban or older, denser settlements. Care is required to preserve large trees, existing infrastructure and significant historical or cultural features.

## LINEAR ROAD AND PEDESTRIAN PATH CONSTRUCTION OPERATIONS

Site disturbance is typically confined to a path or corridor, although lateral connective utilities may require clearing perpendicular to the corridor centerline. Care is required in heavily wooded areas to avoid unnecessary clearing and excessive grading. Construction in existing development requires extra costs associated with traffic control, existing utility protection, and restoration to variable original conditions at adjacent property lines. This work often employs an array of equipment and is built to standards consistent with local codes, and state and federal funding requirements.

C ONSTRUCTION OPERATIONS are commonly sequenced to conserve time (labor), materials, and existing resources. Operations seek to avoid duplication of tasks, extra costs, and environmental damage, both within and outside of the construction zone. The local climate, soil, vegetative cover, regulations and practices influence the actual construction operations and sequences. Contract documents (drawings and specifications) are designed to illustrate and describe each separate construction sequence, as well as coordinate the entire project. The goal of the designer is to accurately prepare documents and to eliminate ambiguity so that the contractor may administer clear field instructions for all phases of work.

## DIAGNOSTIC ASSESSMENT

*What is the scope of the proposed operation?*

The scope of work determines the type of equipment, the degree of site intervention, the time frame, and total cost of the project. Heavy equipment requires a larger disturbance footprint and subsequent restoration may result in additional costs. However, from an operations perspective, it is most efficient to use the largest piece of equipment to accomplish the work required because it results in a lower square unit cost. Light duty equipment or excessive hand labor required in heavily wooded or spatially restricted sites will usually result in a higher per square unit cost, but the disturbance footprint will be more compact.

*Does the site contain any toxic materials, fragile ecological resources, or significant historical or cultural features?*

The cultural and natural history of a site is important to know prior to design so that areas requiring mitigation or preservation may be clearly marked and properly accounted for in the proposed design and the construction operation. A contractor needs to be informed of the existence of all such exceptional areas, and should be expected to develop a bid price, which reflects suitable strategies for addressing the issues. Most contracts contain contingency clauses, which describe unit prices for such work if encountered (e.g. asbestos removal, contaminated soil, uncharted bedrock, etc.).

*Are all construction documents complete enough to calculate accurate quantities for bid purposes?*

Incomplete site surveys and inaccurate or incomplete construction documents create ambiguities and surprises during the bidding and construction process. This typically results in more conservative bidding, and activation of contingency clauses at unit prices, which are higher than the base contract price. It may also lead to an unusually high number of field work change orders leading to a lower probability of achieving the design as envisioned and a higher probability of cost over runs.

*Does the design require any special equipment or construction techniques?*
Experimental or untested design strategies may require special equipment or materials, which call for uncommon construction processes. It is best if this circumstance is understood at the outset so that a cooperative bidding and construction process may be negotiated prior to initiation of work. These experimental strategies commonly involve new stormwater management products, polymer fabrics, and new equipment or fabrications, among others.

## OPERATIONS OBJECTIVES

Figure 9.1 illustrates how a proposed design is installed within a prepared site. Site construction operations are sequenced to achieve the following objectives:

1. Protect identified site resources as required by plans and regulatory authorities.
2. Coordinate various building trades and construction processes.
3. Maintain safe working conditions to prevent injury and limit liability.
4. Eliminate costly delays and material waste to insure timely completion.
5. Deliver completed work as specified in accordance with contractual agreements.

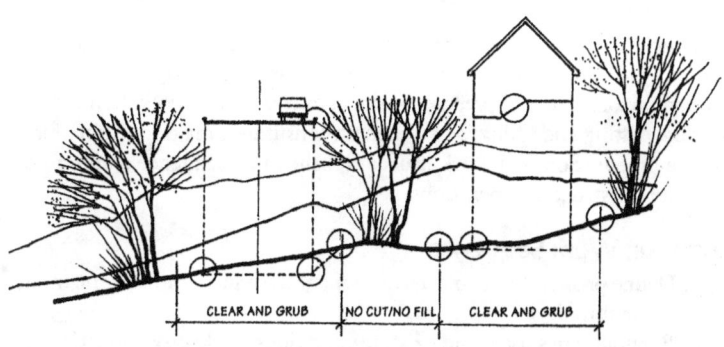

**Figure 9.1. A proposed design is installed within a prepared site. Circled junctions of existing and new require special design attention.**

CLEAR AND GRUB | NO CUT/NO FILL | CLEAR AND GRUB

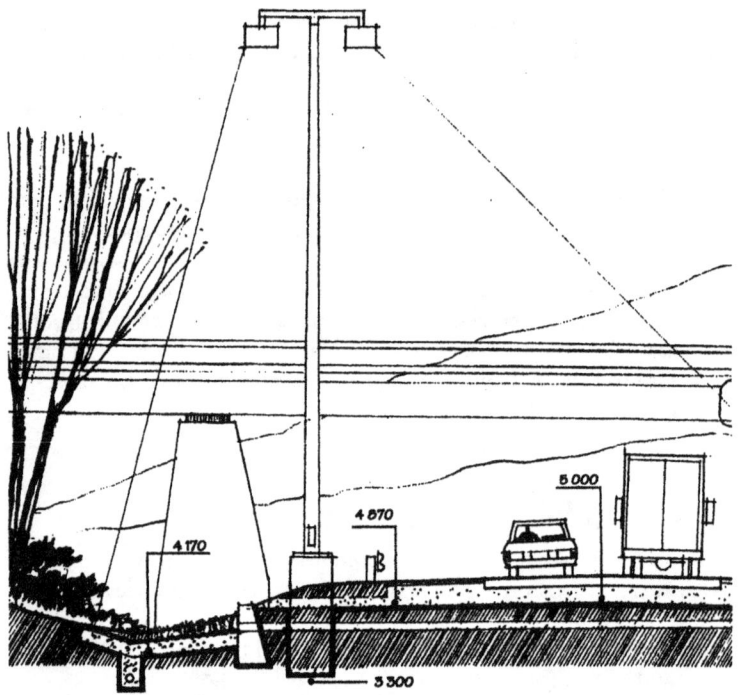

**Figure 9.2. A contractor's perspective of a proposed design concentrates on subgrade elevations.**

## CONTRACTOR'S PERSPECTIVE

Figure 9.2 illustrates a contractor's perspective of a proposed design cross section, which emphasizes the subgrade elevations of all proposed elements. The contractor's task is to prepare the site to receive all new work. Demolition, clearing, cutting and filling, and trenching constitute a major portion of initial site preparation. All work is accomplished in a sequence common to most site construction operations.

### Common Work Sequence

1. Define project scope to determine if light, medium, or heavy methods are required.
2. Examine site survey and existing conditions to identify mitigation requirements.
3. Prepare a quantity take-off and develop a construction strategy to execute required work as specified.

4. Execute a preliminary layout survey and identify all discrepancies between drawings and existing conditions. Make on-site adjustments in concert with the designer and owner.
5. Prepare the site for new construction.
6. Execute all specified work as per construction documents and subsequent field changes.
7. Execute final contract items (cleanup, mechanic's lien waivers, final inspections, punch list, final payment, and certificate of occupancy).

### Bid Preparation

A bid price is estimated based upon the projected cost of implementing all of the provisions of the construction documents within the framework of the general conditions and the agreement. The bid price represents the contractor's cost summary for:

- Preparing the site to receive the design elements.
- Furnishing and installing all materials and fabrications as specified.
- Providing all necessary equipment and labor crews as required.
- Operation overhead expenses and business profit.

### Pricing

Accurate construction documents, which clearly reflect the existing site conditions, tend to result in more accurate bid prices because accurate quantities are more easily obtained and contingency allowances for unknowns are usually more moderate (See Chapter 22: Cost Estimating).

### Project Organization

Projects are commonly managed using a critical path method (CPM) for determining the time required for identified construction tasks. Tasks are arranged on a chart both sequentially and concurrently to determine the amount of time required to execute the entire project. The chart is updated daily to determine if more equipment or personnel is required to maintain the schedule for specific tasks or for the whole project. CPM identifies the most "critical time path," or "task," which if not completed on time, will jeopardize the entire schedule. Figure 9.3 illustrates a bar chart based upon a CPM calculation indicating the critical activities upon which subsequent activities depend if the project completion time is to be achieved.

# SITE CONSTRUCTION OPERATIONS

## Layout survey and staking

The layout survey determines the location of all proposed plan elements and indicates discrepancies between plans and existing site features such as specimen trees, existing buildings, bedrock and wetlands, among others.

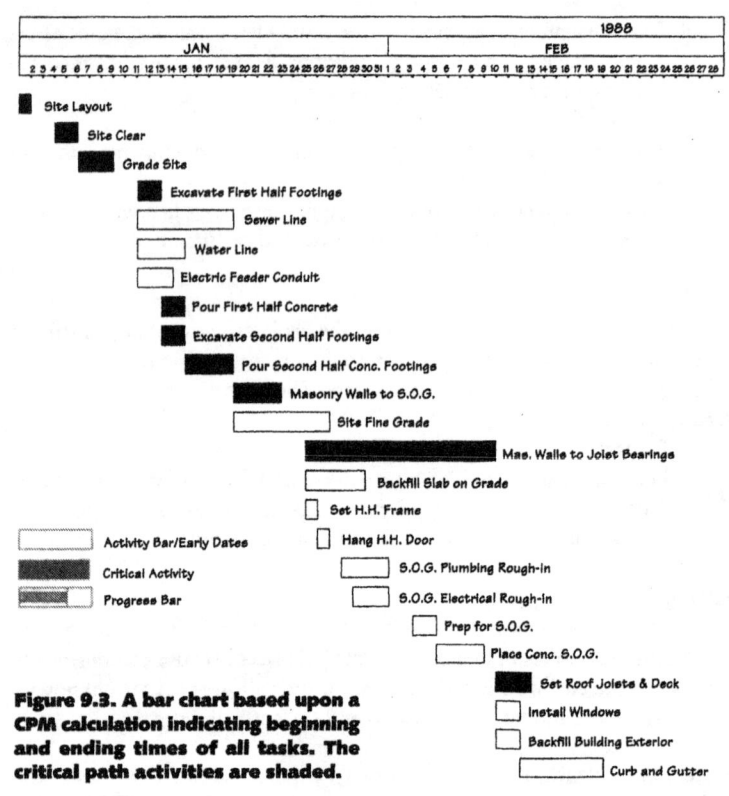

**Figure 9.3. A bar chart based upon a CPM calculation indicating beginning and ending times of all tasks. The critical path activities are shaded.**

Key points of reference include site road PC's (points of curvature), PT's (points of tangency), PI's (points of intersection), and building coordinates (corners or structural column centerlines). Grade differentials and outfall inverts are also checked and staked (See Chapter 8: Layout and Surveying).

### Limit-of-work line

The limit-of-work line establishes the area perimeter, within which all contract work is to occur. All specimen trees or site features designated for protection during the construction process are isolated as specified.

### No cut-no fill line

The no cut-no fill line demarcates the points where all grade changes are to blend into the existing undisturbed site. It indicates areas of saved vegetation within the limit-of-work line, as well as the areas to be cleared of vegetation and topsoil.

# Site Clearing

Before any new work can occur, all vegetation and topsoil (organic matter) and existing structures must be removed from the no cut-no-fill zone as the first step in site preparation.

## Demolition (general and selective)

All designated structures, including buildings, walls, fences, pavements, curbs, buried utilities, basements, pipes, and conduits are commonly removed. It is sound practice when possible to recycle extracted materials. Contaminated structures and soil must be treated as toxic waste and removed according to local regulations.

## Clearing and grubbing (selective clearing)
## tree and stump removal and disposal

All vegetation must be cleared and the roots of all trees must be "grubbed" out of the ground, typically with bulldozers or grub hoes. It is common practice to chip cleared vegetation for use as on-site mulch. Strategic design, which avoids heavy clearing, should be encouraged. Table 9.1 describes area clearing equipment required for different types of vegetative growth and area sizes.

# Topsoil Stripping and Stockpiling

After all vegetation within the no cut–no fill line has been removed, the remaining topsoil is removed to a depth of 100-150 mm (4-6 in) and stockpiled for later use. Areas requiring re-grading must be cleared of all organic matter so that cut and fill operations may proceed. Large projects typically employ heavy-duty scrapers with integral hauling bins, while medium to small scale projects use bulldozers of various sizes. Bulldozers are efficient when push distances are less than 600 m (200 ft).

# Earthwork

Earthwork operations are divided into cut, fill, trenching, and bulk excavation. The site is prepared to create subgrade platforms for all roads, buildings, parking, other pavements, planting areas, lawns, and any other constructed elements specified in the plans. General subgrades are typically set prior to trenching for utilities, or bulk excavation for basements and foundations as shown in Figure 9.4.

## Cut operations

Cut operations use excavators to lower existing grades to the specified subgrade depth required to receive the new work. The results of this cutting

## TABLE 9.1. Area clearing equipment selection.

| | Uprooting Vegetation | Cutting Vegetation At or Above Ground Level |
|---|---|---|
| Small areas 4.0 hectares (10 acres) | Bulldozer blade, axes, grub hoes, and mattocks | Axes, machetes, brush hooks, grub hoes and mattocks, wheel-mounted circular saws |
| Medium areas 40 hectares (100 acres) | Bulldozer blade | Heavy-duty sickle mowers [up to 40 mm (1½") dia.], tractor-mounted circular saws; suspended rotary mowers |
| Large areas 400 hectares (1,000 acres) | Bulldozer blade, root rake, grubber, root plow, anchor chain drawn between two crawler trailers, rails | |

| | Knocking the Vegetation to the Ground | Incorporation of Vegetation Into the Soil |
|---|---|---|
| Small areas 4.0 hectares | Bulldozer blade | Moldboard plows, disc plows, disc harrows |
| Medium areas 40 hectares (100 acres) | Bulldozer blade, rotary mowers, flail-type rotary cutters, rolling brush cutters | Moldboard plows, disc plows, disc harrows |
| Large areas 400 hectares (1,000 acres) | Rolling brush cutter, flail-type cutter, anchor chain drawn between two crawler tractors, rails | Undercutter with disc, moldboard plows, disk plows, disk harrows |

| | Uprooting Vegetation | Cutting Vegetation At or Above Ground Level |
|---|---|---|
| Small areas 4.0 hectares (10 acres) | Bulldozer blade | Axes, crosscut saws, power chain saws, wheel-mounted circular saws |
| Medium areas 40 hectares (100 acres) | Bulldozer blade | Power chain saws, tractor-mounted circular saws mower [up to 100 mm (4 in) diameter] |
| Large areas 400 hectares (1,000 acres) | Shearing blade, angling (tilted), bulldozer blade, rakes, anchor chain drawn between two crawler tractors, root plow | Shearing blade (angling or V-type) |

# TABLE 9.1. Area clearing equipment selection (continued).

|  | Knocking the Vegetation to the Ground | Vegetation into the Soil |
|---|---|---|
| Small areas 4.0 hectares (10 acres) | Bulldozer blades | Heavy-duty disc plow, disc harrow |
| Medium areas 40 hectares (100 acres) | Bulldozer blade, rolling brush cutter [up to 125 mm (5 in) diameter], rotary | Heavy-duty disc plow, disc harrow |
| Large areas 400 hectares (1,000 acres) | Bulldozer blade, flail-type rotary cutter, anchor chain | Bulldozer blade with heavy-duty harrow |

HEAVY CLEARING, VEGETATION
200 MM (8 IN) DIAMETER OR LARGER

|  | Uprooting Vegetation | Cutting Vegetation At or Above Ground Level |
|---|---|---|
| Small areas 4.0 hectares (10 acres) | Bulldozer blade | Axes, crosscut saws, power chain saws |
| Medium areas 40 hectares (100 acres) | Shearing blade, angling (tilted) knockdown beam, rakes, tree stumper | Shearing blade (angling or V-type), tree shear [up to 650 mm (26 in) softwood 350 mm (14 in) hardwood], shearingblade-power saw combination |
| Large areas 400 hectares (1,000 acres) | Shearing blade, angling (tilted) knockdown beam, rakes, tree stumper, anchor chain with ball drawn between two crawler tractors | Shearing blade (angling or V-type), shearing blade-power saw combination |

|  | Knocking the Vegetation to the Ground |
|---|---|
| Small areas 4.0 hectares (10 acres) | Bulldozer blade |
| Medium areas 40 hectares (100 acres) | Bulldozer blade |
| Large areas 400 hectares (1,000 acres) | Anchor chain with ball drawn between two crawler tractors |

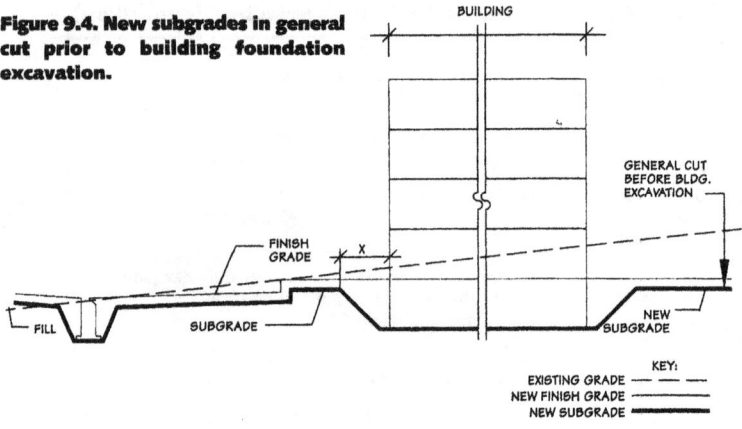

**Figure 9.4. New subgrades in general cut prior to building foundation excavation.**

BUILDING

GENERAL CUT
BEFORE BLDG.
EXCAVATION

FINISH
GRADE

X

FILL

SUBGRADE

NEW
SUBGRADE

KEY:
EXISTING GRADE ⎯ ⎯ ⎯
NEW FINISH GRADE ⎯⎯⎯⎯
NEW SUBGRADE ▬▬▬▬

operation create a series of platforms, which reflect the finished planes of the design. Each finish surface requires a different depth of cut from the finish grade. Table 9.2 indicates common subgrade depths under various finish surfaces. Although natural angles of repose may reach 1:1.5 in some soils, it is recommended that embankments be graded to 1:3 or 1:4 for greater stability and lower maintenance costs over time. Table 9.3 indicates the typical angle of repose values of commonly excavated soils.

- *Pavements:* Pavement subgrades should be free of significant ruts or ridges and excavator tracks should run parallel to the slope direction to prevent damming of infiltration moisture.
- *Footings and Foundations:* Footing trenches should extend beyond the footing edge no less than 600-900 mm (2-3 ft) to allow for form-work operations. The side slope excavation should conform to the limits of the soil type.
- *Trenches:* Trenching for utilities is usually dug with a backhoe, which typically can dig to a depth of 1800-3000 mm (6-10 ft), depending on size of machine. Large trenches require slip-form bracing to prevent side-wall collapse during installation of conduits.
- *Piers and Posts:* Power augers of up to 600 mm (24 in) in diameter are used to excavate cylindrical piers, which do not require footings. Electrical conduits are dug after fiberboard pier forms have been set to avoid wall collapse. Piers requiring footings are dug with a backhoe to allow access. Postholes may be dug with a small 200 mm (8 in) power auger or by hand auger.
- *Rock Removal:* Sound design seeks to avoid bedrock areas. Rock is usually mapped using seismic velocity readings. Readings above 2500 m/sec (8,000 ft/sec) indicate a density requiring blasting. Slower readings indicate removal by mechanical ripping, using a bulldozer equipped with a hydraulic ripping knife.

**TABLE 9.2. Subgrade depths under various finish surfaces.**

| Finish Material | Depth to Subgrade |
|---|---|
| Topsoil (turf) | 150 mm (6 in) |
| Planting Beds | 200-450 mm (8-18 in) |
| Walks and Patios | 200-300 mm (8-12 in) |
| Driveways and Parking | 300-375 mm (12-15 in) |
| Roads and Service Drives | 375-500 mm (15-20 in) |

## Fill operations

All areas requiring fill must be scarified to create a mechanical bond between the subgrade and the fill. Fill must be placed in layers or lifts at depths of 150-300 mm (6-12 in) and mechanically compacted by appropriate machinery to a density of 95%. This process is referred to as "controlled fill placement."

- *Clay Soil Preparation:* Clay soils require compaction using a sheepsfoot roller, because vibration may liquefy the soil. High-density compaction may require 8-12 passes.
- *Granular Soil Preparation:* Granular soils must be rolled and vibrated using a steel or rubber tire roller.

## Types of Fill

- *General Fill:* This fill is typically subsoil taken from excavated portions of the site. It is placed in controlled lifts and consolidated according to soil type.
- *Backfill:* This granular fill is typically placed in controlled lifts in trenches or against foundation walls to prevent differential settlement.

**TABLE 9.3. Typical angle of repose values of excavated soils.**

| Material | Angle of Repose(deg) |
|---|---|
| Clay | 35 |
| Common earth, dry | 32 |
| Common earth, moist | 37 |
| Gravel | 35 |
| Sand, dry | 25 |
| Sand, moist | 37 |

Source: S. W. Nunnally, *Construction Methods and Management,* 1993.

- *Structural Fill:* Structural fill is typically placed under building floor slabs and requires a graded aggregate to be placed in controlled lifts of 100-150 mm (4-6 in) under stringent density rating specifications.

## Drainage and Utilities

Sanitary and storm sewer pipes and basin structures are placed after cut and fill operations are completed. In areas of heavy traffic, new pipes should typically be covered with a minimum of 750 mm (30 in) of soil to prevent crushing during the construction process.

### Structures
- *Basins:* Sanitary and stormwater basin structures require concrete footings placed directly on the excavated subgrade, unless additional preparation is required.
- *Pipes:* Sanitary and stormwater pipes are placed on sand or aggregate setting beds and encased in evenly graded aggregates to maintain proper gradient alignments. Pipes are commonly placed from the outfall to the high point to avoid infiltration from precipitation during construction.
- *Headwalls and Endwalls:* Headwalls and endwalls are retaining walls and require footings to insure that drain pipe inverts do not move with frost-thaw or shrink-swell cycles at discharge or inlet points. Headwall inverts are set flush to the swale invert and endwall inverts are set 150-200 mm (6-8 in) above the swale invert to insure free flow of discharge.
- *Infiltration and Detention Ponds:* These structures are commonly formed with a bulldozer, hydraulic beam bucket, or dragline. Excavation is favored over earthen dams (See Chapter 11: Stormwater Management).
- *Electrical and Telecommunication Lines:* Electrical lines must be buried to a depth of 600 mm (24 in) and rigid conduits are required under paved areas. Telecommunication conduits require separation from electrical lines to avoid magnetic interference (consult local codes).
- *Irrigation Systems:* Irrigation main feeder lines have a shallow depth of 300-450 mm (12-18 in), and are typically last to be installed, often after sodding to insure precise placement of riser heads. Plastic conduit sleeves are placed under walks and pavements to connect planting beds and structural planters during aggregate base placement to allow for later snaking of plastic irrigation pipe through the sleeves. Drip irrigation lines are typically installed just after planting and before mulching (See Chapter 19: Irrigation).

## Grading

Grading operations prepare the site for final placement of pavement aggregates, plantings, and all other site improvements (See Chapter 10: Grading). Final grading stakes are offset from road centerlines so as not to interfere with construction equipment. Stakes are offset 300-600 mm (2-3 ft) from proposed edges. Rough grading is accomplished with bulldozers, road graders, and hand labor to set edges and create uniform slopes. Finish grading refers to final placement of topsoil between pavements and structures. Soil depth varies by planting type.

## Paving and Surfacing

This phase of work involves placement of all aggregate bases, edges, and pavements (See Chapter 14: Paving). The following sequence represents this phase of work:

1. Prepare the subgrade to grading and bearing specifications.
2. Place aggregate base and compact (may consist of multiple layers).
3. Place edges, and set drain and utility access structure grates.
4. Place pavement setting beds, or base courses.
5. Reinforce curbs and utility cover rims (concrete grout).
6. Place wearing surfaces and clean up debris.
7. Paint lines and/or install appurtenances.

## Site Furnishings

Site furnishings is a broad category that encompasses such site improvements as light fixtures, fences and gates, signs, benches, drinking fountains, road and parking appurtenances, etc. At this stage, fixtures are attached to previously placed footings and piers.

## Planting

Planting sequence is highly variable, and depends on site features such as access, and general construction sequence. Generally, major planting of large stock occurs at the completion of rough grading but before finish topsoil is placed so that heavy equipment does not compact the newly placed soil. Small shrubs and herbaceous materials typically are planted after enriched planting medium is placed in the planting bed areas.

- *Trees:* Large specimen trees may be placed within future architecture courtyards and then protected and treated as existing vegetation. Trees and shrubs surrounded by pavements or within structural planters are typically placed before finish pavement installation to avoid machine damage to the pavements. The tree root ball must be set with a surveyor's level to insure proper grades, and then mulched to prevent drying during the final construction operations. It is recommended that trees not be wrapped, and should not be staked or guyed with wire, unless the site is exceptionally windy (See Chapter 12: Planting).

*Construction Operations* • 169

- *Shrubs:* Large shrub groups may be planted and bedded with topsoil prior to placement of finish topsoil for lawns to allow for easier access by equipment.
- *Ground Covers and Herbaceous Plants:* Herbaceous planting beds often require 300-450 mm (12-18 in) depths of enriched planting medium other than the site topsoil. The planting medium is usually placed in the beds and tilled prior to planting. Volume calculations should allow for substantial settlement due to high organic and air content.
- *Seeding and Sodding:* Prior to seeding and sodding, the topsoil must be placed, finely graded and raked to remove stones and imperfections, rolled, fertilized, and corrected for proper pH. Hand raking is required in small confined places. Hydro-seeding, straw mulching or biodegradable netting helps to retain moisture and to prevent washing away of seed during rain or watering operations on slopes or in fine erosive soil conditions.
- *Clean-up and Final Inspection:* A final inspection and punch list tour certifies that all contract items have been furnished and installed as specified in the contract documents and as amended by recorded field change orders. After final acceptance, mechanic's lien waivers are submitted certifying that all subcontractors have been paid. Upon meeting these standards, final payment is made and the contractor is released from bond obligations (This protects the owner from later claims of non-payment by sub-contractors).

## SUGGESTED REFERENCES

Dewberry, Sidney O., (Editor), *Land Development Handbook*, McGraw-Hill Book Co., New York, 1996.

Fee, Sylvia Hollman, *Means Landscape Estimating, 3rd Edition*, R. S. Means Company, Inc., Kingston, MA, 1999.

Harris, Charles W. and Nicholas T. Dines, *Time-Saver Standards for Landscape Architecture, 2nd Edition*, McGraw-Hill, New York, 1998.

Means, R. S., Company, *Means Heavy Construction Handbook*, R. S. Means Company, Inc., Kingston, MA, 1996.

Nunnally, S. W., *Construction Methods and Management*, Prentice-Hall, Inc., Englewood Cliffs, NJ, 1993.

Siddens, R. Scott, *Walker's Building Estimator's Reference Book, 23rd Edition*, Frank R. Walker Company, Lisle, IL, 1989.

# TECHNIQUES

# *Grading*

# 10

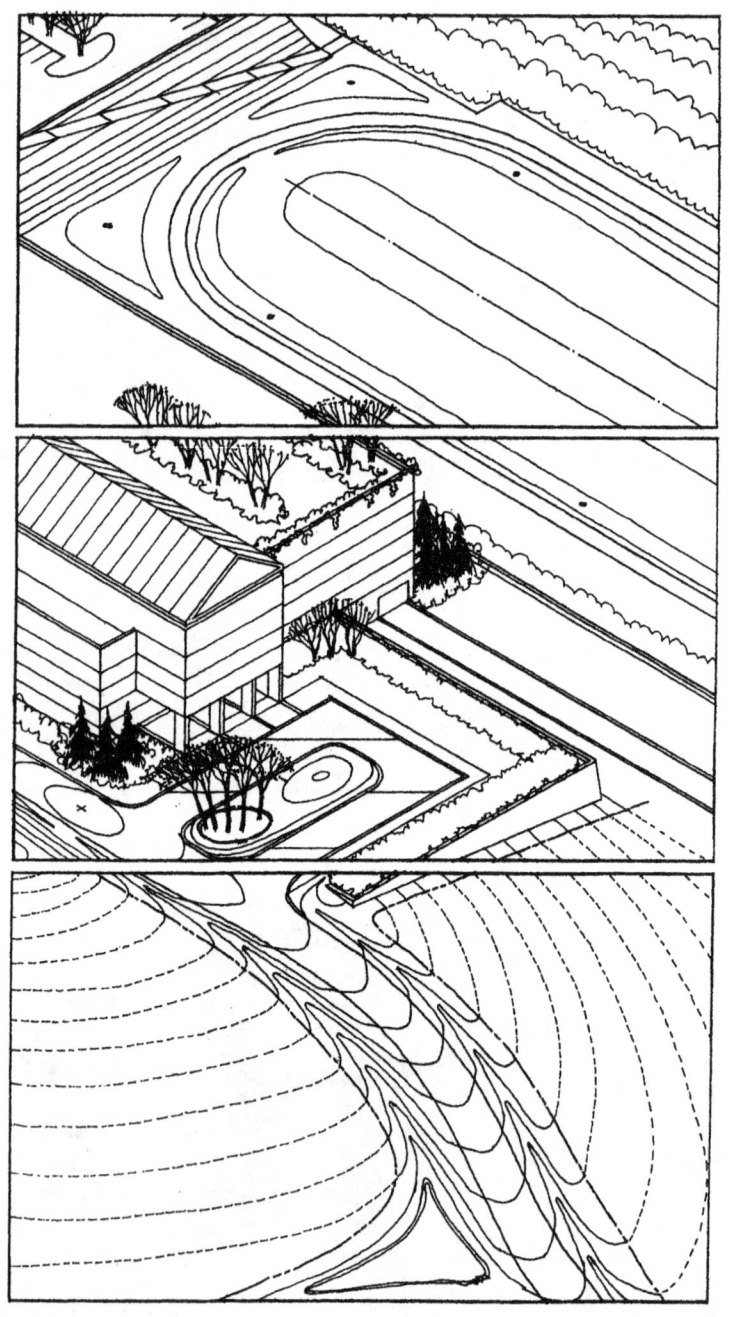

## OPEN GENERAL USE AREAS AND PLAYFIELDS

This grading context requires relatively flat slopes, modest embankments, and accessible ramps. The key visual objective is to create a level appearance while utilizing a low-point drainage system in unobtrusive zones away from intensive activity or playing fields. Contour pattern is typically subtle and requires careful study to achieve graceful transitions. Landforms and significant planting for screening, edge definition, and stormwater diversion are commonly employed.

## BUILDINGS, SURROUNDING SPACES, AND SERVICING INFRASTRUCTURE

Grading in this context needs to accommodate single or multiple building structures and related roads, drives, service bays and parking. The key visual objective is to create a "fit" between large structures and the existing landscape features. This commonly requires the use of retaining structures to improve accessibility and save existing large trees. In partially wooded sites, the designer should consider saving strategically positioned large tree stands to help integrate the new development into the existing landscape. Generally, the structural requirements of the materials, issues of accessibility, and the angle of repose govern slopes.

## LINEAR ROADS, PATHS, DRAINAGE SWALES, PONDS, AND NO-CUT/ NO-FILL TRANSITIONS

This linear type of grading requires careful horizontal and vertical alignment that flows with the landscape contours while avoiding significant vegetation stands, fragile areas, poor soils, or bedrock. The grading should also conform to the kinetic and slope criteria of the particular road or path (speed, drainage, sight-distance, climate, pedestrian access). Longitudinal and cross slope criteria vary by climate zone. Swale centerline and side slopes vary by local precipitation rates and soil texture. No-cut/no-fill transition zones are typically created by parabolic embankments for erosion resistance. To insure tree survival it is generally better practice to be in slight cut or level with the grade at existing tree stands rather than in fill.

THE GOAL OF GRADING DESIGN is to create a topographic fit between existing landscape features and the proposed design layout. The key task is to achieve the design's visual and cultural objectives while at the same time minimizing overall landscape disturbance. Ideally the design should result in the smallest footprint possible to accommodate the program. A smaller footprint results in less erosion during construction.

## DIAGNOSTIC ASSESSMENT

*What general grading considerations help ensure the best environmental, cultural and economic fit between existing and proposed landscape features?*

The careful observation of existing landscape conditions is the first step in attempting to facilitate a design approach that best addresses the environmental, cultural, and economic impacts of reshaping the land. A grading approach that appears to function topographically should be carefully questioned to determine the overall effects on multiple landscape scales.

*What specific grading strategies can be applied to different land-use contexts that will best ensure a topographic fit between existing and proposed landscape features?*

Landscape architects typically address the problem of grading in three different landscape contexts: area grading, comprised of open general use areas and playfields; nodal grading, comprised of buildings, surrounding spaces, and servicing infrastructure; and linear grading, comprised of linear roads, paths, drainage swales, ponds, and no-cut/ no-fill transitions. Specific grading strategies that attempt to create a topographic fit are applicable to each context.

*What types of topographic data are required to calculate the relative appropriateness of a grading scheme?*

Grading requires a thorough understanding of the minimum/maximum ratios of slope gradients and their implication on pedestrian and vehicular accessibility and long-term maintenance. In addition, it is necessary to calculate the amount of earth moving required by any proposed grading scheme with the ultimate goal of balancing cut and fill.

# TYPICAL GRADING METHOD

## Analysis of Existing Conditions

- Diagram existing landform characteristics, including high points, low points, and slope classes, and identify the resulting drainage patterns.
- Note existing conditions that may limit the proposed development: surface rock, soil bearing capacity, water table level, etc.
- Determine fixed control points that cannot, or should not, be disturbed by the proposed development, including existing structures, boundaries, vegetation, topography or subsurface conditions (see Figure 10.1).

## Schematic Design

- Apply the schematic design, setting grades of key elements, slopes of key planes, and the amount and type of grade separation.
- Develop a contoured grading diagram, identifying grades on roads, walks, walls, swales, and other structures, and labeling cross slopes on all surfaces (see Figure 10.2).
- Make certain that all gradients and slopes are within the maximum/minimum criteria for a particular use, e.g., lawn, roadway, terrace, and cut slope or embankment (see Table 10.1 and Figure 10.3).

TECHNIQUES

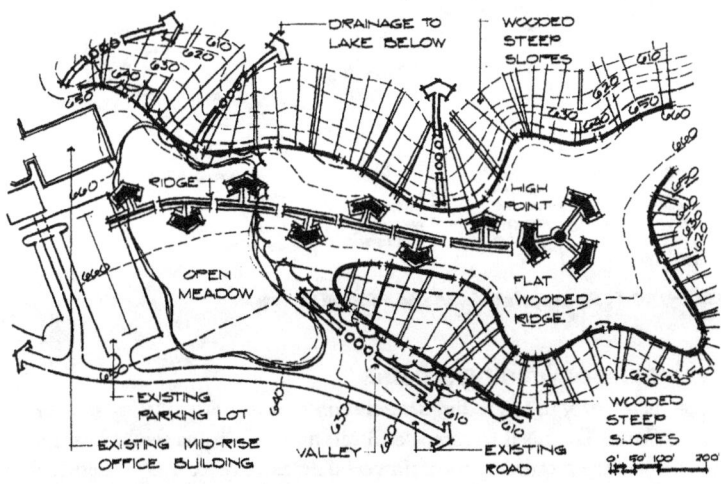

**Figure 10.1. Existing conditions analysis.**

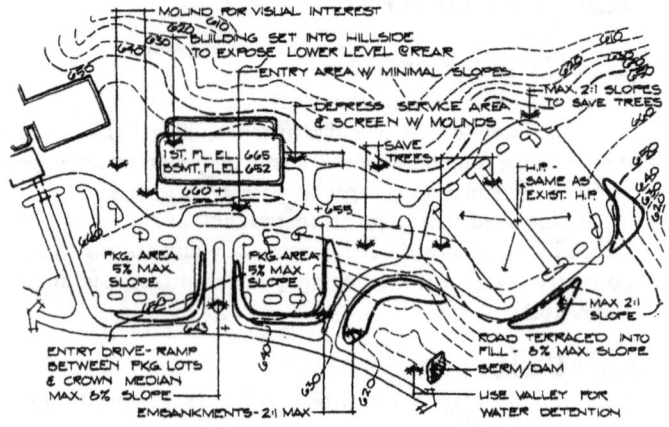

**Figure 10.2. Schematic grading plan.**

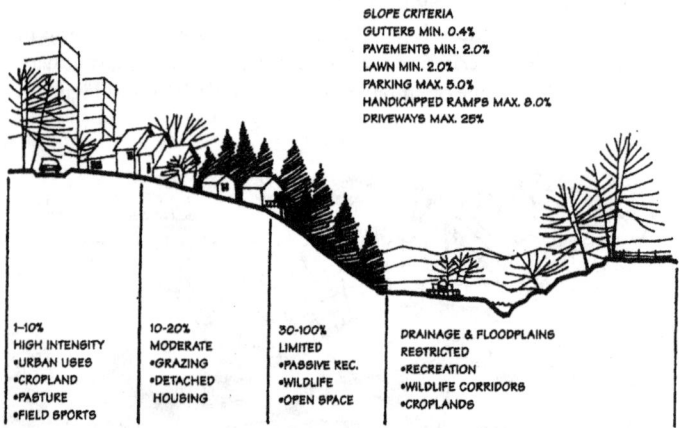

SLOPE CRITERIA
GUTTERS MIN. 0.4%
PAVEMENTS MIN. 2.0%
LAWN MIN. 2.0%
PARKING MAX. 5.0%
HANDICAPPED RAMPS MAX. 8.0%
DRIVEWAYS MAX. 25%

| 1–10%<br>HIGH INTENSITY<br>•URBAN USES<br>•CROPLAND<br>•PASTURE<br>•FIELD SPORTS | 10-20%<br>MODERATE<br>•GRAZING<br>•DETACHED<br>HOUSING | 30-100%<br>LIMITED<br>•PASSIVE REC.<br>•WILDLIFE<br>•OPEN SPACE | DRAINAGE & FLOODPLAINS<br>RESTRICTED<br>•RECREATION<br>•WILDLIFE CORRIDORS<br>•CROPLANDS |

**Figure 10.3. Appropriate land use related to slope.**

## Evaluation of Grading Scheme

- *Is the proposed grading scheme compatible with existing site conditions?* The need for steps and retaining walls, as well as ramps to meet the requirements of universal access, are expensive elements of site development that can be minimized by matching the grading scheme to the site. Steep slopes can cause maintenance difficulties beyond the site development phase.
- *What are the impacts on the adjacent landscape and the larger region?* Intensive grading can have unseen, off-site impacts that should be considered. Point source pollution of the watershed, changes in

the water table, and destruction of wildlife cover and migration corridors are some of the most common threats. Local views and the impact the development will have on the visual quality of the surrounding landscape should be considered.

- *Are the substrate conditions and soil characteristics able to support the proposed grading scheme?* The classifications of soil bearing

## TABLE 10.1. General recommended gradients.

| Types of areas | Maximum, % | Minimum, % | Preferred, % |
|---|---|---|---|
| **STREETS, DRIVEWAYS, AND PARKING AREAS** | | | |
| Crown of improved streets | 3 | 1 | 2 |
| Crown of unimproved streets | 3 | 2 | 2.5 |
| Slope of shoulders | 15 | 1 | 2-3 |
| Longitudinal slope of streets | 20 | 0.5 | 1-10 |
| Longitudinal slope of driveways | 20 | 0.25 | 1-10 |
| Longitudinal slope of parking areas | 5 | 0.25 | 2-3 |
| Cross slope of parking area | 10 | 0.5 | 1-3 |
| **CONCRETE WALKS** | | | |
| Longitudinal slope of sidewalks | 10 | 0.5 | 1-5 |
| Cross slope of sidewalks | 4 | 1 | 2 |
| Approaches, platforms, etc. | 8 | 0.5 | 2 |
| Service areas | 10 | 0.5 | 2-3 |
| **TERRACE AND SITTING AREAS** | | | |
| Concrete | 2 | 0.5 | 1 |
| Flagstone, slate, brick | 2 | 0.75 | 1 |
| **LAWN AREAS** | | | |
| Recreation, games, etc. (noncompetitive) | 5 | 1 | 2-3 |
| Grassed athletic fields | 2 | 0.5 | 1 |
| Lawns and grass areas | 25 | 1 | 5-10 |
| Berms and mounds | 20 | 5 | 10 |
| Mowed slopes | 25 (3:1) | | 20 |
| Unmowed grass banks | Angle of repose | | 25 |
| Planted slopes and beds | 10 | 0.5 | 3-5 |

capacity should be consulted when determining the intensity of development. Engineering practices, such as blasting and removal or importation of soils, are both expensive and ecologically detrimental.

- *Does the amount of cut adequately compensate for the required fill?* In most cases, achieving an approximate balance between the amount of soil being cut from the site and the amount of fill required is the sign of an economical grading scheme. Excessive or unbalanced cut and fill, that requires hauling or importing soil off-site, can become expensive as well as destructive of existing vegetation and other natural resources.
- *Have adequate grading and drainage precautions been taken to minimize on-site and off-site erosion during all phases of project development, including long-term management?* Loss of valuable topsoil through erosion is an environmental and economic expense. Environmental impacts include siltation and loss of existing vegetation. The major economic impact is the cost of replacing lost topsoil. Most important to be avoided during site development are steep and unprotected grades that allow rain and wind to carry off topsoil.

# CONTEXTUAL GRADING STRATEGIES

## Area Grading

Techniques to accommodate open playfields, parking areas, general open space:

- Locate control points at edge of proposed area to capture existing vegetation where appropriate.
- It is generally desirable to run new contours roughly parallel to existing contours to maintain a consistent fit within the existing conditions.
- Place catchment areas and swales at the edges of open surfaces and away from intensive human activities.
- It is better to broadly crown flat turf areas to create enough pitch for adequate runoff, to avoid excessive surface folding and numerous catchment areas (see Figure 10.4).
- Avoid sheet flow distances over 60 m (200 ft) to prevent excess ponding at low points during heavy rains. Parking lot sheet flow distance should be limited to 20-30 m (65-100 ft), especially in frost/thaw climates, or in hot/humid high precipitation areas (see Figure 10.5).

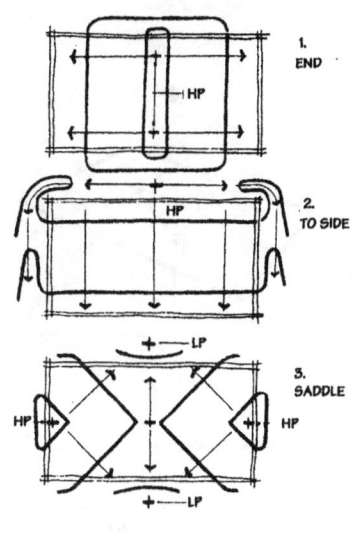

1. END

HP

2. TO SIDE

HP

3. SADDLE

+—LP

HP + + HP

+—LP

**Figure 10.4. Basic field grading.**

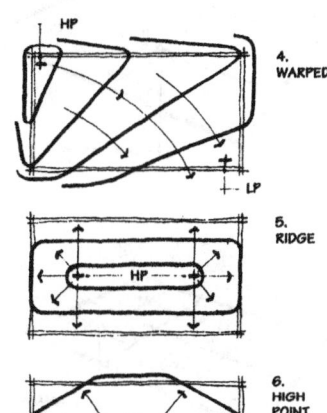

HP

4. WARPED

+ LP

5. RIDGE

HP

6. HIGH POINT

HP

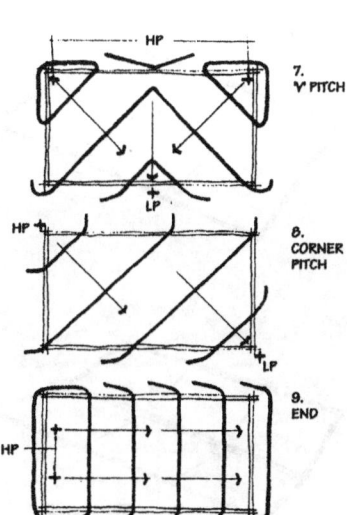

HP

7. 'V' PITCH

+ LP

HP +

8. CORNER PITCH

+ LP

9. END

HP

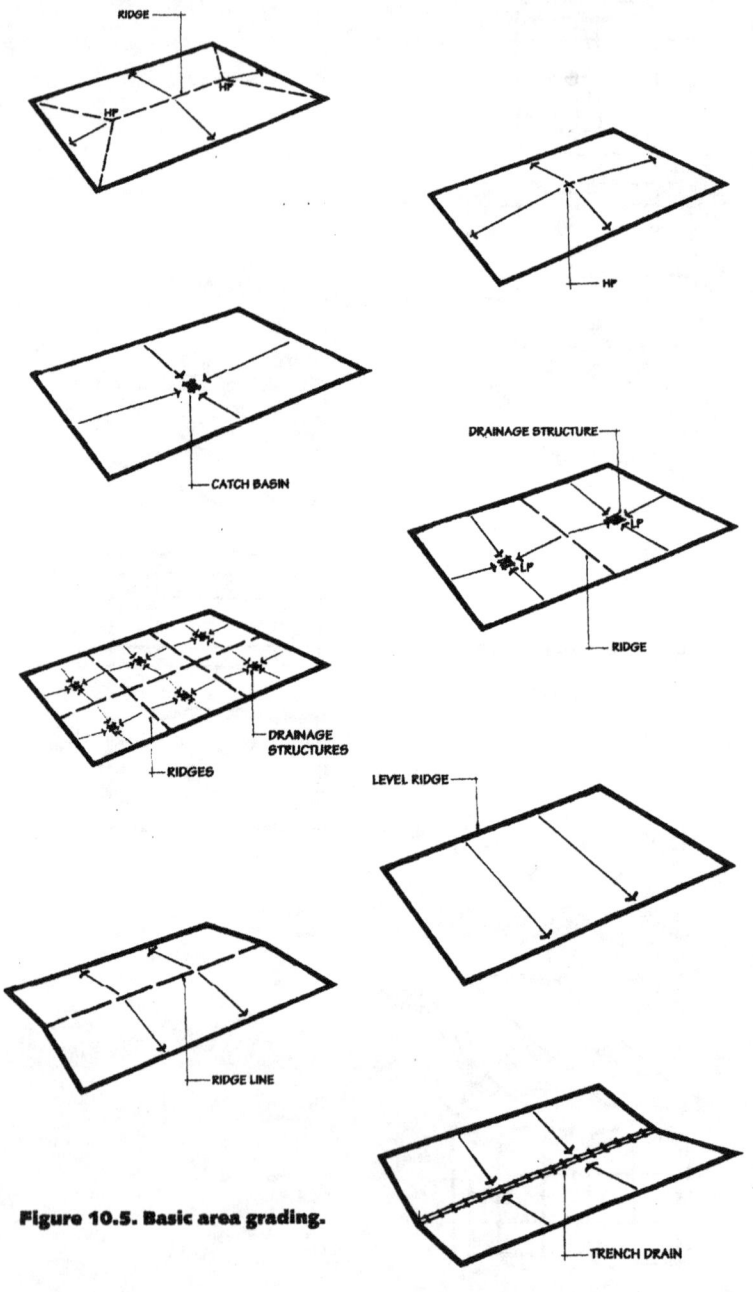

**Figure 10.5. Basic area grading.**

## Nodal Grading

Techniques to accommodate pedestrian transition and vehicular transfer points as found at building entrances and drop-off areas (see Figure 10.6):

- Determine the slope of existing topography at key points in the design: parking area, entrance drive, etc. Check to determine if any existing grades are steeper or flatter than the proposed maximum and minimum standards.
- Study the contour flow and pattern of existing drainage to see how closely the proposed grades might conform to the existing landform.
- Determine the lowest possible elevation of the footing drain, which would still allow gravity flow daylighting.
- Determine the first floor elevation which would result in ramps no steeper than 5% at the entrances, and pavement slopes no greater than the 4% maximum.
- Pedestrian drop-off points should be flush at walkway and pavement edge for unambiguous handicapped accessibility.
- Slope pavements away from building entrances and from pedestrian transition points.
- Locate low points away from human activity zones, or from vehicular maneuvering zones.

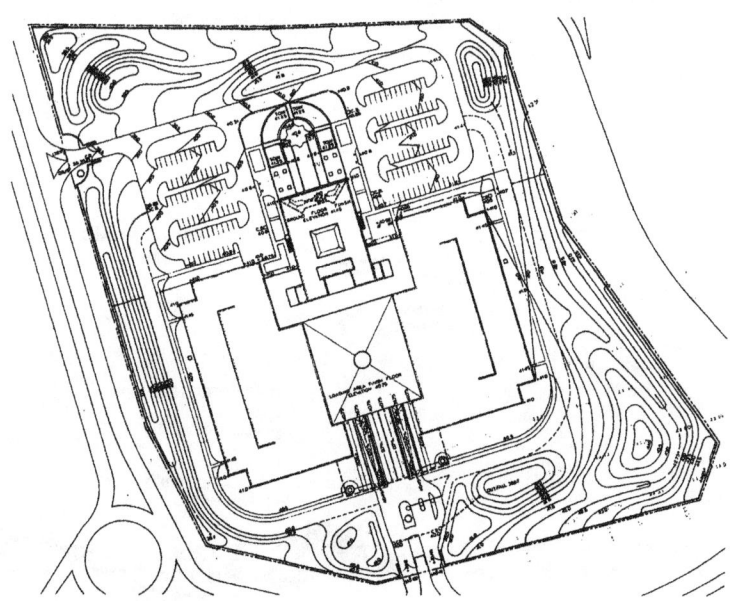

**Figure 10.6. Building area grading.**

- It is best practice for vehicles to ascend, rather than to descend toward a vehicular drop-off area.
- Set tops of curbs to meet existing grades to save existing trees within turnaround circles or at critical spaces between roads, walks, and buildings.

## Linear Grading

Techniques to accommodate linear path and road grading (see Figures 10.7 through 10.11):

- In steeper topography, paths and roads typically traverse the contours diagonally or in broad sweeping curves to maintain slopes within the limits of pedestrian and vehicular safety (see Table 10.2).
- Roads traversing a side slope are commonly built half in fill and half in cut to balance earthwork on either side of the centerline. Weaker soils may require more cut in order to build the bearing portion of the roadbed on undisturbed subgrade.
- Super elevation on curves for both pedestrian and vehicular paths allows for the collection of runoff on the inside edge and away from the outside edge.
- It is proper to drain pavement water onto turf and planted areas, but poor practice to drain turf and planted areas onto pavements due to silting and freeze/thaw cycles.
- It is common to crown two-way roads and to cross-slope single lane paths and driveways.

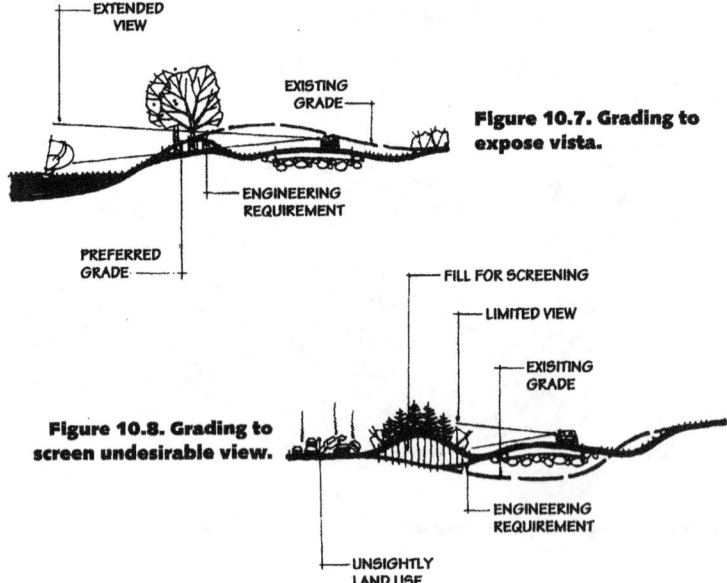

Figure 10.7. Grading to expose vista.

Figure 10.8. Grading to screen undesirable view.

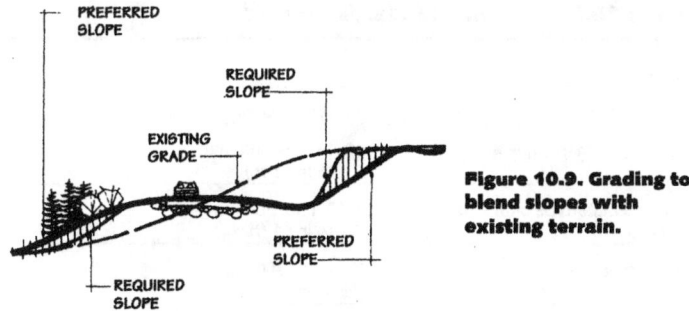

PREFERRED SLOPE

REQUIRED SLOPE

EXISTING GRADE

PREFERRED SLOPE

REQUIRED SLOPE

**Figure 10.9. Grading to blend slopes with existing terrain.**

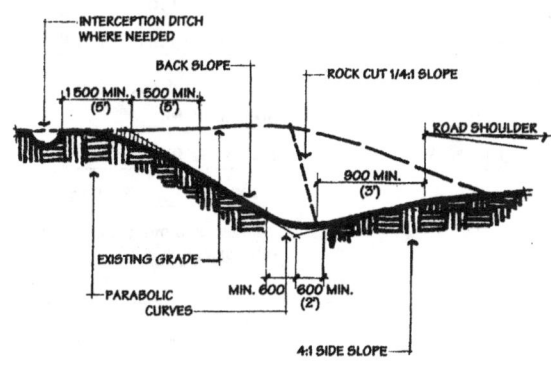

INTERCEPTION DITCH WHERE NEEDED

BACK SLOPE

ROCK CUT 1/4:1 SLOPE

ROAD SHOULDER

1 500 MIN. (5')  1 500 MIN. (5')

900 MIN. (3')

EXISTING GRADE

PARABOLIC CURVES

MIN. 600  600 MIN. (2')

4:1 SIDE SLOPE

**Figure 10.10. Cut side of cross section through road.**

'H' - HEIGHT OF FILL
2:1 SLOPE W/ GUARDRAIL - 'H' MORE THAN 1800 MM (6').
4:1 SLPE W/O GUARDRAIL - 'H' LESS THAN 1 800 MM (6').

SHOULDER

GUARD RAIL

900 mm (3') MIN.

DITCH WHERE NEEDED

2:1    4:1    'H'

750 MIN. (2'-6")

EXISTING GRADE

EARTH FILL

ROCK FILL (1:1 SLOPE)

**Figure 10.11. Fill side of cross section through road.**

*Grading* ▪ 183

## TABLE 10.2. Gradient standards for roads.

| | |
|---|---|
| **Pavement crown** | |
| Natural soil | 15 mm : 300 mm (½ in : 1 ft) |
| Gravel, crushed stone | 10-15 mm : 300 mm (⅜-½ in : 1 ft ) |
| Intermediate-type bituminous | 5-10 mm : 300 mm (¼-⅜ in : 1 ft) |
| High-type bituminous | 3-5 mm : 300 mm (⅛-¼ in : 1 ft) |
| Concrete | 2.5-4 mm : 300 mm (⅒-³⁄₁₆ in : 1 ft) |
| Brick or stone | 5 mm : 300 mm (¼ in : 1 ft) |
| **Shoulders** | |
| Minimum width | 300 mm (1 ft) |
| Minimum desirable width | 600 mm (2 ft) |
| Preferred width | 2 400-3 000 mm (8-10 ft) |
| Slope | 15 mm : 300 mm (½ in : 1 ft) (approximately 4%) |
| **Side slopes** | |
| Slope | 4 : 1 |
| **Back slopes** | |
| Earth, minimum | 1½ : 1 |
| Earth, preferred | 2 : 1 or 3 : 1 |
| Ledge rock, minimum | ¼ : 1 |
| Shale | ½ : 1 |
| **Fill slopes** | |
| Earth, minimum | 2 : 1 |
| Earth, preferred | 4 : 1 |
| **Ditches** | |
| Minimum depth | 300-600 mm (1-2 ft) below shoulder elevation |
| Maximum inslope | 3 : 1 |

Source: From Public Roads Administration, American Association of State Highway Officials, State Highway Departments.

# GRADING CALCULATIONS

## Expressing Slope

Slope is expressed in terms of a percentage, a degree of slope, or a proportional ratio. It is common practice to indicate the rate as well as the direction of slope, using an arrow pointed down the slope.

### Percentage of Slope

The percentage of slope can be calculated by the formula:

$$G = \frac{D}{L} \times 100$$

where:

$G$ = gradient, %
$D$ = vertical rise, m (ft)
$L$ = horizontal distance, m (ft)

This is the most common method of expressing slopes less than 25% in U.S. Units.

### Degree of Slope

Slope may be expressed in degrees, with 0° representing a flat surface and 90° representing a vertical surface. Typically, this method is used only in large-scale earth-moving projects such as strip-mining and other extractive operations.

..............................................................................

FIELD NOTE

# Making a Contour Map

A simple field survey can be created by laying out a temporary grid of stakes at regular intervals on a parcel of land. The elevations of each intersection point are taken with a transit or hand level and the elevation data is plotted on a gridded plan of the site (see Chapter 8 for more information on conducting field surveys). Elevations of critical high or low points that fall between the intersections are also located. Once all spot elevations have been determined, contours at regular intervals can be interpolated and plotted on a map as shown in the figures.

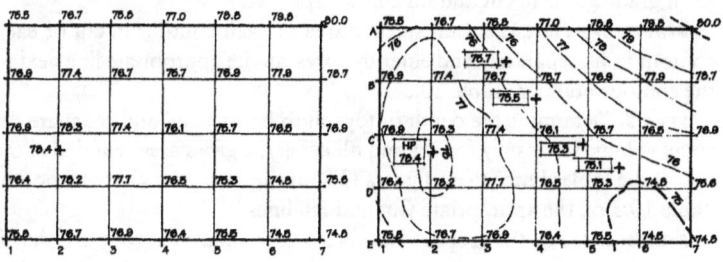

## Proportion of Slope

Slope can also be expressed as a non-dimensional ratio. This is the preferred method of expressing slope in system international (SI) units.

- Using SI units, the vertical component is shown first, and then the horizontal. For slopes less than 45°, the vertical component is unitary (for example 1:4 in the case of a 25% slope). For slopes greater than 45°, the horizontal component is unitary (for example 12:1 in the case of an 85° slope).

- Using U.S. units, the ratio expresses the horizontal distance to the vertical rise, such as 3:1 in the case of a 33% slope. This method is used typically for slopes 4:1 (25%) or steeper.

# Estimating Cut and Fill

## Grid Method

The grid method is relatively simple, quick, and easy to use. It is useful for estimating the excavation of buildings, pools, etc. Figure 10.12 illustrates the grid method and an example calculation.

## Average End-Area Method

The average end-area method is commonly used to estimate volumes on linear elements, such as roads. Cross sections are taken at 15 - 30 m (50-100 ft) intervals perpendicular to the centerline. The simplest average end-area procedure is to average areas and multiply by the distance between them. Figure 10.13 illustrates the average end-area method and an example calculation.

## Contour Method

This method is widely used because it is very accurate for making final grading adjustments and for preparing cost estimates. The step-by-step process for using the contour method is as follows:

**step 1:** Delineate the no-cut/no-fill zone throughout the entire project (Figure 10.14) and calculate the gross area in cut and the gross area in fill. Gross area refers to area delimited by the no-cut / no-fill line and the limits of grading line in cut and fill zones respectively.

**step 2:** Measure the total surface area of each contour in cut or each contour in fill separately and enter this area on the appropriate line next to the contour number (Table 10.3).

**step 3:** Determine the depth of topsoil to be stripped and calculate the cubic volume separately for cut and fill using the gross areas entered at the top of the table. Enter these figures (TS) in the summary chart section of Table 10.3 on the appropriate Cut and Fill lines.

**step 4:** Measure the proposed hardscape areas in the cut zone and the fill zone and enter the measurements under column H area on the respective Cut and Fill lines.

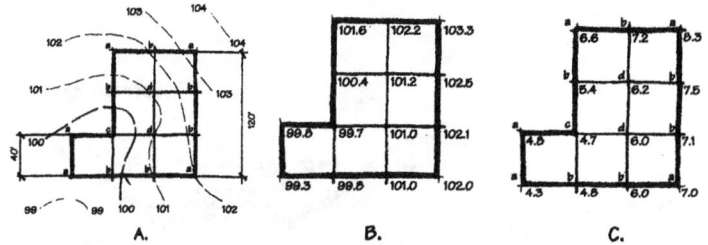

A.                    B.                    C.

The area to be graded is divided into squares and the corners of the squares
are labeled a, b, c, and d, depending on the number of squares each corner per-
tains to. The bottom of the excavation is to be at elevation 95.00. Figure B
shows the existing elevations of the earth surface obtained by interpolating
between the contours. Figure C shows the depth of cut at each of the corners,
obtained as follows:

'a' Corners

| 101.6 | 103.3 | 99.8 | 99.3 | 102.0 |
|-------|-------|------|------|-------|
| −95.0 | −95.0 | −95.0 | −95.0 | −95.0 |
| 6.6 | 8.3 | 4.8 | 4.3 | 7.0 |

= 31.0 total cut

'b' Corners

| 102.2 | 200.4 | 102.5 | 102.1 | 99.8 | 101.0 |
|-------|-------|-------|-------|------|-------|
| −95.0 | −95.0 | −95.0 | −95.0 | −95.0 | −95.0 |
| 7.2 | 5.4 | 7.5 | 7.1 | 4.8 | 6.0 |

= 38.0 total cut

'c' Corners
| 99.7 |
|------|
| −95.0 |
| 4.7  = 4.7 total cut |

'd' Corners
| 101.2 | 101.0 |
|-------|-------|
| −95.0 | −95.0 |
| 6.2 | 6.0 |

= 12.2 total cut

Then, using the formula

$$\text{Volume} = \frac{a + 2b + 3c + 4d \times A}{4}$$

where A = area of grid square, 40 x 40 ft, or
1,600 sq. ft. Then

$$\text{Volume} = \frac{31.0 + 2\,(38.0) + 3\,(4.7 + 4\,(12.2))}{4} \times 1600$$

$$= \frac{31.0 + 76.0 + 14.1 + 48.8}{4} \times 1600$$

$$= \frac{169.9}{4} \times 1600 = 67,960 \text{ cu. ft.}$$

$$\frac{67,960}{27} = 2,517 \text{ cu. yd.}$$

**Figure 10.12. Grid method for estimating earth volume.**

*Grading* ▪ 187

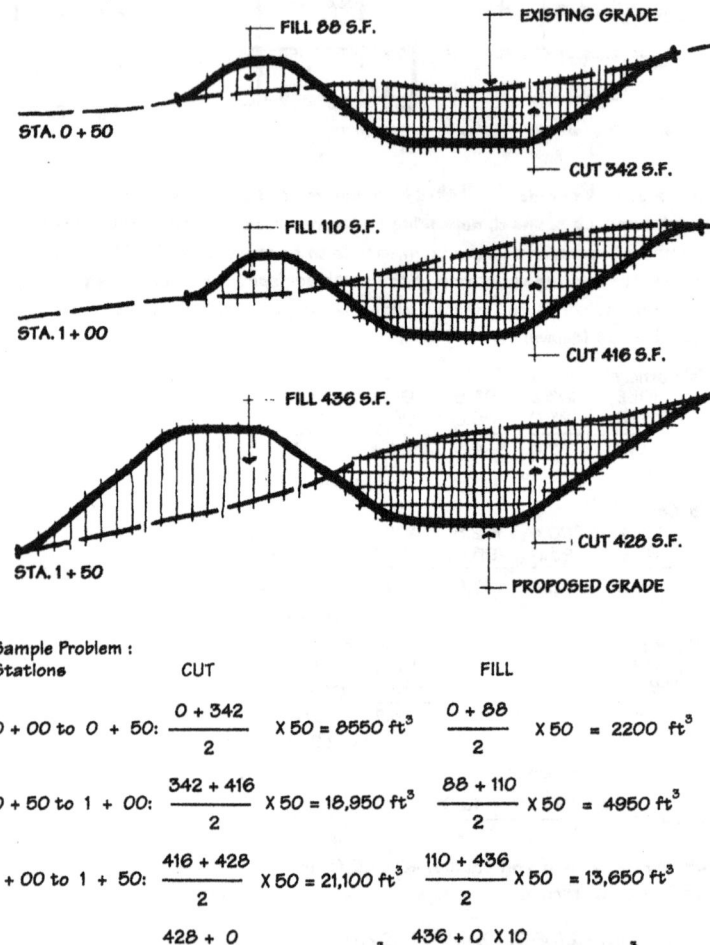

Sample Problem :

| Stations | CUT | | FILL | |
|---|---|---|---|---|

$$0 + 00 \text{ to } 0 + 50: \quad \frac{0 + 342}{2} \times 50 = 8550 \text{ ft}^3 \qquad \frac{0 + 88}{2} \times 50 = 2200 \text{ ft}^3$$

$$0 + 50 \text{ to } 1 + 00: \quad \frac{342 + 416}{2} \times 50 = 18,950 \text{ ft}^3 \qquad \frac{88 + 110}{2} \times 50 = 4950 \text{ ft}^3$$

$$1 + 00 \text{ to } 1 + 50: \quad \frac{416 + 428}{2} \times 50 = 21,100 \text{ ft}^3 \qquad \frac{110 + 436}{2} \times 50 = 13,650 \text{ ft}^3$$

$$1 + 50 \text{ to } 1 + 60: \quad \frac{428 + 0}{2} \times 50 = 2140 \text{ ft}^3 \qquad \frac{436 + 0}{2} \times 10 = 2180 \text{ ft}^3$$

$$= \frac{50,740}{27} \text{ ft}^3 \qquad = \frac{22,980}{27} \text{ ft}^3$$

$$= 1879 \text{ yd}^3 \text{ CUT} \qquad = 851 \text{ yd}^3 \text{ FILL}$$

**Figure 10.13. Average end-area method for estimating earth volume.**

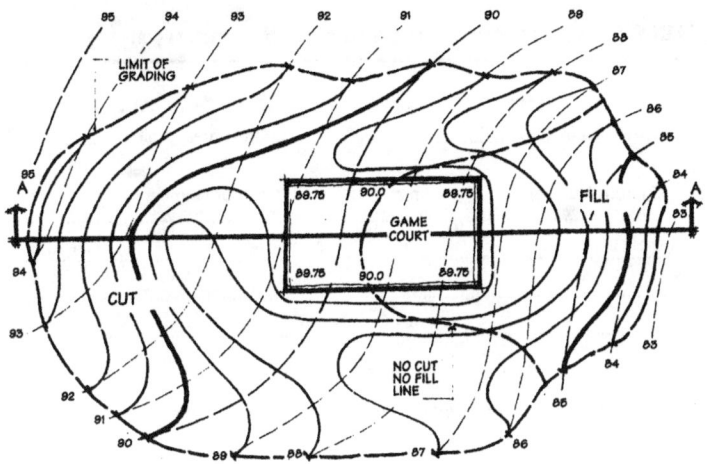

**Figure 10.14. Contour plan method for estimating earth volume.**

**STEP 5:** Calculate the volumes for hardscape in the cut and the fill zones and enter these volumes under H vol. in the summary chart at the appropriate Cut and Fill lines.

**STEP 6:** To determine the total non-paved area to receive topsoil for planting, subtract total hardscape area (H area) from the total no-cut / no-fill zone project area by first, subtracting the area of hardscape in the cut zone from the total area in the cut zone; then, subtracting the area of hardscape in the fill zone from the total area in the fill zone. Enter the resulting area in column S (softscape) at the lines appropriate for Cut and Fill.

**STEP 7:** Determine the thickness to which the topsoil is to be replaced and calculate separately the required volumes for the cut and the fill areas respectively found in Step 6. Enter the volumes in column TR (topsoil replaced) on the appropriate lines for Cut and Fill.

**STEP 8:** Calculate the gross cut and gross fill volume separately by using the formula:

$$V = i\left(\frac{5A_1}{6} + A_2 + A_3 + A_4 + \ldots + \frac{5A_n}{6}\right)$$

where:

  V = Gross volume of cut or fill

  A = area of contour planes measured between original and finished contours

  i = contour interval (vertical distance between contours)

Enter the volume for the cut area under C (cut) on the Cut line. Enter the volume for the fill area under F (fill) on the Fill line.

## TABLE 10.3. Contour method form and summary sheet.

| CUT | | FILL | |
|---|---|---|---|
| Gross area in cut = _____* | | Gross area in fill = _____* | |
| Contour Number | Area | Contour Number | Area |
| .................................................... | | .................................................... | |
| .................................................... | | .................................................... | |
| .................................................... | | .................................................... | |
| .................................................... | | .................................................... | |
| .................................................... | | .................................................... | |
| .................................................... | | .................................................... | |
| .................................................... | | .................................................... | |
| .................................................... | | .................................................... | |

\* Gross area refers to area delimited by no-cut/no-fill line and limits of grading line in cut and fill zones respectively.

Volume in cut or Volume in filll can be calculated as follows:

$$\text{Volume} = i \left( \frac{5A_1}{6} + A_2 + A_3 + A_4 + \dots + \frac{5A_n}{6} \right)$$

Where A = Area of contour planes measured between original and finished contours.
   i = contour interval

Note: If calculating area with a planimeter in square feet, the result of the above equation must be multiplied by the square of the drawing scale divided by 27 in order to yield cubic yards.

### Summary

| | C | SC | F | SF | TS | H Vol. | H Area | TR | S |
|---|---|---|---|---|---|---|---|---|---|
| CUT | | | | | | | | | |
| FILL | | | | | | | | | |
| SUBTOTAL | | | | | | | | | |
| %SHRINKAGE | | | | | | | | | |
| TOTAL | | | | | | | | | |

C= Volume of Cut                    H vol. = Volume of Hardscape (paved)
SC= Subsoil Cut (–C+H vol.+TR–TS)   H area = Area of Hardscape (paved)
 F= Volume of Fill                    TR = Volume of Topsoil Replaced
SF= Subsoil Fill (–F+TS–TR– H vol.)    S = Area of Softscape (non-paved)
TS= Volume of Topsoil Stripped

**TABLE 10.4. Estimating shrink and swell.**

| Material | After excavation during transport or stockpile | Borrow yard* |
| --- | --- | --- |
| Sand | 0.83 m³ (1.11 yd³) 111 % swell | 0.75 m³ (1 yd³) |
| Common earth | 0.94 m³ (1.25 yd³) 125 % swell | 0.75 m³ (1 yd³) |
| Clay | 1.00 m³ (1.43 yd³) 143 % swell | 0.75 m³ (1 yd³) |
| Shot rock | 1.30 m³ (1.67 yd³) 167 % swell | 0.75 m³ (1 yd³) |
| Gravel, loose | | 0.75 m³ (1 yd³) |

| Material | Amount produced by 1 meter (1 yd), replaced with only moderate compaction |
| --- | --- |
| Sand | 0.66 m³ (0.88 yd³) 12 % shrink |
| Common earth | 0.60 m³ (0.82 yd³) 18 % shrink |
| Clay | 0.65 m³ (0.87 yd³) 13 % shrink |
| Shot rock | |
| Gravel, loose | 0.67 m³ (0.89 yd³) 11 % shrink |

* Materials used for compacted subbase will exhibit higher shrinkage levels under the appropriate moisture conditions and compaction technique.

**STEP 9:** Using the formula SC = –C + R + TR – TS, calculate the subsoil cut. Enter the volume cut in column SC (subsoil cut) on the Cut line.

**STEP 10:** Using the formula SF = –F + TS – TR – R, calculate the subsoil fill. Enter the volume fill in column SF (subsoil fill) on the Fill line. (A negative answer can be interpreted as an indication that additional subsoil may need to be removed in order to make room for hardscape materials.)

**STEP 11:** Complete the summary chart by adding the columns vertically and incorporating shrinkage factors where appropriate (Table 10.4).

# SUGGESTED REFERENCES

Harris, Charles W. and Nicholas T. Dines, *Time-Saver Standards for Landscape Architecture, 2nd Edition*, McGraw-Hill, New York, 1998.

Parker and MacGuire, James Ambrose (ed.) *Simplified Site Engineering for Architects and Builders*, Wiley, New York, 1991.

Untermann, Richard K., *Grade Easy*, ASLA Foundation, Washington, DC, 1989.

# TECHNIQUES

# *Stormwater Management*

# 11

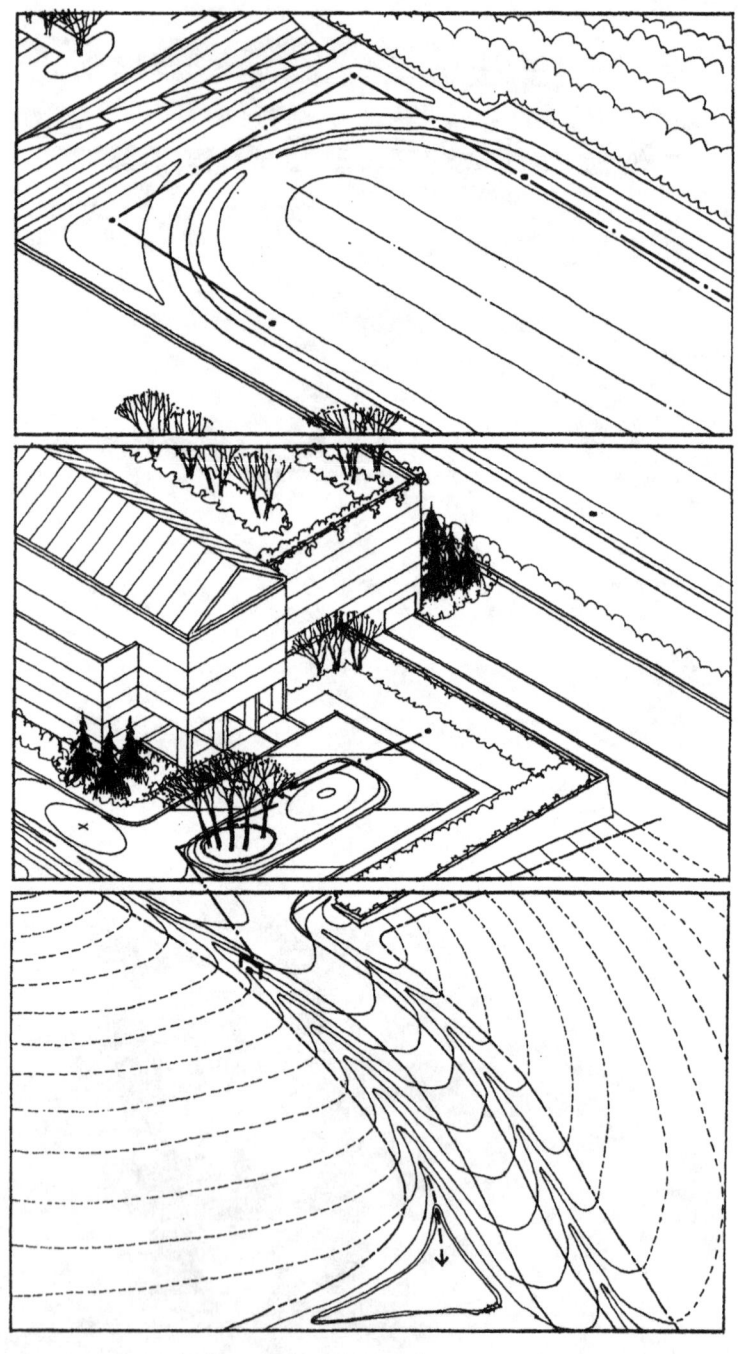

## LARGE PARKING LOTS, ATHLETIC FIELDS AND OPEN VEGETATED AREAS

Typically, high volume sheet runoff is transferred into channel flow, and is subsequently deposited into a collection system. A key goal in this situation is to reduce runoff velocities and volume, while improving water quality. Sheet flow runoff depth should be less than 25 mm (1 in) and velocities should not exceed 0.8-0.9 m/sec (2.5-3 ft/sec) to prevent erosion. Vegetated swales and infiltration devices should be used to convey stormwater flows wherever feasible, due to their ability to reduce velocity and improve quality. Grading is typically parabolic and uniform. Collection is away from use areas. Where appropriate, detention devices may be incorporated to reduce runoff rates to pre-development conditions, provide sediment removal, and infiltration.

## MULTI-SURFACE RUNOFF SITUATIONS IN HIGH-USE AREAS

This condition typically requires quick removal of runoff to maintain human use. Design works to quickly convert sheet flow runoff into channel flow (e.g. pavement to gutter, or turf to swale). Minimum slopes for channels are 0.5-1.0%, and minimum slopes for surfaces are 1.5-2.0%. Storm sewers or other closed systems are typically used to remove channel flow from area, due to space limitations and human activity. Pavement runoff should drain onto vegetated surfaces for infiltration and velocity reduction, but vegetated surface runoff should not drain onto pavements due to increased flow velocities, silting, and organic debris deposition.

## ROADWAYS, PATHWAYS, AND OTHER LINEAR SYSTEMS

Roads are typically crowned or cross-sloped and runoff is collected by curb and gutter systems in urban situations (resulting in increased runoff rates), or vegetated roadside swales where space and site conditions permit (resulting in reduced runoff velocity, filtration and infiltration). Roads and adjacent paved areas require strategically placed collection devices (e.g. drain inlets, gutters, infiltration systems) to prevent ponding. Surfaces commonly are cross-sloped at 2%, and sheet flow should travel no more than 20-30 m (75-100 ft) before being collected. Stormwater flows from roads and adjacent parking areas should be filtered to maintain water quality, and detention is often required to maintain pre-development runoff rates.

T HE HYDROLOGIC CYCLE is the natural process that governs the movement of water through the landscape, consisting of evaporation, condensation, precipitation, runoff and infiltration. Generally speaking, urbanization tends to locally disrupt this cycle by increasing surface runoff and decreasing infiltration. Stormwater management strives to reduce runoff velocity and volumes to pre-development conditions. Therefore, it is a critical component of planning and design at a variety of scales, from the regional watershed to the site. A designer must understand the impact of proposed development on the hydrologic process, in order to specify appropriate management strategies.

## DIAGNOSTIC ASSESSMENT

*What is the objective for stormwater management in the proposed development?*

A comprehensive stormwater management strategy is essential for flood protection and water quality enhancement. This strategy is ideally addressed at the watershed scale, and the components include a major flood protection system, a minor flood protection system, and a water quality protection system. Size, location within the watershed, characteristics of the site, and its proposed use are important criteria in determining the opportunities and responsibilities of a proposed development in meeting the objectives of this comprehensive strategy.

*What are the expected stormwater runoff volumes and peak discharge rates?*

The amount of runoff and the peak discharge rate resulting from a proposed development must be estimated in order to determine specific strategies and size the system. Estimating runoff requires an understanding of precipitation patterns within the region, the size and topographic characteristics of the contributing watershed, as well as the soil characteristics and land cover of the site and contributing watershed.

*What techniques are appropriate for conveyance of stormwater on site?*

A variety of methods are available for facilitating movement of stormwater through a site. These include overland systems such as channels and swales, and closed systems such as culverts and storm sewers. Selection of an appropriate technique is a function of land use, site conditions, stormwater management objectives, and cost.

*What mitigation strategies should be employed to reduce the impact of proposed development on runoff volumes?*

Urbanization tends to increase runoff, raising risks from flooding within the watershed, often depleting groundwater levels through decreased infiltration, and reducing water quality of oceans, streams and lakes. A number of strategies are available for mitigating these adverse impacts, including on-site storage, infiltration and filtration techniques.

# TYPES OF STORMWATER MANAGEMENT SYSTEMS

Table 11.1 describes the primary types of stormwater management systems and design storms commonly used to size these systems. A comprehensive stormwater management strategy includes minor flood protection, major flood protection, and water quality protection for optimum performance.

# ESTIMATING RUNOFF

The most common techniques for estimating runoff in the United States are the Soil Conservation Service (SCS) Runoff Curve Number Method, the Rational Method, and the Small Storm Hydrology WQV Method. The SCS method is a more sophisticated model useful for larger watersheds [up

**TABLE 11.1. Primary stormwater management systems.**

| System | Description | Typical Strategies | Typical Design Storm* |
|---|---|---|---|
| Minor Flood Protection | Minimizes inconveniences from frequently occurring storms | Gutters and storm sewers or swales | 2, 5, or 10 year storm |
| Major Flood Protection | Used during infrequent storms when minor system capacity is exceeded | Streets, and major designed or natural drainageways | 25, 50, 100 year storm |
| Water Quality Protection | Captures and treats runoff from small, frequent storms, removing sediments and pollutants | Storage, filtration and infiltration techniques | 30 mm (1.25 inch) rainfall event |

* Design storms for specific systems may be specified by local law. Design storms for flood protection are specified in terms of duration (usually 24 hour) and probable frequency (in years). For example, a 100 year rainfall event means that in a given year, the probability of a rainfall of this magnitude or greater actually occurring is one percent every time it rains.

to 50 km²(20 square miles)], and larger design storms. The Rational Method is more commonly used for small watersheds [less than 80 hectares (200 acres)], and its simplicity makes it useful for preliminary design estimates. A number of publications listed at the end of this chapter describe the SCS Runoff Curve Number Method in great detail. This chapter presents information for estimating runoff for smaller watersheds using the modified Rational Method and Small Storm Hydrology methods.

## Modified Rational Method

This method for calculating peak runoff rate assumes:.
1. Rainfall intensity is uniform throughout the duration of the storm.
2. Precipitation falls on the entire drainage area for the duration of the storm.
3. Peak discharge occurs at the time of concentration.
4. Duration of the rainfall is equal to at least the time of concentration.
5. Time of concentration is at least 6 minutes.

**STEP 1:** Choose an appropriate design storm, delineate the watershed, identify outlet and calculate watershed area (A) in hectares (acres).

**EXAMPLE (U.S. UNITS)**
Assume a watershed in Kentucky 37 acres in size. Asphalt streets and parking cover 18.1 acres, rooftops cover 6.8 acres, and gently sloping turfgrass with hydrologic soils group C subgrade covering the remaining 12.1 acres. Find the peak discharge from a 25 year rainfall event.

**STEP 2:** Determine appropriate runoff coefficient (C) based on land cover characteristics and hydrologic soil group (Table 11.2). In landscapes with several combinations of land cover and soil type, a composite C value is used. If the design storm return period is greater than 10 years, multiply runoff coefficient (C) by the correction factor (C$_f$) from Table 11.3 to account for antecedent moisture conditions.

| Cover Type | Acres (A) | Runoff Coefficient (C) | C x A |
|---|---|---|---|
| Asphalt | 18.1 | 0.95 | 17.20 |
| Roof | 6.8 | 0.95 | 6.46 |
| Turfgrass, C soils, 2-6% slope | 12.1 | 0.21 | 2.54 |
| Totals | 37.0 | — | 26.2 |

Weighted
Antecedent Moisture Correction
Factor for 25 year storm

$C = 26.2 \div 37.0 = 0.71$

(Table 11.3) $(C_f) = 1.1$

Corrected $C = 1.1 \times 0.71 = 0.78$

**STEP 3:** Calculate the time of concentration for the watershed ($T_c$) in minutes, using the Kirpich formula:

$T_c = KL^{0.77}S^{-0.385}$

Where: K = Constant (0.0195 for SI Units; 0.0078 for US Units)

L = Length of travel in m (ft)

S = Average slope of flow path in m/m (ft/ft)

This formula works for bare earth or mowed grass overland flow. Adjustments should be made for other conditions:

For general overland flow and grassed channels multiply $T_c$ by 2.0

For concrete or asphalt surfaces, multiply $T_c$ by 0.4

For concrete channels multiply $T_c$ by 0.2

Where pathway consists of multiple land cover types, a composite $T_c$ is used.

Assume $T_c$ path is 1700 feet long. The first 1270 feet is turf grass sloping at 5%. The remaining 430 feet is asphalt sloping at 2%.

$T_c$ for turf = $(0.0078)(1270)^{0.77}(0.05)^{-0.385}$

= 6.07 minutes

$T_c$ for asphalt = $(0.0078)(430)^{0.77}(0.02)^{-0.385}$

= 3.75 × 0.4

= 1.50 minutes

Composite $T_c$ = 6.07 + 1.50

= 7.57 minutes

## TABLE 11.2. Recommended Rational Formula Runoff Coefficients (C).

| SURFACE | | C values Min. | Max. |
|---|---|---|---|
| Street, asphalt | | 0.70 | 0.95 |
| Street, concrete | | 0.80 | 0.95 |
| Drives and walks | | 0.75 | 0.85 |
| Roofs | | 0.75 | 0.95 |
| Pervious areas, A soils* | 0-1% slopes | 0.04 | 0.09 |
| | 2-6% slopes | 0.09 | 0.13 |
| | steep slopes | 0.13 | 0.18 |
| Pervious areas, B soils* | 0-1% slopes | 0.07 | 0.12 |
| | 2-6% slopes | 0.12 | 0.17 |
| | steep slopes | 0.18 | 0.24 |
| Pervious areas, C soils* | 0-1% slopes | 0.11 | 0.16 |
| | 2-6% slopes | 0.16 | 0.21 |
| | steep slopes | 0.23 | 0.31 |
| Pervious areas, D soils* | 0-1% slopes | 0.15 | 0.20 |
| | 2-6% slopes | 0.20 | 0.25 |
| | steep slopes | 0.28 | 0.38 |

| COMPOSITE VALUES | | | |
|---|---|---|---|
| Business, downtown areas | | | |
| Neighborhood areas | | | |
| Residential | single-family detached | 0.30 | 0.50 |
| | multi-units, detached | 0.40 | 0.60 |
| | multi-units, attached | 0.60 | 0.75 |
| | suburban lots, < 0.5 acre | 0.25 | 0.40 |
| | suburban lots, ≥ 0.5 acre | 0.30 | 0.45 |
| Apartment dwelling areas | | 0.50 | 0.70 |
| Industrial | light areas | 0.50 | 0.80 |
| | heavy areas | 0.60 | 0.90 |
| Parks and cemeteries | | 0.10 | 0.25 |
| Playgrounds | | 0.20 | 0.40 |
| Railroad yard areas | | 0.20 | 0.40 |
| Unimproved areas | pasture (flat-steep) | 0.10 | 0.42 |
| | cultivated (flat-steep) | 0.31 | 0.44 |

*Use minimum value for dense, layered woods; maximum value for good grass; soils refer to SCS hydrologic groups.

**TABLE 11.3.
Recommended
antecedent moisture
correction factors for the
rational formula
coefficient of runoff (C).**

| Recurrence Interval in Years | Correction Factor $C_f$ |
|---|---|
| 25 | 1.1 |
| 50 | 1.2 |
| 100 | 1.25 |

Note the correction factor is applied:
$C_f$ x C. The product should not exceed
1.0

**STEP 4:** Calculate rainfall intensity (I) using the Steel Formula:

$$I = \frac{K}{T_c + b}$$

Where:

I = Intensity of rainfall in millimeters per hour (in/hour).

$T_c$ = time of concentration in minutes (Step 3).

K and b = coefficients for region of U.S. and design storm frequency (Figure 11.1 and Table 11.4).

**EXAMPLE CONTINUED (US UNITS)**

Kentucky is in Area 3, therefore K = 230 and b = 30

$$I = \frac{230}{7.57 + 30}$$

$$I = 6.12 \ inches/hour$$

**STEP 5:** Calculate the peak discharge (Q) using the formula:

$$Q = KCIA$$

Where:

Q = peak discharge rate in cubic meters per second (ft³/sec)

K = constant (0.0028 for S.I. units; 1.0 for U.S. units)

C = runoff coefficient (Step 2)

I = Rainfall intensity in millimeters or inches per hour (Step 4)

A = Watershed area in hectares or acres (Step 1)

**EXAMPLE CONTINUED (US UNITS)**

Q = (1.0)(0.78)(6.12)(37.0)

Q = 177 ft³/sec

TECHNIQUES

*Stormwater Management* ▪ 201

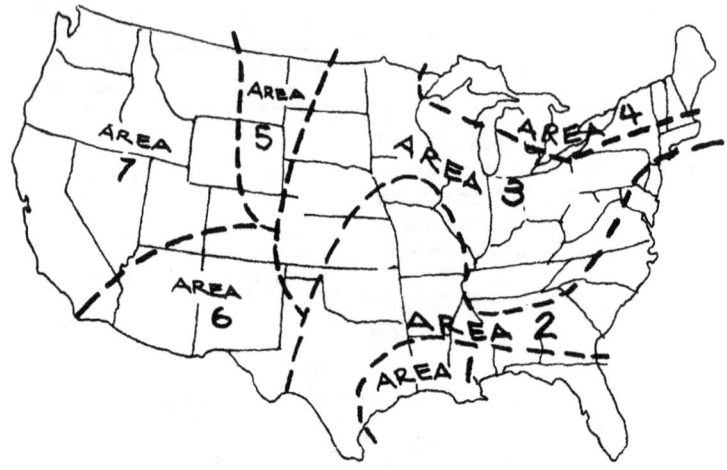

**Figure 11.1. Regions of the United States for use in the Steel Formula.**

**TABLE 11.4. Coefficients for steel formula.**

| Storm Frequency in years | Steel Coefficients | Regions of the United States | | | | | | |
|---|---|---|---|---|---|---|---|---|
| | | 1 | 2 | 3 | 4 | 5 | 6 | 7 |
| 2 | K | 206 | 140 | 106 | 70 | 70 | 68 | 32 |
| | b | 30 | 21 | 17 | 13 | 16 | 14 | 11 |
| 4 | K | 247 | 190 | 131 | 97 | 81 | 75 | 48 |
| | b | 29 | 25 | 19 | 16 | 13 | 12 | 12 |
| 5 | K | 247 | 190 | 131 | 97 | 81 | 75 | 48 |
| | b | 29 | 25 | 19 | 16 | 13 | 12 | 12 |
| 10 | K | 300 | 230 | 170 | 111 | 111 | 122 | 60 |
| | b | 36 | 29 | 23 | 16 | 17 | 23 | 13 |
| 25 | K | 327 | 260 | 230 | 170 | 130 | 155 | 67 |
| | b | 33 | 32 | 30 | 27 | 17 | 26 | 10 |
| 50 | K | 315 | 350 | 250 | 187 | 187 | 160 | 65 |
| | b | 28 | 38 | 27 | 24 | 25 | 21 | 8 |
| 100 | K | 367 | 375 | 290 | 220 | 240 | 210 | 77 |
| | b | 33 | 36 | 31 | 28 | 29 | 26 | 10 |

# Estimating Runoff Volumes for Water Quality

Schueler's Shortcut Method offers a reliable alternative for generating rough runoff volume estimates quickly, using the formula:

$$WQV = (P)(0.05 + 0.009\ I)$$

Where: WQV = water quality volume in watershed millimeters (inches)
P = Design rainfall depth in millimeters (inches) [30 mm (1.25 in) recommended]
I = the percentage of impervious surface (e.g. use 70 to represent 70% impervious surface)

**EXAMPLE (SI UNITS)**

*Assume a 3.3 hectare site with 75% impervious surface from parking, roadways, and rooftops. Calculate for a 30 mm rainfall depth*

$$WQV = (30)(0.05 + 0.009 \times 75)$$
$$WQV = 21.75\ watershed\ millimeters$$

*Convert to cubic meters of runoff for the site:*

$$WQV = \frac{21.75\ mm}{1000\ mm} \times 3.3\ ha \times \frac{10\ 000\ m^2}{1\ ha}$$
$$= 717.75\ m^3\ of\ runoff$$

## Water Quality Management Methods

Design for water quality management focuses on capturing and treating the volume of water produced in smaller storms. The SCS and modified rational methods of converting rainfall to runoff are not calibrated to produce accurate results for these small storms. The preferred method is the Small Storm Hydrology Method, which uses empirical studies to determine runoff coefficients and provides greater accuracy than Schueler's Shortcut Method (see field note). It can be used to calculate peak discharge as well as runoff volumes.

**STEP 1:** Determine design storm rainfall amount. The Center for Watershed Protection in Silver Springs, MD recommends a 30 mm (1.25 in) rainfall event as the design storm for water quality treatment.

**STEP 2:** Determine appropriate runoff coefficient ($R_v$) based on land cover characteristics and hydrologic soil group (Table 11.5). In landscapes with several combinations of land cover and soil type, a composite Rv value is used.

**TABLE 11.5. Small storm volumetric coefficients, rv, for urban runoff.**

| Rainfall (mm) | (Inches) | Flat roofs and large unpaved parking lots | Pitched roofs and large impervious areas (large parking lots | Small impervious areas and narrow streets | Paved streets | Pervious areas, sandy soils group A | Pervious areas, clayey soils groups C &D |
|---|---|---|---|---|---|---|---|
| 1 | 0.04 | 0.00 | 0.25 | 0.93 | 0.26 | 0.00 | 0.00 |
| 3 | 0.12 | 0.30 | 0.75 | 0.96 | 0.49 | 0.00 | 0.00 |
| 5 | 0.20 | 0.54 | 0.85 | 0.97 | 0.55 | 0.00 | 0.10 |
| 10 | 0.39 | 0.72 | 0.93 | 0.97 | 0.60 | 0.01 | 0.15 |
| 15 | 0.59 | 0.79 | 0.95 | 0.97 | 0.64 | 0.02 | 0.19 |
| 20 | 0.79 | 0.83 | 0.96 | 0.67 | n.d. | 0.02 | 0.20 |
| 25 | 1.00 | 0.84 | 0.97 | 0.70 | n.d. | 0.02 | 0.21 |
| 30 | 1.25 | 0.86 | 0.98 | 0.74 | n.d. | 0.03 | 0.22 |
| 38 | 1.50 | 0.88 | 0.99 | 0.77 | n.d. | 0.05 | 0.24 |
| 50 | 2.00 | 0.90 | 0.99 | 0.99 | 0.84 | 0.07 | 0.26 |
| 80 | 3.15 | 0.94 | 0.99 | 0.99 | 0.90 | 0.15 | 0.33 |
| 125 | 4.92 | 0.96 | 0.99 | 0.99 | 0.93 | 0.25 | 0.45 |

n.d. – no data available

Source: Pitt, Robert E. (April 1997) "Section 5. Small Storm Hydrology" text for
*Stormwater Quality Management Through the Use of Detention Basins – A Short
Course on Stormwater Detention Basin Design Basics by Integrating Water Quality
with Drainage Objectives.* Minneapolis, Minnesota: University of Minnesota
Continuing Education and Extension.

**TABLE 11.6. Reduction factors to volumetric runoff coefficients for disconnected impervious surfaces.\***

| Rainfall (mm) | Rainfall (inches) | Strip commercial and shopping center | density residential with paved alleys | density residential without alleys |
|---|---|---|---|---|
| 1 | 0.04 | 0.00 | 0.00 | 0.00 |
| 3 | 0.12 | 0.00 | 0.08 | 0.00 |
| 5 | 0.20 | 0.47 | 0.11 | 0.11 |
| 10 | 0.39 | 0.90 | 0.16 | 0.16 |
| 15 | 0.59 | 0.99 | 0.20 | 0.20 |
| 20 | 0.79 | 0.99 | 0.29 | 0.21 |
| 25 | 1.00 | 0.99 | 0.38 | 0.22 |
| 30 | 1.25 | 0.99 | 0.46 | 0.22 |
| 38 | 1.50 | 0.99 | 0.59 | 0.24 |
| 50 | 2.00 | 0.99 | 0.81 | 0.27 |
| 80 | 3.15 | 0.99 | 0.99 | 0.34 |
| 125 | 4.92 | 0.99 | 0.99 | 0.46 |

\* For low density residential use connected values for pervious surfaces with clayey soil). Source: Pitt, Robert E. (April 1997) "Section 5. Small Storm Hydrology" text for *Stormwater Quality Management Through the Use of Detention Basins – A Short Course on Stormwater Detention Basin Design Basics by Integrating Water Quality with Drainage Objectives*. Minneapolis, Minnesota: University of Minnesota Continuing Education and Extension.

**STEP 3:** Situations where sheet flow drains from impervious surfaces (e.g. pavement) onto pervious surfaces (e.g. grass) are referred to as disconnected imperviousness, and can dramatically reduce runoff. If the pervious area is at least twice the size of the above impervious surface, and the flow path through the pervious area is at least twice as long as the flow path through the above impervious area, then multiply the values from Table 11.6 by the $R_v$ value to determine the corrected coefficient.

**STEP 4:** Find the water quality volume produced by the design storm (WQV), using the formula:

$$WQV = PR_v$$

Where: WQV = volume of runoff in millimeters (inches)

P = design storm rainfall amount in millimeters (inches)

$R_v$ = volumetric runoff coefficient (Step 2)

$WQV = (30)(0.72)$

$WQV = 21.60$ watershed millimeters

Convert to cubic meters of runoff for the site:

$$WQV = \frac{21.60 \text{ mm}}{1000 \text{ mm}} \times 3.3 \text{ ha} \times \frac{10\,000 \text{ m}^2}{1 \text{ ha}}$$

$$= 712.80 \text{ m}^3 \text{ of runoff}$$

Note that this estimate is quite consistent with the quicker Schueler's Shortcut Method described in the field note, due to the lack of disconnected imperviousness (step 3). If disconnected imperviousness of the drainage path is provided consistent with criteria outlined in step 3, WQV would calculated as follows:

Modified $R_v = 0.72 \times 0.22$

$= 0.16$ (modified by reduction factor for high density residential without alleys from table 11.6)

$WQV = (30)(0.16)$

$WQV = 4.80$ watershed millimeters

Convert to cubic meters of runoff for the site:

$$WQV = \frac{4.80 \text{ mm}}{1000 \text{ mm}} \times 3.3 \text{ ha} \times \frac{10\,000 \text{ m}^2}{1 \text{ ha}}$$

$$= 158.40 \text{ m}^3 \text{ of runoff}$$

This illustrates the significant runoff reduction resulting from designs that incorporate disconnected imperviousness.ss

## CONVEYANCE TECHNIQUES

Conveyance of storm water occurs through either open overland techniques such as channels and swales, through closed systems such as culverts or storm sewers, or some combination of open and closed systems. Selection of the proper conveyance system is a function of the intended management strategy (major/minor flood protection or water quality protection), land use, and environmental conditions. In general, open vegetated systems allow greater opportunities for reducing runoff velocity and volume, and should be encouraged to the greatest extent possible. Table 11.7 highlights key characteristics of each type of conveyance.

# MITIGATION STRATEGIES

Many jurisdictions require that post-development runoff rates not exceed rates generated by pre-development conditions. In addition, the adverse impacts of urbanization on water quality must be minimized. A number of strategies for mitigating the impacts of development are available, including site planning techniques, storage, filtration, and infiltration devices.

## Site Planning

- Detain stormwater on site to control runoff velocities in post-development conditions. Use pre-development velocities as a guideline for design.
- Minimize impervious surfaces, and locate them away from drainageways (Figure 11.2).
- Maximize situations where sheet flow drains from impervious surfaces (e.g. pavement) onto pervious surfaces (e.g. grass), to reduce runoff (referred to as disconnected imperviousness). Avoid connected imperviousness, where runoff drains directly from impervious surfaces into drainageways.
- Fit development to the terrain, and place it in the least critical areas of the site, away from drainage pathways, steep slopes, complex plant communities, and porous soils.

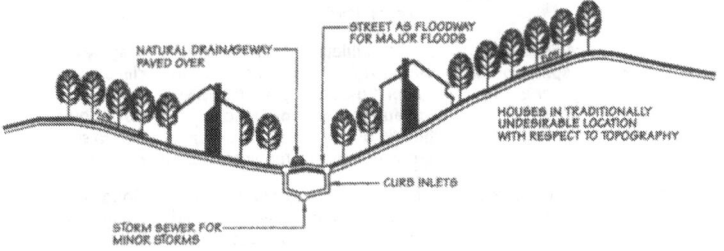

TRADITIONAL DEVELOPMENT LOCATES IMPERVIOUS SURFACES IN DRAINAGEWAYS

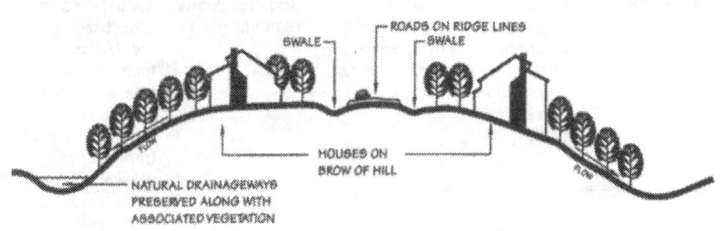

ALTERNATIVE DEVELOPMENT LOCATES IMPERVIOUS SURFACES AWAY FROM DRAINAGEWAYS

**Figure 11.2. Impervious surfaces in conventional and alternative development.**

## TABLE 11.7. Criteria for conveyance systems.

| | Vegetated Swales | Concrete/ Stone Channels | Culverts | Storm Sewers |
|---|---|---|---|---|
| *Stormwater System* | Minor flood protection; water quality protection. | Major and minor flood protection. | Major and minor flood protection. | Minor flood protection. |
| *Design Calculations* | Refer to *Design Charts for Open Channel Flow – Hydraulic Design Series No. 3 (1961)* by the Federal Highway Administration. | Refer to *Design Charts for Open Channel Flow – Hydraulic Design Series No. 3 (1961)* by the Federal Highway Administration. | Refer to *Hydraulic Design of Highway Culverts – Hydraulic Design Series No. 5 (1985)* by the Federal Highway Administration. | Rational Method, using 10 year design storm; work downstream from uppermost inlet. |
| *Application* | Large open spaces; large-lot subdivisions; gradual longitudinal slopes (<4%) with velocities less than 2.1 m/s (7.0 ft/sec). | Large open spaces; large lot subdivisions; steeper longitudinal slopes (>4%); rip-rap helps to dissipate hydraulic energy of channel flow. | Roadway and pedestrian path crossings for swales and channels. | Urban situations; small open spaces where quick removal of stormwater is critical. |
| *Climate* | Wet climates, capable of supporting turf or other vegetative growth. | Arid conditions where vegetation must be irrigated heavily during growing season. | May be costly in climates with periodic heavy downpours, due to sizing requirements. | May be costly in climates with periodic heavy downpours, due to sizing requirements. |
| *Subgrade* | Excellent technique for infiltration in well-drained soils. | Good alternative in highly erodible soils. | Concrete culverts should be used in acid soils. | Good alternative in impermeable soils. |
| *Maintenance* | Requires vegetative maintenance; subject to sedimentation due to lower velocities. | Requires maintenance of concrete and/or rip-rap. | Requires debris removal. | Sumps used to collect sediment/debris; manholes facilitate maintenance; significant problems require trenching to repair. |

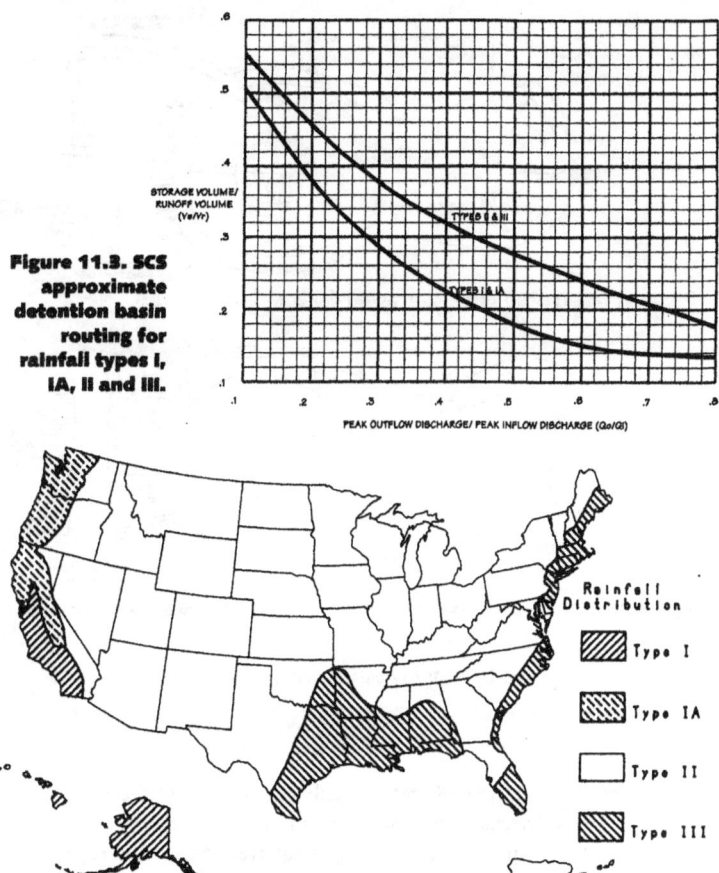

**Figure 11.3. SCS approximate detention basin routing for rainfall types I, IA, II and III.**

STORAGE VOLUME/ RUNOFF VOLUME (Vs/Vr)

PEAK OUTFLOW DISCHARGE/ PEAK INFLOW DISCHARGE (Qo/Qi)

TYPES I & III

TYPES IA & IA

Rainfall Distribution

- ▨ Type I
- ▧ Type IA
- ☐ Type II
- ▩ Type III

**Figure 11.4. SCS storm distribution types for the United States.**

- Use natural drainage systems to transport runoff, wherever possible. Preserve water quality by protecting streams with a minimum of 8 meters (25 ft) of undisturbed vegetation and an additional 15-30 meters (50-100 ft) of managed vegetation, wherever possible.

## Storage

Storage is used to reduce peak discharges from storm events. In situations where the objective is to meet pre-development conditions, the amount of storage required for a given design storm is equal to the volume represented by the difference in post-development ($Q_i$, inflow) and pre-development ($Q_o$, outflow) conditions. Figure 11.3 can be used for initial sizing of storage ponds for four SCS Storm distribution types, whose distribution is shown in Figure 11.4.

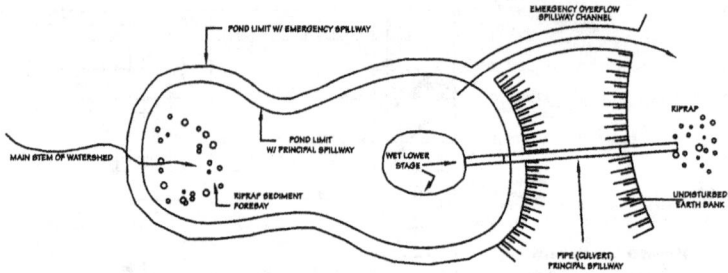

**Figure 11.5. Typical detention pond design.**

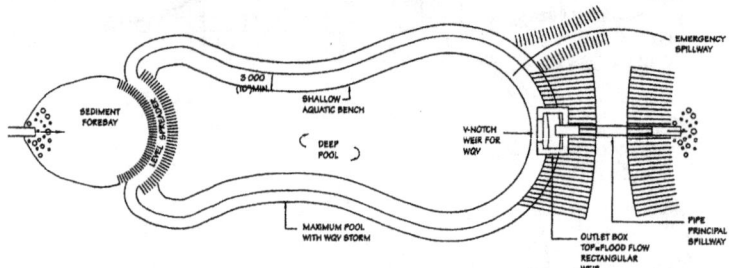

**Figure 11.6. Typical wet detention pond design for sediment removal.**

Pond volume can be roughly estimated by the formula:

$$V = \frac{1}{3} DA$$

Where: V = volume of water in cubic meters (cubic feet)
      D = maximum pond depth in meters (feet)
      A = surface area of pond in square meters (square feet)

Precise pond volumes may be determined using contours and volume calculations. The results may be displayed in a stage-storage curve, a plot of volume stored at each possible water elevation.

- All ponds should have a principal spillway and an emergency overflow spillway (Figure 11.5). Emergency spillway invert elevation is usually 150 mm (6 in) above the principal spillway elevation.
- Wet detention ponds, also know as retention ponds, have a permanent pool of water with additional volume for handling runoff. Principal spillway invert elevation is set at the desired permanent water surface elevation.
- Dry detention ponds are typically designed to drain completely within 72 hours, with the principal spillway invert elevation at the bottom of the pond.

## Filtration

Wet detention ponds, filter strips and sand filters can be employed to enhance water quality by removing sediment and pollutants from stormwater.

- Wet detention ponds are commonly used for sediment removal, often during construction. These ponds should be designed with a fore-bay, storage basin, and outlet structure (Figure 11.6). Regulations for sediment settling typically target a 5 micron or 20 micron particle to gauge performance. Table 11.8 lists minimum pond surface area needed for sediment control for various land uses.
- Filter strips treat sheet flow through filtering and ponding (Figure 11.7). Table 11.9 provides design criteria.
- Sand filters are an alternative where space is limited. Sand traps and strains pollutants from runoff before it is collected by an underdrain system (Figure 11.8). Filter may be located above or below ground.

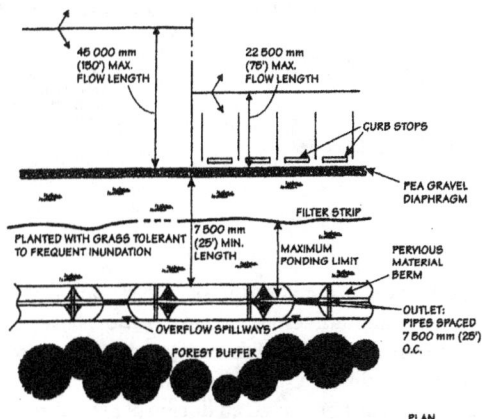

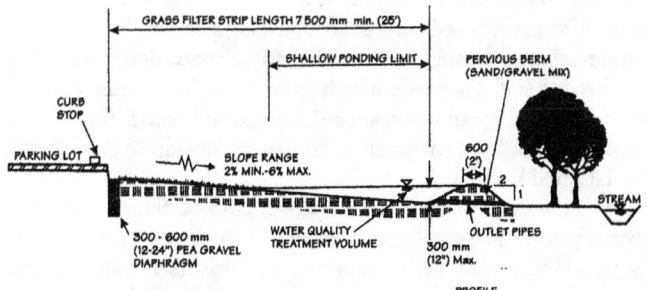

**Figure 11.7. Typical filter strip design.**

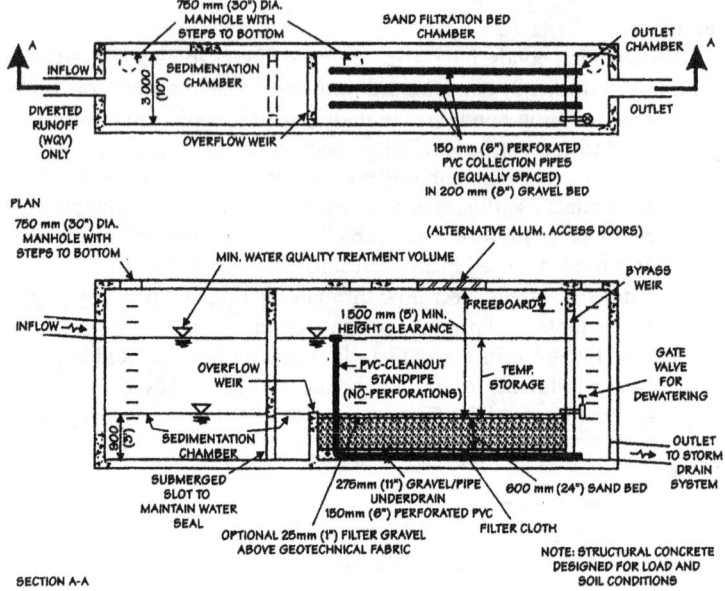

**Figure 11.8. Subsurface sand filter design.**

### Infiltration

Infiltration techniques counter the addition of impervious surfaces resulting from development. Alternatives include infiltration basins, bioretention ponds, recharge trenches, infiltration beds, and infiltration wells. Table 11.10 lists infiltration technique selection criteria.

Areas used for infiltration must be protected during construction to prevent compaction. Compaction and sedimentation are the chief causes of infiltration device failure. Devices should be located off-line of the flood protection systems to prevent sediment scour from large storm flows.

Infiltration basins are essentially dry detention ponds designed to leak into the underlying soil. They have a high failure rate due to sedimentation and must be protected by an upstream sedimentation basin. Inflow should be distributed with a level spreader or fanned by rip-rap to flow evenly across the flat pond bottom.

Bioretention ponds combine infiltration with physical filtering of runoff and biological processing of pollutants (Figure 11.9). A deep layer of planting soil supports a species mix of canopy trees, understory shrubs, and herbaceous ground covers. It is most appropriate for small drainage areas such as parking lots.

**TABLE 11.8. Minimum pond water surface area as a percentage of drainage area for sediment particle control by land use type.**

| Land Use | for 5 micron control | for 20 micron control |
|---|---|---|
| Totally paved areas | 3.0% | 1.1% |
| Freeways (urban) | 2.8% | 1.0% |
| Industrial areas | 2.0% | 0.8% |
| Commercial areas | 1.7% | 0.6% |
| Institutional areas | 1.7% | 0.6% |
| Residential areas | 0.8% | 0.3% |
| Open space areas | 0.6% | 0.2% |
| Construction sites | 1.5% | 0.5% |

Source: Pitt, Robert E. (April 1997) text for *Stormwater Quality Management Through the Use of Detention Basins – A Short Course on Stormwater Detention Basin Design Basics by Integrating Water Quality with Drainage Objectives.* Minneapolis, Minnesota: University of Minnesota Continuing Education and Extension.

**TABLE 11.9. Filter strip design criteria.**

| Parameter | Criteria |
|---|---|
| Size | Length, depth, width needed to provide surface storage of WQV. |
| Width | 8 m (25 ft) minimum. |
| Length | Equal to area draining to filter. |
| Slope | 2% minimum, 6% maximum. |
| Drainage area, pervious surfaces | Maximum overland flow length = 45 m (150 ft). |
| Drainage area, impervious surfaces | Maximum overland flow length = 25 m (75 ft). |

Recharge trenches consist of coarse aggregate and are essentially French drains (Figure 11.10). Aggregate subbase should be wrapped with filter fabric to prevent sediment plugging, with the top surface layer being replaced as needed to maintain porosity.

Infiltration beds are subsurface versions of recharge trenches (Figure 11.11). The infiltration rock and perforated pipe should be wrapped with filter fabric to prevent sediment plugging, and the pipe should be sloped down toward the inlet to concentrate sediment in the sump, where it can be removed.

Infiltration wells are underground devices used to infiltrate roof runoff or other small drainage areas with relatively clean stormwater (Figure 11.12). Aggregate should be wrapped with filter fabric to prevent sediment plugging. Surcharge pipe should be provided to divert overflow to the surface.

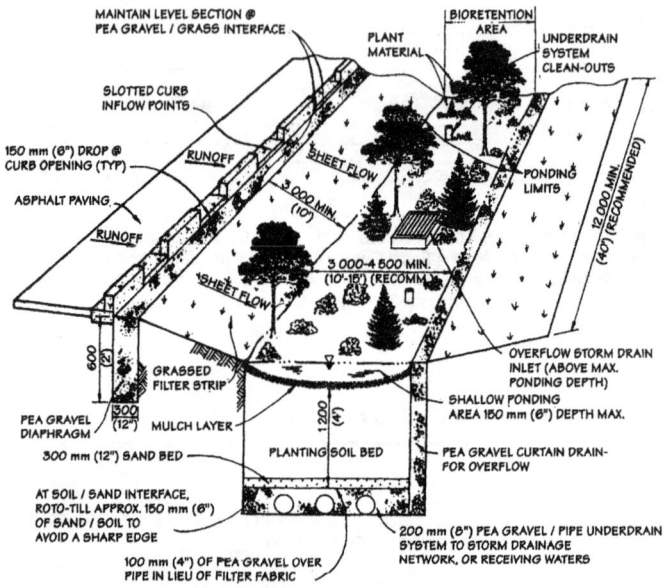

**Figure 11.9. Typical bioretention pond design.**

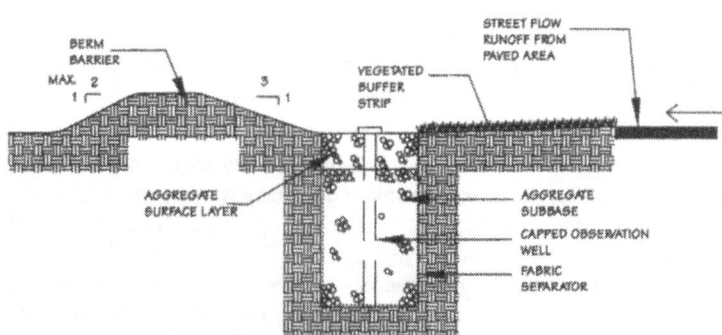

**Figure 11.10. Typical recharge trench design.**

# TABLE 11.10. Infiltration technique selection criteria.

| Technique | Sand 210 (8.27) | Loamy Sand 61 (2.41) | Sandy Loam 26 (1.02) | Loam 13 (0.52) | Silt Loam 7 (0.27) | Sandy Clay Loam 4 (0.17) | Clays <4 (<0.17) |
|---|---|---|---|---|---|---|---|
| | | | | | Soil Type and Minimum Infiltration Rate, mm/hour (inches/hour) | | |
| Filter Strips | • | • | • | • | • | • | |
| Infiltration Basins | • | • | • | • | | | |
| Recharge Trenches | • | • | • | • | | | |
| Bioretention Ponds | • | • | • | • | | | |
| Infiltration Beds | • | • | • | • | | | |
| Infiltration Wells | • | • | • | • | | | |

| | Drainage Area Served, hectacres (acres) | | | | | | |
|---|---|---|---|---|---|---|---|
| | 0-2 (0-5) | 2-4 (5-10) | 4-6 (10-15) | 6-8 (15-20) | 8-10 (20-25) | 10-12 (25-30) | 12-20 (30-50) |
| Filter Strips | • | | | | | | |
| Infiltration Basins | | • | • | • | • | • | • |
| Recharge Trenches | • | • | | | | | |
| Bioretention Ponds | • | • | | | | | |
| Infiltration Beds | • | • | | | | | |
| Infiltration Wells | • | | | | | | |

| | | | Other Restrictions | | | | |
|---|---|---|---|---|---|---|---|
| | Ground-water Table Depth, m (ft) | Slope in Percent | Min. Distance to Well, m (ft) | Min. Distance to Building, m (ft) | Buffer Requirements, m (ft) | Site Constraint | Normal Depth Range, m (ft) |
| Filter Strips | 0.6-1.2 (2-4) | <20 | | | | | |
| Infiltration Basins | 0.6-1.2 (2-4) | <20 | >30 (>100) | >3 (>10) | >6 (>20) | | 0.6-1.5 (2-5) |
| Recharge Trenches | 0.6-1.2 (2-4) | <20 | >30 (>100) | >3 (>10) | >6 (>20) | | 0.6-1.5 (2-5) |
| Bioretention Ponds | 1.8-2.4 (6-8) | <20 | >30 (>100) | >3 (>10) | >6 (>20) | | 0.6-1.5 (2-5) |
| Infiltration Beds | 1.2-1.8 (4-6) | | >30 (>100) | >3 (>10) | >6 (>20) | | |
| Infiltration Wells | 0.6-1.2 (2-4) | <20 | >30 (>100) | >3 (>10) | >6 (>20) | Resid'l. Roof top | 0.6-1.5 (2-5) |

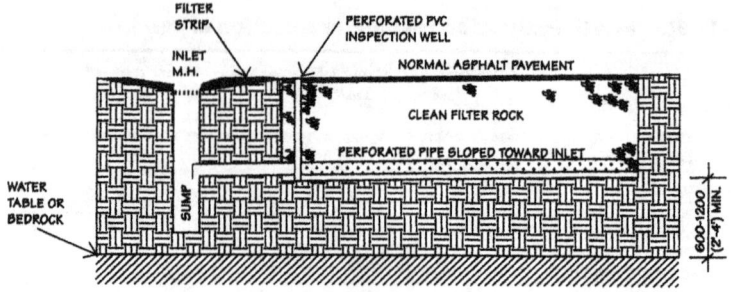

**Figure 11.11. Typical infiltration bed design.**

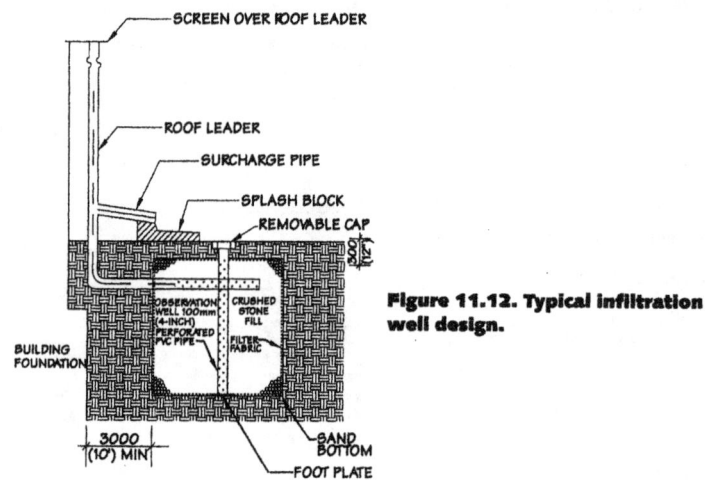

**Figure 11.12. Typical infiltration well design.**

# SUGGESTED REFERENCES

Claytor, Richard A. and Thomas R. Schueler, *Design of Stormwater Filtering Systems*, Center for Watershed Protection, Silver Spring, MD, 1996.

Dewberry and Davis, *Land Development Handbook*, McGraw-Hill, New York, 1996.

Harris, Charles W. and Nicholas T. Dines, *Time-Saver Standards for Landscape Architecture, 2nd Edition*, McGraw-Hill, New York, 1998.

Landphair, Harlow C. and Fred Klatt, *Landscape Architecture Construction*, Elsevier, New York, 1988.

Strom, Steven and Kurt Nathan, *Site Engineering for Landscape Architects*, Van Nostrand Reinhold, New York, 1993.

# Planting

12

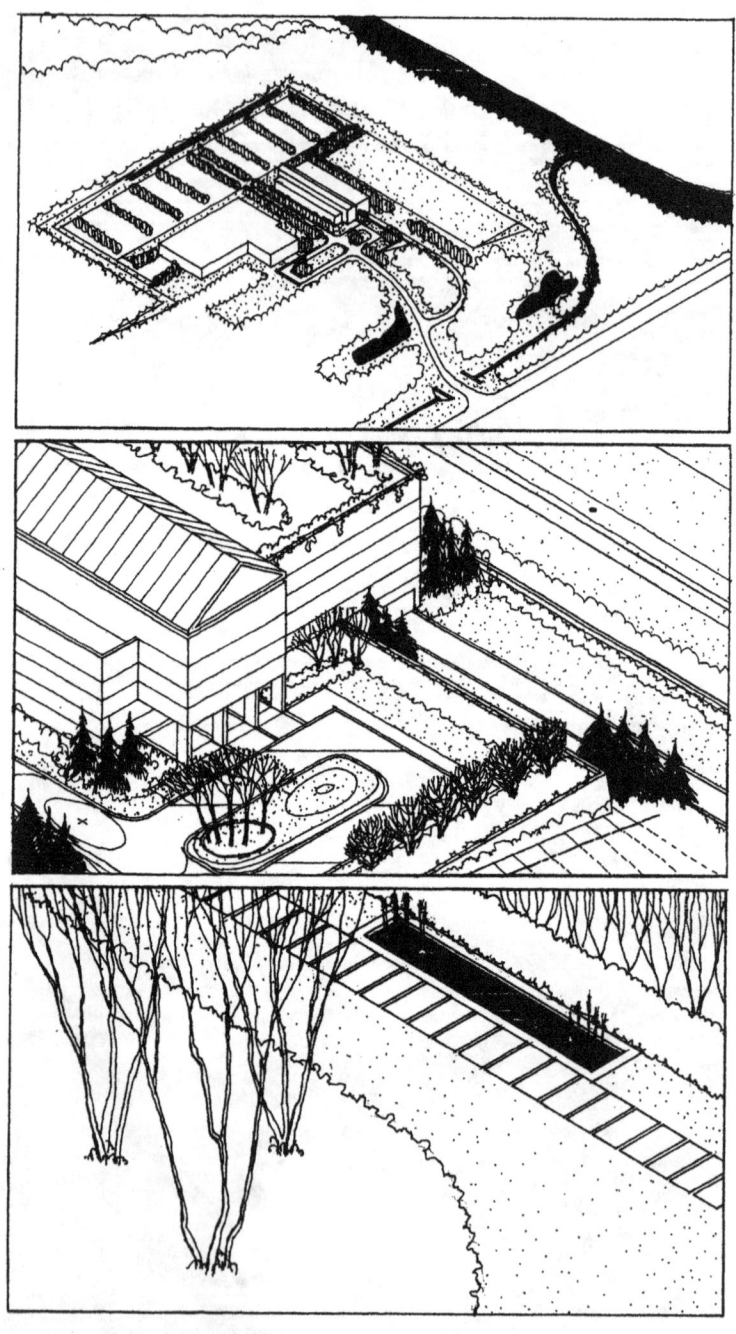

## STRATEGIC APPLICATION OF EXISTING VEGETATION PATTERNS IN LARGE-SCALE DEVELOPMENT

This context commonly involves strategies aimed at preserving existing vegetation cover to maintain species diversity, promote contiguous canopy, or to enhance and expand other vegetated corridors running through a proposed development. Typically, this level of planting design makes strategic use of existing vegetation patterns, which strongly influence land-use decisions and proposed new plantings in large-scale developments. Existing vegetation provides an environmental buffer affecting climate, runoff, views, wildlife, and aesthetics. Plants commonly include large trees, understory plantings, large shrub masses, grasses, and wildflowers.

## INTENSIVE MULTI-USE ACTIVITY AREAS

When applied to this circumstance, plants interrupt expansive paved areas to improve air circulation, absorb runoff, and to alter microclimates. Species are broadly diverse and must tolerate less than ideal soil conditions. The design objective should be to group plants in large connected soil beds, and to eliminate encasing trees in non-porous pavements. Plants chosen from the local species range may be more adaptable to local conditions and soil groups. Long term care and survival probability are critical design criteria. Plant palette often ranges from medium scale trees to richly arranged grasses, perennials, and ground covers.

## SMALL TO MEDIUM SCALE BOTANICAL AND ORNAMENTAL GARDENS

Plants selected for these functions often require larger maintenance and management budgets, but care should be taken to select varieties of hardy species with the aim of staying within local water budgets and for minimizing the need for extreme intervention due to insects and diseases. Visual and compositional objectives should be balanced with ecological compatibility and long-term care requirements with regard to energy and harmful chemicals. Plants range from medium to small trees, shrubs, grasses, groundcovers, and perennial and annual flowers.

T HE ROLE OF PLANT MATERIAL in the designed landscape continues to evolve as new research becomes available within the environmental sciences. The use of plants for aesthetic purposes is still of primary importance, however, designers have not been limited by this single goal. Historically, designers have sought to achieve many functional purposes such as food production, screening, circulation control, and microclimatic improvements using plants. In the 20th century, with the growing awareness of environmental degradation, plants have developed an important role in regenerative design techniques that seek to minimize the amount of natural resource depletion. Recent research in landscape ecology has introduced the need to consider not only specific site issues, but also the impact that proposed planting designs have on regional ecosystems.

## DIAGNOSTIC ASSESSMENT

*What are the regional environmental impacts of the proposed planting scheme?*

The impact of invasive species on regional biodiversity, the demand of irrigation on regional water supplies, and the effect on wildlife resulting from the fragmentation of natural vegetative cover are essential regional considerations in the design process. Mitigating the regional impact of a proposed planting design requires a working knowledge of native plant species and techniques for the preservation of existing vegetation. In addition, further research in the field of landscape ecology is recommended (see Chapter 5: Conservation Standards and the references at the end of this chapter).

*What are the functional requirements of the planting scheme?*

In addition to the essential aesthetic concerns of a planting design, the placement of plants in the landscape can contribute to making a site more comfortable and functional. In some instances, plant material can serve instead of more intensive and invasive engineering practices to stabilize erosion prone slopes. The arrangement of appropriate plant materials can address the cultural requirements of screening and circulation control, as well as provide the environmental benefits of microclimate modification and bioengineering. Inappropriate plantings can cause hazardous conditions for pedestrians.

*What factors contribute to the continued survival and health of installed plant material?*

In developing a planting plan, investigation of relevant environmental factors aids in determining the appropriate type of plant for specific locations. These factors include regional climate, microclimate, available water, and soil profile. Stressed plant material is often a function of poor plant selection for a specific location or improper planting techniques.

# REGIONAL CONSIDERATIONS

## Invasive Species and Biodiversity

Exotic species introduced from outside the native plant population plague many regions. When introduced into the designed landscape, they often spread uncontrollably into surrounding woodlands and beyond. An invasive plant is an exotic species that possess "weedy" characteristics enabling it to spread rapidly and aggressively, competing with the native flora to form dense populations that interfere with the natural development of plant communities. Table 12.1 lists some of the most common invasive plants by region. For a more comprehensive list the USDA Natural Resource Conservation Service Maintains a database of all invasive plants in the United States.

## Landscape Fragmentation

Landscape fragmentation is a concept that has come out of the field of landscape ecology. Fragmentation takes place when human development interrupts large tracts of unbroken woodlands or other continuous ecosystems. Fragmentation turns a continuous habitat into a patchy habitat, which impairs the movement of organisms and can lead to local extinction of vulnerable species over time.

## Demand on Water Resources

All planting schemes should avoid requiring excessive amounts of water to artificially maintain the look of a lush landscape. Xeriscaping is a planting practice that relies on minimal or no irrigation, eschewing heavily watered landscapes in favor of those that combine low water requirements with the unique beauty of plants adapted to the region. For a plant to work in a Xeriscape landscape it must be grouped according to its water needs. For this reason, the use of native plants that are well adapted to the natural soil and rainfall conditions of the region is imperative.

## TABLE 12.1. Invasive plants by region.

| Botanical Name | Common Name | Where Troublesome |
| --- | --- | --- |
| *Acacia melanaoxylon* and many other Acacia species | | Southwestern U.S. |
| *Acer ginnala* | Amur maple | E. Asia |
| *Acer platanoides* | Norway maple | Europe |
| *Ailanthus altissima* | Tree of heaven | Eastern U.S. |
| *Albizia julibrissin* | Mimosa | |
| *Alliaria petiolata* | Garlic mustard | Europe |
| *Ammophila arenaria* | European beach grass | Europe |
| *Bamboo* | | Many parts of the U.S. |
| *Bellis perennis* | English daisy | Northwestern U.S. |
| *Berberis thunbergii* | Japanese barberry | Northeastern and Midwestern U.S. |
| *Bromus inermis* | Smooth brome | Midwestern U.S. |
| *Carduus nutans* | Musk thistle | All of U. S. |
| *Casuarina equisetifolia* | She-oak, ironwood Australian pine | Gulf states (U.S.) |
| *Celastrus orbiculatus* | Leafy spurge, Oriental | Northeastern and Midwestern U.S. |
| *Chrysanthemum leucanthemum* | Oxeye daisy | Northwestern U.S. |
| *Cichorium intybus* | Chicory | Many parts of the U.S. |
| *Cirsium arvense* | Canada thistle | All of U. S. |
| *Coronilla varia* | Crown vetch | Midwestern U.S. |
| *Cortaderia jubata* | Pampas grass | Southwestern U.S. |
| *Cynodon dactylon* | Common Bermudagrass | Southwestern U.S., Gulf states |
| *Cytisus scoparius* | Scotch broom | Northwestern U.S., most species invasive in Southwestern U.S. |
| *Daucus carota* | Queen Anne's lace | |
| *Digitalis purpurea* | Foxglove | Northwestern U.S. |
| *Dipsacus laciniatus* | Cut-leaved teasel | Europe |
| *Dipsacus sylvestris* | Wild teasel | |
| *E. fortunei* | Winter creeper | |
| *E. umbellata* | Autumn olive | Midwestern U.S. |
| *Eichhornia crassipes* | Water hyacinth | S. America |
| *Elaeagnus angustifolia* | Russian olive | Midwestern U.S. |
| *Elaeagnus umbellata* | Autumn olive | East Asia |
| *Elymus arenarius* | European lyme grass | Eurasia |
| *Equisetum hyemale* | Horsetail | Many parts of the U.S. |
| *Eucalyptus spp.* (many) | Gum | Southwestern U.S. |

## TABLE 12.1. Invasive plants by region (continued).

| Botanical Name | Common Name | Where Troublesome |
|---|---|---|
| *Euonymus alata* | Winged wahoo, winged euonymus | |
| *Euphorbia esula* | Leafy spurge | |
| *Festuca elatior* | Tall fescue | |
| *Festuca pratensis* | Tall fescue | Europe |
| *Galium verum* | Yellow bedstraw | Northeastern, Midwestern U.S. |
| *Glechoma hederacea* | Ground ivy | Northwestern U.S. |
| *Hedera helix* | English ivy | |
| *Hungarian brome* | | Southwestern, Northwestern U.S. |
| *Hypericum calycinum* | Aaron's beard, St. John's-wort | Northwestern U.S. |
| *Imperata cylindria* | Cogon grass | Pantropical |
| *Ipomoea spp.* (most) | Morning glory | Many parts of the U.S. |
| *Juniperus virginiana* | Eastern red cedar | |
| *L. maackii* | Amur honeysuckle | |
| *L. tatarica* | Tatarian honeysuckle | Eastern U.S. |
| *Lantana hybrids* | | Gulf states (U.S.) |
| *Lespedeza cuneata* | Sericea lespedeza | |
| *Ligustrum obtusifolium* | Blunt-leaved privet | Japan |
| *Ligustrum vulgare* | Privet | Eastern U.S. |
| *Lonicera japonica* | Japanese honeysuckle | Northeastern, Midwestern U.S. |
| *Lonicera maackii* | Amur honeysuckle | Eurasia |
| *Lonicera tatarica* | Tatarian honeysuckle | |
| *Lysimachia vulgaris* | Garden loosestrife | |
| *Lythrum salicaria* | Purple loosestrife | Northeastern, Midwestern U.S. |
| *M. officinalis* | Yellow sweet clover | |
| *Maclura pomifera* | Osage orange | |
| *Melaleuca quinquenervia* | Punk tree, Cajeput tree | Gulf states (U.S.) |
| *Melia azedarach* | Chinaberry | Asia |
| *Melilotus alba* | White sweet clover | Midwestern U.S. |
| *Melilotus officinalis* | Yellow sweet clover | |
| *Mesembryanthemum ssp.* | Ice plant | Africa |
| *Myriophyllum brasiliense* | Water-feather | |
| *Nasturtium officinale* | Watercress | Many parts of the U.S. |

➤ continued on next page

## TABLE 12.1. Invasive plants by region (continued).

| Botanical Name | Common Name | Where Troublesome |
|---|---|---|
| Pastinaca sativa | Wild parsnip | |
| Paulownia tomentosa | Princess tree | |
| Pennisetum setaceum | Fountain grass | Southwestern U.S. |
| Phalaris arundinacea | Reed canary grass | Midwestern U.S. |
| Phragmites communis | Reed | |
| Pinus nigra | Austrian pine | |
| Pinus sylvestris | Scotch pine | Europe |
| Pinus thunbergii | Japanese black pine | East Asia |
| Poa compressa | Canada bluegrass | |
| Poa pratensis | Kentucky bluegrass | Eurasia |
| Polygnum cuspidatum | Japanese knotweed | Many parts of the U.S. |
| Populus alba | White poplar | |
| Portulaca oleracea | Purslane | Many parts of the U.S. |
| Potamogeton crispus | Pondweed | |
| Pteridium aquilinum | Bracken fern | Northwestern U.S. |
| Pueraria lobata | Kudzu vine | Southeastern U.S. |
| R. frangula | Alder buckthorn | |
| Rhamnus cathartica | Common buckthorn | Midwestern U.S. |
| Rhamnus davurica | Dahurian buckthorn | E. Asia |
| Rhodomyrtus tomentosus | Downy myrtle | E. Asia |
| Robinia pseudoacacia | Black locust | Midwestern U.S. |
| Rosa multiflora | Multiflora rose | Northeastern, Midwestern U.S. |
| Rubus procerus | Himalayan blackberry | Southwestern, Northwestern U.S. |
| Schinus terebinthifolius | Brazilian pepper tree | Gulf states (U.S.) |
| Solidago canadensis | Goldenrod | Northwestern U.S. |
| Sorghum halepense | Johnson grass | |
| Tamarix spp. (many) | Tamarisk | Western U.S. |
| Typha angustifolia | Narrow-leaved cattail | |
| U. pumila | Dwarf elm | |
| Ulmus procera | English elm | |
| V. minor | Common periwinkle | Eastern U.S. |
| Verbascum thapsus | Common mullein | |
| Viburnum lantana | Wayfaringtree | Europe |
| Viburnum opulus | Guelder rose | |
| Vinca major | Large periwinkle | Eastern, Northwestern U.S. |
| Vinca minor common | Periwinkle | Eastern, Northwestern U.S. |

## Existing Vegetation

Existing native vegetation established through succession has proven its adaptability to site conditions by its survival and continued health. The appropriateness of existing plant materials to the site, both aesthetically and functionally, should be considered along with the role the plants play in larger ecological patterns.

The majority of a plant's root system lies within the top 450 mm (18 in) of soil, regardless of the type or size of plant. Ensuring that the root zones of existing plant material are neither compacted nor covered with a material that would restrict the intake of air or moisture, existing plantings need to be protected during periods of construction. A common method for protecting existing plants during construction is to erect a barrier around the plant, enclosing an area as large as the root zone. Figures 12.1 and 12.2 illustrate tree protection methods.

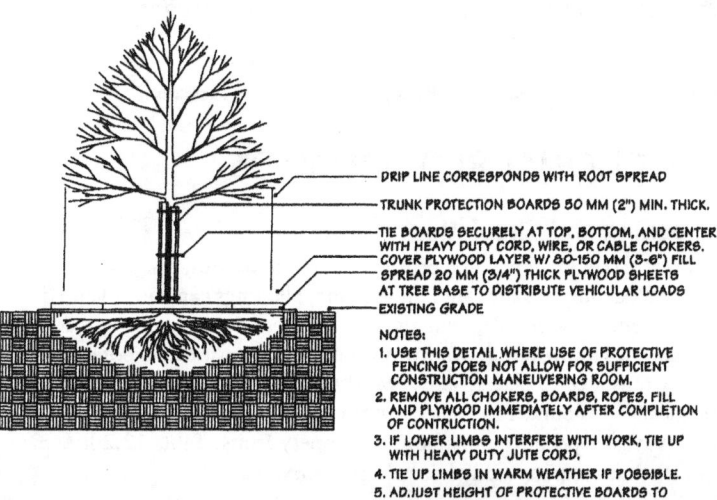

DRIP LINE CORRESPONDS WITH ROOT SPREAD

TRUNK PROTECTION BOARDS 50 MM (2") MIN. THICK.

TIE BOARDS SECURELY AT TOP, BOTTOM, AND CENTER WITH HEAVY DUTY CORD, WIRE, OR CABLE CHOKERS.
COVER PLYWOOD LAYER W/ 80-150 MM (3-6") FILL
SPREAD 20 MM (3/4") THICK PLYWOOD SHEETS AT TREE BASE TO DISTRIBUTE VEHICULAR LOADS
EXISTING GRADE

NOTES:
1. USE THIS DETAIL WHERE USE OF PROTECTIVE FENCING DOES NOT ALLOW FOR SUFFICIENT CONSTRUCTION MANEUVERING ROOM.
2. REMOVE ALL CHOKERS, BOARDS, ROPES, FILL AND PLYWOOD IMMEDIATELY AFTER COMPLETION OF CONTRUCTION.
3. IF LOWER LIMBS INTERFERE WITH WORK, TIE UP WITH HEAVY DUTY JUTE CORD.
4. TIE UP LIMBS IN WARM WEATHER IF POSSIBLE.
5. ADJUST HEIGHT OF PROTECTIVE BOARDS TO

**Figure 12.1. Protection of existing tree during construction.**

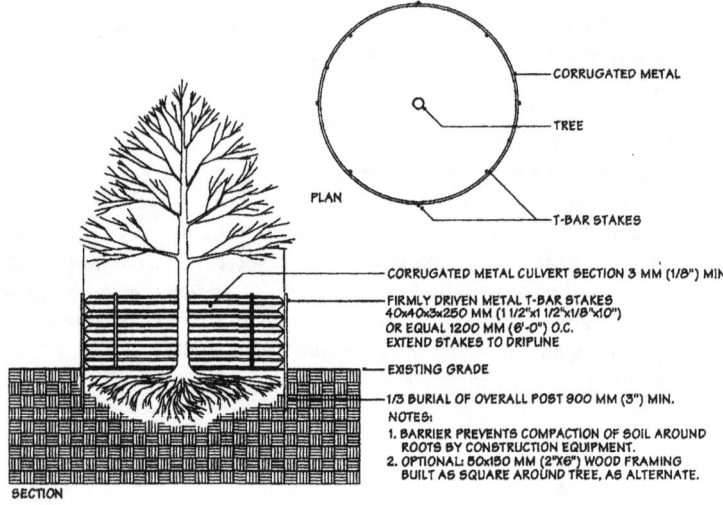

PLAN

CORRUGATED METAL

TREE

T-BAR STAKES

CORRUGATED METAL CULVERT SECTION 3 MM (1/8") MIN.

FIRMLY DRIVEN METAL T-BAR STAKES
40x40x3x250 MM (1 1/2"x1 1/2"x1/8"x10")
OR EQUAL 1200 MM (6'-0") O.C.
EXTEND STAKES TO DRIPLINE

EXISTING GRADE

1/3 BURIAL OF OVERALL POST 900 MM (3") MIN.
NOTES:
1. BARRIER PREVENTS COMPACTION OF SOIL AROUND
   ROOTS BY CONSTRUCTION EQUIPMENT.
2. OPTIONAL: 50x150 MM (2"X6") WOOD FRAMING
   BUILT AS SQUARE AROUND TREE, AS ALTERNATE.

SECTION

**Figure 12.2. Protection of existing tree during construction.**

# FUNCTIONAL REQUIREMENTS

## Screening and Circulation

Plant screens can provide privacy, mark boundaries, discourage intruders, or block unpleasant views. In addition, plantings can control and direct the movement of people, animals, and vehicles.

Plantings along public walkways should not constitute a potential hazard or nuisance to pedestrians. Avoid species with branches that characteristically break under ice or snow, produce excessive litter, droop down over walkways, or produce poisonous or slippery fruits. Table 12.2 lists plant species that are potentially hazardous or noxious.

## Environmental Modification

Outdoor spaces that do not fall within the physical range of human comfort will not be used. Plant materials mitigate the discomforting effects of wind, glare, reflection, temperature, and humidity, contributing to microclimatic comfort as shown in Figure 12.3. In addition, plantings may buffer some unwanted noise near outdoor conversation areas, as shown in Figure 12.4.

## TABLE 12.2. Hazardous and noxious plant species.

| Hazard/nuisance | Species | Comments |
|---|---|---|
| Poisonous plants | Holly, yew, privet, laurel, rhododendron | Children may be tempted to sample bright-colored berries or leaves |
| Debris: fruits and nuts | Crab apple, plum, cherry, oak, chestnut, hickory, walnut | Long, strap-like rods, berries, cones, and nuts can be slippery or difficult to walk on. They are easily tracked into buildings and can stain clothing if sat upon. |
| Cones | Pines, spruce, fir, larch, hemlock | Cones, while having many decorative uses, can cause problems for pedestrians and small-wheeled vehicles on walkway surfaces. |
| Seed pods | Sweetgum, sycamore, London plane tree, honey locust, maple | Pods create unsure footing for pedestrians and hinder the movements of small-wheeled vehicles. |
| Branch breakage | Birch, silver maple, box elder, horse chestnut, poplar, willow, tulip tree, elm | Branch debris is difficult to walk on or to push small wheeled vehicles over. Large branches can cause extensive damage to items on which they might happen to fall, such as cars, small wood-frame structures, etc. |
| Drooping branches | Birch, willow, pin oak, beech, magnolia | Branches can drop below minimum clearances on walkways or streets causing facial or eye injuries to pedestrians and hazards for motorists. |
| Shallow Roots | Willow, red maple, silver maple, beech, cottonwood, poplar varieties | Surface root systems can cause walks to heave and break apart, and pedestrians may trip and fall. Uneven or broken surfaces can be extremely difficult for small-wheeled vehicles. |
| Odor | Siebold viburnum, female ginkgo, Mimosa | Foul-smelling odors not only degrade the aesthetic appeal of an area but also tend to make some people nauseous. |

➤ continued on next page

TECHNIQUES

*Planting* ▪ 227

## TABLE 12.2. Hazardous and noxious plant species (continued).

| Hazard/nuisance | Species | Comments |
|---|---|---|
| *Thorns and spikes* | Barberry, quince, hawthorne, locust, holly, rose varieties, privet | Plants with thorns or spikes can be painful and dangerous to brush against or fall into. Leaves, twigs, and branches that fall to the ground can also be hazardous to people in light footwear or walking bare foot. |
| *Insects and pests* | Fruit trees (crab apple, cherry, plum, etc.), mountain laurel | Because of the severe reaction certain people have to insect bites and stings, the use of plant materials which attract these pests are not recommended for areas near walks and seating. |

Source: Gary Robinette, ed., *Barrier Free Site Design*, Van Nostrand Reinhold, New York, 1985.

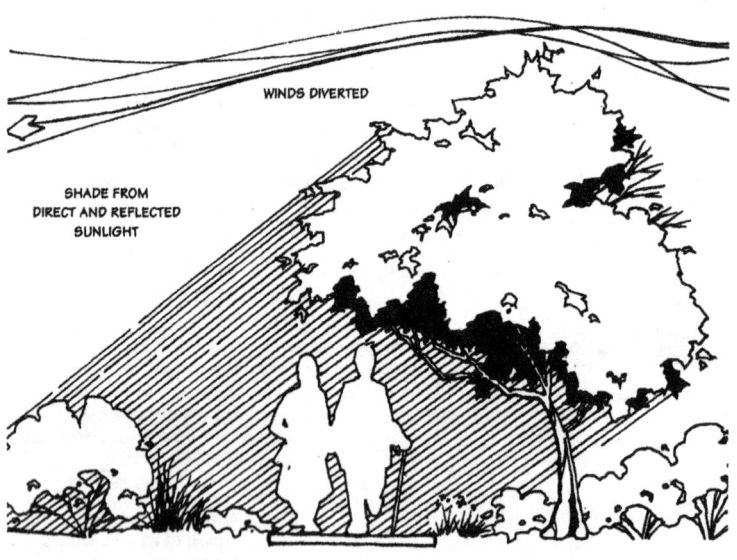

**Figure 12.3. Potential impact of vegetation on microclimate.**

DENSE UNDERGROWTH

EARTH BERM

**Figure 12.4. Noise buffer for easier outdoor conversation.**

## Bioengineering

The natural regenerative tendency of plant material can be used to stabilize eroded banks, revitalize damaged soils, or strengthen wildlife habitats. Plants that are well-suited to these techniques are generally native successional plants that can tolerate moist conditions, have the ability to root quickly from stem nodes, can spread vegetatively and form strong root systems when established. Figure 12.5 shows an example of bioengineering practices used to stabilize a steep slope.

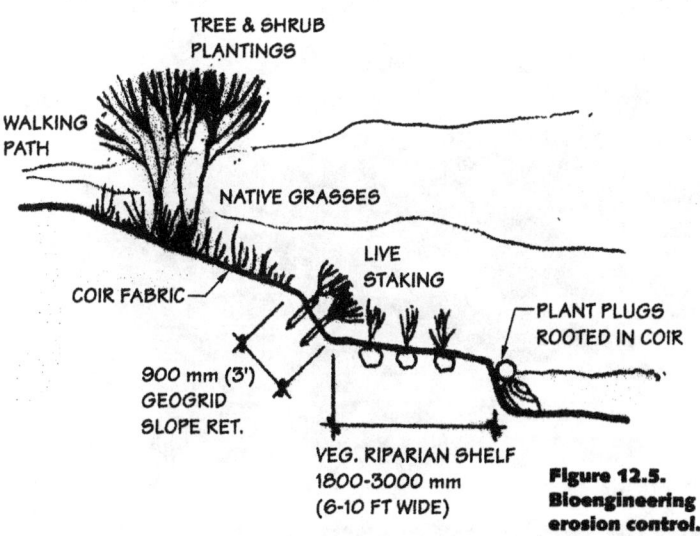

TREE & SHRUB PLANTINGS

WALKING PATH

NATIVE GRASSES

LIVE STAKING

COIR FABRIC

PLANT PLUGS ROOTED IN COIR

900 mm (3') GEOGRID SLOPE RET.

VEG. RIPARIAN SHELF 1800-3000 mm (6-10 FT WIDE)

**Figure 12.5. Bioengineering erosion control.**

*Planting* ▪ 229

# PLANTING CONDITIONS

## Planting Requirements

### Plant Hardiness

Within the United States, the hardiness rating of a given plant material can be checked against the zones for hardiness established by the USDA as shown in Figure 12.6. However, regional hardiness does not guarantee survival if plants are located in inappropriate microclimatic conditions (e.g. shade loving plants located in full sun).

### Soil Characteristics

Soil pH is largely determined by underlying material and the pH level of available water. Choose plants that are adapted to site conditions rather than trying to alter the pH of the soil through amendments. Some planting locations are exposed to seasonal salting by snow removal equipment. Table 12.3 lists a variety of salt tolerant plants. The Natural Resources Conservation Service (NRCS), is responsible for publishing soils data for the United States.

### Precipitation

Appropriate plants are not necessarily constant low-water users. An appropriate plant is one whose growth cycle is well adapted to the specific seasonal pattern of the climate in which it is planted, which may include short periods of intense drought or rain. Plants native to a region will be the best adapted and will be able to survive seasonal extremes.

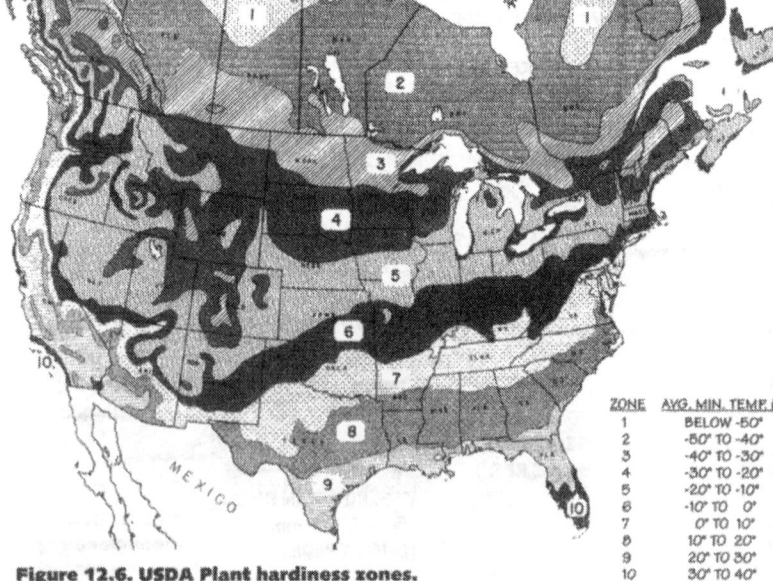

| ZONE | AVG. MIN. TEMP. (F) |
| --- | --- |
| 1 | BELOW -50° |
| 2 | -50° TO -40° |
| 3 | -40° TO -30° |
| 4 | -30° TO -20° |
| 5 | -20° TO -10° |
| 6 | -10° TO 0° |
| 7 | 0° TO 10° |
| 8 | 10° TO 20° |
| 9 | 20° TO 30° |
| 10 | 30° TO 40° |

**Figure 12.6. USDA Plant hardiness zones.**

# How to Plant a Tree

*Note: Tree planting techniques are subject to regional variability.*

**STEP 1.** Ideally planting in the spring or fall, begin with a healthy tree that has no signs of insects or disease, has a strong trunk, and is not root-bound. Choose a site that is large enough for the tree to grow to maturity. Soils that are compacted need to be aerated over the entire area to a minimum depth of 18 inches.

**STEP 2.** Dig a hole that is no deeper than the root ball and at least 3 times as wide (preferably 5 times as wide). This increases root aeration and may greatly increase the lifespan and health of the plant. Place the removed soil aside and use it to backfill the hole.

**STEP 3.** Test the hole for adequate drainage by filling the hole with water. The water should drain out overnight or at least 12 mm (½ in) per hour. If not, find another place, with better drainage or install a drain. Plant only where soils drain and water does not stand during the wet season.

**STEP 4.** Remove non-biodegradable nursery wrappings (i.e. plastic or wire) and unwrap burlap from the top ⅓ of the rootball. Place the tree on undisturbed soil. The top of the rootball should be at grade or slightly above (max 50 mm (2 in)) to keep water, disease, and rot away from the root crown. If the tree has been grafted, face the graft scar away from the direct sun.

**STEP 5.** Backfill soil should be added in alternating layers with water used to help settle the soil. Take care not to tamp or otherwise compact the soil after watering the plant or the soil structure will be damaged. Soil amendments such as compost, peat, and sand have not been show to offer any consistent advantage and may actually inhibit the root penetration of surrounding soil.

**STEP 6.** Cover the prepared area with 75 to 100 mm (3 to 4 in) of coarse, organic mulch (not rocks) directly over the bare soil. (Note: Sheet plastic placed beneath the mulch will kill the tree roots). Mulching will reduce weeds, conserve moisture, and help maintain an even soil temperature. Keep the mulch 6 inches from the tree trunk base.

**STEP 7.** Prune only to correct major form problems, such as branches that may be rubbing.

**STEP 8.** Stake or guy-wire only in conditions of extreme wind. Check ties often to prevent strangulation or bark damage. Remove the stakes after the first growing season. Do not wrap tree trunks. Tree wrapping shelters insect infestations and holds moisture around the bark where fungus or disease may grow.

TECHNIQUES

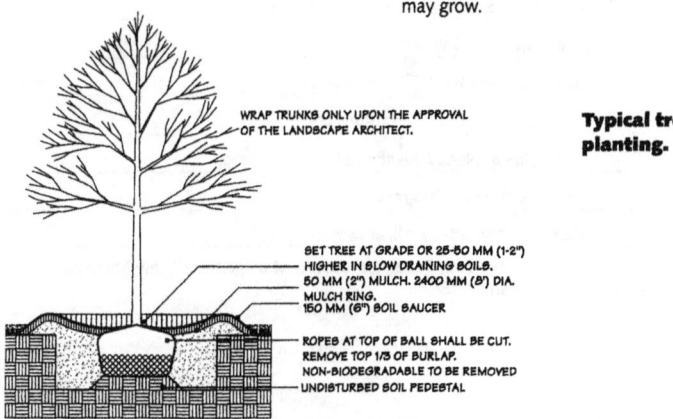

WRAP TRUNKS ONLY UPON THE APPROVAL OF THE LANDSCAPE ARCHITECT.

**Typical tree planting.**

SET TREE AT GRADE OR 25-50 MM (1-2")
HIGHER IN SLOW DRAINING SOILS.
50 MM (2") MULCH. 2400 MM (8') DIA.
MULCH RING.
150 MM (6") SOIL SAUCER

ROPES AT TOP OF BALL SHALL BE CUT.
REMOVE TOP 1/3 OF BURLAP.
NON-BIODEGRADABLE TO BE REMOVED
UNDISTURBED SOIL PEDESTAL

## TABLE 12.3. Salt tolerant plants.

| | Botanical Name / Common Name | |
|---|---|---|
| | **Trees** | **Shrubs** |
| *Moderate Tolerance* | Acer negundo / Box elder<br>Betula populifolia / Gray birch<br>Celtis occidentalis / Hackberry<br>Fraxinus excelsior / European ash<br>F. quadrangulata / Blue ash<br>Juniperus scopulorum / Juniper<br>J. virginiana / Eastern red cedar<br>Koelreuteria paniculata /<br>  Goldenrain tree<br>Maclura pomifera / Osage orange<br>Robinia pseudoacacia / Black locust<br>Sophora japonica /<br>  Japanese pagoda tree,<br>Chinese scholar tree<br>Ulmus pumila / Siberian elm | Caragana arborescens /<br>  Siberian pea shrub<br>Elaeagnus commutata/<br>  Silverberry<br>E. multiflora / Cherry elaeagnus<br>Juniperus chinensis / 'Pfitzerana'<br>J. conferta /<br>  Japanese shore juniper<br>Lonicera tatarica /<br>  Tatarian honeysuckle<br>Rhamnus frangula /<br>  Glossy buckthorn<br>Spiraea vanhouttei /<br>  Vanhoutte spirea |
| *High Tolerance* | Ailanthus altissima / Tree-of-heaven<br>Amelanchier canadensis /<br>  Shadblow serviceberry<br>Crataegus crus galli /<br>  Cockspur hawthorn<br>Elaeagnus angustifolia / Russian olive<br>Pinus thunbergii / Japanese black pine<br>Ptelea trifoliata / Wafer ash<br>Thuja occidentalis /<br>  American arborvitae | Atriplex canescens /<br>  Four-wing saltbush<br>Baccharis halimifolia / Groundsel<br>Cytisus scoparius / Scotch broom<br>Halimodendron /<br>  Salt tree halodendron<br>Hippophae rhamnoides /<br>  Sea buckthorn<br>Myrica pensylvanica / Bayberry<br>Rhamnus cathartica /<br>  Common buckthorn<br>Rosa rugosa / Rugosa rose<br>Shepherdia canadensis /<br>  Buffaloberry<br>Tamarix gallica / Tamarisk<br>T. parviflora |

**Grasses (ranked lowest tolerance to highest tolerance)**

Agrostis palustris / Creeping bentgrass

Agropyron Smithii / Western wheatgrass

A. elongatum / Tall wheatgrass

Elymus canadensis / Canada wildrye

Cynodon dactylon / Bermudagrass

Puccinellia airoides / Alkaligrass

Distichlis stricta / Saltgrass

Sporobolus airoides / Alkali sacaton

Source: Dr. James Feucht and Jack Butler, *Landscape Management* (New York: Van Nostrand Reinhold Company, 1988)

# Plant Mortality

Extreme heat, soil that has been compacted or contaminated with construction fill, and injury from mowers or vehicles are just a few of the challenges for the health of plant material. Table 12.4 lists common causes of plant mortality and suggests some remedies.

**TABLE 12.4. Causes of tree mortality and remedies.**

| Causes | Remedies |
|---|---|
| Soil compaction | Provide large areas of rooting space wherever possible through tree strip trenches rather than pits |
| Sterile or toxic soils | Test soils frequently. Urban soils are by definition highly disturbed, and conditions can vary widely within a small area. Options for dealing with this problem range from replacing soils entirely (i.e. on a large enough scale to provide enough root space horizontally) to planting trees that will tolerate the true conditions of the site. This may mean using "weed" trees. |
| Over-irrigation | Timer irrigation systems frequently do not respond to the real conditions at the roots of a tree. Many trees drown in their pits due to excess water combined with poor drainage. Use timer systems only where absolutely necessary and provide as much drainage as possible. |
| Repeated wounding from trees, maintenance vehicles, vandals | There is no good solution to this type of problem, but damage can be reduced by understanding the zones in which regular activity is likely to occur. Low-branching trees should not be planted right next to the curb or street edge. All street trees need to be located to avoid being whacked by car doors or providing an obstacle to passengers trying to disembark. Studying the needs of the community and involving them in the design process is always a good practice, and can frequently reduce the amount of vandalism trees must endure. |
| Insufficient air space around roots | A side effect of compaction. Structural soils or structural slabs may provide adequate protection in urban conditions. Perforated plastic vent tubes may provide additional air to the root zone. |
| Neglect, failure to remove lines or wraps causing girdling of bark or roots | The best solution to this problem is to avoid using techniques that will require a single visit or unique maintenance after the contractor has left the site. Staking, guying and trunk wrapping should be avoided whenever possible. Consider the maintenance budget when designing, or find some way to make long-term maintenance part of the contract. |

Source: Henry F. Arnold, adapted from *Trees and Urban Design*, 1980

TECHNIQUES

# SUGGESTED REFERENCES

American Association of Nurserymen, *American Standard for Nursery Stock*, Washington, DC.

Bailer, Liberty Hyde, and Ethel Zoe. *Hortus Third*, MacMillan: New York, 1976.

Dines, Nicholas T. and Kyle D. Brown, *Time-Saver Standards Site Construction Details Manual*, McGraw-Hill, New York, 1999.

Dirr, Michael. *Dirr's Hardy Trees and Shrubs, An Illustrated Encyclopedia*, Timber Press, 1997.

Dirr, Michael. *Manual of Woody Landscape Plants*, 4th ed., Stipes Publishing: Champaign, IL, 1990.

Harris, Charles W. and Nicholas T. Dines, *Time-Saver Standards for Landscape Architecture, 2nd Edition*, McGraw-Hill, New York, 1998.

Walker, Theodore D. *Planting Design*, 2nd ed., Van Nostrand Reinhold: New York, 1991.

Wyman, Donald. *Wyman's Gardening Encyclopedia*, 2nd ed., MacMillan: New York, 1986.

STANDARDS

TECHNIQUES

DEVICES

ADMINISTRATION

# Earth Retaining Structures

# 13

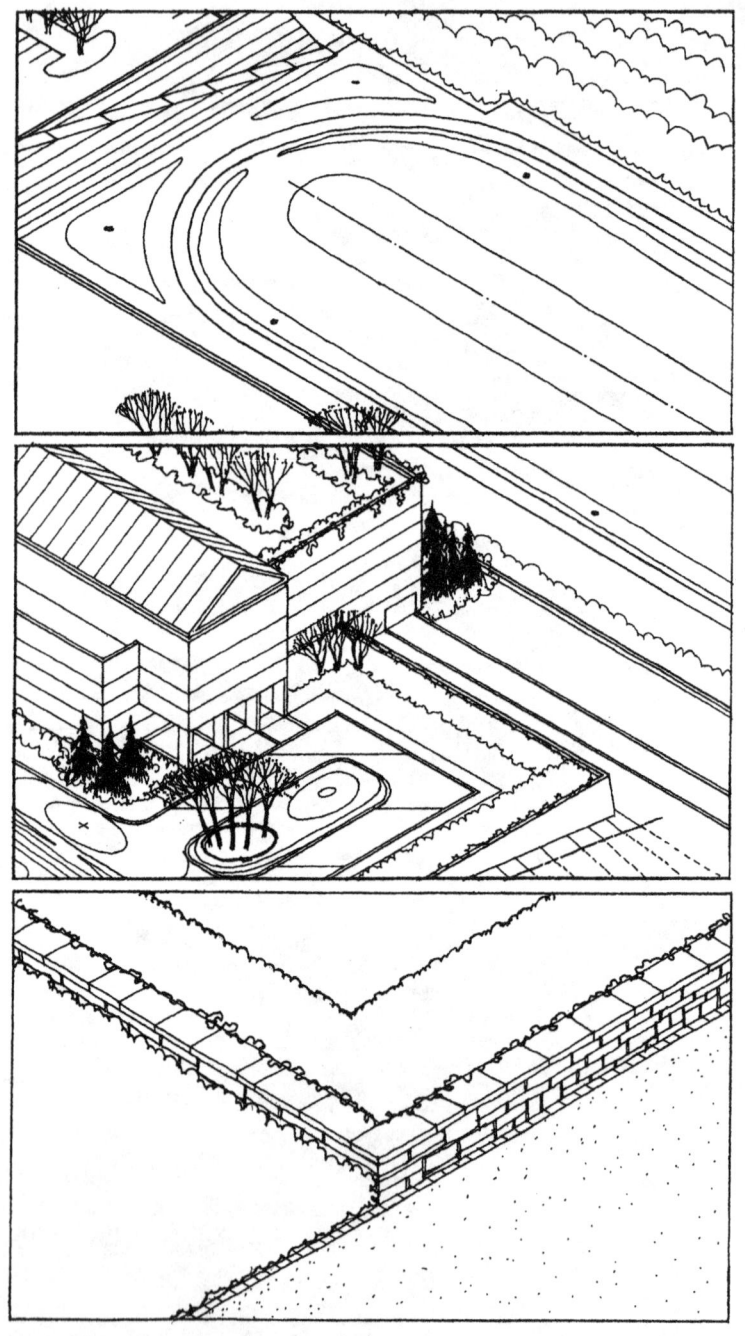

# REINFORCED EMBANKMENT STRUCTURES

Engineered embankments typically slope at a rate no greater than 1:1.5. Steeper slopes should be terraced to ensure long-term stability. Slopes are reinforced with fibrous rooted vegetation, fabrics and meshes, unit masonry, or stone. Key concepts include check swales at the top of slope to prevent surface erosion and swales, subdrains, or inlets at the base of slopes to prevent saturation of the slope foundation, particularly in expansive soils. Embankments are used where space permits, when budgets prevent other options, or when aesthetics are preferred.

# LARGE ARCHITECTURAL WALL STRUCTURES

Major grade transitions ranging from 3-5 meters (10-15 ft) typically employ rigid, segmental, or stack wall systems, when associated with architectural structures requiring precise joinery, or when additional land surface areas are required for use. Systems include rigid concrete walls, fabric reinforced segmental retaining walls, and mortared stone walls. Walls associated with roads, and service areas may include cribbing, and stone filled wire baskets. Larger wall systems typically require footings in cold regions.

DEVICES

# SMALL HUMAN SCALE TRANSITION WALL STRUCTURES

Small walls range from 0.5 -3 meters (2-10 ft) and are often constructed of concrete, masonry stack units, stone, or treated wood timbers. Rigid walls require footings below frost depth in cold climates, but unit walls are often constructed on simple aggregate bases directly on subsoil. Choice of materials is typically governed by proposed use (e. g. seatwall), cost, and aesthetics. Treated wood should not be used for larger walls, especially in expansive soils, or in damp temperate climates due to limited longevity.

ARTH RETAINING STRUCTURES ARE USED WHEN abrupt grade changes are required which exceed the natural angle of repose for the soil (typically 33°-37°). These structures include retaining walls and reinforced embankment structures. Their selection and design is a function of intended use, as well as subgrade conditions of the site. Soil and climate characteristics, such as permeability, bearing capacity, shrink-swell, and frost-thaw cycles, are critical design determinants. A designer must understand these characteristics and fundamental mechanics, in order to appropriately design retaining structures.

## DIAGNOSTIC ASSESSMENT

*What are the subgrade conditions of the site?*

The stability of the soil is the primary indicator of whether or not a retaining structure is indicated. The bearing capacity and friction coefficient of the foundation must be determined, to ensure that the proposed structure will not fail from sliding or excess settlement as a result of the pressure supplied by the structure and the retained soil. In addition, the moisture content of the soil determines appropriate drainage strategies and design specifications.

*What type of retaining structure is appropriate for the site and its proposed use?*

A wide variety of retaining structures are available, including reinforced embankments, segmental and stack wall systems, and rigid retaining walls. Selection of an appropriate structure is a function of application, aesthetics, cost, maintenance desired life expectancy, and access limitations during construction due to tight space or mature vegetation.

*What are the design specifications for the proposed structure?*

Retaining structures must be designed to support the weight of retained soil, while preventing overturning, settlement or crushing at the toe of the structure, and horizontal sliding. Many computer programs and manufacturer design charts are available for assisting in the design of these structures, but an understanding of the fundamentals of these calculations is important to ensure quality design.

*What strategies are appropriate for drainage that preserves the integrity of the retaining structure?*

Care must be taken to maintain proper functioning of the retaining structure over the long term, particularly in situations where property or human life is at risk. Proper drainage, particularly in climates subject to freezing and thawing, is the most important factor in preserving the integrity of earth retaining systems.

# SUBGRADE CONDITIONS

## Weight of Soil

The weight of soil that exceeds the angle of repose contributes to the lateral pressure exerted on a retaining structure. Soil weight is highly variable and is a function of density and moisture content. Typically, a design force of 13 to 17 kN (100 to 110 lbs/ft$^3$) is used for preliminary design calculations, although some jurisdictions may establish stricter guidelines.

## Bearing Capacity

Table 13.1 lists the approximate bearing capacities of various subgrade conditions. Hard bedrock and coarse gravel soils provide the greatest strength, while fine clays provide the least strength.

**TABLE 13.1. Approximate bearing capacities of various soils and rock.** *

| Material | t/m² | kg/m² | Ton/ft² | lb/ft² |
|---|---|---|---|---|
| Alluvial soil | 4.5 | 4500 | ½ | 1,000 |
| Soft clay | 9.5 | 9500 | 1 | 2,000 |
| Firm clay | 19.5 | 4000 | 2 | 4,000 |
| Wet sand | 19.5 | 19 000 | 2 | 4,000 |
| Sand and clay mixed | 19.5 | 19 000 | 2 | 4,000 |
| Fine dry sand | 29.0 | 29 000 | 3 | 6,000 |
| Hard clay | 39.0 | 38 500 | 4 | 8,000 |
| Coarse dry sand | 39.0 | 38 500 | 4 | 8,000 |
| Gravel | 58.5 | 58 000 | 6 | 12,000 |
| Gravel and sand (well-cemented) | 78.0 | 77 500 | 8 | 16,000 |
| Hard pan or hard shale | 97.5 | 97 000 | 10 | 20,000 |
| Medium rock | 195.0 | 194 500 | 20 | 40,000 |
| Hard rock | 780.0 | 779 000 | 80 | 160,000 |

* Tons = U.S. short tons (2000 lb), t = metric tons.

Source: Adapted from Albe E. Munson, *Construction Design for Landscape Architects*, McGraw-Hill, New York, 1975.

## TABLE 13.2. Average coefficients of friction for concrete on various foundation beds.

| Foundation bed | Coefficient of friction |
|---|---|
| Rock (moderate) | 0.7 |
| Rock (hard angular) | 1.0 |
| Gravel | 0.6 |
| Dry clay | 0.5 |
| Sand | 0.4 |
| Wet clay | 0.3 |

*Source: Adapted from Albe E. Munson, Construction Design for Landscape Architects, McGraw-Hill New York, 1975.*

## Friction Coefficient

Table 13.2 lists the coefficient of friction for concrete on various subgrades. Rock foundations provide the greatest resistance to sliding, while wet clay provides the least resistance, and may require a key on the bottom of the footing to prevent wall failure.

## Moisture Content

Clays and highly organic soils are problematic as foundations and backfill because of swelling and shrinkage associated with moisture fluctuations. Design strategies typically focus on stabilizing moisture content by removing expansive material, replace it with non-swelling soil or aggregate, and providing subdrains or other de-watering techniques (Figure 13.1) .

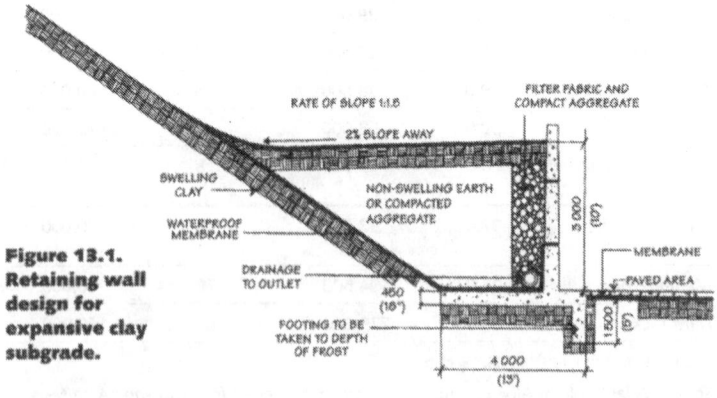

**Figure 13.1. Retaining wall design for expansive clay subgrade.**

## Frost Depth

Figure 13.2 shows average frost depths across the United States. Foundations for rigid retaining structures should extend below frost depths. Flexible structures may be set directly on subsoil above the local frost depth, if constructed on well-drained subgrade with suitable bearing capacity.

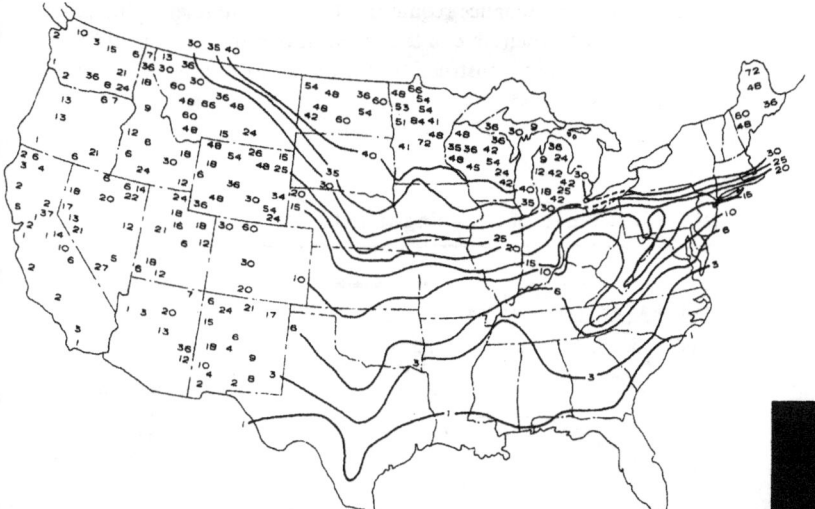

**Figure 13.2. Average frost depth in the United States (in inches)**

## Seismic Conditions

Earthquakes typically result in increased lateral pressures acting on retaining structures. Depending on use and site conditions, a design approach based on permissible displacement of the structure within acceptable limits may be used. In areas susceptible to seismic activity, a geotechnical report should be prepared by a licensed engineer to assess potential consequences of any liquefaction and soil strength loss, including estimation of differential settlement, lateral movement or reduction in foundation soil-bearing capacity. Mitigation measures may include ground stabilization, selection of appropriate foundation type and depths, selection of appropriate structural systems to accommodate anticipated displacements, or any combination of these measures.

# TYPES OF RETAINING STRUCTURES

Table 13.3 describes the common types of retaining structures available. Generally, retaining structures can be classified as reinforced embankments, segmental and stack wall systems, and rigid retaining walls.

- Reinforced embankments are used to stabilize steep slopes. They are typically less expensive to install than other retaining structures, but require greater land area and higher levels of maintenance.

- Segmental and stack wall systems tend to have moderate installation costs and maintenance requirements. They will tolerate limited differential settlement due to their flexible construction. In addition to dry-laid masonry construction, a wide variety of proprietary systems are available.

**TABLE 13.3. Types of retaining structures.**

| Type | Application | Design Standards | Maintenance |
|------|-------------|------------------|-------------|
| **REINFORCED EMBANKMENTS** | | | |
| Turf (fiber mat, sod or seed) | Stabilize cut/fill | 1:2 max. slope; avoid sheet runoff; use check swale at top. | May require irrigation; 1:3 max. slopes preferred for mowing |
| Rip-Rap Stone | Stabilize highly erodible banks | 1:1.5 max. slope; place on aggregate subbase; use check swales at top. | Periodic patching and debris removal |
| Placed Stone or Masonry | Stabilize short slopes with high-quality finish | 1:1.5 max. slope; see Figure 13.3 for design detail. | Periodic weeding and edge repair |
| Cast Concrete | Stabilize steep short slopes (warm climates) | 1:1 max. slope; place on aggregate subbase; provide footing at base of slope; minimize moisture penetration by sealing joints; provide weep holes in wet climates | Very low |

| Type | Application | Design Standards | Maintenance |
|---|---|---|---|
| Root Reinforcement | Stabilize banks in natural settings (wet climates) | 1:1.5 max. slope; fibrous rooted shrub striplings in layers of logs or jute rolls. 1:1.5 max. slope; fibrous rooted shrub striplings in layers of logs or jute rolls. | Periodic trimming to stimulate roots |

**SEGMENTED AND STACK WALL SYSTEMS**

| Type | Application | Design Standards | Maintenance |
|---|---|---|---|
| Dry Laid Stone | Low walls | 3000 mm (10') max. height; place foundation on aggregate base; use aggregate backfill; min. 450 mm (20") width at top of wall; stabilize top courses with recessed mortar | Periodic resetting of stones, particularly along top of wall |
| Gabions | Utilitarian walls; may be hydroseeded or designed to encourage volunteer vegetative growth on wall face | Wire gabions together for strength; provide staggered face or 6° batter for tall walls; place foundation on aggregate base; use aggregate backfill | Periodic inspection and repair of wire fabric; repair top dressing |
| Segmental Retaining Walls(SRW) | Modular systems allow for inexpensive design of short to high walls, from residential to institutional use; easily adaptable to curvilinear alignments | Wide variety of unit options; 3-6° batter for split face masonry units, vertical face for heavy precast "T" type; lateral fabric reinforcement may be required; see Figure 13.4 for design detail of common units | Split face masonry may be susceptible to salt spray and other corrosions |
| Cribbing and Bins | High utilitarian walls; may incorporate vegetative growth on wall face | Typically 3-6° batter; place foundation on aggregate base; use aggregate as fill for cribs/bins, as well as backfill; footing drain may be required; see Figure 13.5 for design detail of concrete crib wall. | Periodic inspection and top dressing |

**RIGID RETAINING WALLS**

| Type | Application | Design Standards | Maintenance |
|---|---|---|---|
| Gravity | Low to moderate walls with high quality finish; typically non-surcharged walls | 3000 mm (10') max. height; place foundation on prepared subgrade, unless prevented by clay soil conditions; provide footing drains and weep holes; see Figure 13.6 for design detail | Periodic grading at top of wall to maintain positive drainage |
| Cantilevered | Moderate to high walls with high quality finish | Place foundation on prepared subgrade, unless prevented by clay soil conditions; provide footing drains and weep holes; see Figure 13.7 for design detail | Periodic grading at top of wall to maintain positive drainage |

DEVICES

*Earth Retaining Structures* ▪ 245

- Rigid retaining walls are concrete structures that are suitable for applications where no differential movement of the structure can be tolerated. These walls are the most expensive to install, but also provide the greatest life span.
- Figures 13.3 through 13.7 illustrate the design of typical retaining structures.

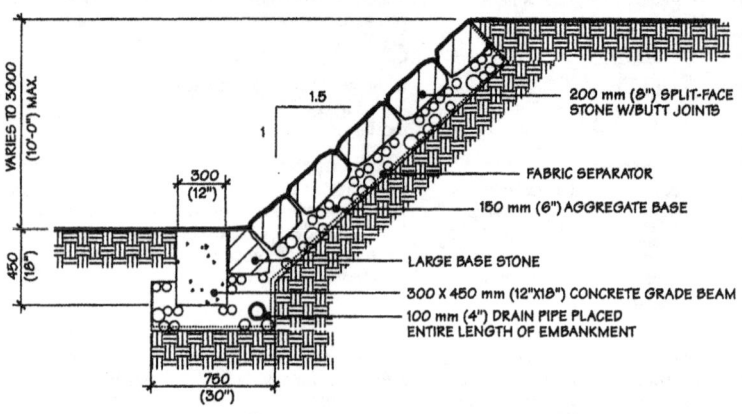

**Figure 13.3. Typical reinforced embankment with placed stone.**

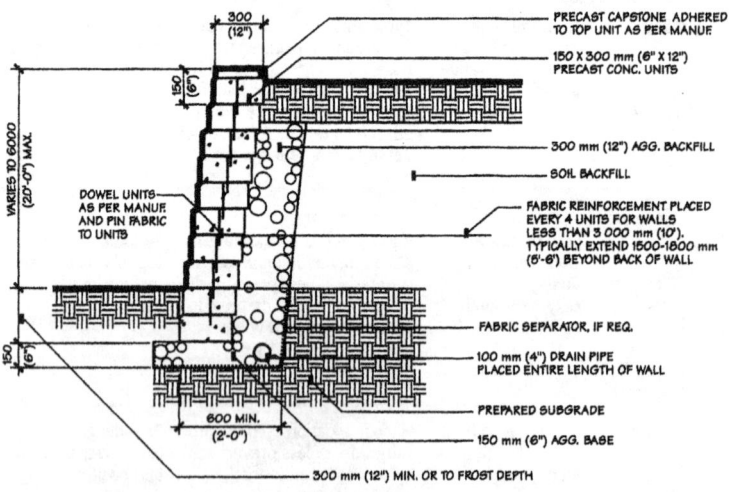

**Figure 13.4. Typical segmental retaining wall (SRW).**

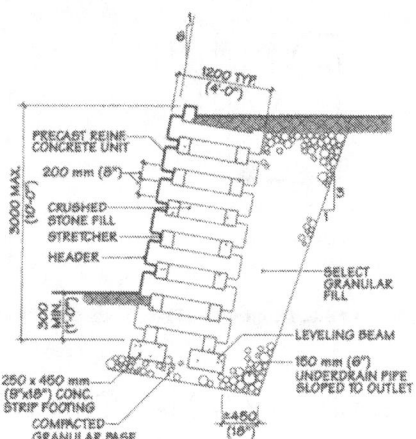

**Figure 13.5. Typical concrete crib wall.**

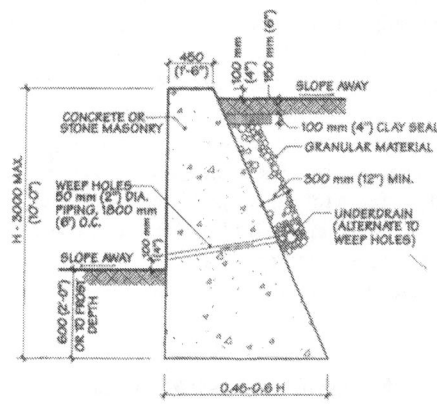

**Figure 13.6. Typical rigid gravity wall.**

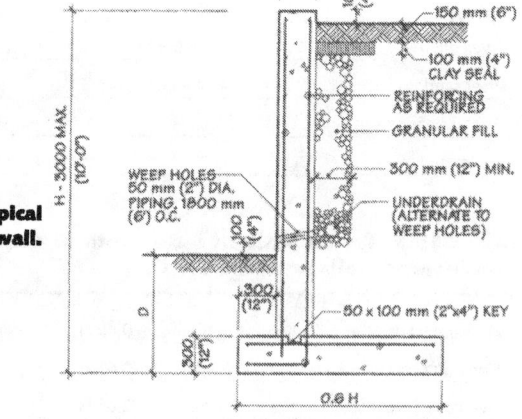

**Figure 13.7. Typical rigid cantilevered wall.**

DEVICES

*Earth Retaining Structures* ▪ 247

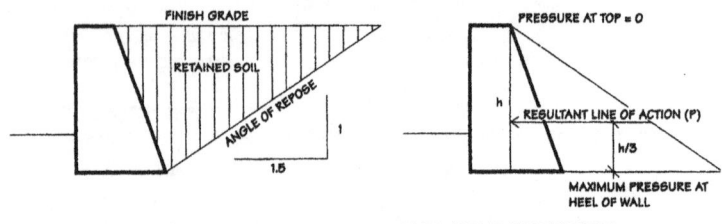

**Figure 13.8. Diagrams of retained soil mass and soil pressure forces.**

# MECHANICS AND DESIGN CALCULATIONS

Figure 13.8 diagrams the forces acting on a typical retaining structure. All retaining structures must be designed to withstand these forces, while preventing overturning, settlement at the toe of the structure, and horizontal sliding. For preliminary design purposes, Tables 13.4 and 13.5 list typical base to height ratios for gravity and cantilevered walls. Many computer programs and manufacturer design charts are available for assisting in the final design calculations of these structures. These programs and charts are based on similar fundamental formulas for calculating lateral and resultant force, as well as testing for stability. Table 13.6 illustrates design calculations using these formulas for a non-surcharged gravity wall in US units. Table 13.7 illustrates calculations for a surcharged cantilevered wall in SI units.

**TABLE 13.4. Recommended base width to height ratios for rigid gravity walls.**

| Soil Type | Ratio | Application |
|---|---|---|
| Well drained gravel | 0.35-0.40 H | Light Duty |
| Wet sand | 0.58-0.60 H | Medium Duty |
| Water bearing soil | 0.65 H | Heavy Duty |
| Fluid mud | 0.75 H | Heavy Dudy |

**TABLE 13.5. Typical ratio of base width to height in cantilevered walls (average soils).**

| | |
|---|---|
| Horizontal Loading | 0.45 H |
| Slope Surcharge Loading | 0.65 H |
| Live Load Surcharge | 0.65 H |

# DRAINAGE

Maintaining positive drainage of the retaining structure's backfill and foundation is essential to long-term performance. Drainage strategies should work to minimize infiltration of water and facilitate the quick removal of water from these areas, particularly in expansive soils, and frost-thaw conditions.

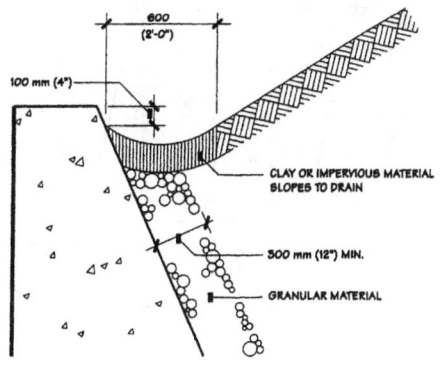

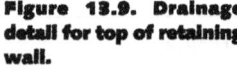

**Figure 13.9. Drainage detail for top of retaining wall.**

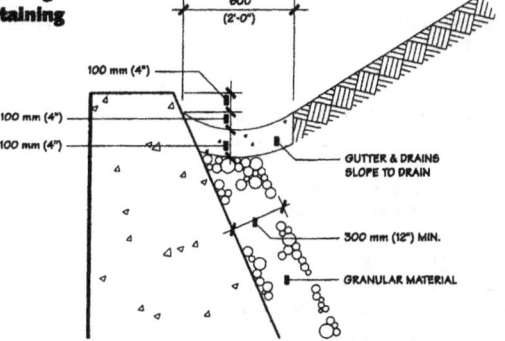

## Surface Runoff

All surface water should be directed away from the top of embankments to avoid slope erosion, and tops of retaining structures to avoid infiltration into the backfill or subgrade. Clay seals or concrete gutters may be used to protect the tops of structures (Figure 13.9) .

## Backfill and Footing Drains

Granular backfill is typically used for retaining structures. Fabric separators are placed between the backfill and subsoil to prevent infiltration of fines. Perforated footing drains may also be used in fine soils subject to infiltration from capillary action and seasonal water table shifts.

*Earth Retaining Structures* ▪ 249

## TABLE 13.6. Sample design calculations for non-surcharged gravity wall (US units).

Concrete gravity wall placed on a sandy-clay foundation

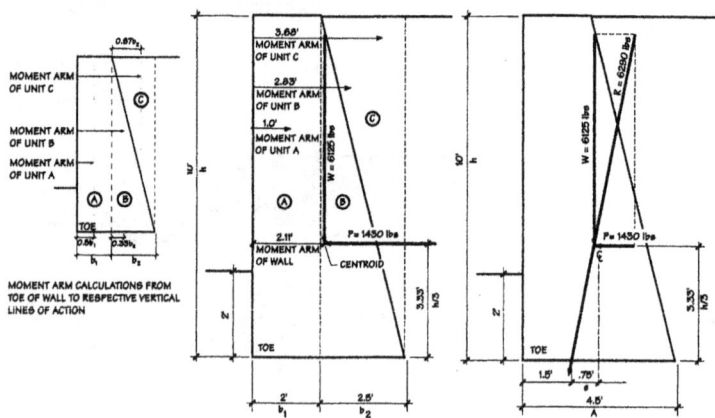

| Procedure | Calculations[a] |
|---|---|
| **DETERMINING LATERAL FORCE (P)** | |
| 1. Calculate pressure of retained soil, acting at h/3 (P): $$P = 0.286 \times \frac{wh^2}{2}$$ | $$P = 0.286 \times \frac{(100)10^2}{2}$$ $$P = 1{,}430 \text{ lbs}$$ |
| **DETERMINING WALL WEIGHT (W)** | |
| 2. Calculate weight of section unit A: ($b_1 \times H \times$ weight of concrete) | $2 \times 10 \times 150 = 3{,}000$ lbs |
| 3. Calculate weight of section unit B: $[0.5(b_2 \times H) \times$ weight of concrete] | $0.5(2.5 \times 10) \times 150 = 1{,}875$ lbs |
| 4. Calculate weight of section unit C: $[0.5(b_2 \times H) \times$ weight of soil] | $0.5(2.5 \times 10) \times 100 = 1{,}250$ lbs |
| 5. Add weights of units A, B & C. This equals the total weight of the wall's cross-section (W) | $3000 + 1875 + 1250 = 6{,}125$ lbs |
| **DETERMINING THE CENTROID** | |
| 6. Calculate the moment arm of unit A from the toe of the wall. The distance of the vertical line of action from the toe in this rectangular section is found by: $(0.5)b_1$ | $(0.5)2 = 1$ ft |
| 7. Calculate the moment arm of unit B from the toe of the wall. The distance of the vertical line of action from the toe in this triangular section is found by: $(0.33)b_2 + b_1$ | $(0.33)2.5 + 2 = 2.83$ ft |
| 8. Calculate the moment arm of unit C from the toe of the wall. The distance of the vertical line of action from the toe in this triangular section is found by: $(0.67)b_2 + b_1$ | $(0.67)2.5 + 2 = 3.68$ ft |

| Procedure | Calculations* |
|---|---|
| 9. Calculate the moment of unit A: (weight x moment arm) | $3000 \times 1 = 3{,}000$ ft lbs |
| 10. Calculate the moment of unit B: (weight x moment arm) | $1875 \times 2.83 = 5{,}306$ ft lbs |
| 11. Calculate the moment of unit C: (weight x moment arm) | $1250 \times 3.68 = 4{,}600$ ft lbs |
| 12. Add moments of units A, B & C to yield the total moment of the wall's cross-section. | $3000 + 5306 + 4600 = 12{,}906$ ft lbs |
| 13. Calculate the moment arm of the wall's entire cross section:<br><br>$\dfrac{\text{Sum of Moments}}{\text{Sum of Weights}}$ | $\dfrac{12906}{6125} = 2.11$ ft |

## DETERMINE THE RESULTANT FORCE (R)

| | |
|---|---|
| 14. Calculate resultant force of earth pressure and wall weight (R):<br>$R = (W^2 + P^2)^{0.5}$ | $(6125^2 + 1430^2)^{0.5} = 6{,}290$ lbs |
| 15. Graphically construct a parallelogram of forces and draw in the resultant (R). Extend diagonal until it intersects base of wall. If it passes within the middle ⅓ of the base, the wall is considered generally stable. The distance from the centerline of the wall base to the point where the resultant force cuts the base is the eccentricity (e). | The wall is generally stable (see figure)<br>$e = 0.75$ ft |

## TESTING FOR OVERTURNING

| | |
|---|---|
| 16. Divide the resisting moment by the overturning moment to check for tendency to overturn. A safety factor of 2 or more is acceptable.<br><br>$\dfrac{W \times \text{Moment Arm}}{P \times \text{Moment Arm}}$ | Resisting moment:<br>$6125 \times 2.11 = 12{,}924$ ft lbs<br>Overturning moment:<br>$1430 \times 3.33 = 4{,}762$ ft lbs<br>$\dfrac{12924}{4762} = 2.7$ Acceptable |

## TESTING FOR SETTLEMENT AT THE TOE (CRUSHING)

| | |
|---|---|
| 17. Test for Settlement:<br><br>$f = \dfrac{W}{\text{Area of base (A)}}\left(1 + \dfrac{6e}{\text{width of footing (d)}}\right)$<br><br>In the case of a wall test strip, $d = A$<br>Compare results with Table 13.1. | $f = \dfrac{6125}{4.5}\left(1 + \dfrac{6(0.75)}{4.5}\right)$<br><br>$f = 1361\,(2)$<br>$f = 2{,}722$ psf<br>Acceptable for sandy-clay foundation |

## TESTING FOR SLIDING

| | |
|---|---|
| 18. Calculate the tendency to slide. A safety factor of 1.5 or more is acceptable:<br><br>$\dfrac{W \times \text{Coefficent of Friction (Table 13.2)}}{P}$ | $\dfrac{6125(0.4)}{1430} = 1.7$<br><br>Acceptable for sandy foundation |

\* Assumes a 1 ft thick test strip for calculation

## TABLE 13.7. Sample design calculations for surcharged cantilevered wall (SI units).

Surcharged concrete cantilevered wall placed on a sandy-clay foundation

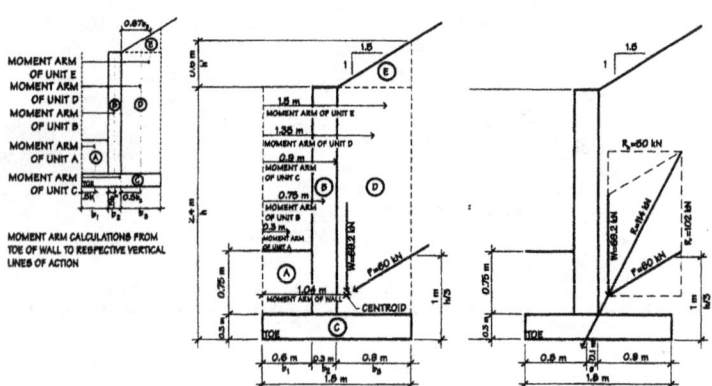

| Procedure | Calculations* |
|---|---|
| **DETERMINING LATERAL FORCE (P)** | |
| 1. Calculate pressure of retained soil, acting at (h+h')/3 (P): $$P = 0.833 \times \frac{w(h + h')^2}{2}$$ | $$P = 0.833 \times \frac{16(2.4 + 0.6)^2}{2}$$ $$P = 60 kN$$ |
| **DETERMINING WALL WEIGHT (W)** | |
| 2. Divide cross-section into series of rectangle and triangle-shaped units (A, B, C, D, E). | |
| 3. Calculate weight of section unit A: ($b_1 \times H \times$ weight of soil) | $0.6 \times 0.75 \times 16 = 7.2$ kN |
| 4. Calculate weight of section unit B: ($b_2 \times H \times$ weight of concrete) | $0.3 \times 2.1 \times 23.5 = 14.8$ kN |
| 5. Calculate weight of section unit C: $[(b_1+b_2+b_3) \times H \times$ weight of concrete] | $1.8 \times 0.3 \times 23.5 = 12.7$ kN |
| 6. Calculate weight of section unit D: ($b_3 \times H \times$ weight of soil) | $0.9 \times 2.1 \times 16 = 30.2$ kN |
| 7. Calculate weight of section unit E: $[0.5(b_3 \times H) \times$ weight of soil] | $0.5(0.9 \times 0.6) \times 16 = 4.3$ kN |
| 8. Add weights of all units. This equals the total weight of the wall's cross-section (W) | $7.2 + 14.8 + 12.7 + 30.2 + 4.3 = 69.2$ kN |

| Procedure | Calculations* |
|---|---|

## DETERMINING THE CENTROID

| Procedure | Calculations* |
|---|---|
| 9. Calculate the moment arm of unit A from the toe of the wall. The distance of the vertical line of action from the toe in this rectangular section is found by: <br> $(0.5)b_1$ | $(0.5)0.6 = 0.3$ m |
| 10. Calculate the moment arm of unit B from the toe of the wall. The distance of the vertical line of action from the toe in this rectangular section is found by: <br> $(0.5)b_2 + b_1$ | $(0.5)0.3 + 0.6 = 0.75$ m |
| 11. Calculate the moment arm of unit C from the toe of the wall. The distance of the vertical line of action from the toe in this rectangular section is found by: <br> $(0.5)$base of wall | $(0.5)1.8 = 0.9$ m |
| 12. Calculate the moment arm of unit D from the toe of the wall. The distance of the vertical line of action from the toe in this rectangular section is found by: <br> $(0.5)b_3 + b_2 + b_1$ | $(0.5)0.9 + 0.3 + 0.6 = 1.35$ m |
| 13. Calculate the moment arm of unit E from the toe of the wall. The distance of the vertical line of action from the toe in this triangular section is found by: <br> $(0.67)b_3 + b_2 + b_1$ | $(0.67)0.9 + 0.3 + 0.6 = 1.5$ m |
| 14. Calculate the moment of unit A: <br> (weight × moment arm) | $7.2 \times 0.3 = 2.2$ kN·m |
| 15. Calculate the moment of unit B: <br> (weight × moment arm) | $14.8 \times 0.75 = 11.1$ kN·m |
| 16. Calculate the moment of unit C: <br> (weight × moment arm) | $12.7 \times 0.9 = 11.4$ kN·m |
| 17. Calculate the moment of unit D: <br> (weight × moment arm) | $30.2 \times 1.35 = 40.8$ kN·m |
| 18. Calculate the moment of unit E: <br> (weight × moment arm) | $4.3 \times 1.5 = 6.5$ kN·m |
| 19. Add moments of all units to yield the total moment of the wall's cross-section. | $2.2 + 11.1 + 11.4 + 40.8 + 6.5 = 72$ kN·m |
| 20. Calculate the moment arm of the wall's entire cross section: <br> $\dfrac{\text{Sum of Moments}}{\text{Sum of Weights}}$ | $\dfrac{72}{69.2} = 1.04$ m |
| 21. Graphically construct a parallelogram of forces, extending P from the centroid in a line parallel to the slope of the surcharged soil (1:1.5 in example). Graphically determinethe vertical ($R_v$) and the horizontal ($R_h$) components of the constructed parallelogram of forces through scaling (see dashed lines in figure). | $R_v = 102$ kN <br> $R_h = 50$ kN |

➤ continued on next page

DEVICES

**TABLE 13.7. Sample design calculations for surcharged cantilevered wall (SI units) (continued).**

| Procedure | Calculations* |
|---|---|
| **DETERMINE THE RESULTANT FORCE (R)** | |
| 22. Draw in the resultant (R). Extend diagonal until it intersects base of wall. If it passes within the middle ⅓ of the base, the wall is considered generally stable. The distance from the centerline of the wall base to the point where the resultant force cuts the base is the eccentricity (e). | The wall is generally stable (see figure) $e = 0.1$ m |
| **TESTING FOR OVERTURNING** | |
| 23. Divide the resisting moment by the overturning moment to check for tendency to overturn. A safety factor of 2 or more is acceptable: $$\frac{R_v \times \text{Moment Arm}}{R_h \times \text{Moment Arm}}$$ | Resisting moment: $102 \times 1.04 = 106$ kN·m Overturning moment: $50 \times 1 = 50$ kN·m $$\frac{106}{50} = 2.1 \text{ Acceptable}$$ |
| **TESTING FOR SETTLEMENT AT THE TOE (CRUSHING)** | |
| 24. Test for Settlement: $$f = \frac{R_v}{\text{Area of Base (A)}}\left(1 + \frac{6e}{\text{width of footing (d)}}\right)$$ In the case of a wall test strip, d=A Compare results with Table 13.1 | $$f = \frac{102}{1.8}\left(1 + \frac{6(0.1)}{1.8}\right)$$ $f = 57(1.3)$ $f = 74.1$ kN or 7560 kg/m² Acceptable for sandy-clay foundation |
| **TESTING FOR SLIDING** | |
| 25. Calculate the tendency to slide. A safety factor of 1.5 or more is acceptable: $$\frac{R_v \times \text{Coefficient of Friction (Table 13.2)}}{R_h}$$ | $$\frac{102\,(0.4)}{50} = 0.8$$ Requires a shear key to prevent sliding |

\* Assumes a 1 m thick test strip for calculation

## Weep Holes

Weep holes are essential for most rigid wall construction to allow further opportunities for drainage of backfill. Spacing varies from 900 to 3000 mm (3-10 ft) depending on soil porosity (fine soils require closer spacing to relieve pressure).

# SUGGESTED REFERENCES

Harris, Charles W. and Nicholas T. Dines, *Time-Saver Standards for Landscape Architecture, 2nd Edition*, McGraw-Hill, New York, 1998.

Landphair, Harlow C. and Fred Klatt, *Landscape Architecture Construction*, Elsevier, New York, 1988.

Munson, Albe E, *Construction Design for Landscape Architects*, McGraw-Hill, New York, 1975.

Ramsey/Sleeper, *Architectural Graphic Standards*, 9th Ed., Wiley, New York, 1994.

DEVICES

# Paving

# 14

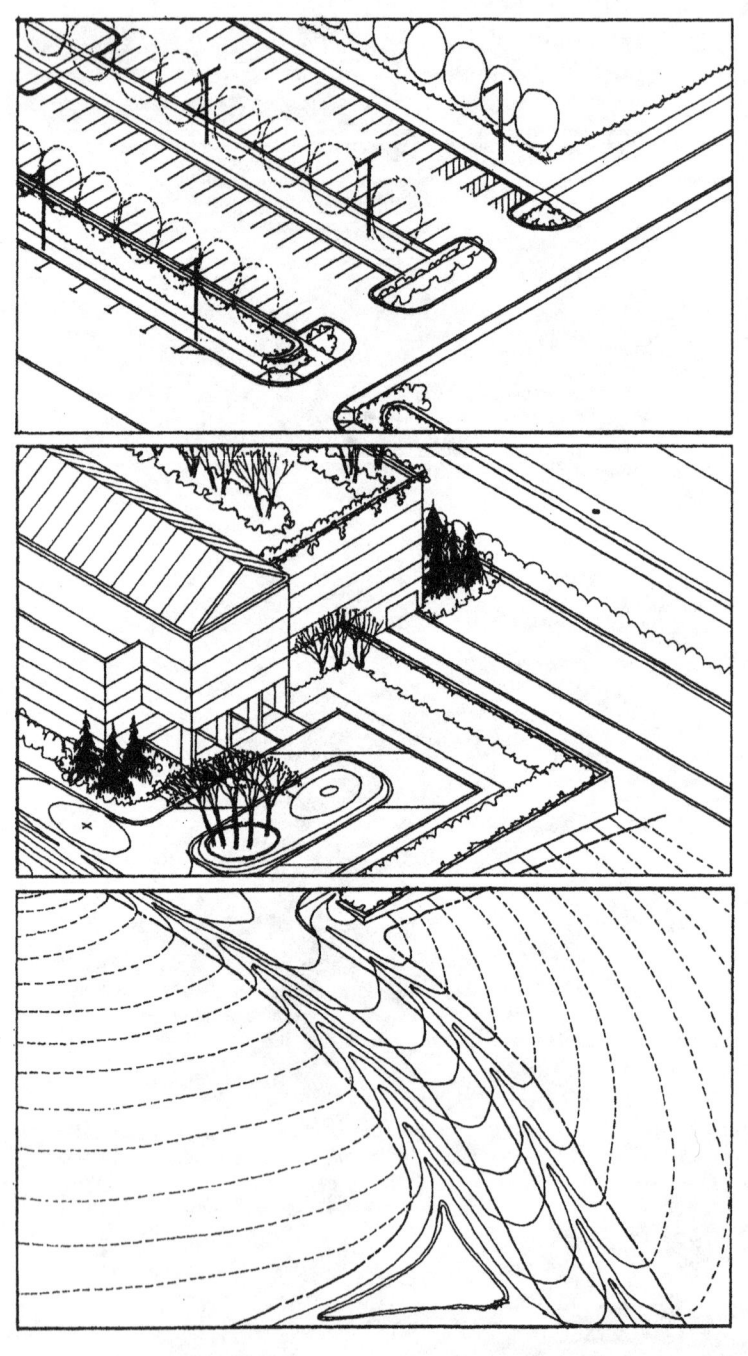

## LARGE CONTIGUOUS PAVEMENT SURFACE AREAS

These pavements include large parking lots, pedestrian plazas, athletic surfaces, and reinforced turf. Key objectives are to maintain uniform performance and to accommodate highly variable subgrades, climate extremes, and maintenance practices required by the regional climate conditions. Additionally, stormwater runoff typically requires periodic drain inlets to interrupt the surface, creating potentials for differential settlement and silting. Color, texture, reflectivity, and pattern choices are often limited by climate and use intensity factors. Costs are commonly lower per square unit due to scale economies and uniformity of construction.

## CONNECTIVE NODAL TRANSITION PAVEMENT AREAS

Pavements are commonly defined by vehicular and pedestrian transitions and often require separation by curbs, ramps, flush transition materials, or bollards. Key objectives in this area are pedestrian safety, aesthetic expression, and cultural appropriateness. Costs tend to be higher per square unit due to use intensity, variable edge and pattern conditions, and multipurpose loading requirements.

## LINEAR ROAD AND PATH PAVEMENTS

Roads and paths must safely accommodate vehicles, cyclists, and pedestrians. Linear pavements have unique design requirements including slope, velocity, and alignment factors. Pavement design must maintain uniform strength, consistant edge and joint conditions, and must shed stormwater runoff in a predictable manner. Costs tend to be more easily calculated due to the consistent cross section required and the common availability of installation equipment.

DEVICES

THE DESIGN OF PAVEMENTS for both pedestrian and vehicular applications requires knowledge of the intensity of intended use, the nature of the subsoil or substrate, the climate, and the short-term and the long-term budget allocation (installation and on-going maintenance costs). These factors, together with aesthetics and the cultural setting are typically combined to produce a particular pavement design recommendation. Extensive impermeable pavements may have negative effects on stormwater runoff quantity and quality. Project design should aim to minimize the use of pavements in general, and to substitute permeable pavements in areas where use, subsoil, and climate circumstances permit.

## DIAGNOSTIC ASSESSMENT

*What are the land use context and anticipated levels of service for the pavement?*

A pavement's level of service refers to its capacity to support heavy, medium, or light duty loading during sustained use. The land use context also indicates the cultural and aesthetic environment adjacent to the proposed pavement. These combined factors indicate the pavement bearing requirements and appropriate finishes, edge, and visual design details.

*What is the existing subgrade condition?*

The subgrade condition determines the soil's structural bearing capacity and indicates pavement and aggregate base thickness requirements. Colloidal (clay) soil requires special design details due to its potential for swelling and shrinking during uneven moisture conditions. Well-drained sands and aggregates provide superior subgrade conditions for pavements due to high bearing capacity and stability in varying moisture conditions.

*What are the regional climate characteristics?*

Extreme fluctuations in daily or annual temperature, frost-thaw cycles, precipitation rates and frequencies are key regional climate factors, which strongly affect both vehicular and pedestrian pavement design. Hot arid, hot humid, temperate, and cold climates possess specific limiting factors (color, porosity, flexibility, texture, thickness, etc.) that need to be accommodated to insure sustained utility.

*What is the budget for installation and on-going maintenance?*

Most paving projects are limited by the initial installation budget. However, the annual budget available to properly maintain the pavement and to sustain its long-term utility is equally important. Factors such as anticipated length of service, climate, proprietary coatings, and specialized maintenance equipment should be included when calculating the true cost of a particular pavement design.

*What are the advantages and disadvantages of various types of pavement applications?*

Pavements may be categorized as rigid monolithic, flexible monolithic, rigid unit, or flexible unit. The performance of a particular pavement is related to its strength, durability, safety, aesthetic characteristics, ease of repair and maintenance, and adaptability to climate extremes. Together, these performance factors affect both initial and on-going costs, and serve as a primary basis for comparison (Refer to Table 14.2).

# DESIGN CRITERIA

## Land use Contexts

- *Public Plaza:* Pavements are subject to medium to heavy loads and must accommodate emergency vehicles and mechanized maintenance practices. Costs are typically high, often 10 times higher than light duty pavements due to loading, edging and reinforcement requirements.
- *Townscape:* Pavements tend to reflect suburban and exurban surroundings and range from light to medium duty. Installation and maintenance costs tend to be moderate on average, reaching 4-5 times the cost of typical light duty pavements.
- *Athletic Facility:* Surfaces range from light to medium duty, with the exception of those multi-use exposition arenas, which often accommodate heavy vehicular loads. Pavements associated with track, field, and court sports have high installation costs and high maintenance costs due to requirements for uniformity and special drainage and maintenance of proprietary products.
- *Highway:* Pavements are heavy duty due to speed, high use, and maintenance requirements, and typically use heavy multi-layered construction methods. Both installation and maintenance costs are high to insure safety at high speeds, but vary by climate zone.
- *Urban Street:* Pavements are often heavy duty, but lower speeds provide opportunities for a greater variety of materials and a range of aesthetic choices. Installation and maintenance costs are typically high.

- *Parking Lot:* Pavements are light to medium duty due to low speed and weight requirements, and may include porous paving options as subsoil and climate allows. Costs are low to moderate and are greatly influenced by climate factors.
- *Public Garden:* Pavements may vary from light to heavy duty, depending on the complexity of the development program. Large crowds, heavy service, and special festival or concert events may require medium to high installation and maintenance costs.
- *Roof Garden:* Pavements are typically designed to achieve minimum loads on the roof structure and require special substrate and drainage details. Costs are very high to achieve long service, minimal maintenance, and ease of access for repair of utility systems as required.
- *Private Garden:* Pavements are often small in scale, but may also include heavy-duty applications in special circumstances. Costs are more related to aesthetic choices rather than heavy use. A broad range of choices is available.

## Pavement Structure

All pavements are built from the bottom up, but designers tend to think of pavements from the top down. Figure 14.1 illustrates the common components of a composite pavement structure presented for illustrative purposes.
- *Wearing Surface:* Whether flexible or rigid, the wearing surface receives the pedestrian or vehicular load and transfers it to the supporting pavement structure and aggregate base.
- *Aggregate Base:* The aggregate base transfers the load to the subgrade, prevents upward migration of capillary moisture, and drains infiltration moisture. It is typically extended 150-200 mm (6-8 in) beyond the wearing surface edge for stability and drainage.
- *Edge Restraint:* All unit pavements and heavily loaded asphalt pavements require an edge restraint to resist lateral migration due to loading and vibration (typically a curb is used in roadwork).
- *Aggregate Subbase:* Heavy duty pavements or those on unstable subgrades require a second layer of course aggregate to spread the load over a broader subbase area. The subbase is often extended to form a turf or paved shoulder.
- *Prepared Subgrade:* The subgrade is prepared to receive the aggregate by grading, and vibration, or in the case of clay, by sheeps foot roller passes. In poorly drained soils, fabric reinforcement is placed directly on the prepared subgrade to help bind the aggregate subbase layer, and to resist deformation. The subgrade typically slopes to reflect surface grading.
- *Subdrain:* In cold climates or in clay soil conditions, a subdrain is placed in a fabric lined trench and surrounded by a clean stone back-

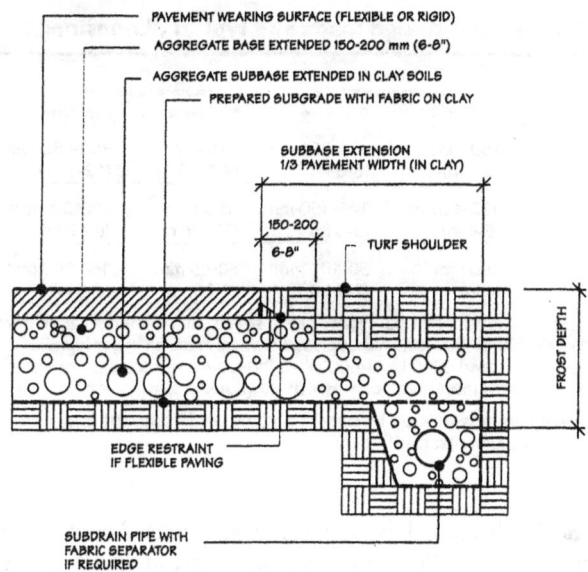

PAVEMENT WEARING SURFACE (FLEXIBLE OR RIGID)

AGGREGATE BASE EXTENDED 150-200 mm (6-8")

AGGREGATE SUBBASE EXTENDED IN CLAY SOILS

PREPARED SUBGRADE WITH FABRIC ON CLAY

SUBBASE EXTENSION
1/3 PAVEMENT WIDTH (IN CLAY)

150-200
6-8"    TURF SHOULDER

FROST DEPTH

EDGE RESTRAINT
IF FLEXIBLE PAVING

SUBDRAIN PIPE WITH
FABRIC SEPARATOR
IF REQUIRED

**Figure 14.1. Illustrative composite pavement diagram. The cross section indicates a variety of paving elements required in severe conditions.**

fill to draw moisture away from the aggregate base to prevent heaving. Pipes must rest below frost depth.

## Pavement Loading

Pedestrian pavements in public settings should be designed to accommodate the weight of service or maintenance vehicles, commonly exerting a minimum static wheel load of about 910 kg (2000 lbs). Wheel loads for streets and service areas range from 910 – 4500 kg (2000-10,000 lbs.), and up to 6000 kg (14,000 lbs) for highways and freight ways. Table 14.1 indicates minimum total pavement thickness for light, medium, and heavy duty pavement loads on soils suitable for construction.

## Subgrade Conditions

Existing subgrade conditions directly influence pavement design choices. Well-drained sands and aggregates are ideal, and poorly drained clays are problematic. The key to stable pavement design in colloidal soil is to maintain even moisture conditions to avoid shrink and swell cycles. Remedies include: extra aggregate subbase courses, subdrains, and fabric reinforcement (to bind aggregate bases and to guard against deformation), and significant aggregate base extension beyond the pavement edge (See Figure 14.1). The aggregate base for medium duty roads may double in thickness from 300 mm to 600 mm (12 in to 24 in) to compensate for weak subsoils.

DEVICES

## TABLE 14.1. Pavement design loads and typical dimensions.

| | Rigid Pavements** | | Flexible Pavements | |
| | Pavement | Agg. Base | Pavement | Agg. Base |
|---|---|---|---|---|
| *Heavy Duty* | 150-200 mm* (6-8 in) | 150-200 mm (6-8 in) | 115 mm (4½ in) | 300-450 mm (12-18 in) |
| *Medium Duty* | 125-150 mm (5-6 in) | 125-150 mm (5-6 in) | 65-75 mm (2½-3 in) | 200-300 mm (8-12 in) |
| *Light Duty* | 100 mm (4 in) | 50-100 mm (2-4 in) | 50-65 mm (2-2½ in) | 150-200 mm (6-8 in) |

*Static wheel loads on most municipal service paths, streets, and roads can range from 910 kg-4500 kg (2,000-10,000 lbs). Although static wheel loads on major highways and freight ways can exceed 6000 kg (14,000 lbs), this table is restricted to the lesser loads of streets and roads more commonly associated with site construction.

**Rigid pavement thickness will vary by cement content, reinforcing, and aggregate specification (Reinforcing is assumed).

## Climate

- Hot Arid: Use lighter colors to avoid heat absorption. Porous finishes are permitted due to low humidity. Unit pavers and rigid monolithic pavements are common. A wide variety of pavement options are available.

- Hot Humid: Drainage is important to prevent the growth of moss and algae, and to accommodate intense periods of precipitation. Light colors are used to reflect heat. A wide variety of pavement options are available.

- Temperate: Darker colors are used to absorb radiant solar heat. Frost-thaw cycles may require thicker aggregate bases and the use of subdrains. Heavy snow regions may require abrasive snow clearing equipment. Mortared unit pavers may require extensive pointing and repair, while concrete may deteriorate due to chemical ice melting products.

- Cold: Cold climates are similar to temperate zones but have more restrictions due to extreme temperature changes. Flexible monolithic and unit pavements are preferred over reinforced concrete pavements. Reinforcing steel is subject to corrosion from salts, which infiltrate small tensile surface fissures. Mortared unit pavers are not recommended in this zone.

## Cost and Maintenance

Initial installation cost is calculated by adding the cost of all materials, labor and machine time required to prepare the construction area, install the pavement, and clear away debris, plus the contractor's business overhead and profit requirements. Cost per square unit increases if more expensive materials are used or if the pavement design requires multiple layers, special edging, or proprietary operations during installation. Long-term costs are a function of annual maintenance and repair expenditures over the life of the pavement. More durable materials typically have a longer utility and often cost less per year of operation than less expensive pavements with a shorter utility life and high annual maintenance, or frequent repair requirements. Life-cycle costing is important in public or institutional installations (See Chapter 22: Cost Estimating).

## PAVEMENT PERFORMANCE COMPARISONS

Table 14.2 identifies pavement characteristics and an assessment of positive and negative factors, which may affect design decisions.

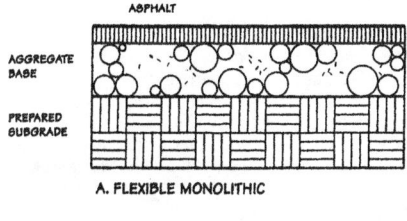

A. FLEXIBLE MONOLITHIC

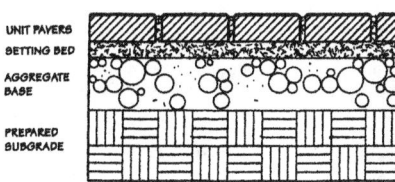

B. FLEXIBLE UNIT

**Figure 14.2. Typical flexible pavement section showing monolithic (A) and unit (B) types. Fabric separator subgrade reinforcing is often used in weaker soils to maintain structural integrity and to guard against deformation. Unit pavers subject to vehicular loading should use high silica content sand, rather than stone dust.**

**Figure 14.3. Typical rigid pavement section showing monolithic (A) and unit (B) types. Although many local practices place rigid pavements directly onto prepared subgrades, especially in warm climates, it is highly recommended to use an aggregate base for best long-term results.**

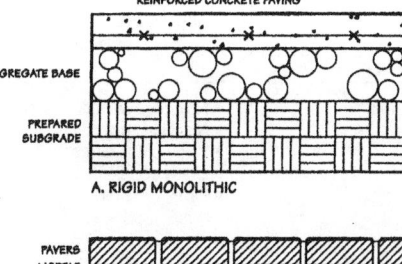

A. RIGID MONOLITHIC

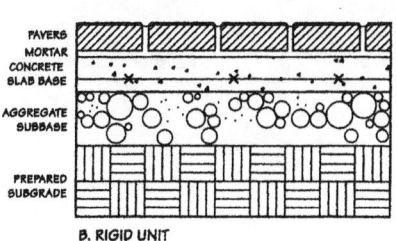

B. RIGID UNIT

## TABLE 14.2. Pavement checklist of advantages and disadvantages of various pavement types.

| Type of paving | Advantages | Disadvantages |
|---|---|---|
| **IN-SITU PAVING** | | |
| Concrete | • Relatively easy to install<br>• Available with several finishes, many colors and various textures<br>• Durable surface<br>• Year-round and multiple usage<br>• Low lifetime maintenance costs<br>• Long-lasting<br>• Low heat absorbency<br>• Hard, nonresilient surface<br>• Adaptable to curvilinear forms | • Joints are required<br>• Some surfaces are aesthetically unappealing<br>• Can disintegrate if not properly installed<br>• Difficult to color evenly and permanently<br>• Light color is reflective and can cause glare<br>• Some types can deteriorate from deicing salts<br>• Relatively low tensile strength: can crack easily<br>• Low resiliency |
| Asphalt | • Low heat and light reflectivity<br>• Year-round and multiple use<br>• Durable<br>• Low maintenance costs<br>• Dust-free surface<br>• Resiliency can vary depending on mixture<br>• Water repellent surface<br>• Adaptable to curvilinear forms<br>• Can be made porous | • Will fray at edges if not supported<br>• Can soften in warm weather<br>• Soluble by gasoline, kerosene, and other petroleum solvents<br>• Susceptible to freeze damage if water penetrates base |
| Synthetic Surfacing Systems (proprietary) | • Can be designed for a specific purpose (e.g., court games, track)<br>• Wide color range<br>• More resilient than concrete or asphalt<br>• Sometimes can be applied over old concrete or asphalt | • Specially trained labor may be required for installation or repair<br>• More costly than asphalt or concrete |
| **UNIT PAVING** | | |
| Brick | • Nonglare surface<br>• Nonskid surface<br>• Wide color range<br>• Good scale<br>• Easily repaired | • High installation cost<br>• Difficult to clean<br>• Can disintegrate in freezing weather<br>• Susceptible to differential settlement<br>• Efflorescence |
| Tiles | • Polished indoor/outdoor appearance | • Suitable only for milder climates<br>• High installation costs |

## TABLE 14.2. Pavement checklist of advantages and disadvantages of various pavement types (continued).

| Type of paving | Advantages | Disadvantages |
|---|---|---|
| Adobe Bricks | • Fast and easy installation<br>• Can last indefinitely if base contains an adequate amount of asphaltic stabilizer<br>• Rich color and texture | • Tend to crumble at the edges<br>• Store considerable amounts of heat<br>• Fragile; require level foundations (fracture easily)<br>• Dusty<br>• Suitable only for warm and nonhumid areas |
| Flagstones | • Very durable if properly installed<br>• Natural weathering qualities | • Moderately expensive to install<br>• Might seem cold, hard, or quarry-like in appearance<br>• Color and random pattern sometimes difficult to work with aesthetically<br>• Can become smooth and slippery when wet or worn |
| Granite | • Hard and dense<br>• Very durable under extreme weathering conditions<br>• Will support heavy traffic<br>• Can be polished to a hard gloss surface that is durable and easily cleaned | • Hard and dense; difficult to work with<br>• Some types are subject to a high rate of chemical weathering<br>• Relatively expensive |
| Limestone | • Easy to work with<br>• Rich color and texture | • Susceptible to chemical weathering (especially in humid climates and urban environments) |
| Sandstone | • Easy to work with<br>• Durable | • Susceptible to chemical weathering (especially in humid climates and urban environments) |
| Slate | • Durable<br>• Slow to weather<br>• Range of colors | • Relatively expensive<br>• Can be slippery when wet |
| Molded Units (synthetic) | • Can be designed or selected for various purposes (i.e., firm, soft)<br>• Short installation time<br>• Easy installation, removal, and replacement usually without specialized labor<br>• Wide color range | • Subject to vandalism<br>• Higher installation costs than asphalt or concrete |

DEVICES

➤ continued on next page

*Paving* ▪ 267

**TABLE 14.2. Pavement checklist of advantages and disadvantages of various pavement types (continued).**

| Type of paving | Advantages | Disadvantages |
|---|---|---|
| **SOFT PAVING** | | |
| Aggregates | • Economical surfacing material<br>• Range of colors | • Requires replenishment every few years depending on amount of use<br>• Potential for weeds<br>• Requires edging |
| Organic Materials | • Relatively inexpensive<br>• Compatible with natural surroundings<br>• Quiet, comfortable walking surface | • Suitable only for light traffic<br>• requires periodic replenishment or replacement |
| Turfgrass | • Colorful<br>• Nonabrasive<br>• Dust-free<br>• Good drainage characteristics<br>• Quiet, comfortable walking surface<br>• Ideal for many types of recreation<br>• Relatively low installation costs | • Difficult and expensive to maintain, especially in areas of heavy use |
| Turf Blocks | • Same as turf alone but has added stability to withstand light vehicular loads | • Requires high levels of maintenance (frequent watering, etc.) |
| Artificial Turf | • Same as turf surface<br>• Can be used sooner after rains without wet spots<br>• Allows flat grading of playing surface<br>• Available with built-in markings, etc.<br>• No irrigation or maintenance problems as with natural turfgrass | • Results in a higher number of player injuries (regarding field sports)<br>• Results in faster and higher ball roll and bounce<br>• Initial installation costs higher than natural turfgrass |

NOTE: No one surface will meet the needs of all outdoor activities. Each activity has its own surface requirements.

## Pavement Structure Types

Figures 14.2 and 14.3 illustrate four key paving concepts: flexible monolithic and flexible unit pavements, and rigid monolithic and rigid unit pavements.

# PAVEMENT INSTALLATION

All pavements require proper subgrade preparation and careful placement of a granular base prior to installation. Aggregate base thickness and composition varies with each pavement type.

## Aggregate Base Placement

### Roads and Parking Lots

After cutting and filling to the desired subgrade elevation, the construction surface is prepared as specified (vibration, rolling, etc.). The surface must slope to drain and be free of significant ruts or ridges. Colloidal or weak soils may require a fabric layer to be installed at this point. The aggregate base or subbase is placed in 150-200 mm (6-8 in) lifts and compacted as specified until the desired thickness is achieved. Edges such as in-situ concrete curbs, cut stone, or staked metal or plastic edge restraints may be installed at this point. After sufficient fine grading and surface preparation, the aggregate base is now ready to receive the paving material and any additional setting beds (for unit pavers) if required.

### Walks and Plazas

Residential pavements typically require only a single sand or aggregate base. The subgrade should be smooth and well tamped or consolidated. The aggregate base is typically placed in a single lift, since depths rarely exceed 150 mm (6 in) is such settings. The base should extend at least 100 mm (4 in) beyond the pavement edge. In the case of unit pavers, it is best practice to place the pavers on a thin 25 mm (1 in) sand setting bed, which is placed on an aggregate base, rather than using the traditional method of a single 100 mm (4 in) layer of sand. Aggregate base depth should allow for maintenance or service vehicle loading as required. Public plazas are typically required to support the weight of a variety of service and emergency vehicles, including fire fighting equipment and must be designed using deeper bases and thicker wearing surfaces, even though the pavement is primarily for pedestrian use.

## Paving material placement

- *Asphalt:* Most asphalt pavements are installed in two courses consisting of a coarse aggregate base course and a finer aggregate wearing course. Where required, a liquid asphalt binder penetration may be placed on the aggregate base prior to receiving the asphalt base course. If no curbs or edges are used, the asphalt base course typically extends 50-100 mm (2-4 in) beyond the finish wearing course to allow for edge reinforcement, and is commonly referred to as a tamped or tapered edge.

- *Concrete:* Concrete pavement is placed on a prepared base and is contained by wood, plastic, or metal forms. Pedestrian walks are often constructed using high strength concrete without reinforcing mesh or bars in slabs ranging from 100-125 mm (4-5 in) in thickness. Walks subject to vehicular loading are typically 150 mm (6 in) thick and may be reinforced with a wire mesh. Local practices vary widely with regard to steel reinforcing in walkways and driveways and are related to area freeze-thaw cycles, subsoil conditions, and temperature and moisture extremes. Minimum slab thickness is typically 100 mm (4 in). All steel reinforcing bars should be held back from the concrete surface by at least 50 mm (2 in). Isolating expansion joints are required every 7500 mm (25 ft) in most circumstances. Highway loads require steel bar reinforcing to maintain strength and resistance to vibration.

- *Unit Pavers:* It is common practice to set unit pavers on a 25 mm (1 in) sand setting bed over a 100-150 mm (4-6 in) aggregate base. Unit pavers must be placed within edge restraints to prevent lateral spreading with use. Joints are dry grouted with sand or stone dust. Units may be sealed with a clear liquid sealant to preserve finish color and to consolidate the sand grout. Driveways and parking areas require deeper aggregate bases ranging from 150-300 mm (6-12 in). A fabric binder may be used to reinforce expansive sub soils (See Figure 14.1).

## SUGGESTED REFERENCES

Dines, Nicholas T. and Kyle D. Brown, *Time-Saver Standards Site Construction Details Manual*, McGraw-Hill, New York, 1999.

Harris, Charles W. and Nicholas T. Dines, *Time-Saver Standards for Landscape Architecture, 2nd Edition*, McGraw-Hill, New York, 1998.

Means, R. S., *Site Work and Landscape Cost Data*, R. S. Means Company, Inc., Kingston, MA, 2000.

# Fences
# and Walls

# 15

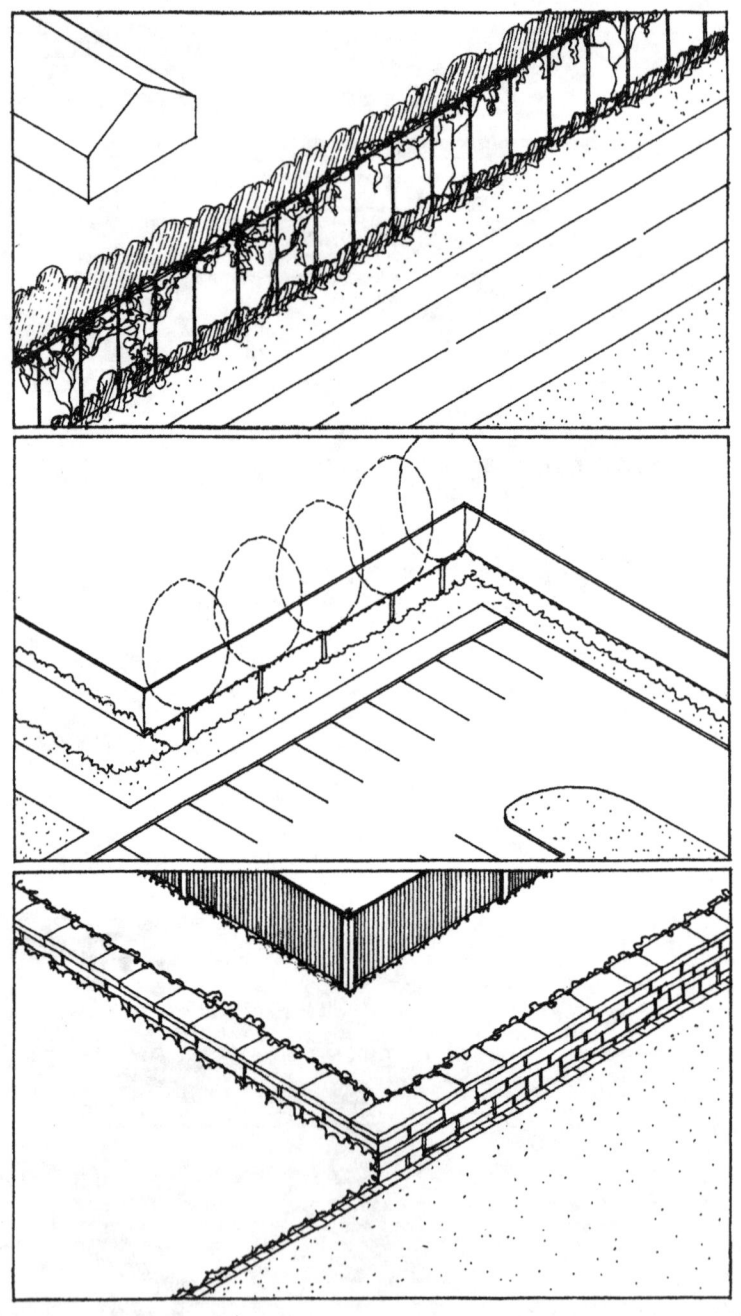

## LARGE SCALE ACOUSTICAL
## BARRIER AND SCREENING WALLS

Large-scale barriers ranging from 3000-4500 mm (10-15 ft) are common-ly employed to serve as acoustical deflection devices at the edge of high-ways, train corridors, or other wind borne noise producing activities. Materials are typically wood or pre-cast masonry. Support posts require deep footings and stable soils to withstand lateral wind loads and frost action where applicable. Local ordinances may require these devices and commonly regulate materials, finishes, dimensions, and construction methods.

## INSTITUTIONAL AND COMMERCIAL
## BARRIER FENCES AND WALLS

These devices are commonly used to delimit property lines for safety and secu-rity, and to channel pedestrian circulation toward portals or gateways. Opaque masonry walls may be required by local fire and building codes in some locations. Institutional fences may be semi-transparent wrought iron, or opaque timber and board construction. Heights may vary from 2000-3000 mm (6-10 ft).

## RESIDENTIAL AND GARDEN SCALE
## SCREENS AND WALLS

Residential and garden scale screens and walls commonly range from 1000-2000 mm (3-6 ft) in height, but may also include heights up to 2400 mm (8 ft). Local ordinances restrict the height, setback, and materials of such screens and walls. Placement of plantings should allow for periodic main-tenance and repair access. Placement requires a registered property line sur-vey to prevent unintended encroachment.

F ENCES AND WALLS are barrier devices that help define spatial enclosure, screen out negative off-site features such as wind, noise, or unpleasant views, and provide a feeling of security and privacy. These structures are indicated when a vegetative barrier is not sufficient for meeting functional or aesthetic goals. In the process of improving a site, fences and walls should not create an unpleasant off-site environment for abutting properties by adversely affecting the microclimate, limiting access to views, or altering stormwater runoff patterns.

## DIAGNOSTIC ASSESSMENT

*What functional requirements suggest using a barrier device?*

Certain functional requirements, such as privacy, security, sound abatement, or environmental modification may require using a barrier device. Plant material, especially in the form of hedges, is often used as a barrier; however, where space is limited or where a more opaque and sound deflecting barrier is required, a fence or freestanding wall may be more appropriate.

*What type of fence or wall is appropriate for the site and its proposed use?*

There are numerous structural barrier options available, including wood and metal fences, brick and concrete walls, and stone walls. Selecting the appropriate type, size, and material of fence or wall is guided by the purpose of the barrier, the landscape context, the site conditions, and long-term maintenance requirements.

*What are the aesthetic and structural considerations when designing wood or metal fences?*

The aesthetic impact of wood and metal fences is modulated through the repetition of boards or pickets and the detailing of posts, caps, and other connection points. Careful materials selection and appropriate joining methods will reduce maintenance requirements. Fence height determines the degree of enclosure and is often regulated by local ordinances.

*What are the aesthetic and structural considerations when designing brick and concrete block walls?*

The aesthetic impact of a brick wall is modulated through the choice of brick pattern and texture, and the articulation of details that create shadow lines. Brick walls are non-load bearing structures that carry only their own weight plus lateral wind loads, and require reinforcement based on height and width. Access for routine pointing and coating is an important long-term maintenance consideration.

*What are the aesthetic and structural considerations when designing stone walls?*

The aesthetic impact of a stone wall is modulated through the choice of stone and the stonework pattern employed. Ashlar, or cut stone provides a sharp contrast to split faced field stone. Depending on the intensity of use and the height, stone walls may be either dry-laid or mortared.

# FUNCTIONAL REQUIREMENTS

Determining the need for a barrier device in a project requires a careful consideration of the purposes of barriers in the landscape:

- **Privacy:** Privacy requires a degree of protection against visual and/or physical intrusion. The extent of privacy desired and its context will greatly influence the design and materials used for privacy barriers, as shown in Figure 15.1
- **Safety and Security:** Barriers can discourage deliberate trespassing, keep people away from such potentially dangerous items as mechanical equipment, transformers, or swimming pools, and keep children and animals in safe areas.
- **Boundary Definition:** Fences and walls are commonly used to define boundaries and to prevent or discourage trespassing.
- **Circulation Control:** Barriers can control and direct the movement of people, animals, or vehicles. Low walls can channel or direct pedestrian traffic while discouraging unauthorized or unsafe shortcuts.
- **Environmental Modification:** Barriers can reduce or eliminate heavy winds, noise, drifting snow, glare, and strong sunlight. Strategically placed windbreaks and shaded areas can reduce the energy required for heating and cooling, as shown in Figure 15.2.

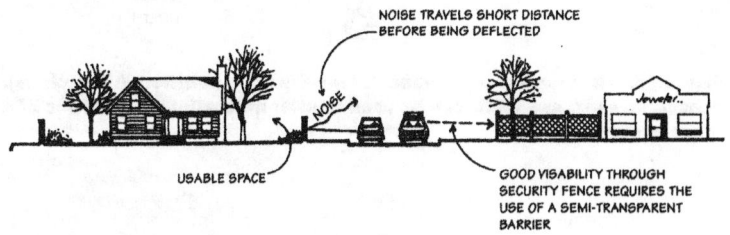

NOISE TRAVELS SHORT DISTANCE BEFORE BEING DEFLECTED

NOISE

USABLE SPACE

GOOD VISABILITY THROUGH SECURITY FENCE REQUIRES THE USE OF A SEMI-TRANSPARENT BARRIER

**Figure 15.1. Placement of privacy barriers.**

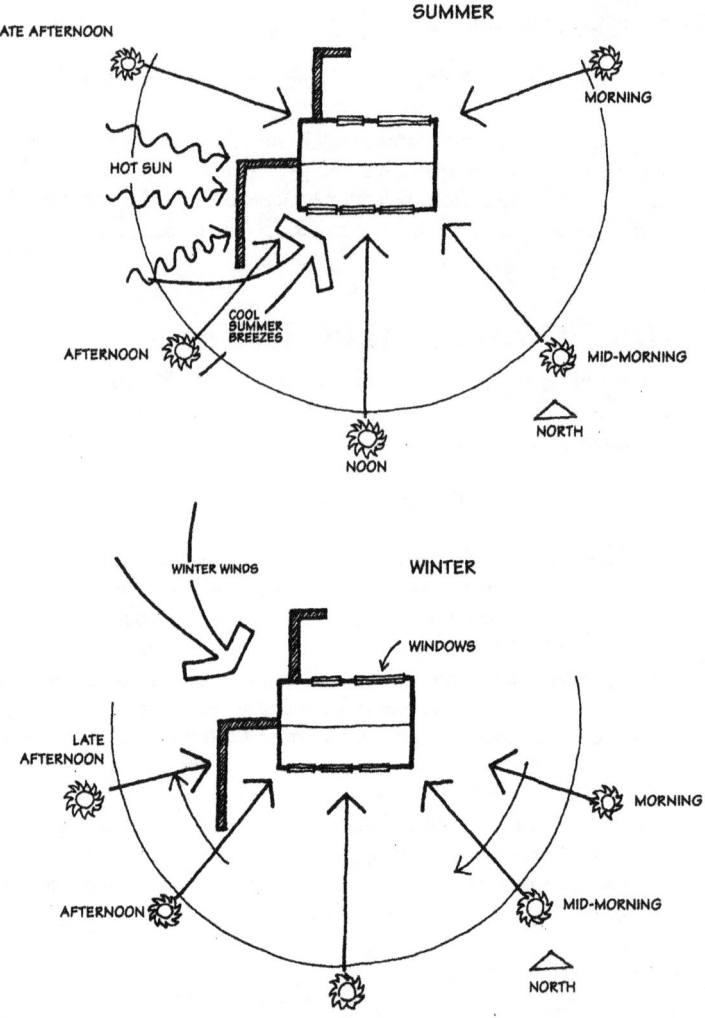

**Figure 15.2. Barriers for environmental modification (northern hemisphere). Fences, screens, and walls can be used to alter microclimatic qualities of a space in several ways.**

# BARRIER DESIGN

## Design Criteria

Site context and off-site impacts are key considerations in determining barrier type, size, and material. Adjacent architectural styles, scale, drainage patterns, topography, and site lines are key considerations. As shown in Figure 15.3, poorly styled or improperly built fences, screens or walls can detract from the appearance of adjacent properties. The type and nature of barrier device will be influenced by the following design considerations:

- Whether the barrier is an aesthetic feature, a practical boundary, or both
- Whether the barrier is to provide a strong sense of privacy or security
- Whether the barrier is solid or allows some degree of visual accessibility
- Whether the barrier is in harmony or in contrast with other features
- Whether areas near the barrier are to be planted

## Legal and Feasibility Considerations

A proposed barrier must also comply with all relevant legal and building codes, as well as cost and maintenance considerations.

- Most sites are highly constrained by legal regulations regarding setbacks, dimensions, and in some cases, materials and colors.
- Low initial costs should be balanced against annual maintenance costs and eventual replacement. A more permanent screen may require a heavier initial investment.
- Maintenance access should guide design layout and materials selection to provide ease of routine maintenance on both sides of the barrier.

## Footings and Foundations

All barrier types will require consideration of methods for anchoring the fence or wall to the ground. A structural engineer familiar with local

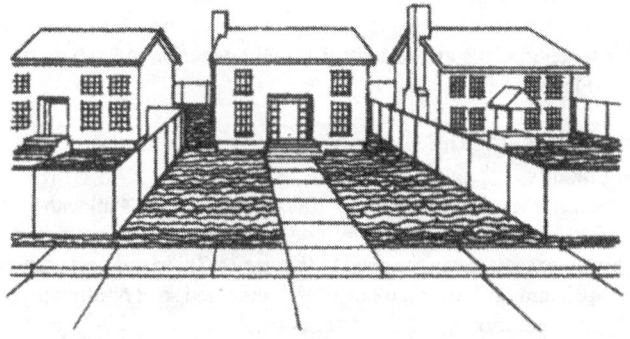

**Figure 15.3. Problem of off-site impacts. In this example, the adjacent residence is fenced in, contrary to desires.**

DEVICES

conditions, code requirements, and standard practices should be consulted for major structures, such as high masonry walls, in difficult soil conditions.

## Footing Depth

Top of footing for walls and masonry piers is typically 300 mm (1 ft) below finish grade in warm, non-frost areas, and below or at the frostline in cold regions to provide a safety factor equal to the footing thickness. At a minimum, bottom of footing should be set 50 mm (2 in) below local frost line (check local codes).

## Soil Conditions

Extremely sandy, heavy clay, expansive or very wet soil conditions may require deeper and wider footings to insure stability against lateral wind load stresses.

## Drainage

Freeze/thaw processes in cold climates can cause heaving of posts, footings, and foundations. Surface water should not be allowed to collect adjacent to, and should be drained away from the base of fences, screens, and walls.

## Response to Terrain

Figure 15.4 illustrates methods for responding to changes in terrain. Some types of fences and walls can run parallel to a sloping or rolling landscape, while others require some method of stepping down of panels between posts or piers.

# WOOD AND METAL FENCES

## Aesthetic Considerations

As shown in Figure 15.5, horizontal rails attach to posts and make a basic framework for supporting various combinations of pickets, panels, or other fencing. Caps are added for visual appeal or to keep water off the posts (Figure 15.6).

## Structural Consideration

### Components

Wooden fence posts are typically 100 × 100 mm (4 × 4 in) with 150 × 150 mm (6 × 6 in) posts at corners for additional stability. Various methods are employed to set posts in the ground (Figure 15.7). Metal posts can be made of 25-100 mm (1-4 in) square or round tempered steel or aluminum tubing set in concrete footings. Pickets are normally made of 20-25 mm (¾-1 in) square or round tempered steel or aluminum tubing or solid bars.

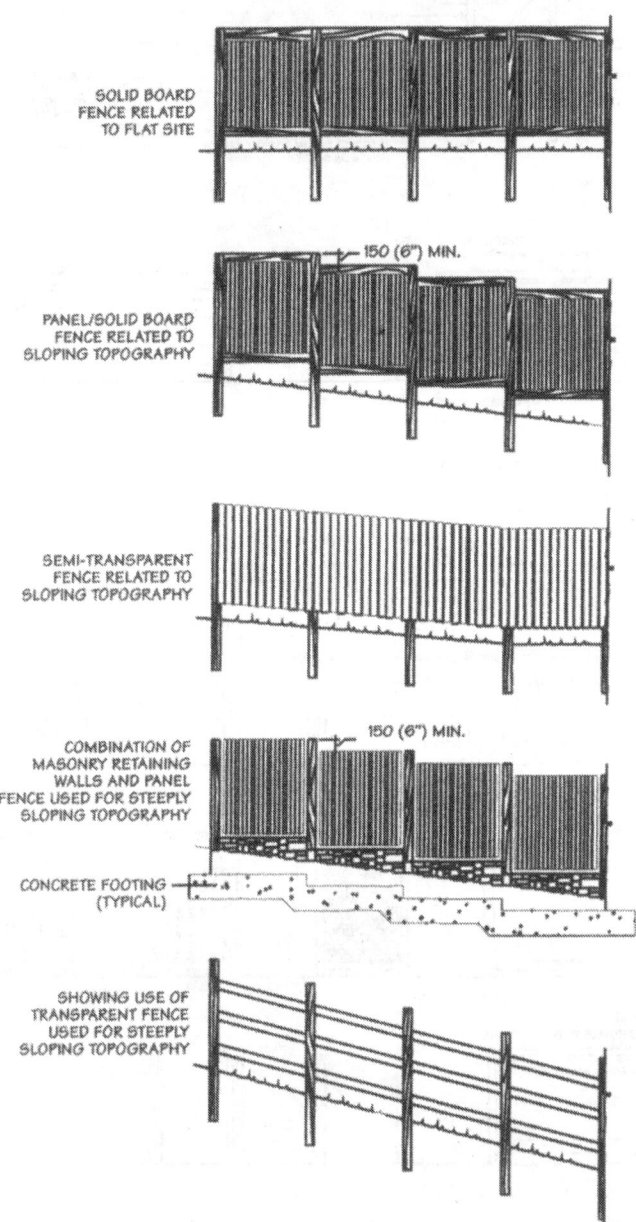

SOLID BOARD FENCE RELATED TO FLAT SITE

PANEL/SOLID BOARD FENCE RELATED TO SLOPING TOPOGRAPHY

150 (6") MIN.

SEMI-TRANSPARENT FENCE RELATED TO SLOPING TOPOGRAPHY

COMBINATION OF MASONRY RETAINING WALLS AND PANEL FENCE USED FOR STEEPLY SLOPING TOPOGRAPHY

150 (6") MIN.

CONCRETE FOOTING (TYPICAL)

SHOWING USE OF TRANSPARENT FENCE USED FOR STEEPLY SLOPING TOPOGRAPHY

DEVICES

**Figure 15.4. Methods for responding to terrain.**

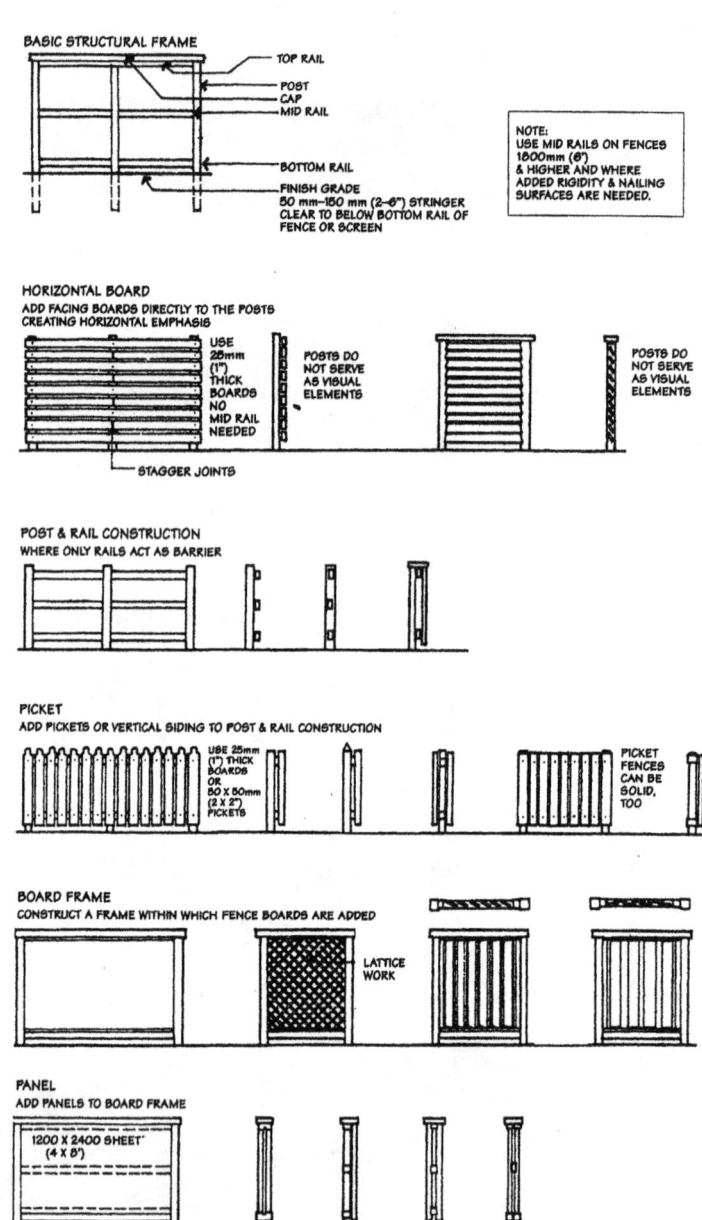

**Figure 15.5. Various types of fence construction.**

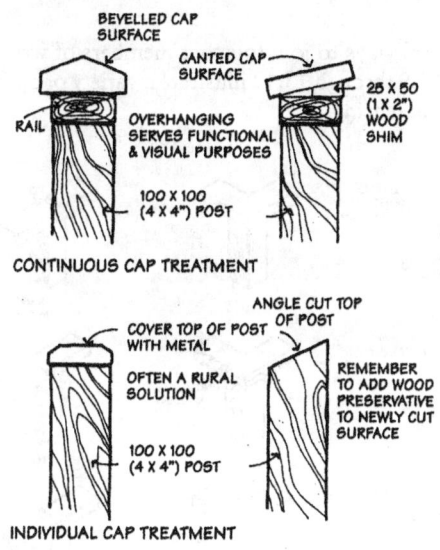

BEVELLED CAP
SURFACE

CANTED CAP
SURFACE

25 X 50
(1 X 2")
WOOD
SHIM

RAIL

OVERHANGING
SERVES FUNCTIONAL
& VISUAL PURPOSES

100 X 100
(4 X 4") POST

CONTINUOUS CAP TREATMENT

COVER TOP OF POST
WITH METAL

ANGLE CUT TOP
OF POST

OFTEN A RURAL
SOLUTION

REMEMBER
TO ADD WOOD
PRESERVATIVE
TO NEWLY CUT
SURFACE

100 X 100
(4 X 4") POST

INDIVIDUAL CAP TREATMENT

**Figure 15.6. Typical cap details.**

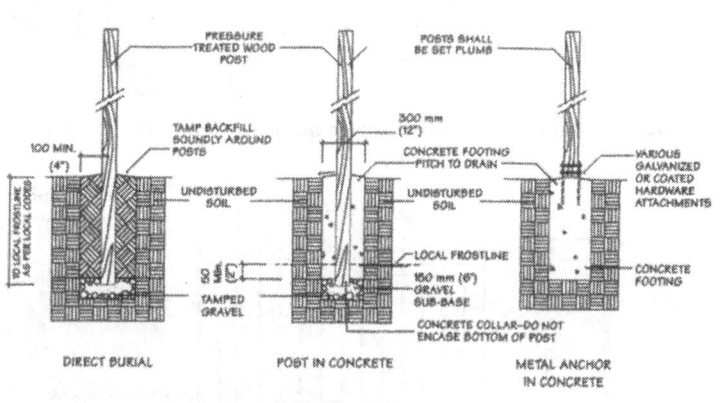

PRESSURE
TREATED WOOD
POST

POSTS SHALL
BE SET PLUMB

TAMP BACKFILL
SOUNDLY AROUND
POSTS

300 mm
(12")

100 MIN.
(4")

CONCRETE FOOTING
PITCH TO DRAIN

VARIOUS
GALVANIZED
OR COATED
HARDWARE
ATTACHMENTS

UNDISTURBED
SOIL

UNDISTURBED
SOIL

TO LOCAL FROSTLINE
AS PER LOCAL CODES

LOCAL FROSTLINE

150 mm (6")
GRAVEL
SUB-BASE

CONCRETE
FOOTING

TAMPED
GRAVEL

CONCRETE COLLAR-DO NOT
ENCASE BOTTOM OF POST

DIRECT BURIAL

POST IN CONCRETE

METAL ANCHOR
IN CONCRETE

**Figure 15.7. Typical post and footing details.**

DEVICES

## Construction

Figure 15.8 shows several ways to join together members of wooden fences or screens. Figures 15.9 through 15.12 illustrate a variety of options for the construction of metal fencing.

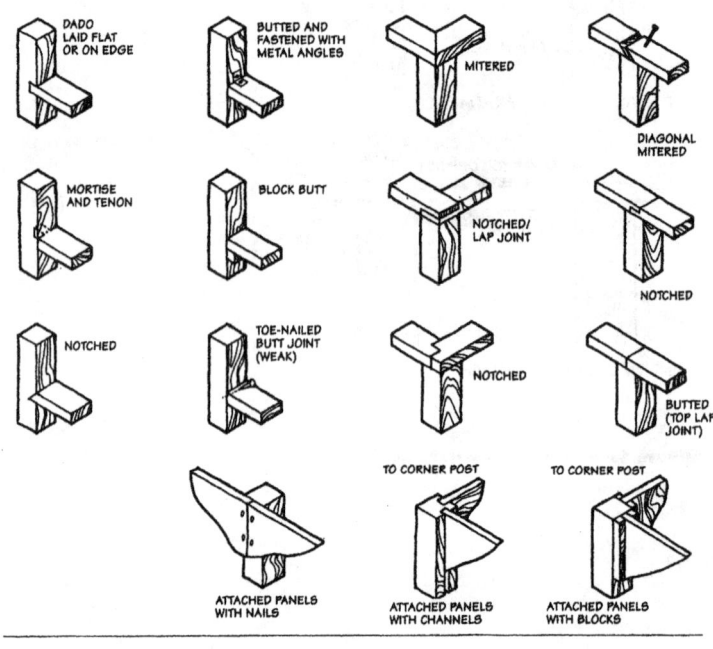

**Figure 15.8. Typical joining techniques for wood fences and screens.**

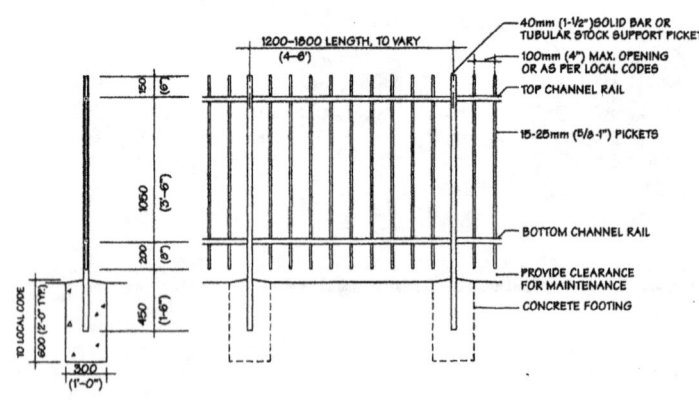

**Figure 15.9. Typical metal picket fence construction.**

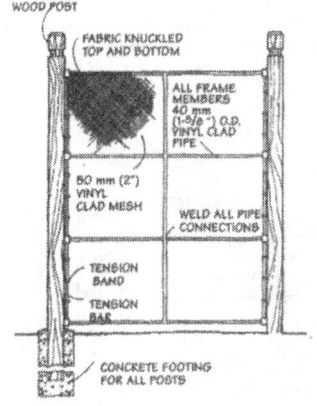

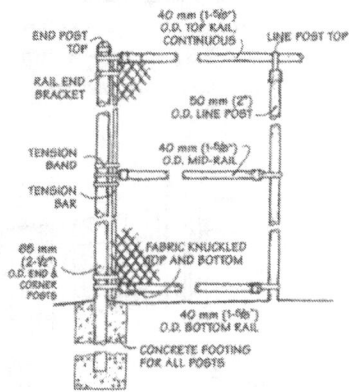

**Figure 15.10. Metal fabric fencing with wood post construction.**

**Figure 15.11. Typical chain link fencing.**

# BRICK AND CONCRETE BLOCK WALLS

## Aesthetic Considerations

Figure 15.13 shows some of the more common bonds used in bricklaying. Caps can be made from standard bricks, special brick cap units, precast concrete, or other materials such as wood or cut stone (Figure 15.14).

## Structural Considerations

### Components

Masonry walls require continuous footings that are generally constructed of cast-in-place reinforced concrete. The wall is then built upon these footings as shown in figure 15.15 . Many codes require footings for non-load bearing walls to extend a minimum of 150 mm (6 in) on either side of the wall. Generally, the size of the footing will not be less than 250 mm (10 in) deep by 400 mm (16 in) wide with two continuous reinforcing bars as required by site conditions.

### Construction

Figure 15.16 illustrates common construction methods for masonry walls. The Brick Institute recommends that for 49 kg/m² (10 lbs/ft²) of wind pressure, a straight brick wall should not be higher than ¾ of the wall thickness squared. A 200 mm (8 in) wall for example, would be limited to a maximum 1200 mm (4 ft) height. Therefore, taller walls are often constructed of reinforced concrete piers with a masonry veneer, as shown in figures 15.17 and 15.18 .

*Fences and Walls* ▪ 283

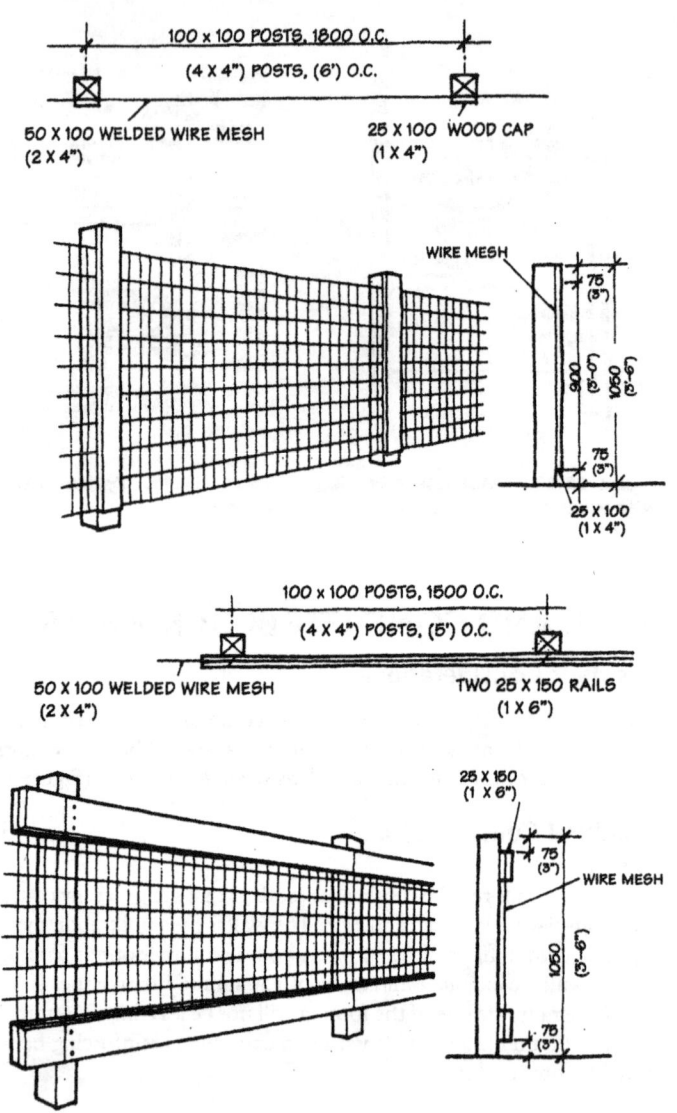

100 x 100 POSTS, 1800 O.C.
(4 X 4") POSTS, (6') O.C.

50 X 100 WELDED WIRE MESH
(2 X 4")

25 X 100  WOOD CAP
(1 X 4")

WIRE MESH

75
(3")

900
(3'-0")
1050
(3'-6")

75
(3")

25 X 100
(1 X 4")

100 x 100 POSTS, 1500 O.C.
(4 X 4") POSTS, (5') O.C.

50 X 100 WELDED WIRE MESH
(2 X 4")

TWO 25 X 150 RAILS
(1 X 6")

25 X 150
(1 X 6")

75
(3")

WIRE MESH

1050
(3'-6")

75
(3")

**Figure 15.12. Application of metal fabrics.**

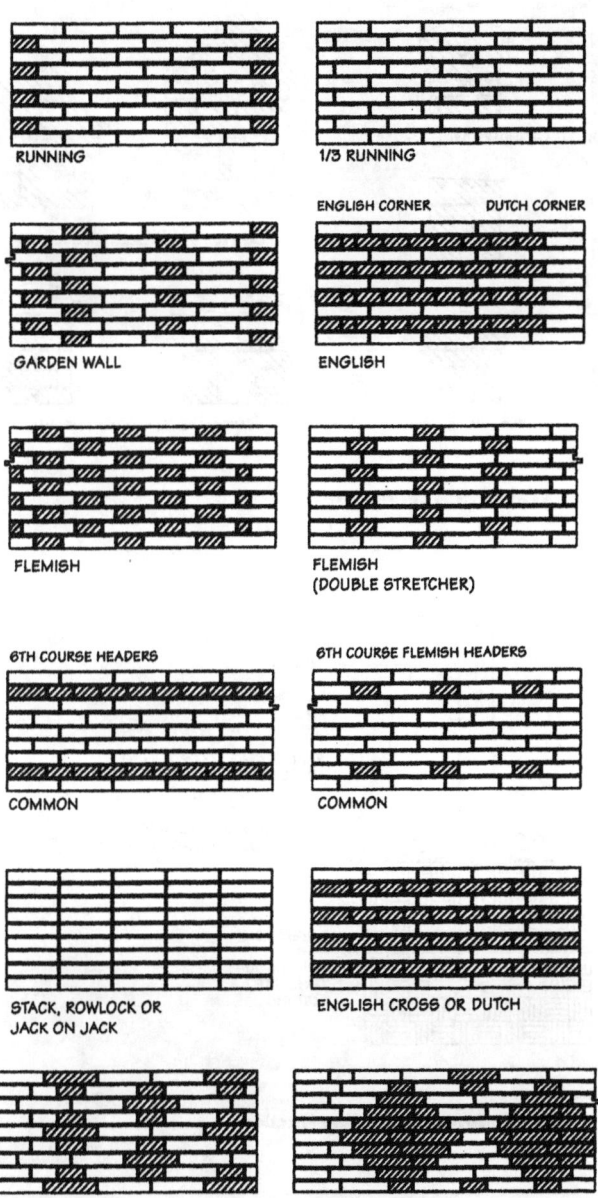

RUNNING

1/3 RUNNING

GARDEN WALL

ENGLISH CORNER    DUTCH CORNER

ENGLISH

FLEMISH

FLEMISH
(DOUBLE STRETCHER)

6TH COURSE HEADERS

COMMON

6TH COURSE FLEMISH HEADERS

COMMON

STACK, ROWLOCK OR
JACK ON JACK

ENGLISH CROSS OR DUTCH

FLEMISH (CROSS)

FLEMISH (DIAGONAL)

**Figure 15.13. Common brickwork patters.**

DEVICES

*Fences and Walls* ▪ 285

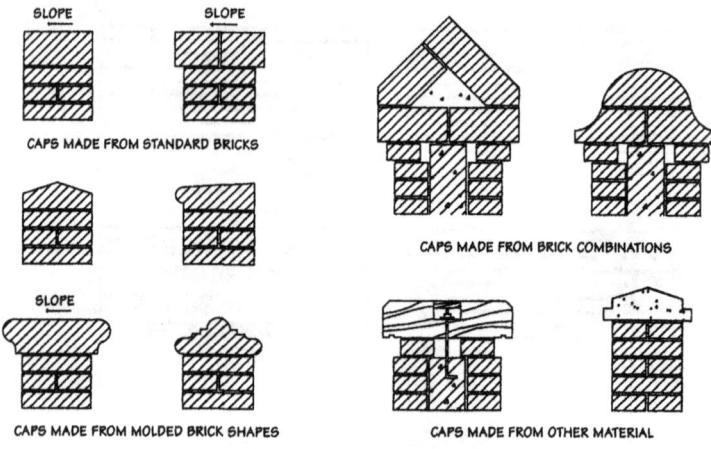

CAPS MADE FROM STANDARD BRICKS

CAPS MADE FROM BRICK COMBINATIONS

CAPS MADE FROM MOLDED BRICK SHAPES

CAPS MADE FROM OTHER MATERIAL

**Figure 15.14. Typical caps for masonry walls.**

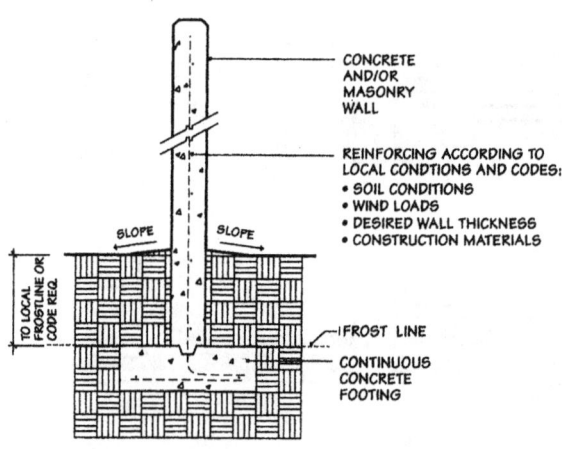

CONCRETE AND/OR MASONRY WALL

REINFORCING ACCORDING TO LOCAL CONDTIONS AND CODES:
• SOIL CONDITIONS
• WIND LOADS
• DESIRED WALL THICKNESS
• CONSTRUCTION MATERIALS

SLOPE        SLOPE

TO LOCAL FROSTLINE OR CODE REQ.

FROST LINE

CONTINUOUS CONCRETE FOOTING

**Figure 15.15. Continuous footing construction.**

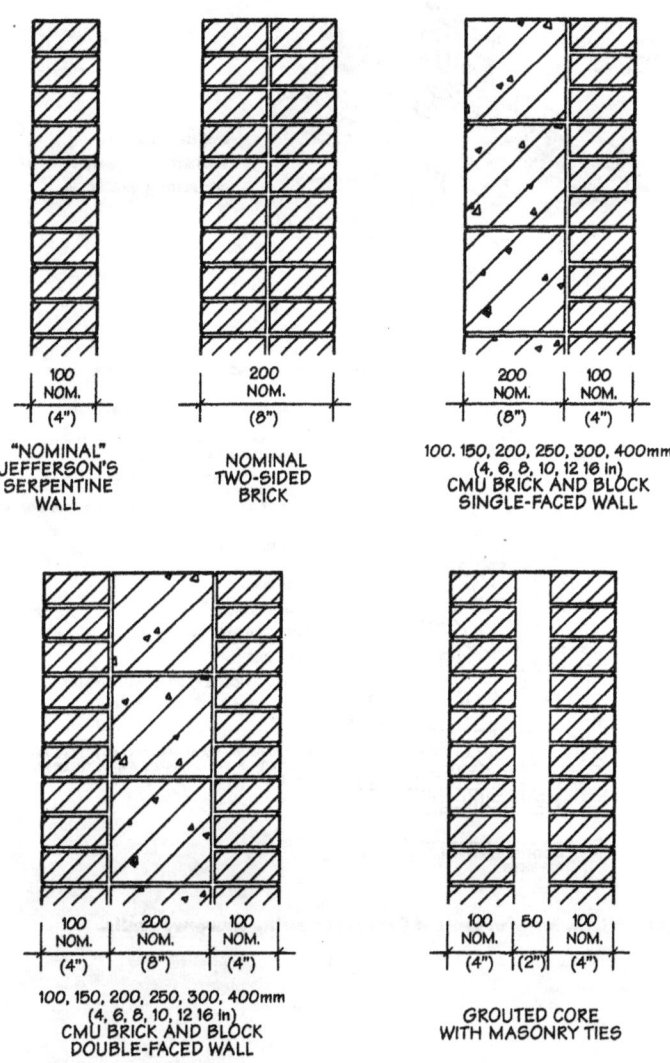

**Figure 15.16. Typical brick wall construction.**

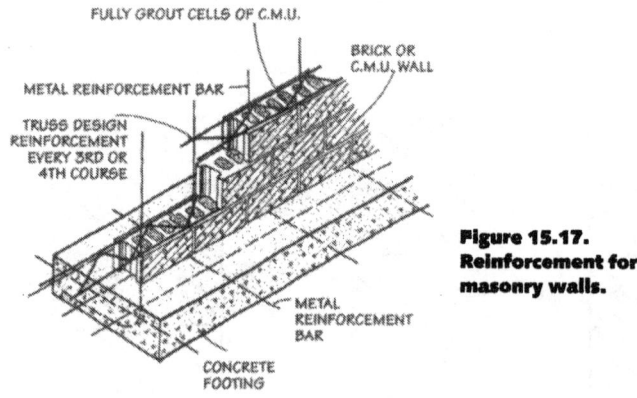

FULLY GROUT CELLS OF C.M.U.

BRICK OR
C.M.U. WALL

METAL REINFORCEMENT BAR

TRUSS DESIGN
REINFORCEMENT
EVERY 3RD OR
4TH COURSE

METAL
REINFORCEMENT
BAR

CONCRETE
FOOTING

**Figure 15.17.
Reinforcement for
masonry walls.**

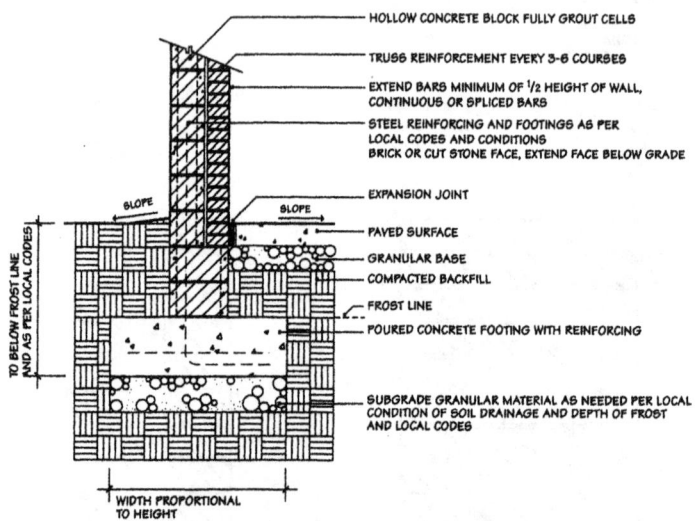

HOLLOW CONCRETE BLOCK FULLY GROUT CELLS

TRUSS REINFORCEMENT EVERY 3-6 COURSES

EXTEND BARS MINIMUM OF 1/2 HEIGHT OF WALL,
CONTINUOUS OR SPLICED BARS

STEEL REINFORCING AND FOOTINGS AS PER
LOCAL CODES AND CONDITIONS
BRICK OR CUT STONE FACE, EXTEND FACE BELOW GRADE

EXPANSION JOINT

PAVED SURFACE

GRANULAR BASE

COMPACTED BACKFILL

FROST LINE

POURED CONCRETE FOOTING WITH REINFORCING

SUBGRADE GRANULAR MATERIAL AS NEEDED PER LOCAL
CONDITION OF SOIL DRAINAGE AND DEPTH OF FROST
AND LOCAL CODES

SLOPE

SLOPE

TO BELOW FROST LINE
AND AS PER LOCAL CODES

WIDTH PROPORTIONAL
TO HEIGHT

**Figure 15.18. Reinforcement for freestanding masonry walls.**

# STONE WALLS

## Aesthetic Considerations

Two basic stonework patterns used in wall construction are random rubble and ashlar (Figures 15.19 and 15.20). Ashlar typically consists of flat surfaces and a limited range of sizes, and therefore, is more easily laid. Rubble usually consists of locally available stone and is often less expensive than ashlar. Rubble, however, is irregular in shape and difficult to cut. Regardless of the type of stone used, some method of capping the top of the wall will be necessary. Figure 15.21 illustrates several options for stone wall caps.

UNCOURSED RANDOM WITH ROUGHLY SQUARED RUBBLE

COURSED RANDOM WITH ROUGHLY SQUARED RUBBLE

UNCOURSED RANDOM WITH ROUGH RUBBLE

**Figure 15.19. Random rubble masonry patterns. Units are squared and dressed by stone masons in the field.**

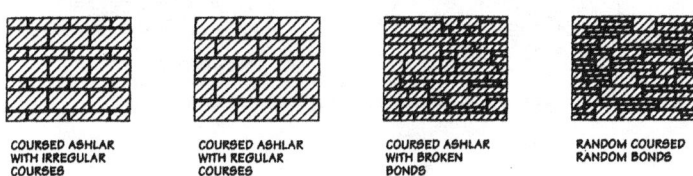

COURSED ASHLAR WITH IRREGULAR COURSES

COURSED ASHLAR WITH REGULAR COURSES

COURSED ASHLAR WITH BROKEN BONDS

RANDOM COURSED RANDOM BONDS

**Figure 15.20. Ashlar stone masonry patterns. Units are precut and dressed before delivery to the site.**

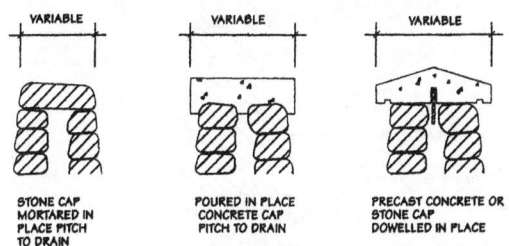

VARIABLE

VARIABLE

VARIABLE

STONE CAP MORTARED IN PLACE PITCH TO DRAIN

POURED IN PLACE CONCRETE CAP PITCH TO DRAIN

PRECAST CONCRETE OR STONE CAP DOWELLED IN PLACE

**Figure 15.21. Caps for stone walls.**

DEVICES

## Structural Considerations

### Components

Dry stone walls are an example of flexible construction that can tolerate a certain amount of differential settlement and do not require a base or footing that extends below the frostline. Mortar-laid stone walls have continuous footings and are therefore stronger and can be built higher (Figure 15.22).

### Construction

Stone walls can be laid up in two rough wythes with rubble fill or bond stones laid across the wall tying the wall faces together as in Figure 15.23. A good rule of thumb is to place a minimum of one bond stone for every 1 m² (10 ft²) of wall surface.

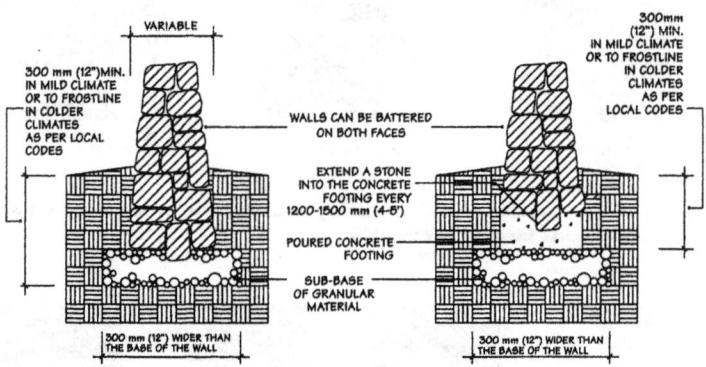

**Figure 15.22. Typical stone wall footing construction.**

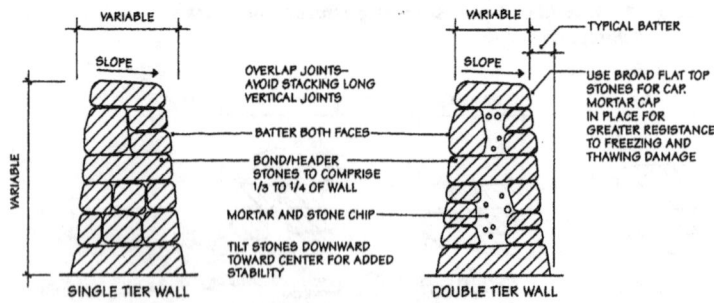

**Figure 15.23. Typical stone wall construction.**

# SUGGESTED REFERENCES

Dines, Nicholas T. and Kyle D. Brown, *Time-Saver Standards Site Construction Details Manual*, McGraw-Hill, New York, 1999.

Harris, Charles W. and Nicholas T. Dines, *Time-Saver Standards for Landscape Architecture, 2nd Edition*, McGraw-Hill, New York, 1998.

Landphair, Harlow C. and Fred Klatt, *Landscape Architecture Construction*, Elsevier, New York, 1988.

Vivian, John, *Building Fences of Wood, Stone, Metal and Plants*, Williamson Publishing, Charlotte, Vermont, 1987.

**DEVICES**

SUGGESTED REFERENCES

# Decks

16

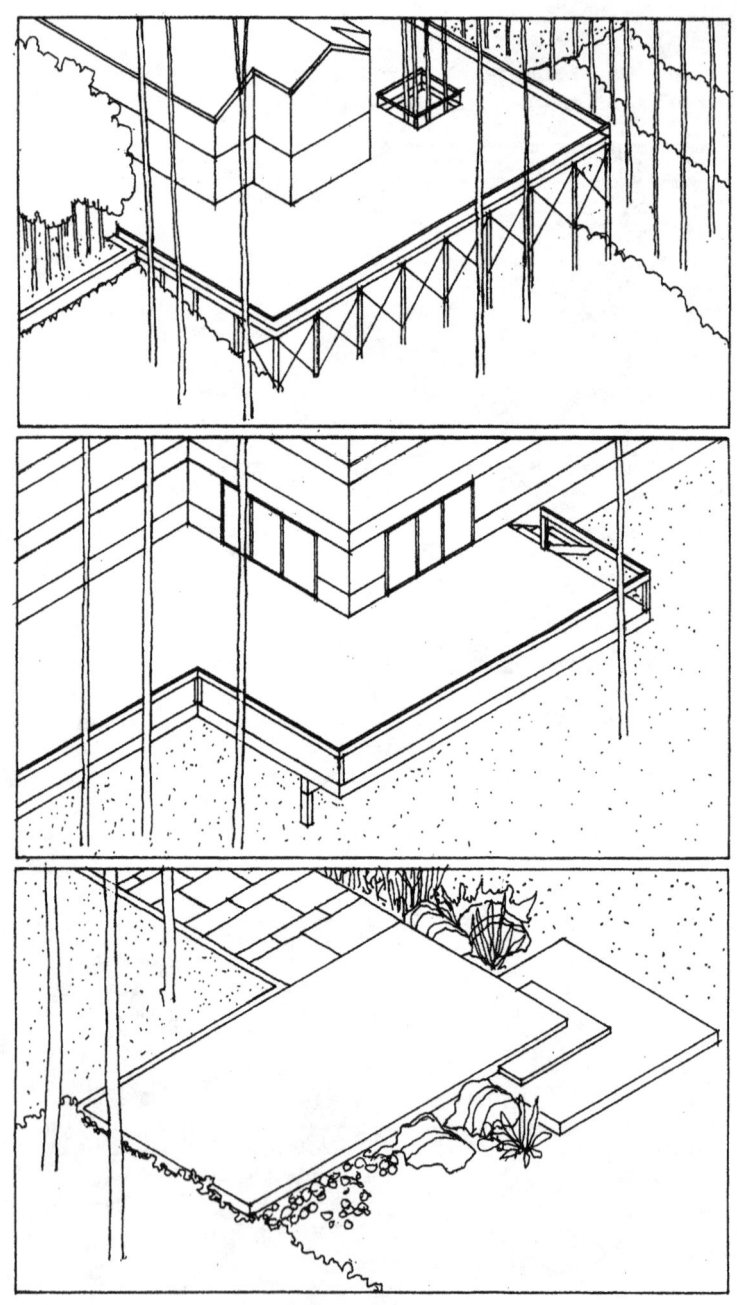

## HEAVY DUTY LARGE CAPACITY PUBLIC DECKS

This type of deck is often found in large commercial amusement parks, national, state, and local parks and piers, and in heavy-duty residential settings. It is characterized by significant square unit design loads, commercial grade timbers and sizing, and high annual maintenance to insure structural integrity and to withstand heavy use.

## MEDIUM DUTY RESIDENTIAL AND LIGHT COMMERCIAL DECKS AND BOARDWALKS

This type of deck structure is designed to sustain moderate loading and use. It is characterized by a wide variety of design expressions, ranging from utilitarian porches to elaborate and finely detailed construction. Utility and design details vary by climate zone and local codes. Maintenance centers on finishes and coatings.

DEVICES

## SMALL SCALE LIGHT DUTY DECKS AND BOARDWALKS

This type of structure is found in fragile landscapes such as conservation areas with limited access. Structures typically have small footprints and are limited in their spatial dimension by architectural, regulatory, or other factors. Loading is light to moderate and the structural system is typically simple. Maintenance commonly involves periodic replacement of components rather than annual coatings.

WOOD DECKS AND BOARDWALKS MAY BE USED to provide outdoor pedestrian space when at-grade hardscape is not feasible or desired. Decks or boardwalks may be indicated when the grade is too steep for accessibility, when surface conditions are ecologically sensitive (such as a wetland), or when an overlook or raised/upper-story platform is desired. An appropriate framing plan for the construction of a wood deck or boardwalk requires a survey of site conditions, assessment of functional requirements, calculation of design loads, and sizing of deck components.

## DIAGNOSTIC ASSESSMENT

*What are the design requirements for the proposed deck or boardwalk?*

The functional areas of a proposed deck must fall within the limitations of existing site conditions, which include all legal setback distances and other regulatory restrictions, as well as physical limitations of access and proper soil bearing capacity. The area requirements for each activity must be calculated before a preliminary framing plan may be explored.

*What are the structural properties of the materials for the deck or boardwalk?*

The structural properties of the deck timber and hardware components must be compatible with the calculated loads and use intensity, the local climate cycles, the desired degree of finish detailing, and the aesthetic appearance. Most local codes require that only stamped agency approved lumber be allowed in residential and commercial construction applications.

*What steps have been taken to assure the structural stability of the proposed deck or boardwalk?*

The deck design must be analyzed for weight distribution on all components to insure that the timber sizes and proposed spans fall within accepted parameters for the species and grade of lumber selected. Footings, attachments, framing, and joinery must conform to local structural codes.

## DESIGN REQUIREMENTS

### Function of the Deck

Certain functional requirements or programmatic elements may best be resolved through a deck and/or boardwalk system. The following is a list of possible functions that may require the use of wood decks or boardwalks:

- *Transition between levels:* The transition between two grade levels or from a building to a lower grade through a progression of terraced wood deck spaces may be preferable to long sets of steps.
- *Continuation of indoor space:* Both indoor and outdoor spaces benefit when there is a graceful transition between the two, each borrowing a sense of greater area and openness from the other.
- *Bringing commonly indoor uses outdoors:* Most interior functions can also be accommodated outdoors when weather permits. Decks are often conceived of as spaces for entertaining, dining, and cooking; however, they can also be private and secluded spaces for sleeping, hot tubs, and even showers. The amount of exterior space devoted to each function should be about ⅓ greater than the corresponding interior space.
- *Platforms and overlooks:* Constructing decks high above grade or off a precipice provides pedestrians a perspective that they don't often have, allowing for expansive views or the feeling of being up in the trees.
- *Pedestrian paths:* Wood boardwalks are used most often when surface conditions are ecologically sensitive, such as wetlands or steep slopes, or where accessibility requires ramping to transition between grades.

## Site Analysis

Where and how to construct the deck should be informed by a careful consideration of site conditions:
- *Legal:* Local codes, zoning ordinances, and permitting processes may limit the style, materials, location, and construction methods of a deck or boardwalk, and should be investigated early in the design process.
- *Climate and microclimate:* A basic understanding of ecological site design will guide the landscape architect in addressing issues such as sun exposure and wind mitigation. In addition, in cold and temperate climates the designer must calculate the potential loading impact of large snowfalls. Snowdrifts of 1.5-1.8 m (5-6 ft) can weigh as much as 390-490 kg per m$^2$ (80-100 lbs per ft$^2$). Many high snowfall areas have minimum building codes for snow loading.
- *Topography:* Soil stability is an issue in areas with steep slopes or very sandy soils. Soil or structural engineers should be consulted.

## Framing Method

The choice of framing method is a function of cost comparison, aesthetic preference, regional practice, and the amount of cross-sectional space available for the deck profile.

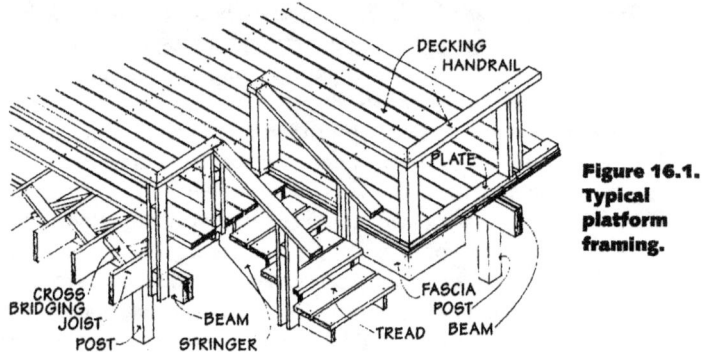

Figure 16.1.
Typical
platform
framing.

DECKING
HANDRAIL
PLATE
CROSS
BRIDGING
JOIST
POST
BEAM
STRINGER
FASCIA
POST
TREAD BEAM

## Platform Framing

Platform framing is a beam-and-joist method of construction (Figure 16.1). Few beams are necessary because joists carry the load over a wide area. Platform framing results in a deeper (thicker) deck profile than plank-and-beam framing due to the inclusion of joists. It is a very common framing system, especially in cold and temperate zones, and provides opportunities for constructing decks using fewer footings and support columns.

## Plank-and-Beam Framing

Plank-and-beam framing refers to a beam-and-decking method of construction (Figure 16.2). No joists are used because the beams are spaced close enough together to function like joists. A major advantage of plank-and-beam framing over platform framing is its shallow profile, which gives it a simple and clean appearance. It is commonly employed in warm dry climates where footings are shallow and relatively easy to install, and in boardwalk construction and near-grade decking. In dry climates, planks may be tongue and groove, or thick squared dimension lumber. In cool wet climates, the plank decking may be covered with a roofing membrane and finished with another material.

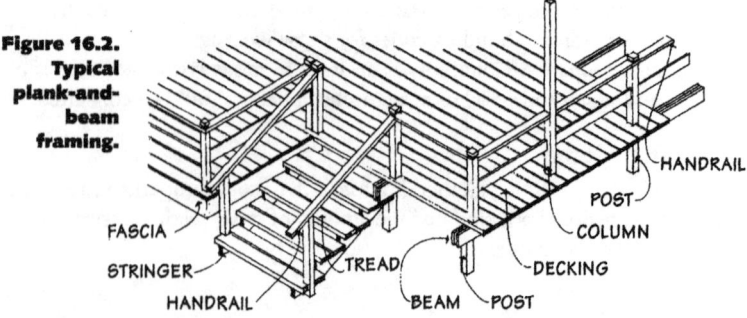

Figure 16.2.
Typical
plank-and-
beam
framing.

HANDRAIL
POST
COLUMN
FASCIA
TREAD
DECKING
STRINGER
HANDRAIL
BEAM
POST

# MATERIALS

## Basic Components

### Decking

Decking refers to the surface walked upon and is supported by joists or beams. The appearance and finish of decking is usually more important than the appearance of substructure hidden out of the view of users. The following design factors should be considered:

- Decking is usually laid flat but can also be laid on edge.
- Decking material should be greater than 25 mm (1″) nominal thickness. 30 mm (1¼″) planking is acceptable but 50 mm (2″) material is more common.
- The space between planks should be no more than 3 mm (⅛″) or the equivalent of a 16d nail unless the wood is not completely dry in which case the planks should be laid without a space to allow for shrinkage.
- Decking should be less than 150 mm (6″) wide because of the propensity to warp.
- Decking should be laid bark side up to avoid cupping and consequent drainage problems unless higher grade vertical grain wood is used.

### Joists

Joists are used in platform framing and support decking material of relatively short spans. The following design factors should be considered:

- Dimensioned lumber as classified by the National Forest Products Association (NFPA) should be specified for joists and should be oriented with the narrow dimension up.
- Ideally, joists should be supported on each end by a beam, a ledger, or metal hangers.
- Bridging is sometimes used between joists to minimize lateral movement.
- When fastening joists or beams, especially with bolts, care must be taken to prevent weakening of the member.

### Beams

Beams function to support the weight of joists and decking, transferring the load to posts or directly to a foundation. The following design factors should be considered:

- There are 5 common types of beam support systems:
  1. *Simple beam:* rests on a support at each end.
  2. *Cantilevered:* supported at one end only.
  3. *Overhanging:* projects beyond one or both sides.
  4. *Continuous:* rests on three or more supports.
  5. *Fixed:* fixed at both ends.

- Graded lumber should be specified for beams (NFPA) and they should be placed so the narrow dimension is vertical.

## Posts

Posts carry the weight of the entire deck structure to the foundation. Posts are not necessary when beams can rest directly on the foundation. The following design factors should be considered:

- Lumber for posts should be classified as post and timbers graded to carry longitudinal loads.
- Square posts have the least propensity to twist or warp.
- Wood posts are often sized beyond their recommended dimension as calculated for the proposed load in order to add "visual strength" and promote user confidence.
- Posts extended up through the deck or boardwalk can also serve as railing components. The exposed top end of the post should be angle cut, capped, or covered in order to prevent moisture infiltration.
- There should be a clearance or barrier between the bottom of the post and the footing pier to avoid moisture infiltration.

## Footings

Footings anchor a deck or boardwalk to the ground, supporting its weight and its expected live load. The following design factors should be considered:

- In cold and temperate climates, the footing must extend below the local frost line.
- Expansive clay soils, unstable organic soils, and deep fills require pier-and-beam foundations.
- Footings should be protected from the possibility of soil erosion.

## Wood

Tables 16.1 and 16.2 provide comparative information on various species of wood commonly used for deck construction. The use of higher grade, decay resistant lumber is always preferable but must be balanced with cost factors. When naturally decay resistant lumbers such as redwood or cedar are not used, penetrating stains are recommended. It should be noted, however, that copper-arsenic based pressure treated products should be used only for framing and not in areas of human contact. Table 16.3 lists standard nominal wood dimensions and their shrinkage factors.

## Hardware

Wood members are typically fastened together using various types of metal hardware such as nails, wood screws, and bolts. Stainless steel fasteners are recommended to prevent rusting from exposure to the elements, however, plated, aluminum, or hot-dipped galvanized fasteners are also

## TABLE 16.1. Relative comparison of various qualities of wood used in deck construction.

| | Douglas Fir-Larch | Southern Pine | Hemlock Fir* | Soft Pines† |
|---|---|---|---|---|
| Hardness | Fair | Fair | Poor | Poor |
| Warp resistance | Fair | Fair | Fair | Good |
| Ease of working | Poor | Fair | Fair | Good |
| Paint-holding | Poor | Poor | Poor | Good |
| Stain acceptance‡ | Fair | Fair | Fair | Fair |
| Nail-holding | Good | Good | Poor | Poor |
| Heartwood-decay resistance | Fair | Fair | Poor | Poor |
| Proportion of heartwood | Good | Poor | Poor | Fair |
| Bending strength | Good | Good | Fair | Poor |
| Stiffness | Good | Good | Good | Poor |
| Strength as a post | Good | Good | Fair | Poor |
| Freedom from pitch | Fair | Poor | Good | Fair |

| | Western Red Cedar | Redwood | Spruce | Cypress |
|---|---|---|---|---|
| Hardness | Poor | Fair | Poor | Fair |
| Warp resistance | Good | Good | Fair | Fair |
| Ease of working | Good | Fair | Fair | Fair |
| Paint-holding | Good | Good | Fair | Good |
| Stain acceptance‡ | Good | Good | Fair | Fair |
| Nail-holding | Poor | Fair | Fair | Fair |
| Heartwood-decay resistance | Good | Good | Poor | Good |
| Proportion of heartwood | Good | Good | Poor | Good |
| Bending strength | Poor | Fair | Fair | Fair |
| Stiffness | Poor | Fair | Fair | Fair |
| Strength as a post | Fair | Good | Fair | Fair |
| Freedom from pitch | Good | Good | Good | Good |

*Includes West Coast and eastern hemlocks.

†Includes western and northeastern pines.

‡Categories refer to semitransparent oil base stain.

Source: C.G. Ramsey and H. R. Sleeper, *Architectural Graphic Standards*, 9th Ed., John R. Hoke, ed., Wiley, New York, 1994.

DEVICES

**TABLE 16.2. Strength groupings of common softwood species.**

| Strength Group | Species |
|---|---|
| High | • Douglas Fir<br>• Hemlock, western<br>• Larch, western<br>• Pine:<br>  – Loblolly†<br>  – Longleaf†<br>  – Pitch<br>  – Slash<br>  – Shortleaf<br>  – Virginia<br>• Spruce<br>  – Canadian coastal<br>  – Coast Sitka |
| Moderate | • Cedar, western red<br>• Cypress<br>• Douglas fir (south)<br>• Fir<br>  – Subalpine<br>  – White<br>• Hemlock<br>  – Eastern<br>  – Western<br>• Pine<br>  – Eastern white<br>  – Lodgepole<br>  – Ponderosa<br>  – Red<br>  – Sugar<br>  – Western white<br>• Redwood, California<br>• Spruce<br>  – Eastern<br>  – Engelmann<br>  – Sitka<br>• Tamarack |
| Low | • Cedar, northern white |

\* No. 1 or better.

† Also known as southern pine.

Source: Adapted from *U.S. Department of Agriculture Construction Guides for Exposed Wood Decks*, U.S.D.A. Handbook No. 432, 1972.

**TABLE 16.3. Lumber shrinkage (inches).**

| Nominal | Dry | Green |
|---|---|---|
| 1 | $3/4$ | $25/32$ |
| 2 | $1^1/2$ | $1^9/16$ |
| 4 | $3^1/2$ | $3^9/16$ |
| 6 | $5^1/2$ | $5^5/8$ |
| 8 | $7^1/4$ | $7^1/2$ |
| 10 | $9^1/4$ | $9^1/2$ |
| 12 | $11^1/4$ | $11^1/2$ |

used. Anchors, hangers, and plates are used to facilitate easy and strong connections between structural members.

# STRUCTURAL DESIGN

## Estimating Design Load

Table 16.4 lists the recommended live loads for different deck uses. The span tables that follow are calculated for light to medium duty applications (40-60 lb/ft²) such as residential decks and should not be relied on for heavier duty applications. It is recommended that local code enforcing agencies and a structural engineer be consulted when finalizing decks or boardwalks that will receive unusually heavy loads.

## Span Tables

Figure 16.3 illustrates the relationship between decking, joist, and beam spans. For the purpose of preliminary design or light duty applications, the following span tables are provided (all spans should be measured center-to-center):

- *Plank sizing:* Table 16.5 shows maximum decking spans as modified by species and decking size. Decking span is also referred to as joist spacing.
- *Joist sizing:* Table 16.6 provides joist span data for various wood species, joist sizes, and spacing values. Joist span is also referred to as beam spacing.
- *Beam sizing:* Tables 16.7-16.9 list beam span data for various wood species, beam sizes, and tributary load widths (ft). It should be noted that solid wood beams are rated for greater spans than are compos-

## TABLE 16.4. Recommended live loads for different decking uses.

| Type of Deck | Load: kg/m² | (lb/ft²) |
|---|---|---|
| Residential decks | 195-290 | (40-60) |
| Public decks | 390-490 | (80-100) |
| Foot bridges | 490 | (100) |
| Light vehicular bridge | 980-1 470 | (200-300) |

The average dead load allowance (weight of decking plus fasteners, etc. per m² (ft²) is 49 kg/m² (10 lb/ft²).

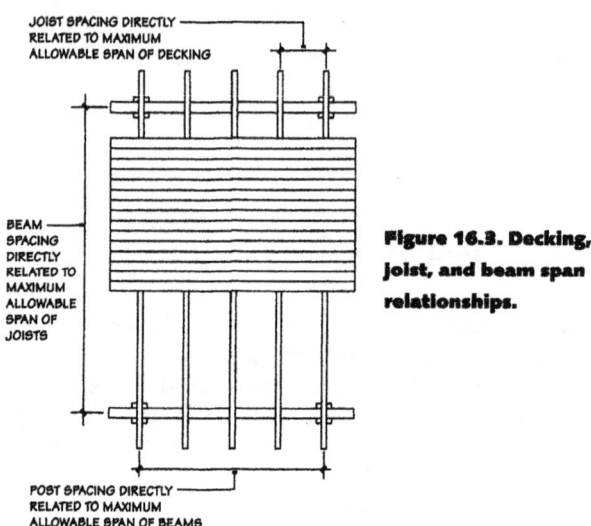

JOIST SPACING DIRECTLY RELATED TO MAXIMUM ALLOWABLE SPAN OF DECKING

BEAM SPACING DIRECTLY RELATED TO MAXIMUM ALLOWABLE SPAN OF JOISTS

POST SPACING DIRECTLY RELATED TO MAXIMUM ALLOWABLE SPAN OF BEAMS

**Figure 16.3. Decking, joist, and beam span relationships.**

ite beams fashioned from double or triple 2 in. stock. Beam span is also referred to as post spacing.

- *Post height:* Table 16.10 gives maximum post height data for various wood species, post heights, post sizes, and tributary load areas (ft²) (total area loading on a post). Post height is measured from the top of the footing to the bottom of the beam to which it is attached.

## TABLE 16.5. Maximum decking spans (joist spacing).

| Species | Nominal Decking Size | Recommended Span |
|---|---|---|
| Douglas-Fir, Southern Pine, | RED [a] | 16"[c] |
| Hem-Fir, SPF, SPF (south), | 2 x 4 [b] | 24" |
| Ponderosa Pine, Redwood, Western Cedar | 2 x 6 [b] | 24" |

[a] RED is radius edge decking, 4" to 6" widths.

[b] Grade is No. 2 or better.

[c] Southern Pine RED can span 24".

Source: Adapted from McDonald et.al, *Wood Decks: Materials, Construction, and Finishing*, Forest Products Laboratory, Madison, WI, 1996.

## TABLE 16.6. Maximum joist spans (beam spacing).

| Species | Joist Size[†] | 40 lb./ft² Live Load [*] | | | 60 lb./ft² Live Load[*] | | |
|---|---|---|---|---|---|---|---|
| | | 12" | 16" | 24" | 12" | 16" | 24" |
| Douglas Fir, | 2 × 6 | 10'4" | 9'5" | 7'10" | 9'0" | 8'2" | 6'8" |
| Southern Pine | 2 × 8 | 13'8" | 12'5" | 10'2" | 11'11" | 10'6" | 8'7" |
| | 2 × 10 | 17'5" | 15'5" | 12'7" | 15'0" | 13'0" | 10'7" |
| | 2 × 12 | 20'0" | 17'10" | 14'7" | 17'5" | 15'1" | 12'4" |
| Hem-Fir,SPF | 2 × 6 | 9'2" | 8'4" | 7'3" | 8'0" | 7'3" | 6'3" |
| SPF (south) | 2 × 8 | 12'1" | 10'11" | 9'6" | 10'6" | 9'6" | 8'0" |
| | 2 × 10 | 15'4" | 14'0" | 11'7" | 13'5" | 12'0" | 9'10" |
| | 2 × 12 | 18'8" | 16'6" | 13'6" | 16'1" | 14'0" | 10'10" |
| Ponderosa Pine, | 2 × 6 | 8'10" | 8'0" | 7'0" | 7'9" | 7'0" | 5'11" |
| Redwood, | 2 × 8 | 11'8" | 10'7" | 8'10" | 10'2" | 9'2" | 7'6" |
| Western Cedar | 2 × 10 | 14'10" | 13'3" | 10'10" | 12'11" | 11'2" | 9'2" |
| | 2 × 12 | 17'9" | 15'4" | 12'7" | 15'0" | 13'0" | 10'7" |

[*] Includes 10 lb./ft² dead load

[†] Joists are on edge, and Grade is No. 2 or better

Source: Adapted from McDonald, et.al, *Wood Decks: Materials, Construction, and Finishing*, Forest Products Laboratory, Madison, WI, 1996

**TABLE 16.7. Maximum beam spans (post spacing) for Douglas fir and southern pine.**

| Beam Size† | Tributary Load Width, ft | | | | | | | | | | | | |
|---|---|---|---|---|---|---|---|---|---|---|---|---|---|
| | 4' | 5' | 6' | 7' | 8' | 9' | 10' | 11' | 12' | 13' | 14' | 15' | 16' |
| 40 LB./FT² LIVE LOAD DECK DESIGN* | | | | | | | | | | | | | |
| (2) 2×6 | 7' | 6' | | | | | | | | | | | |
| (2) 2×8 | 9' | 8' | 7' | 7' | 6' | | | | | | | | |
| (2) 2×10 | 11' | 10' | 9' | 8' | 8' | 6' | | | | | | | |
| (3) 2×8 | 12' | 11' | 10' | 9' | 8' | 8' | 7' | 6' | 6' | 6' | 6' | | |
| (2) 2×12 | 13' | 12' | 10' | 10' | 9' | 8' | 8' | 7' | 7' | 7' | 6' | 6' | 6' |
| (3) 2×10 | 15' | 13' | 12' | 11' | 10' | 10' | 9' | 9' | 8' | 8' | 8' | 7' | 7' |
| (3) 2×12 | 16' | 15' | 14' | 13' | 12' | 11' | 11' | 10' | 10' | 9' | 9' | 8' | 8' |
| 4×6 | 7' | 7' | 6' | | | | | | | | | | |
| 4×8 | 10' | 9' | 8' | 7' | 7' | 6' | 6' | 6' | | | | | |
| 6×8 | 12' | 10' | 9' | 9' | 8' | 8' | 7' | 7' | 6' | 6' | 6' | 6' | 6' |
| 4×10 | 12' | 11' | 10' | 9' | 8' | 8' | 7' | 7' | 7' | 6' | 6' | 6' | 6' |
| 4×12 | 14' | 13' | 11' | 10' | 10' | 9' | 9' | 8' | 8' | 7' | 7' | 7' | 7' |
| 6×10 | 15' | 13' | 12' | 11' | 10' | 10' | 9' | 9' | 8' | 8' | 7' | 7' | 7' |
| 6×12 | 16' | 16' | 15' | 13' | 12' | 12' | 11' | 10' | 10' | 10' | 9' | 9' | 8' |

**TABLE 16.7. Maximum beam spans (post spacing) for Douglas fir and southern pine (continued).**

| Beam Size† | Tributary Load Width, ft | | | | | | | | | | | | |
|---|---|---|---|---|---|---|---|---|---|---|---|---|---|
| | 4' | 5' | 6' | 7' | 8' | 9' | 10' | 11' | 12' | 13' | 14' | 15' | 16' |
| **60 LB./FT² LIVE LOAD DESIGN** | | | | | | | | | | | | | |
| (2) 2 × 6 | 6' | | | | | | | | | | | | |
| (2) 2 × 8 | 7' | 7' | 6' | | | | | | | | | | |
| (2) 2 × 10 | 9' | 8' | 7' | 7' | 6' | | | | | | | | |
| (3) 2 × 8 | 10' | 9' | 8' | 7' | 7' | 6' | 6' | | | | | | |
| (2) 2 × 12 | 11' | 10' | 9' | 8' | 7' | 7' | 6' | 6' | 6' | | | | |
| (3) 2 × 10 | 12' | 11' | 10' | 9' | 9' | 8' | 8' | 7' | 7' | 6' | 6' | 6' | 6' |
| (3) 2 × 12 | 14' | 13' | 12' | 11' | 10' | 9' | 9' | 8' | 8' | 8' | 7' | 7' | 6' |
| 4 × 6 | 6' | | | | | | | | | | | | |
| 4 × 8 | 8' | 7' | 6' | 6' | | | | | | | | | |
| 6 × 8 | 10' | 9' | 8' | 7' | 7' | 6' | 6' | | | | | | |
| 4 × 10 | 10' | 9' | 8' | 7' | 7' | 6' | 6' | 6' | | | | | |
| 4 × 12 | 12' | 10' | 9' | 9' | 8' | 8' | 7' | 7' | 6' | 6' | 6' | | |
| 6 × 10 | 12' | 11' | 10' | 9' | 9' | 8' | 8' | 7' | 7' | 6' | 6' | 6' | 6' |
| 6 × 12 | 15' | 13' | 12' | 11' | 10' | 10' | 9' | 9' | 8' | 8' | 8' | 7' | 7' |

\* Includes 10 lb/ft² dead load. † Number in parentheses is number of full-length nailed laminations.

Source: Adapted from McDonald, et. al, *Wood Decks: Materials, Construction, and Finishing,* Forest Products Laboratory, Madison, WI, 1996.

DEVICES

# TABLE 16.8. Maximum beam spans (post spacing) for hem-fir, SPF, and SPF (south).

| Beam Size | Tributary Load Width, ft | | | | | | | | | | | | |
|---|---|---|---|---|---|---|---|---|---|---|---|---|---|
| | 4' | 5' | 6' | 7' | 8' | 9' | 10' | 11' | 12' | 13' | 14' | 15' | 16' |
| **40 LB./FT² LIVE LOAD DECK DESIGN·** | | | | | | | | | | | | | |
| (2) 2×6 | 6' | 6' | | | | | | | | | | | |
| (2) 2×8 | 8' | 7' | 6' | 6' | | | | | | | | | |
| (2) 2×10 | 10' | 9' | 8' | 7' | 7' | 6' | 6' | | | | | | |
| (3) 2×8 | 11' | 10' | 9' | 8' | 7' | 7' | 6' | 6' | 6' | | | | |
| (2) 2×12 | 11' | 10' | 9' | 8' | 8' | 7' | 7' | 6' | 6' | 6' | | | |
| (3) 2×10 | 13' | 12' | 11' | 10' | 9' | 8' | 8' | 8' | 7' | 7' | 6' | 6' | |
| (3) 2×12 | 15' | 14' | 12' | 11' | 11' | 10' | 9' | 9' | 8' | 8' | 8' | 7' | 7' |
| 4×6 | 7' | 6' | 6' | | | | | | | | | | |
| 4×8 | 9' | 8' | 7' | 6' | 6' | 6' | | | | | | | |
| 6×8 | 9' | 8' | 8' | 7' | 7' | 6' | 6' | 6' | 6' | | | | |
| 4×10 | 11' | 10' | 9' | 8' | 7' | 7' | 6' | 6' | | | | | |
| 4×12 | 13' | 11' | 10' | 9' | 9' | 8' | 7' | 7' | 7' | 6' | 6' | 6' | |
| 6×10 | 12' | 11' | 10' | 9' | 8' | 8' | 7' | 7' | 7' | 6' | 6' | 6' | 6' |
| 6×12 | 15' | 13' | 12' | 11' | 10' | 10' | 9' | 9' | 8' | 8' | 7' | 7' | 7' |

**TABLE 16.8. Maximum beam spans (post spacing) for hem-fir, SPF, and SPF (south) (continued).**

| Beam Size | Tributary Load Width, ft | | | | | | | | | | | | |
|---|---|---|---|---|---|---|---|---|---|---|---|---|---|
| | 4' | 5' | 6' | 7' | 8' | 9' | 10' | 11' | 12' | 13' | 14' | 15' | 16' |
| **60 LB./FT² LIVE LOAD DESIGN** | | | | | | | | | | | | | |
| (2) 2 × 6 | 5' | | | | | | | | | | | | |
| (2) 2 × 8 | 7' | 6' | | | | | | | | | | | |
| (2) 2 × 10 | 8' | 7' | 7' | 6' | | | | | | | | | |
| (3) 2 × 8 | 9' | 8' | 7' | 7' | 6' | | | | | | | | |
| (2) 2 × 12 | 10' | 9' | 8' | 7' | 6' | 6' | | | | | | | |
| (3) 2 × 10 | 11' | 10' | 9' | 8' | 8' | 7' | 6' | 6' | | | | | |
| (3) 2 × 12 | 13' | 11' | 10' | 9' | 9' | 8' | 8' | 7' | 6' | 6' | 6' | | |
| 4 × 6 | 5' | | | | | | | | | | | | |
| 4 × 8 | 7' | 6' | | | | | | | | | | | |
| 6 × 8 | 8' | 7' | 7' | 6' | | | | | | | | | |
| 4 × 10 | 9' | 8' | 7' | 7' | 6' | | | | | | | | |
| 4 × 12 | 10' | 9' | 8' | 8' | 7' | 7' | 6' | 6' | | | | | |
| 6 × 10 | 10' | 9' | 8' | 8' | 7' | 7' | 6' | 6' | 6' | | | | |
| 6 × 12 | 12' | 11' | 10' | 9' | 9' | 8' | 8' | 7' | 6' | 6' | 6' | 6' | 6' |

* Includes 10 lb/ft² dead load. † Number in parentheses is number of full-length nailed laminations.

Source: Adapted from McDonald, et.al, *Wood Decks: Materials, Construction, and Finishing*, Forest Products Laboratory, Madison, WI, 1996.

DEVICES

# TABLE 16.9. Maximum beam spans (post spacing) for ponderosa pine, redwood, and western cedar.

| Beam Size | 4' | 5' | 6' | 7' | 8' | 9' | 10' | 11' | 12' | 13' | 14' | 15' | 16' |
|---|---|---|---|---|---|---|---|---|---|---|---|---|---|
| **40 LB./FT² LIVE LOAD DECK DESIGN\*** | | | | | | | | | | | | | |
| (2) 2 × 6 | 6' | | | | | | | | | | | | |
| (2) 2 × 8 | 8' | 7' | 6' | 6' | | | | | | | | | |
| (2) 2 × 10 | 9' | 8' | 8' | 7' | 6' | 6' | 6' | | | | | | |
| (3) 2 × 8 | 10' | 9' | 8' | 8' | 7' | 7' | 6' | 6' | | | | | |
| (2) 2 × 12 | 11' | 10' | 9' | 8' | 7' | 7' | 7' | 6' | 6' | | | | |
| (3) 2 × 10 | 13' | 11' | 10' | 9' | 8' | 8' | 7' | 7' | 7' | | | | |
| (3) 2 × 12 | 15' | 13' | 12' | 11' | 10' | 9' | 9' | 8' | 8' | 8' | 7' | 7' | 7' |
| 4 × 6 | 7' | 6' | | | | | | | | | | | |
| 4 × 8 | 9' | 8' | 8' | 7' | 6' | 6' | 6' | | | | | | |
| 6 × 8 | 9' | 8' | 8' | 7' | 7' | 6' | 6' | 6' | | | | | |
| 4 × 10 | 10' | 9' | 8' | 8' | 7' | 7' | 6' | 6' | 6' | | | | |
| 4 × 12 | 12' | 11' | 10' | 9' | 8' | 8' | 7' | 7' | 6' | 6' | 6' | 6' | |
| 6 × 10 | 12' | 11' | 10' | 9' | 8' | 8' | 7' | 7' | 7' | 6' | 6' | 6' | |
| 6 × 12 | 15' | 13' | 12' | 11' | 10' | 9' | 9' | 8' | 8' | 8' | 7' | 7' | 7' |

Tributary Load Width, ft

**TABLE 16.9. Maximum beam spans (post spacing) for ponderosa pine, redwood, and western cedar (continued).**

| Beam Size† | | | Tributary Load Width, ft | | | | | | | | | | | | |
|---|---|---|---|---|---|---|---|---|---|---|---|---|---|---|---|
| | 4' | 5' | 6' | 7' | 8' | 9' | 10' | 11' | 12' | 13' | 14' | 15' | 16' |
| 60 LB./FT² LIVE LOAD DESIGN | | | | | | | | | | | | | |
| (2) 2 × 8 | 6' | 6' | | | | | | | | | | | |
| (2) 2 × 10 | 8' | 7' | 6' | 6' | | | | | | | | | |
| (3) 2 × 8 | 9' | 8' | 7' | 6' | 6' | | | | | | | | |
| (2) 2 × 12 | 9' | 8' | 7' | 7' | 6' | 6' | | | | | | | |
| (3) 2 × 10 | 11' | 9' | 8' | 8' | 7' | 7' | 6' | 6' | | | | | |
| (3) 2 × 12 | 12' | 11' | 10' | 9' | 8' | 8' | 7' | 7' | 6' | 6' | | | |
| 4 × 8 | 7' | 6' | 6' | | | | | | | | | | |
| 6 × 8 | 8' | 7' | 6' | 6' | | | | | | | | | |
| 4 × 10 | 9' | 8' | 7' | 6' | | | | | | | | | |
| 4 × 12 | 10' | 9' | 8' | 7' | 7' | 6' | 6' | | | | | | |
| 6 × 10 | 10' | 9' | 8' | 7' | 7' | 6' | 6' | 6' | | | | | |
| 6 × 12 | 12' | 11' | 10' | 9' | 8' | 8' | 7' | 7' | 7' | 6' | 6' | 6' | |

* Includes 10 lb/ft² dead load. † Number in parentheses is number of full-length nailed laminations.

Source: Adapted from McDonald, et.al, *Wood Decks: Materials, Construction, and Finishing*, Forest Products Laboratory, Madison, WI, 1996.

DEVICES

*Decks* ▪ 311

# TABLE 16.10. Maximum post heights.

| Species | Post Size | Tributary Load Area to Post, ft² | | | | | | | | | | | | | | | | | | |
|---|---|---|---|---|---|---|---|---|---|---|---|---|---|---|---|---|---|---|---|---|
| | | 36 | 48 | 60 | 72 | 84 | 96 | 108 | 120 | 132 | 144 | 156 | 168 | 180 | 192 | 204 | 216 | 228 | 240 | 256 |
| **40 LB/FT² LIVE LOAD DECK DESIGN\*** | | | | | | | | | | | | | | | | | | | | |
| Southern Pine, Douglas-Fir | 4 × 4 | 10' | 10' | 10' | 9' | 9' | 8' | 8' | 7' | 7' | 6' | 6' | 6' | 6' | 5' | 5' | 5' | 4' | 4' | 4' |
| | 4 × 6 | 14' | 14' | 13' | 12' | 11' | 10' | 10' | 9' | 9' | 8' | 8' | 8' | 7' | 7' | 7' | 7' | 6' | 6' | 6' |
| | 6 × 6 (No.1) | 17' | 17' | 17' | 17' | 17' | 17' | 17' | 17' | 17' | 17' | 17' | 16' | 16' | 15' | 15' | 14' | 14' | 14' | 13' |
| | 6 × 6 (No.2) | 17' | 17' | 17' | 17' | 17' | 17' | 17' | 17' | 16' | 16' | 15' | 15' | 14' | 13' | 13' | 12' | 12' | 12' | 12' |
| Hem-Fir, SPF | 4 × 4 | 10' | 10' | 10' | 9' | 9' | 8' | 8' | 7' | 7' | 6' | 6' | 6' | 6' | 5' | 5' | 5' | 4' | 4' | 4' |
| | 4 × 6 | 14' | 14' | 14' | 11' | 11' | 11' | 10' | 10' | 9' | 9' | 8' | 8' | 8' | 7' | 7' | 7' | 7' | 6' | 6' |
| | 6 × 6 (No.1) | 17' | 17' | 17' | 17' | 17' | 17' | 17' | 17' | 17' | 17' | 17' | 16' | 16' | 15' | 15' | 14' | 14' | 14' | 13' |
| | 6 × 6 (No.2) | 17' | 17' | 17' | 17' | 17' | 17' | 17' | 17' | 16' | 16' | 15' | 15' | 14' | 14' | 13' | 13' | 13' | 12' | 12' |
| Ponderosa Pine, Redwood, Western cedar, SPF (south) | 4 × 4 | 10' | 10' | 9' | 8' | 7' | 7' | 6' | 6' | 5' | 4' | | | | | | | | | |
| | 4 × 6 | 14' | 13' | 12' | 11' | 10' | 9' | 8' | 8' | 7' | 7' | 7' | 6' | 6' | 5' | 5' | 4' | | | |
| | 6 × 6 (No.1) | 17' | 17' | 17' | 17' | 17' | 17' | 17' | 17' | 16' | 15' | 15' | 14' | 14' | 13' | 13' | 12' | 12' | 11' | 11' |
| | 6 × 6 (No.2) | 17' | 17' | 17' | 17' | 16' | 16' | 13' | 7' | | | | | | | | | | | |
| **60 LB/FT² LIVE LOAD DECK DESIGN\*** | | | | | | | | | | | | | | | | | | | | |
| Southern Pine, Douglas-Fir | 4 × 4 | 10' | 10' | 9' | 8' | 7' | 7' | 6' | 6' | 5' | 5' | 5' | | | | | | | | |
| | 4 × 6 | 14' | 12' | 11' | 10' | 9' | 9' | 8' | 8' | 7' | 7' | 7' | 6' | 6' | 6' | 5' | 5' | 5' | 5' | |
| | 6 × 6 (No.1) | 17' | 17' | 17' | 17' | 17' | 17' | 17' | 16' | 16' | 15' | 14' | 14' | 13' | 13' | 12' | 12' | 11' | 11' | 10' |
| | 6 × 6 (No.2) | 17' | 17' | 17' | 17' | 16' | 15' | 15' | 14' | 13' | 12' | 11' | 9' | 6' | | | | | | |
| Hem-Fir, SPF | 4 × 4 | 10' | 10' | 9' | 8' | 7' | 7' | 6' | 6' | 6' | 5' | 5' | | | | | | | | |
| | 4 × 6 | 14' | 13' | 11' | 10' | 9' | 9' | 8' | 8' | 7' | 7' | 7' | 6' | 6' | 6' | 5' | 5' | | | |
| | 6 × 6 (No.1) | 17' | 17' | 17' | 17' | 17' | 17' | 16' | 16' | 15' | 14' | 13' | 13' | 12' | 11' | 10' | 10' | 9' | 8' | 7' |
| | 6 × 6 (No.2) | 17' | 17' | 17' | 17' | 16' | 16' | 14' | 12' | 10' | | | | | | | | | | |

**TABLE 16.10. Maximum post heights (continued).**

| Species | Post Size | Tributary Load Area to Post, ft² | | | | | | | | | | | | | | | | | | |
|---------|-----------|-----|-----|-----|-----|-----|-----|-----|-----|-----|-----|-----|-----|-----|-----|-----|-----|-----|-----|-----|
| | | 36 | 48 | 60 | 72 | 84 | 96 | 108 | 120 | 132 | 144 | 156 | 168 | 180 | 192 | 204 | 216 | 228 | 240 | 256 |
| Ponderosa Pine, | 4 × 4 | 10' | 9' | 7' | 7' | 6' | 5' | | | | | | | | | | | | | |
| Redwood, | 4 × 6 | 13' | 11' | 10' | 9' | 8' | 7' | 7' | 6' | 5' | 5' | | | | | | | | | |
| Western cedar, | 6 × 6 (No.1) | 17' | 17' | 17' | 17' | 17' | 16' | 15' | 14' | 13' | 13' | 12' | 11' | 11' | 10' | 10' | 9' | 9' | 8' | 6' |
| SPF (south) | 6 × 6 (No.2) | 17' | 17' | 17' | 15' | 9' | | | | | | | | | | | | | | |

*Includes 10 lb/ft² dead load

Source: Adapted from McDonald et.al., *Wood Decks: Materials, Construction, and Finishing,* Forest Products Laboratory, Madison, WI 1996.

DEVICES

*Decks* ▪ 313

# SUGGESTED REFERENCES

Goetz, Karl-Heinz. *Timber Design and Construction Source Book*, McGraw-Hill, New York, 1989.

Harris, Charles W. and Nicholas T. Dines, *Time-Saver Standards for Landscape Architecture, 2nd Edition*, McGraw-Hill, New York, 1998.

McDonald, et al., *Wood Decks: Materials, Construction, and Finishing*, Forest Products Laboratory, Madison, WI, 1996.

National Forest Products Association (NFPA). *National Design Specifications for Wood Construction*, 1986.

Ramsey, C.G. and H.R. Sleeper. *Architectural Graphic Standards*, 8th ed., Robert T. Packard, ed., Wiley, New York, 1994.

DEVICES

# *Water Features*

17

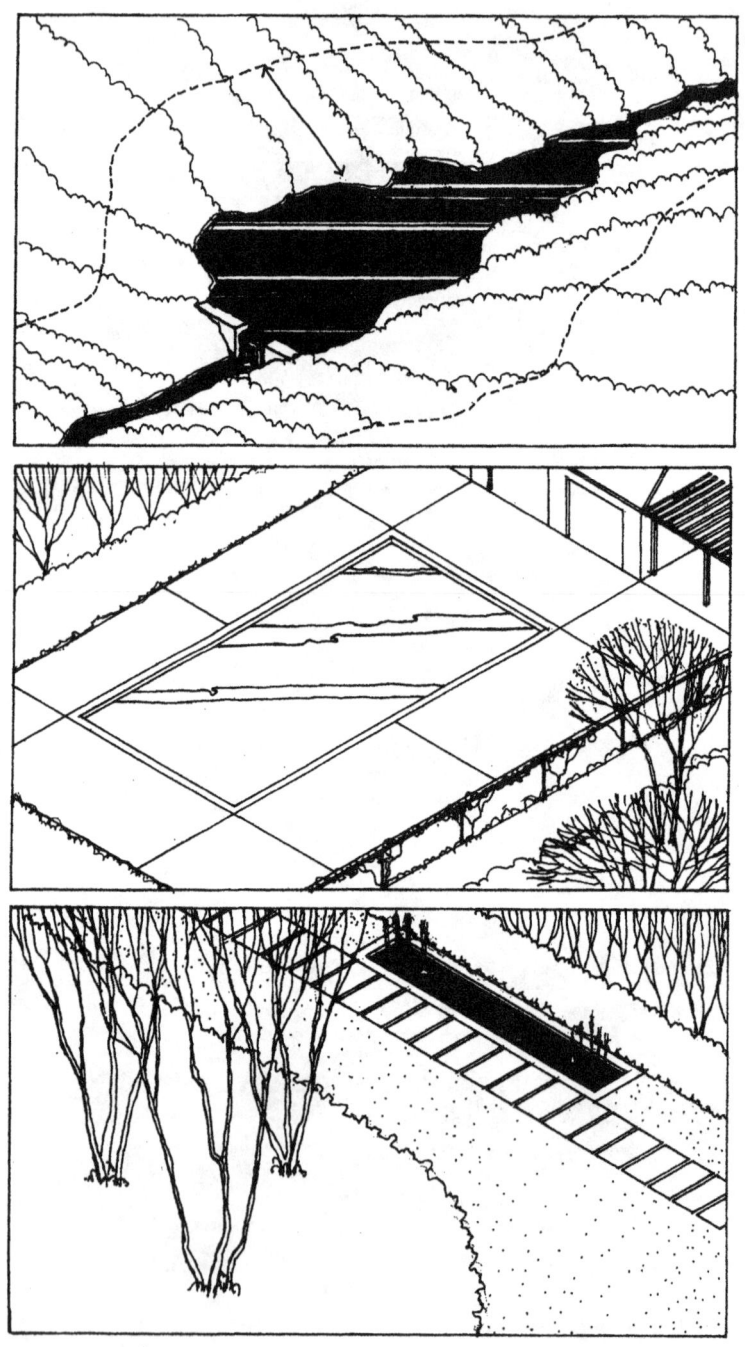

## STORMWATER DETENTION AND IRRIGATION PONDS

Ponds designed to collect stormwater and to serve as an irrigation source or as an ornamental feature may be lined or unlined, depending on soils and water table conditions. Key considerations include fabric filter layers to control turbidity at the pond edge in influent circumstances, and adequate overflow provisions to accommodate large storms. These ponds often require small earthen dams and masonry weirs to control pool elevation. A depth of 2.5-3.0 meters (7.5-10 ft) is recommended to create temperature stratification and biological conditions to sustain aquatic life. Spray displays may be used to add oxygen to the water.

## SWIMMING AND LARGE ORNAMENTAL POOLS

These pools typically require full recirculating filtration and chlorination due to human contact. Liners vary from polymers, polymer coated metal, reinforced concrete and masonry, or reinforced sprayed concrete (gunite). Surfaces are commonly finished with epoxy paint, smooth stucco, or tile to ease cleaning and to provide a suitable surface for human contact. Pools often are combined with water display features including cascades, sprays, and jets. As a matter of public health, many local codes require full filtration and treatment of public ornamental pools and fountains. Circulating pumps, water treatment, and seasonal maintenance are key long-term economic considerations.

## SMALL GARDEN POOLS AND ORNAMENTAL PONDS

These more intimate scale features may vary in size from 2 to 75 square meters (6 to 800 sq ft) in area. They are typically constructed with a polymer or rubber liner, resting on a sand cushion directly on the subgrade, but may include mesh-reinforced gunite in larger applications. Due to shallow depths of less than 450 mm (18″), water must be circulated to increase oxygen, and $CO_2$ levels and pH must be monitored to accommodate aquatic life. Recirculating pumps, display features, and heavily planted edges are commonly found in these features. Recycled water is often used as a water source in arid regions.

**DEVICES**

WATER FEATURES contribute recreational and aesthetic amenities to a design. They include water display elements, such as spouting fountains or cascading waterfalls, pool structures, and ornamental pond systems. A designer must understand the hydraulics and structural issues associated with the design of a proposed feature, as well as its impact on the perceptual qualities of the site, human use, and regional water resources.

## DIAGNOSTIC ASSESSMENT

*What issues should be considered in determining the appropriateness of water features?*

The use of water features should be carefully considered. Issues of safety, impacts on regional water resources, impacts of climatic conditions on the proposed display, as well as installation and maintenance costs should be analyzed prior to determining that a water feature should be included in the design.

*What are desirable display characteristics of the proposed water feature?*

Water features are typically incorporated into a design as a visual or recreational amenity, but they may also provide significant auditory, climatic, and sensory effects as well. Selecting an appropriate water effect depends on the design objectives, as well as climatic and site constraints.

*What reservoir structures are appropriate for the proposed effect?*

A water feature typically incorporates a pool structure or pond as its principal display and/or reservoir. However, some motion effects such as water walls or spout jets may utilize a hidden reservoir system below grade, to facilitate human interaction or accommodate site conditions. Selection of materials for reservoir structures is a function of cost, the intended application, and desired finish.

*What system specifications are appropriate for the proposed feature?*

The water feature's operating system, piping, display heads, and lighting must be carefully selected for the intended purpose and site conditions. Pumps for smaller features may be submersible, while larger displays typically employ remote pumps located under the reservoir wherever possible. Pipes, display heads, fittings, and valves, must be selected to ensure adequate pressure is delivered to the display to achieve the desired effect.

# CONSIDERATIONS IN USE
# OF WATER FEATURES

Water features are powerful design elements, capable of transforming people's perceptions of the environment. But a number of factors should be considered when deciding whether to include a water feature:

- Safety should always be a primary concern in the design of water features. Alternatives, such as displays without surface pools, should be considered in landscapes where unsupervised children are present. Most jurisdictions require perimeter fencing around features that exceed specified depths or design standards.

- The use of water features in arid climates with stressed water supplies should be carefully considered. Displays should be designed to recirculate water through the system for continued use. Alternatives to potable water supplies should be used wherever possible. Many jurisdictions require the use of recycled water for ornamental fountains.

- Water features are subject to significant water loss through evaporation, particularly in hot arid climates. Windy sites, large shallow surface pools, and displays with significant water spray and movement are subject to the greatest losses from evaporation. Human activity in swimming pools or displays may also increase evaporation rates as much as 40-70%. Some jurisdictions restrict the use of spray displays or limit the total surface area of water features on a site.

- In cold climates, consideration should be given to the design effect of the display, during the winter months it is inactive. Also, thermal covers should be provided for heated pools in cooler climates.

- Design and installation costs for water features are very high, and are a function of display size, complexity, material selection, and site conditions. Water features that satisfy multiple objectives (e.g. aesthetics, recreation, wildlife habitat, irrigation, fire protection, stormwater management) may justify their costs more rapidly than single-purpose displays.

- Maintenance is also quite expensive. Pools typically require on-going treatment of the water, as well as continual cleaning and repair. Long-term management must be carefully considered to protect the initial investment in feature design and installation.

# WATER EFFECTS

Table 17.1 describes characteristics of different water feature effects. Effects are typically categorized as still water features or moving water features that utilize gravity or applied pressure to generate motion. Selection of an appropriate effect is a function of design purpose and site conditions.

## TABLE 17.1. Water effect characteristics.

| | Effect | Visibility | Sound Levels | Splash | Wind Stability |
|---|---|---|---|---|---|
| **STILL WATER** | | | | | |
| | Reflector – Dark container | Good | None | None | Excellent |
| | Window - Light Container | Fair | None | None | Excellent |
| | Texture – Reflector w/surface disturbance | Good | Nominal | None | Excellent |
| | Activator – Window w/surface disturbance | Fair | Nominal | None | Excellent |
| **FALL EFFECTS** | | | | | |
| | Full Sheet – Continuous weir w/high flowrate | Good | High | Substantial | Good |
| | Interrupted Sheet – Intermittent weir | Good | Moderate | Substantial | Good |
| | Broken Sheet — Continuous weir w/low flowrate | Fair | Low | Moderate | Fair |
| | Gravity Spout – Circular discharge opening | Good | Moderate | Substantial | Good |
| **FLOW EFFECTS** | | | | | |
| | Smooth Waterwall – Low flowrate | Fair | Low | None | Excellent |
| | Aerated Waterwall – Textured surface w/moderate flowrate | Excellent | Moderate | Moderate | Good |

**TABLE 17.1. Water effect characteristics (continued).**

| | Effect | Visibility | Sound Levels | Splash | Wind |
|---|---|---|---|---|---|
| **FLOW EFFECTS (CONTINUED)** | | | | | |
| | Quiet Stream – Low velocity, shallow shape | Fair | Nominal | None | Excellent |
| | Turbulent Stream – High velocity, interrupted flow | Good | Low | Nominal | Excellent |
| **CASCADE EFFECTS** | | | | | |
| | Cascading waterfall – vertical orientation | Good | Moderate | Substantial | Good |
| | Stepped forms – Irregular steps, >1:1 | Excellent | Moderate | Moderate | Good |
| | Water Stairs – Regular steps, >1:1 | Excellent | Moderate | Moderate | Good |
| | Stepped pools | Good | Moderate | Moderate | Excellent |
| **SPOUTING EFFECTS** | | | | | |
| | Clear column – Circular discharge, minimal turbulence | Good | Moderate | Substantial | Fair |
| | Aerated Mass – Circular discharge, significant turbulence | Excellent | Moderate | Moderate | Fair |
| | Spray – Discharge broken into droplets | Good | Low | Nominal | Poor |
| | Sheet – Linear discharge, minimal turbulence | Good | Low | Nominal | Poor |

DEVICES

# RESERVOIR STRUCTURES

All water features incorporate a reservoir structure. With the exception of some spouting water features that use a hidden reservoir, this reservoir is typically incorporated into the overall display in the form of a pool structure or pond system. Selection of a reservoir type is primarily a function of design intent.

## Pools Structures

- Table 17.2 describes materials commonly used in the construction of pools. Material selection is a function of aesthetics, climate conditions, cost, and site conditions (subgrade, construction access, etc.).
- Figure 17.1 illustrates a variety of edge conditions for pool structures. The most common solution is a cantilevered coping edge to contain waves and conceal stains caused by variations in water level.
- Figure 17.2 shows critical dimensions for ornamental pool design with a cantilevered edge.
- Figure 17.3 shows a typical construction detail for a swimming pool with a gunite concrete structure.
- Adjacent surfaces should be sloped to drain away from the pool to preserve water quality. However, surfaces should slope towards pools with larger displays for at least 600 mm (2 ft) to provide for overflow resulting from splash.

### Depth

- Pool depth for ornamental displays varies between 300 and 450 mm (12-18″). In the United States, depths in excess of 450 mm (18″) are typically considered swimming pools and are subject to further regulation, including the erection of perimeter fencing or other barriers.
- Reservoirs for spouting displays typically require a minimum depth of 300 mm (12″).

### Freeboard

- Freeboard requirements (distance between waterline and top of pool edge) vary as a function of the edge condition. Trough solutions, also known as infinity edges, are designed to provide no freeboard. Cantilevered and stepped edges require minimal freeboard [25 mm (1″)], while seatwalls or planted edges may require greater freeboard [150 mm (6″)].
- When multiple pools are involved, lower pools must be designed to accommodate higher non-operating water levels, as well as lower levels provided during operation. The difference is due to water that is built up behind weirs and other display devices during operation.

## TABLE 17.2. Pool materials.

| Material | Application | Finish | Construction | Life Expectancy |
|----------|-------------|--------|--------------|-----------------|
| Cast-in-place Concrete | Large ornamental and recreational pools and displays | May be colored, textured, coated, or tiled | Use concrete mix rich in Portland cement, with fine-graded aggregate; features are formed and finished on site | Long |
| Precast Concrete | Smaller displays; useful where precise control of configuration, dimensions, or finish is required | May be colored, coated, or tiled | Joints must be sealed, waterproofed, and carefully controlled at weirs and waterwalls | Long |
| Gunite Concrete | Ornamental displays and swimming pools, where naturalistic or curvilinear forms are desired; light weight suitable for on-structure use | May be colored, coated, tiled, or textured to simulate natural stone. | Wire mesh formwork laid on site, concrete is sprayed into place. Benches are formed on site to receive stones or submersed in pots later. | Long |
| Stone | Ornamental displays, seeking richness and permanence, or naturalistic character | May be used in naturalistic boulder or stone shapes, or cut with smooth or rough finish | Stone is applied as a mortared veneer, or may be placed on a membrane cushioned by drain matting. | Long |
| Brick | Ornamental displays; integrates well with brick paving or adjacent structures | Brick may be glazed or sealed with clear coating to ease maintenance. | Require sealing; Joints must be carefully controlled particularly in weirs and waterwalls | Moderate to Long |
| Metal | Smaller installations and structures; good where leaks present major concern | High quality polished finish | Typically coated with polymer sheathing or epoxy sealants. | Moderate |
| Fiberglass | Smaller installations; good lightweight alternative for on-structure conditions | Usually finished smooth | Typically prefabricated and coated after installation. | Moderate |

DEVICES

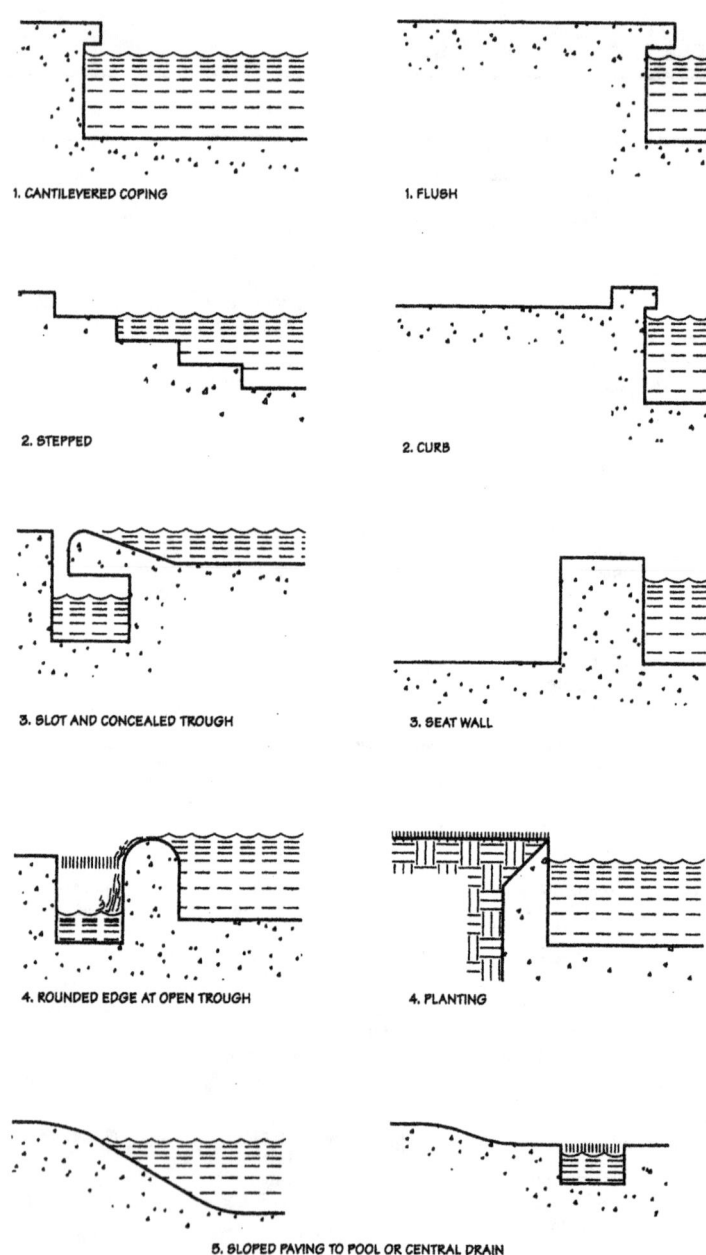

1. CANTILEVERED COPING

1. FLUSH

2. STEPPED

2. CURB

3. SLOT AND CONCEALED TROUGH

3. SEAT WALL

4. ROUNDED EDGE AT OPEN TROUGH

4. PLANTING

5. SLOPED PAVING TO POOL OR CENTRAL DRAIN

**Figure 17.1. Common pool edge conditions.**

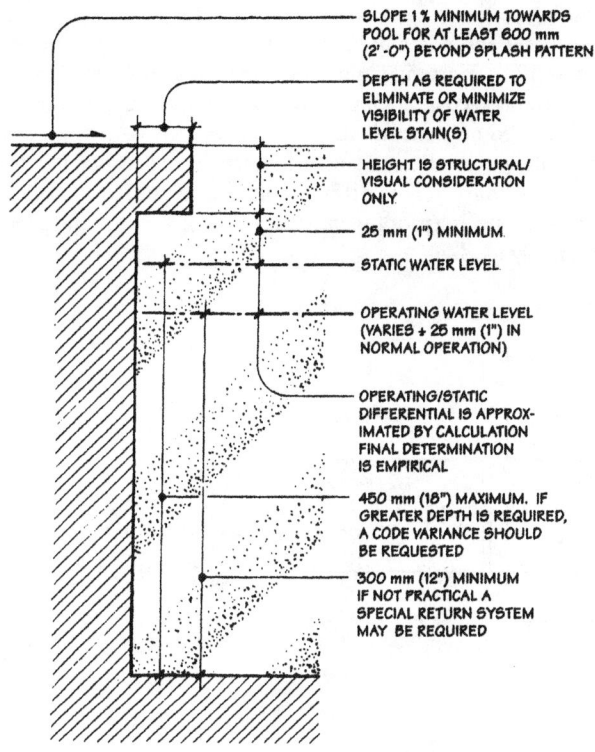

SLOPE 1 % MINIMUM TOWARDS POOL FOR AT LEAST 600 mm (2'-0") BEYOND SPLASH PATTERN

DEPTH AS REQUIRED TO ELIMINATE OR MINIMIZE VISIBILITY OF WATER LEVEL STAIN(S)

HEIGHT IS STRUCTURAL/ VISUAL CONSIDERATION ONLY

25 mm (1") MINIMUM

STATIC WATER LEVEL

OPERATING WATER LEVEL (VARIES + 25 mm (1") IN NORMAL OPERATION)

OPERATING/STATIC DIFFERENTIAL IS APPROX- IMATED BY CALCULATION FINAL DETERMINATION IS EMPIRICAL

450 mm (18") MAXIMUM. IF GREATER DEPTH IS REQUIRED, A CODE VARIANCE SHOULD BE REQUESTED

300 mm (12") MINIMUM IF NOT PRACTICAL A SPECIAL RETURN SYSTEM MAY BE REQUIRED

**Figure 17.2. Typical pool design with cantilevered edge.**

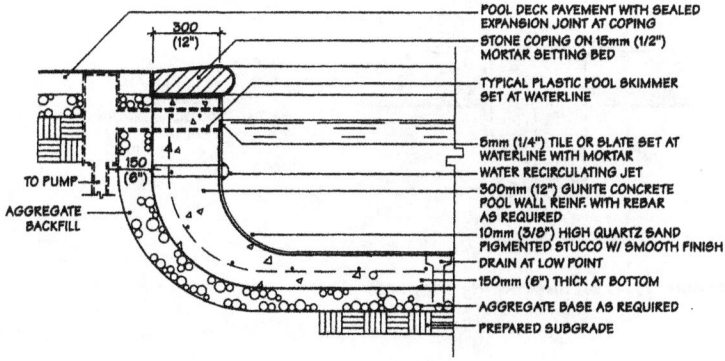

POOL DECK PAVEMENT WITH SEALED EXPANSION JOINT AT COPING

STONE COPING ON 15mm (1/2") MORTAR SETTING BED

TYPICAL PLASTIC POOL SKIMMER SET AT WATERLINE

5mm (1/4") TILE OR SLATE SET AT WATERLINE WITH MORTAR

WATER RECIRCULATING JET

300mm (12") GUNITE CONCRETE POOL WALL REINF. WITH REBAR AS REQUIRED

10mm (3/8") HIGH QUARTZ SAND PIGMENTED STUCCO W/ SMOOTH FINISH

DRAIN AT LOW POINT

150mm (6") THICK AT BOTTOM

AGGREGATE BASE AS REQUIRED

PREPARED SUBGRADE

300 (12")

150 (6")

TO PUMP

AGGREGATE BACKFILL

**Figure 17.3. Typical gunite swimming pool design.**

*Water Features* ▪ 325

## Waterproofing

- Waterstops should be used at all slab joints and pipe penetrations (Figure 17.4). Plastering, tiling, or coating the pool with epoxy paint or elastomeric coating may provide additional waterproofing.
- Pools placed on structure or in expansive soils require greater waterproofing protection because of threats from leakage. In addition, weight of materials is often a concern in rooftop landscapes. Continuous waterproof membranes, fiberglass or metal shells are commonly used.

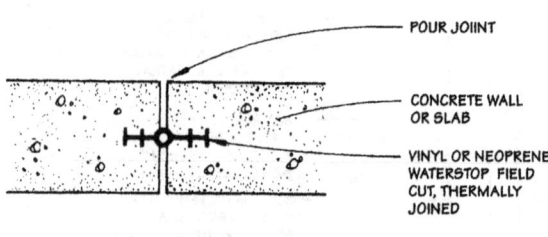

POUR JOIINT

CONCRETE WALL OR SLAB

VINYL OR NEOPRENE WATERSTOP FIELD CUT, THERMALLY JOINED

POOL WATERSTOP

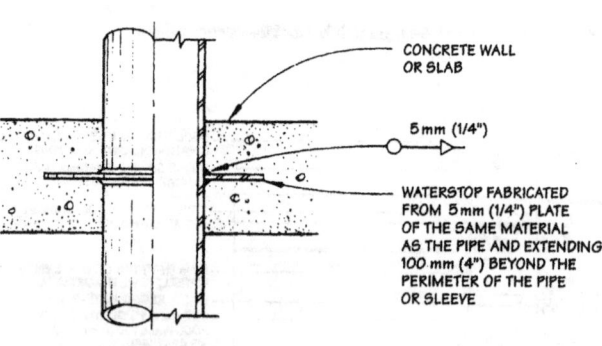

CONCRETE WALL OR SLAB

5 mm (1/4")

WATERSTOP FABRICATED FROM 5 mm (1/4") PLATE OF THE SAME MATERIAL AS THE PIPE AND EXTENDING 100 mm (4") BEYOND THE PERIMETER OF THE PIPE OR SLEEVE

PIPE PENETRATION WATERSTOP

**Figure 17.4. Waterproofing for pools.**

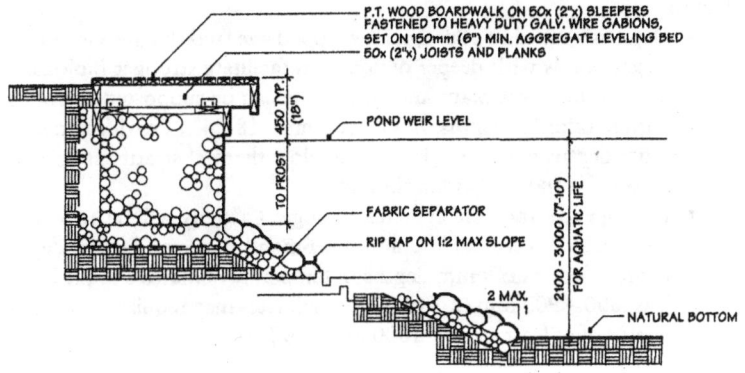

**Figure 17.5. Pond edge reinforced with gabions to facilitate boardwalk.**

## Pond Systems

Pond systems may be designed to incorporate natural inflows of water through stream impoundment, the presence of locally high water tables that feed excavated ponds, or stormwater runoff. However, this section focuses on the more common situation of ornamental ponds that are fed by artificial water supplies. Refer to Chapter 11: Stormwater Management for information on the design of ponds for stormwater detention.

- Synthetic liners or clay lenses are used to retain water for pond systems. Liners are protected by a fine granular base, which often rests upon a fabric filter if a clay lens is used. Plants are typically planted in pots.
- Edge conditions vary from vegetated slopes, to rip-rap or more finished surfaces. In areas of intense human activity or significant wave action, edges should be reinforced with concrete, stone, or gabion baskets, to prevent erosion and facilitate access (Figure 17.5).
- Larger ponds should be designed with gradual slopes (less than 3:1), to provide a measure of safety. Where vegetated wetland edges are desired, a planting shelf with a more gradual 10:1 slope should be provided (Figure 17.6).
- Nutrient intake must be carefully controlled in ornamental and recreational ponds, to inhibit excessive algae growth. Runoff should be diverted around the pond.
- Aeration is typically required to sustain biological growth, and reduce water temperature in hot climates. This may be provided by spouting, or other display features that also possess aesthetic interest.

## Depth

- Depth is a function of design intent, pond size, and climate. Generally, larger ponds with deeper designs will facilitate stronger biological activity, however plant and animal life can be supported in ponds with maximum depths of 450-600 mm (18-24"). Providing maximum depths over 3 m (10 ft) will allow thermal stratification and seasonal turnovers within the pond.

- In temperate and cold climates, biological activity will be adversely affected by "freeze-out" during winter months, unless adequate depth is provided. Maximum depths in temperate climates should be at least 600 – 900 mm (2-3 ft). Colder climates may require maximum depths of at least 1500 – 1800 mm (5-6 ft).

# SYSTEM REQUIREMENTS

## Display Pumps

Display pumps may be submersible within the water reservoir, or part of a remote system located adjacent to the water feature (Figure 17.7). Submersible systems are generally limited to installations of up to 10 square meters (100 ft2), in features that are routinely drained, cleaned, and re-filled in lieu of filtering. Larger, more complex features typically employ remote systems.

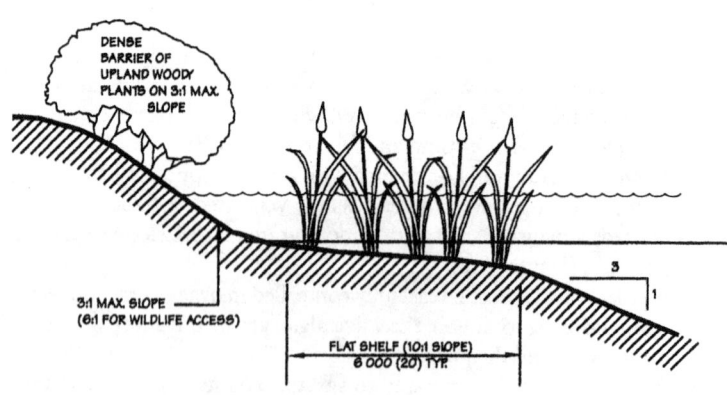

DENSE BARRIER OF UPLAND WOODY PLANTS ON 3:1 MAX. SLOPE

3:1 MAX. SLOPE (6:1 FOR WILDLIFE ACCESS)

3

1

FLAT SHELF (10:1 SLOPE)
6 000 (20) TYP.

**Figure 17.6. Vegetated pond edge.**

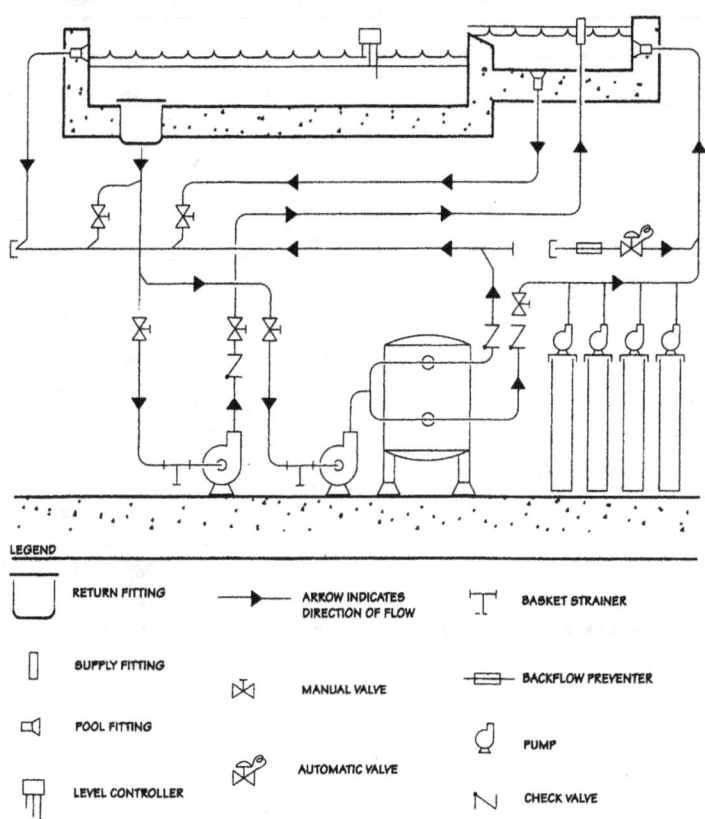

LEGEND

| | RETURN FITTING | | ARROW INDICATES DIRECTION OF FLOW | | BASKET STRAINER |
| | SUPPLY FITTING | | MANUAL VALVE | | BACKFLOW PREVENTER |
| | POOL FITTING | | AUTOMATIC VALVE | | PUMP |
| | LEVEL CONTROLLER | | | | CHECK VALVE |

**Figure 17.7. Schematic fountain diagram.**

DEVICES

## TABLE 17.3. Flowrates for various jets and weirs (US units).

### FLOWRATE FOR SOLID STREAM JETS (GPM)

| Height (ft) | 2 | 4 | 6 | 8 | 10 | 15 | 20 | 30 | 50 | 75 | 100 |
|---|---|---|---|---|---|---|---|---|---|---|---|
| Head (ft) | 3 | 5 | 8 | 10 | 14 | 20 | 27 | 41 | 69 | 97 | 150 |
| 1/4" orifice | 2 | 2.8 | 3.4 | 4 | 5 | 6 | - | - | - | - | - |
| 3/8" orifice | 4 | 6 | 7 | 8 | 9 | 12 | 15 | 20 | | | - |
| 1/2" orifice | 7 | 11 | 12 | 15 | 19 | 22 | 26 | 33 | - | - | - |
| 3/4" orifice | 16 | 21 | 26 | 31 | 35 | 50 | 58 | 74 | 93 | - | - |
| 1" orifice | 37 | 46 | 50 | 56 | 60 | 82 | 106 | 127 | 167 | 199 | 238 |
| 1 1/2" orifice | - | - | - | - | 159 | 199 | 233 | 304 | 368 | 444 | 518 |
| 2" orifice | - | - | - | - | 309 | 357 | 410 | 526 | 650 | 780 | 938 |
| 3" orifice | - | - | - | - | - | - | 965 | 1220 | 1640 | 1750 | 1905 |

### FLOWRATE FOR RECTANGULAR WEIRS.

| Depth over weir | 1/4" | 1/2" | 3/4" | 1" | 1 1/2" | 2" | 2 1/2" | 3" | 4" | 5" | 6" |
|---|---|---|---|---|---|---|---|---|---|---|---|
| GPM per linear ft. | 4.5 | 13 | 23 | 36 | 65 | 101 | 141 | 185 | 285 | 399 | 524 |

### FLOWRATE FOR CASCADE-TYPE AERATED STREAM JETS.

| Height (ft) | | 2 | 4 | 6 | 8 | 10 | 12 | 15 | 20 | 25 | 30 |
|---|---|---|---|---|---|---|---|---|---|---|---|
| 3/4" orifice | GPM | 18 | 21 | 26 | 30 | - | - | - | - | - | - |
| | Head | 30 | 43 | 61 | 77 | - | - | - | - | - | - |
| 1 1/2" orifice | GPM | 28 | 32 | 40 | 46 | 50 | 56 | 67 | - | - | - |
| | Head | 15 | 27 | 37 | 50 | 60 | 70 | 83 | - | - | - |
| 3" orifice | GPM | 71 | 110 | 142 | 157 | 171 | 186 | 210 | 246 | 312 | 330 |
| | Head | 9 | 16 | 26 | 32 | 36 | 44 | 56 | 66 | 108 | 134 |

Figure 17.8 shows a typical pump curve provided by a pump manufacturer. Selecting the proper pump size is a function of required flowrate, pressure, and net positive suction head available.

### Flowrate

Flowrate is express in liters per minute (LPM) in SI units or gallons per minute (GPM) in US units. Table 17.3 lists flowrate requirements of typical display features in US units. Manufacturer data should be used for pre-

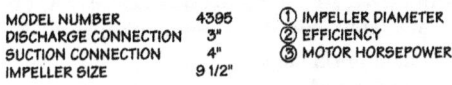

TYPE: END SUCTION CENTRIFUGAL

MODEL NUMBER            4395     ① IMPELLER DIAMETER
DISCHARGE CONNECTION    3"       ② EFFICIENCY
SUCTION CONNECTION      4"       ③ MOTOR HORSEPOWER
IMPELLER SIZE           9 1/2"

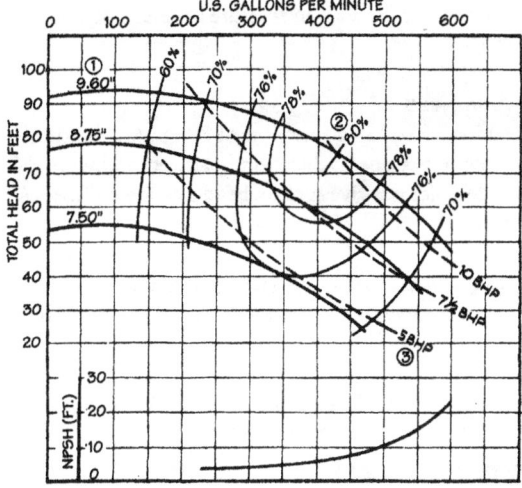

**Figure 17.8. Typical pump curve.**

cise calculations. Required flowrates for all display elements should be summed to determine pump needs. The required flow at any weir may be reduced by the amount that jets or other weirs contribute to the source of that weir.

### Pressure

Water pressure is expressed in kilopascals or meters of head in SI units (1 m of head = 9.80 kPa), and pounds per square inch or feet of head in US units (1 ft of head = 0.433 psi). The manufacturer provides water pressure requirements for spout jets, with Table 17.3 providing general guidelines in US units. Pressure loss resulting from the delivery system must be calculated to ensure adequate pressure exists for each display:

- Table 17.4 lists pressure loss from friction in commonly used pipes in US units.
- Friction loss due to pipe fittings should be considered, and is estimated at 10% of the loss from the entire system.

- Pressure loss from valves, strainers and other devices must be calculated using data available from the manufacturer, with Table 17.5 providing general data in US units.
- Each meter (foot) of vertical rise or fall throughout the system results in an increase or decrease in pressure of one meter head (ft head) or 9.80 kPa (0.433 psi).

### Net Positive Suction Head

Net positive suction head is a function of the pump suction system. Manufacturers provide net positive suction head requirements (NPSHR) for each pump model. Net positive suction head available (NPSHA) is calculated by the formula:

$$NPSHA = \text{Atmospheric pressure} + (\text{reservoir water elevation} - \text{pump elevation}) - \text{friction losses in suction line}$$

**TABLE 17.4. Pipe Sizing and head loss chart (US units).**

| Velocity | 2 ft per sec. | | 5 ft per sec. | | 7 ft per sec. | | 10 ft per sec. | |
|---|---|---|---|---|---|---|---|---|
| Function | Gravity return | | Return (< 30); Gravity drain | | Return (>30); Pressure supply or drain (<30) | | Pressure supply or drain (>30) | |
| Size | GPM | Head Loss* | GPM | Head Loss* | GPM | Head Loss* | GPM | Head Loss* |
| ½" | 2 | 7.4 | 5 | 38.3 | 7 | 70.5 | 10 | 134.8 |
| ¾" | 3 | 5.9 | 8 | 28.6 | 12 | 50.2 | 17 | 95.1 |
| 1" | 5 | 3.8 | 13 | 20.4 | 19 | 38.0 | 27 | 73.7 |
| 1 ¼" | 10 | 2.9 | 23 | 14.6 | 32 | 27.1 | 46 | 53.1 |
| 1 ½" | 13 | 2.2 | 32 | 12.2 | 44 | 23.3 | 63 | 44.0 |
| 2" | 19 | 1.8 | 49 | 9.5 | 68 | 17.7 | 98 | 34.5 |
| 2 ½" | 31 | 1.3 | 76 | 7.3 | 103 | 13.8 | 151 | 26.5 |
| 3" | 44 | 1.1 | 110 | 6.0 | 152 | 11.0 | 220 | 21.5 |
| 4" | 78 | 0.78 | 195 | 4.0 | 273 | 8.0 | 393 | 15.0 |
| 5" | 125 | 0.60 | 308 | 3.3 | 428 | 6.1 | 612 | 11.8 |
| 6" | 177 | 0.48 | 440 | 2.6 | 616 | 4.9 | 881 | 9.7 |
| 8" | 315 | 0.34 | 780 | 1.8 | 1090 | 3.5 | 1560 | 6.7 |
| 10" | 490 | 0.27 | 1240 | 1.4 | 1657 | 2.7 | 2450 | 5.2 |
| 12" | 725 | 0.23 | 1760 | 1.2 | 2466 | 2.2 | 3550 | 4.2 |
| 14" | 950 | 0.18 | 2400 | 0.99 | 3354 | 1.8 | 4761 | 3.6 |
| 16" | 1250 | 0.15 | 3127 | 0.98 | 4387 | 1.6 | 6255 | 3.0 |
| 20" | 1960 | 0.12 | 4900 | 0.65 | 6910 | 1.2 | 9850 | 2.3 |
| 24" | 2830 | 0.09 | 7100 | 0.55 | 9970 | 0.97 | 14400 | 1.9 |
| 30" | 4400 | 0.08 | 11022 | 0.40 | 15400 | 0.95 | 21500 | 1.4 |
| Velocity head | | 0.06 | | 0.39 | | 0.76 | | 1.55 |

*Per 100 ft of pipe

**TABLE 17.5. Head loss chart for strainers and valves (US units)*.**

**Butterfly valve**

| Velocity (ft per sec.) | 3" | 4" | 6" | 8" | 10" | 12" | 14" | 16" | 20" | 24" | 30" |
|---|---|---|---|---|---|---|---|---|---|---|---|
| 5 | – | – | – | – | – | – | – | – | – | 0.18 | 0.17 |
| 7 | 0.53 | 0.34 | 0.57 | 0.115 | – | – | – | – | – | 0.35 | 0.37 |
| 10 | 1.31 | 1.06 | 1.38 | 0.78 | 0.69 | 0.46 | 0.57 | 0.60 | 0.50 | 0.75 | 0.70 |

**Basket strainer**

| Velocity (ft per sec.) | 3" | 4" | 6" | 8" | 10" | 12" | 14" | 16" | 20" | 24" | 30" |
|---|---|---|---|---|---|---|---|---|---|---|---|
| 5 | 2.35 | 1.73 | 1.50 | 1.10 | 0.80 | 0.64 | 0.36 | 0.25 | 0.23 | 0.23 | – |
| 7 | 5.77 | 4.15 | 3.00 | 2.07 | 1.51 | 1.03 | 0.64 | 0.55 | 0.46 | 0.46 | 0.46 |
| 10 | 11.55 | 6.43 | 6.46 | 4.62 | 2.77 | 3.01 | 1.38 | 1.15 | 0.80 | 0.92 | 0.87 |

**Silent check valve**

| Velocity (ft per sec.) | 2" | 2½" | 3" | 4" | 6" | 8" | 10" | 12" | 14" | 16" | 20" | 24" |
|---|---|---|---|---|---|---|---|---|---|---|---|---|
| 5 | 4.38 | 4.15 | 4.15 | 4.50 | 4.62 | 4.85 | 4.96 | 3.90 | 4.85 | 3.90 | 1.73 | 1.61 |
| 7 | 6.00 | 6.23 | 6.69 | 6.69 | 7.16 | 7.85 | 7.39 | 5.31 | 6.00 | 6.00 | 6.00 | 3.11 |
| 10 | 11.08 | 11.08 | 11.31 | 11.31 | 12.01 | 13.86 | 13.16 | 9.24 | 10.39 | 11.55 | 2.70 | 23.10+ |

**Diaphragm valve – globe**

| Velocity (ft per sec.) | 1" | 1½" | 2" | 2½" | 3" | 4" | 6" | 8" | 10" | 12" | 14" | 16" |
|---|---|---|---|---|---|---|---|---|---|---|---|---|
| 7 | 6.2 | 6.4 | 4.1 | 5.7 | 4.6 | 1.6 | 1.6 | 4.8 | 2.0 | 4.6 | 5.7 | 5.7 |
| 10 | 11.5 | 13.4 | 9.0 | 11.5 | 10.4 | 7.8 | 4.4 | 8.0 | 11.0 | 9.4 | 11.5 | 11.5 |
| 12 | 20.7 | 20.3 | 12.7 | 18.5 | 15.7 | 11.8 | 12.0 | 13.1 | 15.9 | 13.8 | 16.1 | 16.1 |

**Diaphragm valve – angle**

| Velocity (ft per sec.) | 1½" | 2" | 3" | 4" | 6" | 8" | 10" | 12" | 14" | 16" |
|---|---|---|---|---|---|---|---|---|---|---|
| 7 | 5.5 | 3.2 | 3.2 | 2.3 | 2.3 | 2.8 | – | 2.3 | 2.8 | 2.3 |
| 10 | 11.0 | 6.5 | 5.8 | 5.5 | 4.6 | 4.6 | 4.6 | 4.1 | 4.9 | 4.8 |
| 12 | 16.1 | 8.3 | 9.5 | 7.4 | 6.7 | 7.8 | 6.5 | 6.2 | 7.2 | 7.0 |

*Expressed in feet of head lost.

DEVICES

Atmospheric pressure is 10.400 m (34 ft) at sea level, decreasing approximately 0.120 mm (1.2 ft) with each 100 m (1000 ft) rise in elevation. NPSHR for the selected pump must not exceed NPSHA. For this reason, pumps are typically located below reservoir water elevation whenever possible.

## Filtration Systems

Fountain filters are usually high-rate sand filters, sized on the basis of pool area. Table 17.6 lists typical filter characteristics in US units. A standard of 400 mm$^2$ (4 ft$^2$) of filter area should be used for each 100 000 mm$^2$ (1000 ft$^2$) of reservoir area. Filter pumps must be selected using similar sizing procedures for display pumps.

## Piping

Table 17.7 lists maximum pipe sizes and corresponding velocities for different types of piping. Return piping size must be carefully considered with regard to NPSHR.

**TABLE 17.6. High rate sand filter data (US units).**

| Filter tank diameter | Sand bed area (ft$^2$) | Pool size (ft$^2$) |
|---|---|---|
| 1' – 4" | 1.4 | 350 |
| 1' – 8" | 2.2 | 550 |
| 2' – 0" | 3.1 | 775 |
| 2' – 6" | 4.9 | 1225 |
| 3' – 0" | 7.1 | 1775 |
| 3' – 6" | 9.6 | 2400 |
| 4' – 0" | 12.6 | 3150 |
| 4' – 6" | 15.9 | 3975 |
| 5' – 0" | 19.6 | 4900 |
| 5' – 6" | 23.7 | 5925 |
| 6' – 0" | 28.3 | 7075 |
| 6' – 6" | 33.2 | 8300 |
| 7' – 0" | 38.5 | 9625 |
| 7' – 6" | 44.2 | 11,050 |
| 8' – 0" | 50.3 | 12,575 |

**TABLE 17.7. Sizing of Gravity Flow Piping**

| Type of piping | Sizing | Sized for maximum velocity of: |
|---|---|---|
| Gravity return piping | Sizing is critical & must be carefully calculated for long piping runs & minimal slopes | 600 mm/sec. (2 fps) |
| Return piping | 75 mm (3") & smaller<br>100 mm (4") & larger | 1.5 m/sec (5 fps)<br>2.1 m/sec (7 fps) |
| Supply piping | 75 mm (3") & smaller<br>100 mm (4") & larger | 2.1 m/sec. (7 fps)<br>3.04 m/sec. (10 fps) |
| Gravity drawn and overflow piping | | 1.5 m/sec. (5 fps) |
| Pumped drain piping | 75 mm (3") & smaller<br>100 mm (4") & larger | 2.1 m/sec. (7 fps)<br>3.04 m/sec. (10 fps) |
| Fill/make up piping | | 3.04 m/sec. (10 fps) |

## Lighting

- Daylighting is effective for illuminating motion displays. In the northern hemisphere, a southerly exposure is optimal for daylighting water features. Northerly exposures generally offer little enhancement to the readability of the display.
- The effects of floodlighting are similar to daylighting. Care must be taken to minimize glare from the light source.
- Underwater lighting can be very dramatic, as the water refracts and diffuses the light. However, each fixture costs 3 to 5 times as much as open-air lighting fixtures due to physical requirements for submersion.
- For optimal human perception, the brightness of a primary display should be at least 10 times the surrounding ambient light level and 3 times the subordinate displays.
- If uniform lumination is desired, a minimum of two fixtures should be used for spout displays.
- A maximum spacing of 1000 mm (3 ft) for uplights should be used for uniform illumination of waterfall features.

DEVICES

# SUGGESTED REFERENCES

Dines, Nicholas T. and Kyle D. Brown, *Time-Saver Standards Site construction Details Manual,* McGraw-Hill, New York, 1999.

Harris, Charles W. and Nicholas T. Dines, *Time-Saver Standards for Landscape Architecture, 2nd Edition,* McGraw-Hill, New York, 1998.

Landphair, Harlow C. and Fred Klatt, *Landscape Architecture Construction,* Elsevier, New York, 1988.

# Lighting

18

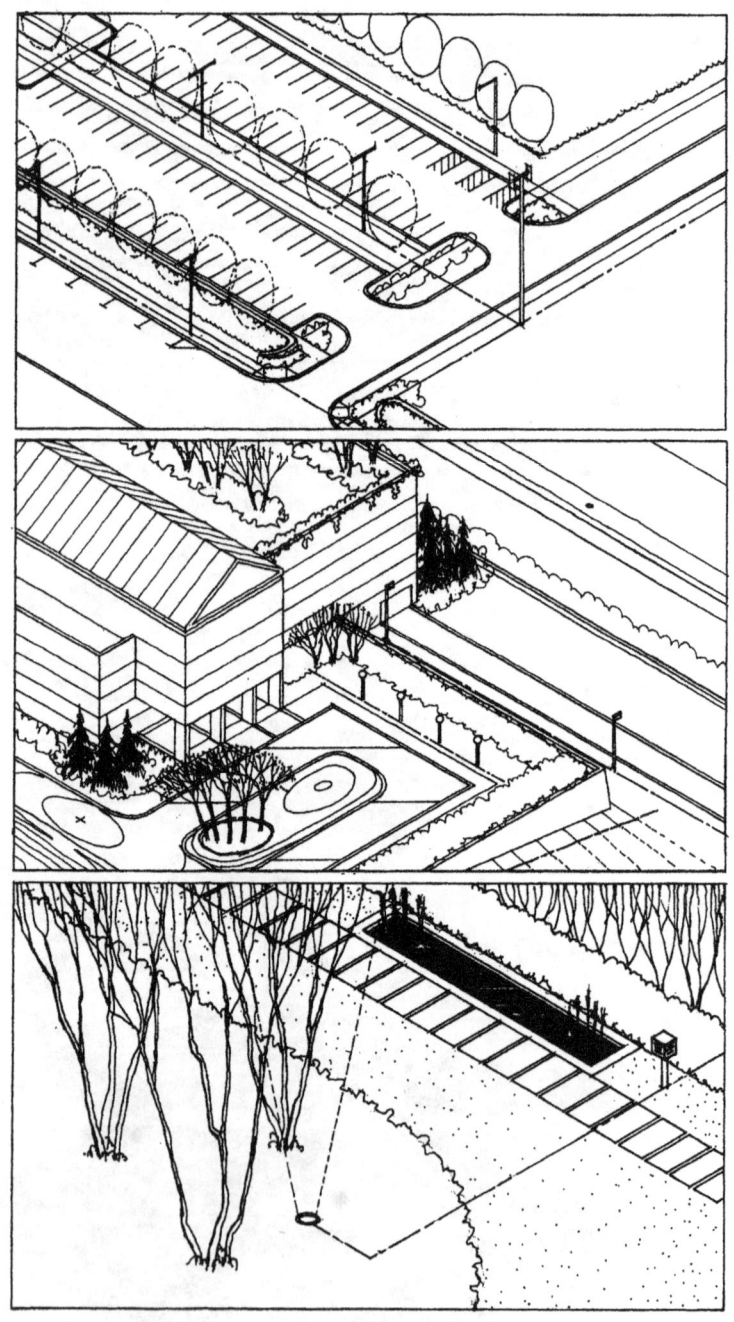

## LARGE SCALE HIGHWAY, STADIUM, AND PARKING LOT LIGHTING

Large scale lighting uses mounting standards that range from 18 to 30 m (60 to 100 ft) in height and requires extensive footing depths to counter lateral wind loads and weight. Lamps are high intensity and require special lenses to inhibit side glare and to direct light on the field of play or subject area. Tall lights require lowering devices to gain access to light fixtures for maintenance.

## RESIDENTIAL STREETS, URBAN PEDESTRIAN CORRIDORS, AND ARCHITECTURAL LIGHTING

Medium scale lighting standards range from 6 to 9 m (20 to 30 ft) and include special architectural illumination fixtures. Distribution patterns maintain even lighting levels for safety and clarity of way finding. A wide variety of designs and finishes are available.

## PUBLIC AND SMALL SCALE GARDEN LIGHTING

Small to intermediate scale lighting heights range from 3 to 4.5 m (10 to 15 ft) and include continuous wash pedestrian lighting to focused spot and feature lighting. Distribution patterns are highly varied employing a broad range of fixture design and finishes. Small scale or low level lighting often employs direct current low wattage and solar power electrical sources.

O UTDOOR LIGHTING is a requirement for all landscapes that are to remain functional spaces for human use at night. The purposes of outdoor lighting include: (1) improving the legibility of critical nodes, landmarks, circulation routes and activity zones in the landscape; (2) facilitating the safe movement of pedestrians and vehicles, promoting a more secure environment, and minimizing the potential for personal harm and damage to property; and (3) helping to reveal the salient features of a site at a desired intensity of light in order to encourage nighttime use.

## DIAGNOSTIC ASSESSMENT

*How will outdoor lighting support the overall objectives of the design?*

A well-designed and functional outdoor space may become unsafe and underused at night without appropriate lighting. Elements such as plantings, sculpture, and pedestrian and vehicular circulation paths, may require specific lighting strategies to retain aesthetic character, function, and safety.

*What lighting effects best accomplish the desired function?*

Lighting options are determined by clearly delineated functional requirements, influencing light intensity, coverage pattern, and fixture type. Options range from soft accent washes to high intensity spotlights aimed at architectural features or high use areas.

*What kind of lighting fixture will create the desired effect?*

Lights are generally categorized by height, which is a function of the scale of the space to be lit, and the intensity of coverage required. For example, highway lighting requires a pattern and intensity of light that is qualitatively and functionally different from that of pedestrian plaza lighting.

*How much light is appropriate for the proposed function of the fixture?*

The intensity of light a fixture gives off is determined by the programmed use of the space. Where safety is the concern, intensity is not as important as coverage and the elimination of dark spots. However, uses such as sports fields will require a level of intensity that would be inappropriate in other contexts.

# LIGHTING OBJECTIVES

## Orientation and Identification

Driver and pedestrian orientation can be aided by providing a hierarchy of lighting effects that correspond to the different zones and uses of a site. As shown in Figure 18.1 subtle distinctions can be made between major and minor roads, paths, and use areas by varying the distribution and brightness of light and the height, spacing, and color of lamps.

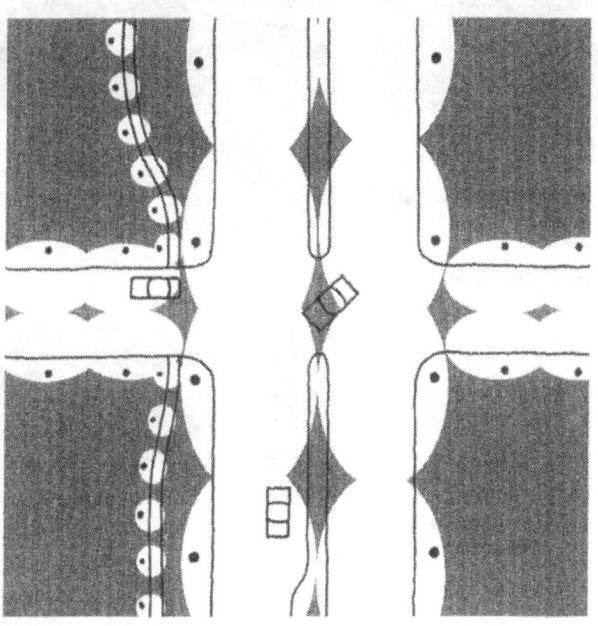

**Figure 18.1. Lighting hierarchy.**

## Safety and Security

Figure 18.2 illustrates the importance of providing clear lighting patterns and sufficient coverage to help insure the safety of pedestrians. The placement of appropriate light fixtures that eliminate dark spots in potentially vulnerable areas help to provide a sense of security (Figure 18.3).

DEVICES

## Atmosphere and Character

The design intent of outdoor spaces in the daytime can be reinforced at night through the bright illumination of objects of interest, the unobtrusive illumination of background spaces, and the modulation of color.

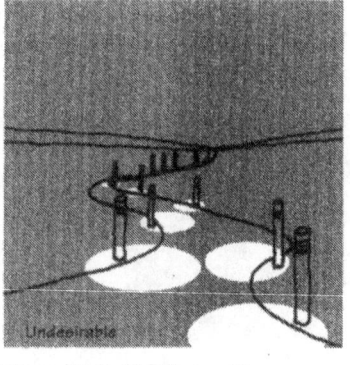 

**Figure 18.2. Lighting patterns.**

**Figure 18.3.
Walkway lights.**

# LIGHTING EFFECTS

## Uplighting

Figures 18.4 and 18.5 illustrate the uplighting effect provided by above grade accent lights and below ground well lights with louvers.

## Moonlighting

In Figure 18.6 lights are placed in trees to create a sense of hidden light source and dappled shadows on the ground.

## Silhouette Lighting

Plants or sculptural elements can be dramatically expressed when silhouetted against a wall or building facade as shown in Figure 18.7.

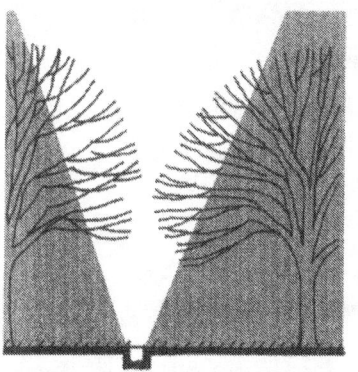
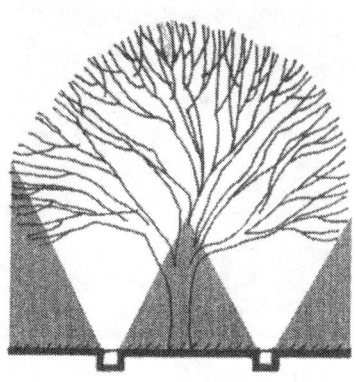

**Figure 18.4. Uplighting (well lights).**

**Figure 18.5. Uplighting (above grade light).**

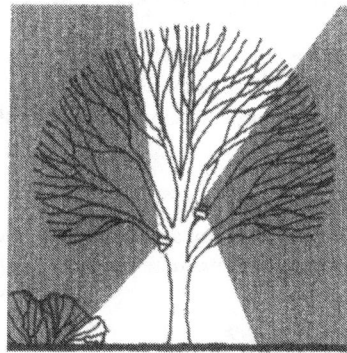

**Figure 18.6. Moonlighting.**

**Figure 18.7. Silhouette lighting.**

DEVICES

**Figure 18.8. Spotlighting.**

## Spotlighting

Special objects such as statues, sculpture, or specimen plantings can be lighted with well-shielded fixtures using spot lamps (Figure 18.8).

## Spread Lighting

Figure 18.9 shows how spread lights can be used to produce circular patterns of illumination to soften shadows while creating a uniform lighting effect.

## Path Lighting

Figures 18.10 and 18.11 illustrate how spread lights can be used at lower heights to illuminate pedestrian paths.

# FIXTURES

## Definitions

*Lumen:* A quantitative unit of measurement referring to the total amount of light energy emitted by a light source, without regard to the direction of its distribution.

*Footcandle (fc):* A U.S. unit of measurement referring to incident light. Footcandles can be derived from lumens (1 fc = 1 lumen/sq. ft.) or candelas (fc = candelas/distance$^2$).

*Lux (lx):* The International Standard (SI) measure of incident light. It is equal to one lumen uniformly distributed over an area of one square meter (10.7 lx = 1 fc).

*Candlepower:* The unit of intensity of a light source in a specific direction, often referred to as candela. One candela directed perpendicular to a surface one foot away generates one footcandle of light.

*Illuminance:* Incident light, or light striking a surface.

*Luminance:* Light leaving a surface, whether due to the surface's reflectance, or because it is the surface of a light-emitting object (like a light bulb). Luminance is the measurable form of brightness, which is a subjective sensation.

**Figure 18.9. Spread lighting.**

**Figure 18.10. Path lighting.**

**Figure 18.11. Wall lights.**

*Efficacy:* A measure of how efficiently a lamp converts electric power (watts) into light energy (lumens) without regard to the effectiveness of its illumination. It should not be assumed that a lamp with high efficacy would give better illumination than a less efficient lamp.

*Light depreciation:* Lamp output (lumens) will depreciate over its effective life to 50-70% of original illumination. New installations are routinely designed to deliver 1.5 to 2 times as much illumination as needed, to avoid insufficient lighting over the anticipated life of the lamp.

*Color:* Two measures used to describe the color characteristics of lamps are (1) the apparent color and (2) the color rendering index. Apparent color refers to the warmth or coolness of the light source and the color rendering index is a measurement of the degree to which object colors are faithfully rendered. Figure 18.12 compares the apparent color of various light sources with the color rendering index.

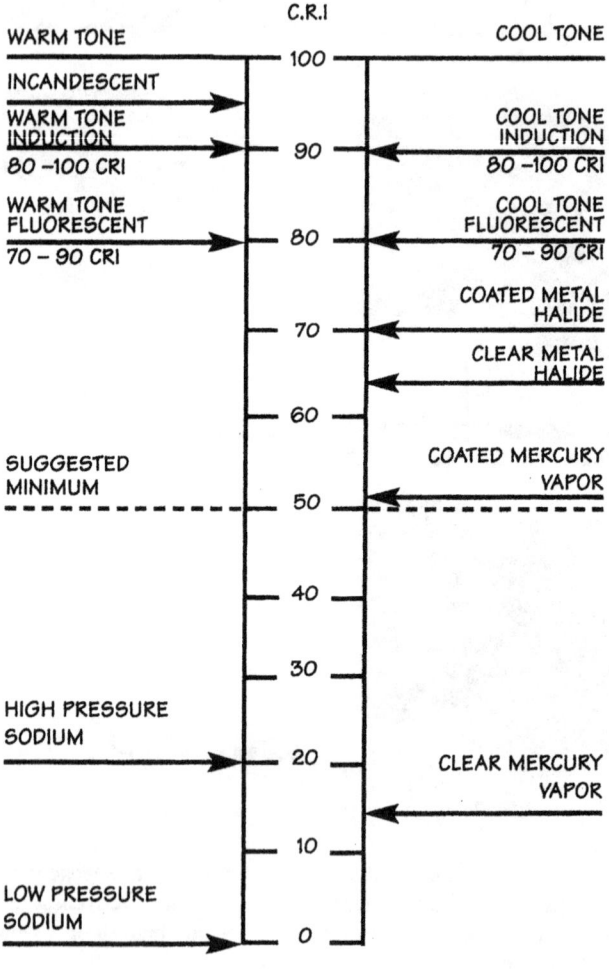

**Figure 18.12. Color rendering index.**

*Uniformity:* a ratio that typically compares the average illumination with the minimum footcandle value of a particular field. Low ratios appear evenly lit and uniform while high ratios have high contrast and may appear spotty. See Table 18.1 for general descriptions of different uniformity ratios.

## TABLE 18.1. Uniformity Ratios

| Uniformity ratio | | Visual description of illuminated field |
|---|---|---|
| Average, lux (fc) | Minimum, lux (fc) | |
| 21.4 (2) | 10.7 (1) | Just a visible difference in light intensities |
| 32.3 (3)* | 10.7 (1)* | The high values of the field are twice as bright as the low values |
| 43.0 (4)† | 10.7 (1)† | — |
| 107.6 (10) | 10.7 (1) | Very distinct focal highlights; spotty |

\* Average and minimum uniformity ratios usually recommended for roads.
† Average and minimum uniformity ratios usually recommended for walkways.

## Categories

Various categories of light fixtures commonly used in outdoor lighting situations are described in Figure 18.13.

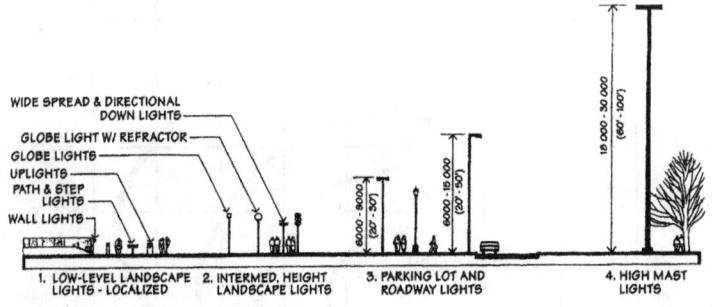

**Figure 18.13. Categories of light fixtures.**

## Lamp Characteristics

When selecting the appropriate lamp the designer must weigh factors such as cost, efficiency, life span, and color rendering with the desired effect of the light. Table 18.2 is a summary of these factors for each lamp type.

# LAMP INTENSITY

## Photometric Charts

The manufacturers' photometric charts illustrate illumination data for outdoor lighting fixtures. These charts illustrate the actual light patterns and intensity levels on horizontal and vertical planes. Examples of photometric charts are shown in Figures 18.14 and 18.15.

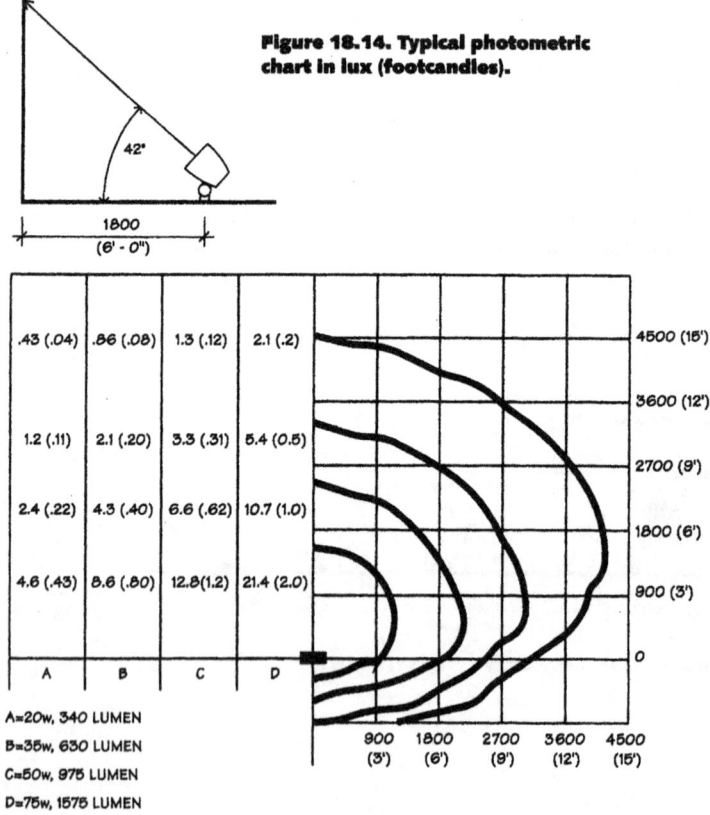

**Figure 18.14. Typical photometric chart in lux (footcandles).**

A=20w, 340 LUMEN
B=35w, 630 LUMEN
C=50w, 975 LUMEN
D=75w, 1575 LUMEN

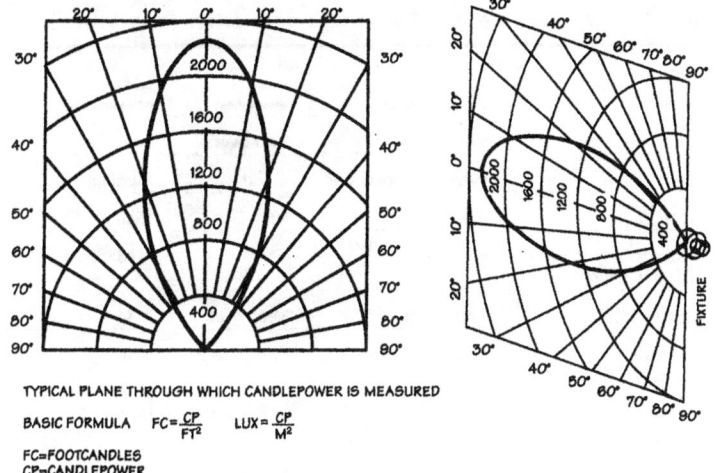

TYPICAL PLANE THROUGH WHICH CANDLEPOWER IS MEASURED

BASIC FORMULA    $FC = \dfrac{CP}{FT^2}$    $LUX = \dfrac{CP}{M^2}$

FC=FOOTCANDLES
CP=CANDLEPOWER
FT= DISTANCE FROM FIXTURE TO OBJECT IN FT
M=DISTANCE FROM FIXTURE TO OBJECT IN METERS

**Figure 18.15. Typical photometric chart in candela and conversion formula.**

## TABLE 18.2. Summary of Lamp Characteristics.

| Lamp | Wattage range | Efficacy, lumen/watt* | Average life, hrs |
|---|---|---|---|
| Incandescent | 3-300 (10-1000) | 10-25 | 750-2000 |
| Fluorescent | 4.5-64.5 (15-215) | 40-80 | 7500-15,000 |
| Induction | 16.5-25.5 (55-85) | 63-70 | 100,000 |
| Mercury vapor (deluxe white) | 12-300 (40-1000) | 25-60 | 24,000 |
| Metal halide | 52.5-450 (175-1500) | 65-105 | 7500-20,000 |
| High-pressure sodium (STP) | 10.5-300 (35-1000) | 60-120 | — |
| 'White' high-pressure sodium | 45-75 (150-250) | 75-80 | — |
| Low-pressure sodium | 5.4-54 (18-180) | 70-150 | — |

*Includes ballast losses

➤ continued on next page

**TABLE 18.2. Summary of Lamp Characteristics (continued).**

| Lamp | Apparent color | Color rendering | Initial cost of equipment |
|---|---|---|---|
| Incandescent | Warm white | Best overall | Low |
| Fluorescent | Warm to cool white | Good | Medium |
| Induction | White | Very Good | High |
| Mercury vapor (deluxe white) | Cool white | Good | Medium |
| Metal halide | Cool white | Very good | Med to High |
| High-pressure sodium (STP) | Orange-yellow | Poor | High |
| 'White' high-pressure sodium | Warm white | Very good | High |
| Low-pressure sodium | Intense yellow | Very poor | High |

## Recommended Levels of Illumination

The levels of illumination listed in Table 18.3 represent current standards in the lighting industry.

**TABLE 18.3. Recommended Levels of Illumination.**

| Area/activity Outdoor facilities | Lux (lx) | Footcandles (fc) |
|---|---|---|
| **BUILDING EXTERIOR** | | |
| *Entry* | | |
| Active use | 50 | 5.0 |
| Locked or infrequent use | 10 | 1.0 |
| *Vital locations or structures* | 50 | 5.0 |
| *Building surrounds* | 10 | 1.0 |
| **BUILDING AND MONUMENTS (FLOODLIGHTED)** | | |
| *Bright Surroundings* | | |
| Light surfaces | 150 | 15.0 |
| Medium light surfaces | 200 | 20.0 |
| Medium dark surfaces | 300 | 30.0 |
| Dark surfaces | 500 | 50.0 |

## TABLE 18.3. Recommended Levels of Illumination (continued).

| Area/activity   Outdoor facilities | Lux (lx) | Footcandles (fc) |
|---|---|---|
| **BUILDING AND MONUMENTS (FLOODLIGHTED)** | | |
| *Dark surroundings* | | |
| Light surfaces | 50 | 5.0 |
| Medium light surfaces | 100 | 10.0 |
| Medium dark surfaces | 150 | 15.0 |
| Dark surfaces | 200 | 20.0 |
| **BIKEWAYS** | | |
| *Along roadside* | | |
| Commercial areas* | 10 | 0.9 |
| Intermediate areas* | 5 | 0.5 |
| Residential areas* | 2 | 0.2 |
| *Distant from roadside* | 5 | 0.5 |
| **BULLETIN AND POSTERBOARDS, SIGNS** | | |
| *Bright surroundings* | | |
| Light surfaces | 5 | 0.5 |
| Dark surfaces | 1000 | 100.0 |
| *Dark surroundings* | | |
| Light surfaces | 200 | 20.0 |
| Dark surfaces | 500 | 50.0 |
| **ROADWAYS** | | |
| *Expressways* | | |
| Commercial areas* | 14 | 1.4 |
| Intermediate areas* | 12 | 1.2 |
| Residential areas* | 9 | 0.9 |
| *Major Roads* | | |
| Commercial areas* | 17 | 1.7 |
| Intermediate areas* | 13 | 1.3 |
| Residential areas* | 9 | 0.9 |

**DEVICES**

➤ continued on next page

## TABLE 18.3. Recommended Levels of Illumination (continued).

| Area/activity   Outdoor facilities | Lux (lx) | Footcandles (fc) |
|---|---|---|
| **ROADWAYS** | | |
| *Collector roads* | | |
| Commercial areas* | 12 | 1.2 |
| Intermediate areas* | 9 | 0.9 |
| Residential areas* | 6 | 0.6 |
| *Local Roads* | | |
| Commercial areas* | 9 | 0.9 |
| Intermediate areas* | 7 | 0.6 |
| Residential areas* | 4 | 0.4 |
| **WALKWAYS** | | |
| *Along roadside* | | |
| Commercial areas* | 10 | 0.9 |
| Intermediate areas* | 5 | 0.5 |
| Residential areas* | 2 | 0.2 |
| *Distant from roadside* | 5 | 0.5 |
| *Park walkways* | 5 | 0.5 |
| *Pedestrian tunnels* | 20 | 2.0 |
| *Pedestrian overpasses* | 2 | 0.2 |
| *Pedestrian stairways* | | |
| Light surfaces | 200 | 20.0 |
| Dark surfaces | 500 | 50.0 |
| **GARDENS** | | |
| *General lighting* | 5 | 0.5 |
| *Path, steps away from home* | 10 | 1.0 |
| *Backgrounds, fences, walls, trees, shrubbery* | 20 | 2.0 |
| *Flower beds, rock gardens* | 50 | 5.0 |
| *Trees, shrubs (when emphasized)* | 50 | 5.0 |
| *Focal points (large)* | 100 | 10.0 |
| *Focal points (small)* | 200 | 20.0 |
| *Loading and unloading platforms* | 200 | 20.0 |

**TABLE 18.3. Recommended Levels of Illumination (continued).**

| Area/activity | Outdoor facilities | Lux (lx) | Footcandles (fc) |
|---|---|---|---|
| **PARKING AREAS** | | | |
| | Self parking | 10 | 1.0 |
| | Attendant parking | 20 | 2.0 |
| **PIERS** | | | |
| | Freight | 200 | 2.0 |
| | Passenger | 200 | 2.0 |
| | Active shipping area surrounding | 50 | 5.0 |
| **PLAYGROUND** | | 50 | 5.0 |
| **Badminton (outdoor)** | | | |
| | Recreational | 100 | 10 |
| | Club | 200 | 20 |
| **Baseball** | | | |
| | Recreational | | |
| | Infield | 105 | 15 |
| | Outfield | 100 | 10 |
| | Junior League (Class I and II) | | |
| | Infield | 300 | 30 |
| | Outfield | 200 | 20 |
| | Semi-pro and municipal league | | |
| | Infield | 200 | 20 |
| | Outfield | 150 | 15 |
| | On seats during game | 20 | 2 |
| | On seats before and after game | 50 | 5 |
| **Basketball (outdoor) recreational** | | 100 | 10 |
| **Football** | | | |
| | Distance from nearest sideline to the farthest rows of spectators: | | |
| | Class I (over 30,000 spectators) over 100 ft (30 m) | 1000 | 100 |

➤ continued on next page

DEVICES

# TABLE 18.3. Recommended Levels of Illumination (continued).

| Area/activity | Outdoor facilities | Lux (lx) | Footcandles (fc) |
|---|---|---|---|
| | Class II (10 to 15,000 spectators) 15 to 30 m (50 to 100 ft) | 500 | 50 |
| | Class III (5 to 10,000 spectators) 9 to 15 m (30 to 50 ft) | 300 | 30 |
| | Class IV (under 5,000 spectators) under 9 m (30 ft) | 200 | 20 |
| | Class V (no fixed seating facilities) | 100 | 10 |
| **Handball and racquetball (outdoor)** | | | |
| | Recreational (two-court) | 100 | 10 |
| | Club (two-court) | 200 | 20 |
| **Hockey (outdoor)** | | | |
| | Recreational | 100 | 10 |
| | Amateur | 200 | 20 |
| **Horse shows** | | | |
| | Recreational | 50 | 5 |
| | Tournament | 100 | 10 |
| **Shuffleboard** | | | |
| | Recreational | 50 | 5 |
| **Skating** | | | |
| | Roller rink | 100 | 10 |
| | Ice rink (outdoor) | 50 | 5 |
| | Lagoon, pond, or flooded area | 10 | 1 |
| **Ski slope** | | 10 | 1 |
| **Soccer (see Football)** | | | |
| **Softball** | | | |
| | Slow pitch, recreational (6 pole) | | |
| | Infield | 100 | 10 |
| | Outfield | 70 | 7 |

**TABLE 18.3. Recommended Levels of Illumination (continued).**

| Area/activity Outdoor facilities | Lux (lx) | Footcandles (fc) |
|---|---|---|
| *Slow pitch, tournament* | | |
| Infield | 200 | 20 |
| Outfield | 150 | 15 |
| *Recreational (6-pole)* | | |
| Infield | 100 | 10 |
| Outfield | 70 | 7 |
| *Industrial League* | | |
| Infield | 200 | 20 |
| Outfield | 150 | 15 |
| *Semiprofessional* | | |
| Infield | 300 | 30 |
| Outfield | 200 | 20 |
| *Professional and championship* | | |
| Infield | 500 | 50 |
| Outfield | 300 | 30 |
| **Swimming (outdoor)** | | |
| *Recreational* | 100 | 10 |
| *Underwater* | 600 | 60 |
| *Exhibitions* | 200 | 20 |
| **Tennis (outdoor)** | | |
| *Recreational* | 100 | 10 |
| *Club* | 200 | 20 |
| *Tournament* | 300 | 30 |
| **Volleyball** | | |
| *Recreational* | 100 | 10 |
| *Tournament* | 200 | 20 |

*Areas are defined as follows:

Commercial areas: Dense business districts with heavy vehicular and pedestrian traffic throughout the day and night.

Intermediate areas: Moderately heavy pedestrian traffic during nights (libraries, recreation centers, large apartment complex, neighborhood retail stores).

Residential areas: Predominantly a residential area with light pedestrian traffic at night (single family,multifamily apartments).

# SUGGESTED REFERENCES

Callwey Munchen, *Landscape Lighting Design Book,* Illuminating Engineering Society of North America, 1999.

Harris, Charles W. and Nicholas T. Dines, *Time-Saver Standards for Landscape Architecture,* 2nd Edition, McGraw-Hill, New York, 1998.

Illuminating Engineering Society of North America, *Lighting for Exterior Environments: an IESNA Recommended Practice,* 1999.

Illuminating Engineering Society of North America, *Lighting Handbook: Reference & Application,* 9th Edition, 1999.

Moyer, Jan Lennox. *The Landscape Lighting Book,* John Wiley & Sons, New York, 1992.

Randall Whitehead, *The Art of Outdoor Lighting,* Illuminating Engineering Society of North America, 1999.

# Irrigation

19

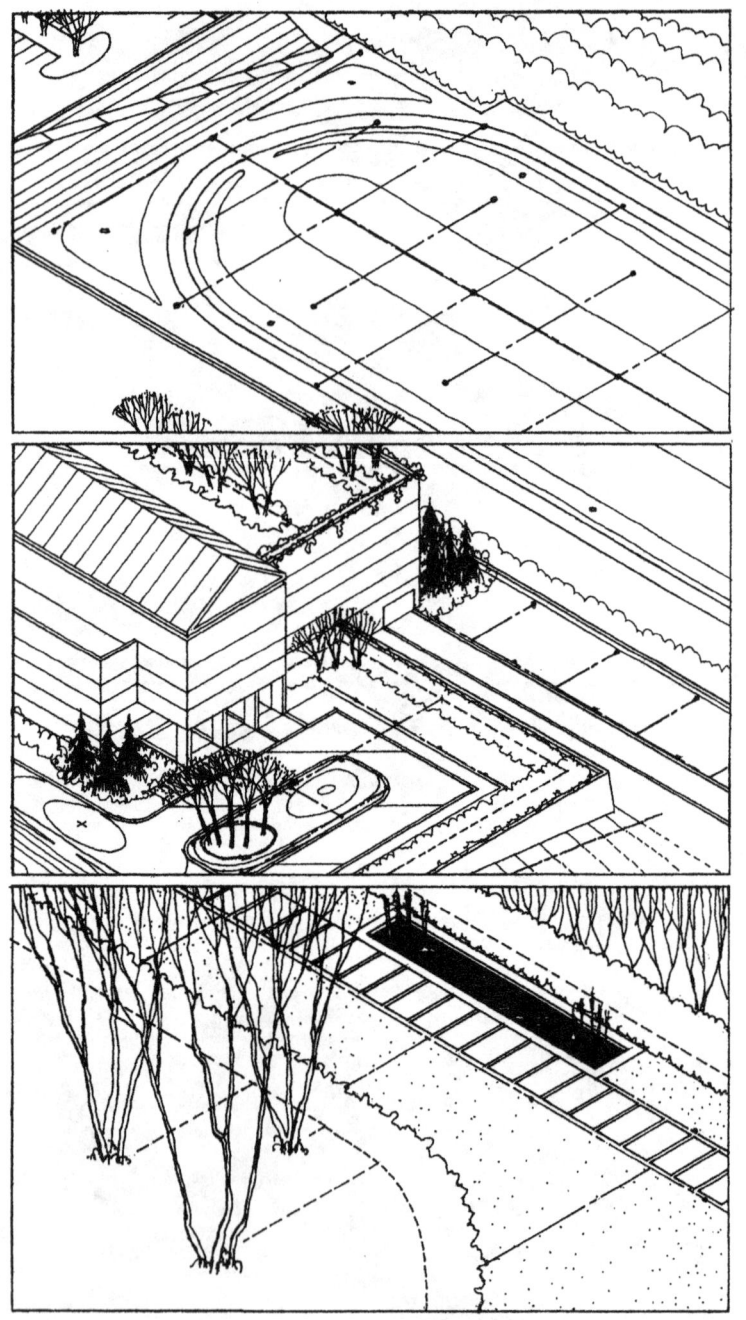

## LARGE AREA TURF SYSTEMS

This type generally uses impulse spray heads, with large radii for efficiency. High static pressure is required to deliver the m³/h (gpm) indicated by the spray heads. These systems are typically used to irrigate large athletic fields, parks, golf courses, auto parkways, and other open expanses of turf. The application rate should not exceed the infiltration rate of the soil to avoid wasteful runoff, and should be calculated using the local evapotranspiration rate.

## COMBINED SPRAY AND DRIP SYSTEMS

This type is commonly applied to the areas surrounding buildings, pedestrian traffic parking lots, urban parks, and gardens. Systems are designed to accommodate the moisture requirement of different types of plant materials, including turf, groundcovers, annuals and perennial flowers, shrubs, and trees, while at the same time allowing for human use. Key components involve pop-up spray heads, bubbler heads, drip emitters, and root soaker tubes. Area humidity, plant fungus susceptibility, and types of human use determine system design.

## LOW VOLUME DRIP EMITTERS AND DIRECT ROOT SOAKER CONDUIT SYSTEMS

This type of system is a good alternative for hot-arid climates and regions with limited water supplies. It is designed to apply only the absolute minimum water required to sustain plant life. The system requires less pressure and longer wetting times, and may also feature direct feeding of roots. Alternating infiltration trenches may also harvest residual irrigation water for later re-use.

DEVICES

THE HYDROLOGIC CYCLE IS the natural process that governs the movement of water through the landscape, consisting of evaporation, condensation, precipitation, runoff and infiltration. While this natural cycle may be sufficient to support indigenous vegetative growth under natural conditions, irrigation may be necessary to maintain the functional and aesthetic character of a landscape, particularly in the context of introduced plant species, or high-stress environments. Irrigation may alter the functioning of the natural hydrologic cycle, depending on the source of water, soil characteristics and runoff conditions. Therefore, a designer must understand the impact of a proposed irrigation scheme on this natural process, in order to specify appropriate strategies.

## DIAGNOSTIC ASSESSMENT

*What are the climatic conditions within the region?*

The growing season for plants, the amount and timing of precipitation within a region, and the evaporation and transpiration rates in the landscape are critical for the selection of appropriate plant material and the design of irrigation systems. These data establish a baseline for the natural water budget during the critical growing season, as well as indicate the type of plant material that may be appropriate, and the availability of water for use in irrigation. In addition, the microclimate of the site must be taken into consideration when calculating water needs for different portions of the site.

*What are the soil characteristics of the site?*

The ability of soil to hold moisture will greatly affect irrigation design and scheduling. Percolation rates will influence the type of system used, as well as application rates. Generally, highly permeable soils indicate the use of conventional sprinkler systems, whereas drip systems may be more appropriate in impermeable soils.

*What are the water requirements of vegetation on the site?*

The quantity of water necessary for desired plant growth must be determined in order to properly design an irrigation system. Water requirements are a function of local evapotranspiration rates, characteristics of particular plant species, planting density, and microclimatic conditions. In addition, a number of plants may favor specific irrigation techniques, due to susceptibility to mildew or diseases.

*What sources of irrigation water are available?*

Most design projects use potable water provided by local water districts. Increasingly however, non-potable sources are being used for irrigation, particularly in regions with stressed water resources. Alternative sources include recycled water and graywater from residential housing units

*What type of irrigation distribution system is appropriate for the project?*

Irrigation systems may be broadly categorized as conventional sprinkler or low-volume drip irrigation systems. Selection of the appropriate system is a function of application, climate, soil conditions, installation considerations, and maintenance concerns. Each type has specific components and procedures for designing and layout of the delivery and distribution system.

# CLIMATIC CONDITIONS

## Growing Season

The growing season is the annual period that supports plant growth. For most climates, this period falls between the last frost in spring, and the first frost in fall. However, mild climates may experience a year-round growing season, and hot climates may have their growing season interrupted by extreme heat in summer months. Irrigation design considers the precipitation and evapotranspiration rates during the growing season in water budget calculations. Data on the growing season is typically available from local weather services, regional gardening and agricultural resources.

## Precipitation

Annual precipitation data is needed with monthly breakdowns, to determine the amount of rainfall provided to landscape plants during the growing season. In addition, this data may be useful for calculating storage volumes for cisterns or other on-site retention techniques that may be useful sources of irrigation water. Data on average monthly precipitation is typically available from local weather services.

## Evapotranspiration Rate

Evapotranspiration is the amount of water that is lost to the atmosphere by the combination of evaporation and transpiration from the growth of plants. Potential evapotranspiration (ET) is calculated for each month based on average temperature and length of daylight. Data on average montly ET rates are typically available from local weather services, regional gardening resources, or agricultural bureaus. Table 19.1 lists estimated ET rates in mid-summer for different climatic conditions. This "worst-case" ET scenario may serve as a useful guideline for preliminary design of irrigation

DEVICES

## TABLE 19.1. Evapotranspiration rates (ET) and application efficiency for different climate zones.

| Climate | Characteristics (mid-summer) | ET (worst case, millimeters per day) | ET (worst case, inches per day) | Application Efficiency (Sprinkler) | Application Efficiency (Drip) |
|---|---|---|---|---|---|
| Cool Humid | < 20° C (70° F) > 50% humidity | 3–4 | 0.10 – 0.15 | 0.80 | 0.95 |
| Cool Dry | < 20° C (70° F) < 50% humidity | 4–5 | 0.15 – 0.20 | 0.80 | 0.95 |
| Warm Humid | 20°–30° C (70°–90° F) > 50% humidity | 4–5 | 0.15 – 0.20 | 0.75 | 0.90 |
| Warm Dry | 20°–30° C (70°–90° F) < 50% humidity | 5–6 | 0.20 – 0.25 | 0.75 | 0.90 |
| Hot Humid | > 30° C (90° F) > 50% humidity | 5–8 | 0.20 – 0.30 | 0.70 | 0.85 |
| Hot Dry | > 30° C (90° F) < 50% humidity | 8–11 | 0.30 – 0.45 | 0.65 | 0.85 |

Source: Adapted from *Low-Volume Landscape Irrigation Design Manual*, Donald B. Clark (ed.), Rainbird, Inc., 1994.

systems, however its strict application may also result in unnecessary overwatering during much of the growing season.

## SOIL CHARACTERISTICS

Percolation rates and the potential for lateral water movement through capillary action are important characteristics of soil when designing irrigation systems. Coarser, sandy soils tend to indicate the use of conventional or micro-spray systems, because they have greater percolation rates and do not allow for significant horizontal spread of water by capillary action. Low volume drip emitters may be appropriate in medium and fine soils, as capillary action may be sufficient to facilitate significant horizontal movement of water through the soil. Table 19.2 lists infiltration rates and available water held by various types of soils.

## CALCULATING WATER REQUIREMENTS OF LANDSCAPE PLANTINGS

### Landscape Coefficient (K_L)

When combined with growing season and precipitation data, ET rates can reveal a surplus or deficit in water required to sustain turf grass under nat-

**TABLE 19.2. Infiltration rates and available water capacity of soils.**

| Soil type | Maximum Infiltration Rate | Available Water (AW) |
|---|---|---|
| Coarse (sandy loam) | 18 – 30 mm/hr (0.72 – 1.25 in/hr) | 115 mm/m (1.4 in/ft) |
| Medium (loam) | 5 – 20 mm/hr (0.25 – 0.75 in/hr) | 165 mm/m (2.0 in/ft) |
| Fine (clay loam) | 3 – 5 mm/hr (0.13 – 0.25 in/hr) | 210 mm/m (2.5 in/ft) |

Source: Adapted from *Low-Volume Landscape Irrigation Design Manual*, Donald B. Clark (ed.), Rainbird, Inc., 1994.

ural conditions. For other plant types a landscape coefficient ($K_L$) must be calculated using the formula:

$$K_L = k_s \times k_d \times k_{mc}$$

Where:  $k_s$ = species factor based on species water requirements (Table 19.3)

$k_d$ = density factor based on density of plantings (Table 19.4)

$k_{mc}$ = microclimate factor based on relative water needs of different conditions (Table 19.5)

**EXAMPLE**

*You're designing a planting area that contains densely planted ground covers that have low water requirements, but the area is located on an exposed, south-facing slope, adjacent to a building. Therefore the ground cover species factor is low (0.2), the density factor is high (1.1), and the microclimate factor is high (1.2).*

*To calculate $K_L$ you multiply:*

$$0.2 \times 1.1 \times 1.2 = 0.26$$

## Water Requirements for Densely Planted Areas

Water Requirement (milliliters or inches per day) = $K_L \times ET$

**EXAMPLE (US UNITS)**

*The site is located in a warm dry climate, suggesting a maximum ET rate of 0.25 inches per day (Table 19.1). $K_L$ has been calculated at 0.26.*

$$Water\ requirement = 0.26 \times 0.25$$
$$Water\ requirement = 0.07\ inches\ per\ day$$

## TABLE 19.3. Estimated species factor $k_s$ used to determine landscape coefficient ($K_L$).

| Vegetation Type | Low Water Req. | Average Water Req. | High Water Req. |
|---|---|---|---|
| Trees | 0.2 | 0.5 | 0.9 |
| Shrubs | 0.2 | 0.5 | 0.7 |
| Ground Covers | 0.2 | 0.5 | 0.7 |
| Mixed Trees, Shrubs and Ground Covers | 0.2 | 0.5 | 0.9 |

Source: Adapted from Costello, Laurence R. et al. *Estimating Water Requirements of Landscape Plantings.* University of California Cooperative Extension, 1991.

## TABLE 19.4. Estimated density factor $k_d$ used to determine landscape coefficient ($K_L$).

| Vegetation Type | Low Density | Average Density | High Density |
|---|---|---|---|
| Trees | 0.5 | 1.0 | 1.3 |
| Shrubs | 0.5 | 1.0 | 1.1 |
| Ground Covers | 0.5 | 1.0 | 1.1 |
| Mixed Trees, Shrubs and Ground Covers | 0.6 | 1.1 | 1.3 |

Source: Adapted from Costello, Laurence R. et al. *Estimating Water Requirements of Landscape Plantings.* University of California Cooperative Extension, 1991.

## TABLE 19.5. Estimated microclimate factor $k_{mc}$ used to determine landscape coefficient ($K_L$).

| Vegetation Type | Low | Average | High |
|---|---|---|---|
| Trees | 0.5 | 1.0 | 1.4 |
| Shrubs | 0.5 | 1.0 | 1.3 |
| Ground Covers | 0.5 | 1.0 | 1.2 |
| Mixed Trees, Shrubs and Ground Covers | 0.5 | 1.0 | 1.4 |

Source: Adapted from Costello, Laurence R. et al. *Estimating Water Requirements of Landscape Plantings.* University of California Cooperative Extension, 1991.

## Water Requirement for Individual Plants

Water requirements for individual plants are measured in liters or gallons per day. First you must calculate the area of the plant's root zone, based on the area of the plant's canopy when it is mature.

Canopy Area in square meters (sq. ft) = $0.7854 \times$ Diameter in meters (ft.)$^2$

To calculate the water requirement for an individual plant, you must know the mature canopy area, its $K_L$, the ET rate for the area and the application efficiency of the irrigation system.

$$\text{Water Requirements (liters or gallons per day)} = \frac{0.623 \times \text{Canopy Area} \times K_L \times \text{ET}}{\text{Application Efficiency}}$$

# SOURCES OF IRRIGATION WATER

Most projects use potable water provided by the local water district. Available volume and water pressure are key considerations when using this source. Table 19.6 lists the recommended available volumes of standard water meters. Pressure should be measured on site, as it will vary depending on a number of conditions, including time of day. Backflow

DEVICES

**TABLE 19.6. Maximum recommended capacities of standard water meters (US Units).**

| Meter Size (inches) | Available Water Volume (gallons per minute) |
|---|---|
| 5/8" | 20 gpm |
| 3/4" | 30 gpm |
| 1" | 50 gpm |
| 1 1/2" | 100 gpm |
| 2" | 160 gpm |
| 3" | 300 gpm |
| 4" | 500 gpm |

Source: Landphair, Harlow C. and Fred Klatt. *Landscape Architecture Construction.* New York: Elsevier, 1988.

preventers are required to prevent contamination of potable supplies from irrigation systems.

A number of alternatives to irrigation sources are often available, and should be considered in an effort to conserve potable resources wherever possible. These alternatives include surface water, wells, recycled water and graywater.

## Surface Water

Lakes, ponds, reservoirs, streams and rivers are a potential irrigation source, depending on riparian rights dictated by federal, state and local law. Pumping requirements, filtration of water, and seasonal changes in water availability must be considered with this option.

## Wells

High water tables are good sources of irrigation water. Pumping requirements, water availability, and the relative purity of the water should be considered.

## Recycled Water

Recycled water is liquid effluent that has been treated by a sewage plant and may be used for agricultural and landscape irrigation. It is commonly used for golf courses, college campuses, parks, and other large landscapes, particularly in regions with limited water supplies. Levels of nitrogen, phosphorous and potassium found in recycled water often reduce the amount of fertilizer required on these landscapes.

## Graywater

Increasingly, regulatory agencies are providing for the use of graywater in irrigation systems, particularly in regions with limited water supplies. Graywater is untreated household wastewater that has not come into con-

**TABLE 19.7. Estimated graywater flows from residential units.**

| Source | Volume in liters per day (gallons per day) |
|---|---|
| Showers, Bathtubs and Wash Basins | 95 LPD (25 GPD) per occupant |
| Laundry | 55 LPD (15 GPD) per Occupant |

Source: Adapted from 1994 Uniform Plumbing Code.

**TABLE 19.8. Minimum irrigation/leaching area for graywater.**

| Soil Type | Minimum Area per 100 Liters of Graywater Discharge per Day (Square Meters) | Minimum Area per 100 Gallons of Graywater Discharge per Day (Square Feet) |
|---|---|---|
| Coarse Sand or Gravel | 0.5 | 20 |
| Fine Sand | 0.6 | 25 |
| Sandy Loam | 1.0 | 40 |
| Sandy Clay | 1.5 | 60 |
| Clay with Considerable Sand or Gravel | 2.2 | 90 |
| Clay with Small Amounts of Sand or Gravel | 3.0 | 120 |

Source: Adapted from 1994 Uniform Plumbing Code.

tact with toilet waste. It includes wastewater from bathtubs, showers, bathroom sinks, washing machines and laundry tubs. It does not typically include wastewater from kitchen sinks or dishwashers, or waste from manufacturing or processing. Most jurisdictions allow only subsurface irrigation with graywater, and some limit its use to single family residential dwellings. Table 19.7 lists estimated graywater flows from residential dwellings, and Table 19.8 lists minimum irrigation/leaching areas based on soil types. In some instances graywater may be a valuable supplement to conventional or low-volume drip irrigation.

# DELIVERY SYSTEMS

Most irrigation systems use a network of pipe, with controlled valves to regulate and direct the flow of water in the system. Pipe will be either polyvinyl chloride (PVC) or flexible polyethylene tubing.

Pressure loss resulting from the delivery and distribution system must be calculated to ensure proper functioning of the system:

- Table 19.9 lists pressure loss from friction in commonly used PVC pipe.
- Table 19.10 estimates pressure loss through typical water meters. Meter manufacturers provide more precise data.

# TABLE 19.9. Friction-loss table for pipe (PVC 1120–1220 class 160 in).*

| GPM | Velocity | Loss per pipe length noted, psi | | | | | | | | | | |
|---|---|---|---|---|---|---|---|---|---|---|---|---|
| | | 5 | 10 | 20 | 30 | 40 | 50 | 60 | 70 | 80 | 90 | 100 |
| **1/2-IN. PIPE, 0.720-IN-INSIDE DIAMETER** | | | | | | | | | | | | |
| 1 | 0.8 | 0.01 | 0.02 | 0.04 | 0.06 | 0.08 | 0.10 | 0.12 | 0.14 | 0.16 | 0.18 | 0.20 |
| 2 | 1.6 | 0.04 | 0.07 | 0.15 | 0.22 | 0.30 | 0.37 | 0.44 | 0.52 | 0.59 | 0.67 | 0.74 |
| 3 | 2.4 | 0.08 | 0.16 | 0.31 | 0.47 | 0.62 | 0.78 | 0.94 | 1.09 | 1.25 | 1.40 | 1.56 |
| 4 | 3.2 | 0.13 | 0.27 | 0.54 | 0.80 | 1.07 | 1.34 | 1.61 | 1.88 | 2.14 | 2.41 | 2.68 |
| 5 | 4.0 | 0.20 | 0.40 | 0.81 | 1.21 | 1.62 | 2.02 | 2.42 | 2.83 | 3.23 | 3.64 | 4.04 |
| 6 | 4.8 | 0.29 | 0.58 | 1.15 | 1.73 | 2.30 | 2.88 | 3.46 | 4.03 | 4.61 | 5.18 | 5.76 |
| 7 | 5.6 | 0.38 | 0.77 | 1.53 | 2.30 | 3.06 | 3.83 | 4.60 | 5.36 | 6.13 | 6.89 | 7.66 |
| 8 | 6.4 | 0.49 | 0.98 | 1.96 | 2.93 | 3.91 | 4.89 | 5.87 | 6.85 | 7.82 | 8.80 | 9.78 |
| **3/4-IN. PIPE, 0.930-IN-INSIDE DIAMETER** | | | | | | | | | | | | |
| 2 | 0.9 | 0.01 | 0.02 | 0.04 | 0.07 | 0.09 | 0.11 | 0.13 | 0.15 | 0.18 | 0.20 | 0.22 |
| 4 | 1.9 | 0.04 | 0.08 | 0.16 | 0.23 | 0.31 | 0.39 | 0.47 | 0.55 | 0.63 | 0.70 | 0.78 |
| 6 | 2.8 | 0.09 | 0.17 | 0.34 | 0.50 | 0.66 | 0.83 | 1.00 | 1.16 | 1.34 | 1.49 | 1.66 |
| 8 | 3.8 | 0.14 | 0.28 | 0.56 | 0.85 | 1.14 | 1.42 | 1.70 | 1.99 | 2.27 | 2.56 | 2.84 |
| 10 | 4.7 | 0.22 | 0.43 | 0.86 | 1.29 | 1.72 | 2.15 | 2.58 | 3.01 | 3.45 | 3.87 | 4.30 |
| 12 | 5.7 | 0.30 | 0.60 | 1.20 | 1.80 | 2.40 | 3.00 | 3.60 | 4.20 | 4.80 | 5.40 | 6.00 |
| 14 | 6.6 | 0.40 | 0.80 | 1.60 | 2.40 | 3.20 | 4.00 | 4.80 | 5.60 | 6.40 | 7.20 | 8.00 |

TABLE 19.9. Friction-loss table for pipe (PVC 1120-1220 class 160 in)* (continued).

| GPM† | Velocity‡ | Loss per pipe length noted, psi § | | | | | | | | | | |
|---|---|---|---|---|---|---|---|---|---|---|---|---|
| | | 5 | 10 | 20 | 30 | 40 | 50 | 60 | 70 | 80 | 90 | 100 |
| 1-IN PIPE, 1.195-IN-INSIDE DIAMETER | | | | | | | | | | | | |
| 6 | 1.7 | 0.03 | 0.05 | 0.10 | 0.15 | 0.20 | 0.24 | 0.29 | 0.34 | 0.39 | 0.44 | 0.48 |
| 8 | 2.3 | 0.04 | 0.08 | 0.16 | 0.25 | 0.34 | 0.42 | 0.50 | 0.59 | 0.67 | 0.76 | 0.84 |
| 10 | 2.9 | 0.07 | 0.13 | 0.26 | 0.38 | 0.50 | 0.63 | 0.76 | 0.88 | 1.02 | 1.13 | 1.26 |
| 12 | 3.4 | 0.09 | 0.18 | 0.36 | 0.53 | 0.71 | 0.89 | 1.07 | 1.25 | 1.43 | 1.60 | 1.78 |
| 14 | 4.0 | 0.12 | 0.24 | 0.48 | 0.71 | 0.94 | 1.18 | 1.42 | 1.65 | 1.89 | 2.12 | 2.36 |
| 16 | 4.5 | 0.15 | 0.30 | 0.60 | 0.91 | 1.21 | 1.52 | 1.82 | 2.12 | 2.43 | 2.73 | 3.04 |
| 18 | 5.1 | 0.19 | 0.38 | 0.76 | 1.13 | 1.50 | 1.88 | 2.26 | 2.63 | 3.01 | 3.38 | 3.76 |
| 20 | 5.7 | 0.23 | 0.46 | 0.92 | 1.37 | 1.82 | 2.28 | 2.74 | 3.19 | 3.65 | 4.10 | 4.56 |
| 22 | 6.3 | 0.28 | 0.55 | 1.10 | 1.65 | 2.20 | 2.75 | 3.30 | 3.85 | 4.40 | 4.95 | 5.50 |
| 24 | 6.8 | 0.38 | 0.65 | 1.30 | 1.94 | 2.58 | 3.23 | 3.88 | 4.52 | 5.23 | 5.81 | 6.46 |

*Name of pipe and its pressure grouping. The C value constant used in determining friction losses, based on relative smoothness of the interior of the pipe, is 150.

† Gallons per minute flow is given in equal increments with logical increment spacing to satisfy most designer needs.

‡ Velocity of water through pipe. In no instance are friction losses given where the velocity exceeds 7 fps as this should be the extreme limit of velocity in design.

§ Friction loss of water through pipe in increments of 10 ft up to 100 ft with an additional column for 5 ft. This enables rapid selection of loss in all length pipe runs.

DEVICES

## TABLE 19.10. Pressure loss (psi) through water meters (US Units).

| Flow (GPM) | 5/8" | 3/4" | 1" | 11/2" | 2" |
|---|---|---|---|---|---|
| 15 | 8.3 | 3.6 | 1.2 | | |
| 16 | 9.4 | 4.1 | 1.4 | 0.4 | |
| 17 | 10.7 | 4.6 | 1.6 | 0.5 | |
| 18 | 12.0 | 5.2 | 1.8 | 0.6 | |
| 19 | 13.4 | 5.8 | 2.0 | 0.7 | |
| 20 | 15.0 | 6.5 | 2.2 | 0.8 | |
| 22 | | 7.9 | 2.8 | 1.0 | |
| 24 | | 9.5 | 3.4 | 1.2 | |
| 26 | | 11.2 | 4.0 | 1.4 | |
| 28 | | 13.0 | 4.6 | 1.6 | |
| 30 | | 15.0 | 5.3 | 1.8 | 0.7 |
| 32 | | | 6.0 | 2.1 | 0.8 |
| 34 | | | 6.9 | 2.4 | 0.9 |
| 36 | | | 7.8 | 2.7 | 1.0 |
| 38 | | | 8.7 | 3.0 | 1.2 |
| 40 | | | 9.6 | 3.3 | 1.3 |
| 42 | | | 10.6 | 3.6 | 1.4 |
| 44 | | | 11.7 | 3.9 | 1.5 |
| 46 | | | 12.8 | 4.2 | 1.6 |
| 48 | | | 13.9 | 4.5 | 1.7 |
| 50 | | | 15.0 | 4.9 | 1.9 |
| 55 | | | | 6.0 | 2.1 |
| 60 | | | | 7.2 | 2.7 |
| 65 | | | | 8.3 | 3.2 |
| 70 | | | | 9.8 | 3.7 |
| 75 | | | | 11.3 | 4.3 |
| 80 | | | | 12.8 | 4.9 |
| 90 | | | | 16.1 | 6.2 |
| 100 | | | | 20.0 | 7.8 |

Source: Landphair, Harlow C. and Fred Klatt. *Landscape Architecture Construction.* New York: Elsevier, 1988.

- Friction loss due to pipe fittings should be considered, and is estimated at 10% of the loss from the entire system.
- Pressure loss from valves, backflow preventers and other devices must be calculated using data available from the manufacturer.
- Each meter (foot) of vertical rise or fall throughout the system results in an increase or decrease in pressure of 9.80 kPa (0.433 psi)
- Wherever practical, a loop delivery system should be used to distribute pressure evenly to each irrigation zone (Figure 19.1).

# DISTRIBUTION SYSTEMS

Irrigation systems may be broadly categorized as conventional sprinkler or low-volume drip irrigation systems. Table 19.11 lists criteria for selection of the appropriate type of system. Often a mixture of conventional and drip irrigation is an appropriate solution for a site.

## Conventional Sprinkler Systems
### Head Selection and Layout

Manufacturers produce a wide variety of sprinkler heads to accommodate varying conditions. Pop-up spray heads (Figures 19.2 and 19.3) are available in full or partial circle patterns, as well as other specialty patterns for unique conditions. They are typically used for small turf areas and shrub or groundcover planting. Bubbler heads (Figure 19.4) are used to soak planting areas where foliage should not be wetted, such as flowerbeds. Rotary heads have one or more nozzles that deliver water in streams, and are used to cover large turf areas. These heads may have sprinkling radii in excess of 15 meters (50 feet).

The area to be irrigated should be divided into zones that have similar water requirements and similar head selection. Each zone is typically connected to the delivery system by a valve, which controls it operation. Calculating pressure supplied to each head in the zone is essential to ensure uniform application. There should be no greater than 10% difference in pressure supplied to each head.

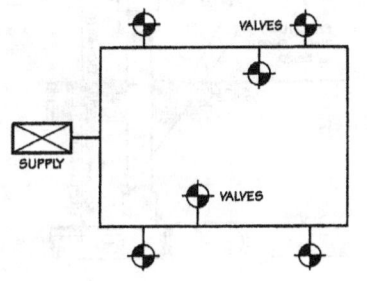

**Figure 19.1. Loop delivery system.**

DEVICES

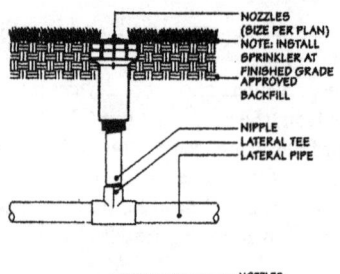

NOZZLES
(SIZE PER PLAN)
NOTE: INSTALL
SPRINKLER AT
FINISHED GRADE
APPROVED BACKFILL

NIPPLE
LATERAL TEE
LATERAL PIPE

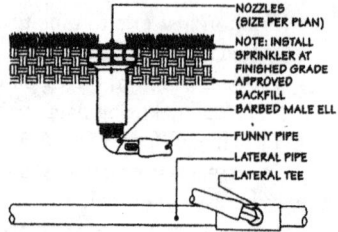

NOZZLES
(SIZE PER PLAN)
NOTE: INSTALL
SPRINKLER AT
FINISHED GRADE
APPROVED
BACKFILL
BARBED MALE ELL

FUNNY PIPE

LATERAL PIPE
LATERAL TEE

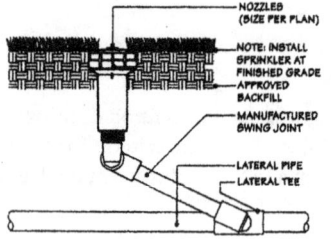

NOZZLES
(SIZE PER PLAN)

NOTE: INSTALL
SPRINKLER AT
FINISHED GRADE
APPROVED
BACKFILL

MANUFACTURED
SWING JOINT

LATERAL PIPE
LATERAL TEE

**Figure 19.2. Typical pop-up spray heads.**

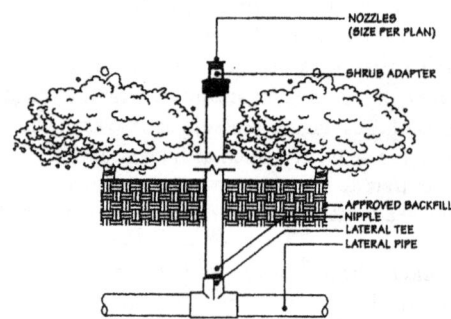

NOZZLES
(SIZE PER PLAN)

SHRUB ADAPTER

APPROVED BACKFILL
NIPPLE
LATERAL TEE
LATERAL PIPE

**Figure 19.3. Typical shrub head.**

**Figure 19.4. Typical bubbler head.**

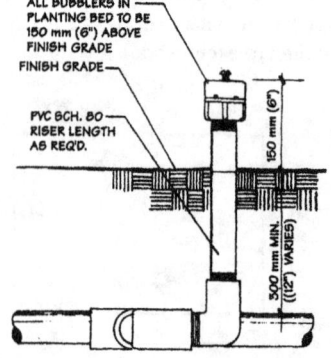

ALL BUBBLERS IN
PLANTING BED TO BE
150 mm (6") ABOVE
FINISH GRADE
FINISH GRADE

PVC SCH. 80
RISER LENGTH
AS REQ'D.

150 mm (6")

300 mm MIN.
((12") VARIES)

**TABLE 19.11. Irrigation system selection criteria.**

| Criteria | Conventional Sprinkler Irrigation | Low-Volume Drip Irrigation |
|---|---|---|
| Application | • Best alternative for large open turf areas.<br>• A wide variety of head types are available to meet various landscape conditions, including narrow strips and planting beds.<br>• Applications in and around large shrubs and trees may result in sprinkler "shadows" from trunks or foliage, that receive less moisture.<br>• May result in overspray onto walks and buildings in tight locations.<br>• Good alternative in locations where regular cleansing of foliage is desired. | • Not appropriate for turf applications.<br>• Good alternative for dense and sparsely planted areas, where foliage should not be wetted, such as flowerbeds.<br>• Eliminates problems of sprinkler "shadows" in densely planted areas.<br>• Good alternative in tight locations where overspray presents would present a problem |
| Climate | • Application efficiency is greatly decreased in hot arid climates, requiring greater water use.<br>• Sprinklers susceptible to windy conditions common to coastal and other environments, which will distort coverage. | • Application efficiency is less affected by climate and wind,. making drip irrigation a good alternative for hot arid and windy climates. |
| Soil Conditions | • Good alternative for well-draining coarse soils.<br>• Impermeable soils may result in runoff due to higher application rates. | • Well-draining coarse soils may prevent adequate capillary action to distribute water to the root zone.<br>• Good alternative for medium and fine (clay) soils which facilitate significant horizontal movement. |
| Installation | • Typically requires trenching for installation. | • In warm climates, installation may be at or near grade, minimizing need for trenching. |
| Maintenance | • Leaks or other problems are easy to spot with conventional systems.<br>• Delivery/Distribution problems typically require trenching to repair.<br>• Solvents are required to repair pipes. | • Clogged systems are more common due to emitter size. Water filtration may be required.<br>• Clogs, leaks or other problems are less noticeable with drip systems.<br>• Depending on climate and installation, repairs may be much quicker and easier than conventional systems.<br>• Solvents not typically required to repair materials. |

DEVICES

*Irrigation* • 373

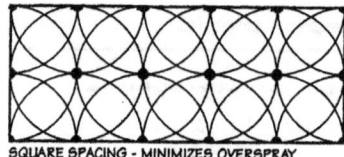

SQUARE SPACING - MINIMIZES OVERSPRAY

SQUARE SPACING - MINIMIZES OVERSPRAY

**Figure 19.5. Typical spacing patterns for sprinkler heads**

Figure 19.5 illustrates typical spacing patterns for conventional sprinkler heads. Triangular spacing is most efficient, and is commonly used for large turf areas, such as athletic fields. Square spacing is more common in smaller rectalinear areas, where overspray onto sidewalks or a building is a concern. Spacing is described as a percentage of the sprinkler diameter. Generally, heads should be spaced so that the spray from one head reaches the adjacent head, although windy sites should provide closer spacing.

### Precipitation Rate

With conventional sprinkler systems, the main objective is to apply water at a rate that the soil can accept, without causing runoff. Table 19.2 lists percolation rates of soils. Precipitation rates for each head used should not exceed these rates. Calculate the precipitation rate (PR) in millimeters per hour (inches per hour) as follows:

Precipitation rate formula for layouts with square spacing:

$$PR = \frac{m^3/hr \text{ applied by sprinkler} \times 1000}{\text{head spacing in } m^2}$$

$$\left( PR = \frac{GPM \text{ applied by sprinkler} \times 96.3}{\text{head spacing in } ft^2} \right)$$

Precipitation rate formula for layouts with triangular spacing:

$$PR = \frac{m^3/hr \text{ applied by sprinkler} \times 1000}{\text{head spacing in } m^2 \times 0.866}$$

$$\left( PR = \frac{GPM \text{ applied by sprinkler} \times 96.3}{\text{head spacing in } ft^2 \times 0.866} \right)$$

Average precipitation rate for heads that are not matched or in areas of irregular spacing can be averaged using the formula:

$$PR = \frac{\text{Total } m^3/hr \text{ applied to area irrigated} \times 1000}{\text{area irrigated in } m^2}$$

$$\left( PR = \frac{\text{Total GPM applied to area irrigated} \times 96.3}{\text{area irrigated in } ft^2} \right)$$

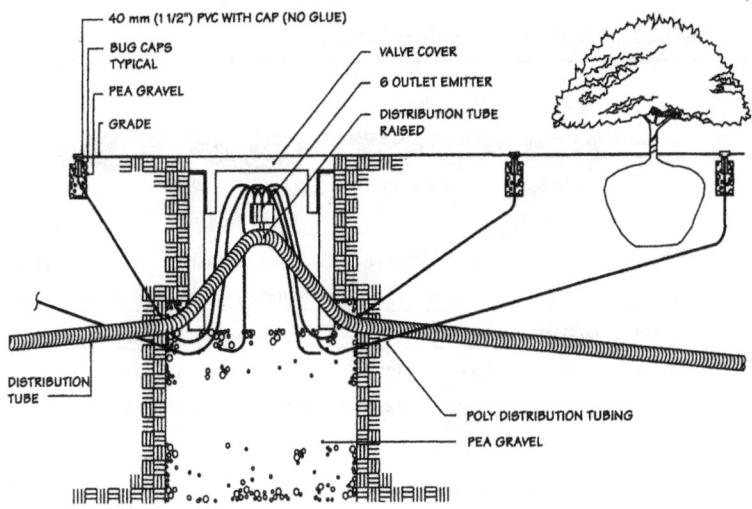

**Figure 19.6. Multiple-outlet drip emitter installation.**

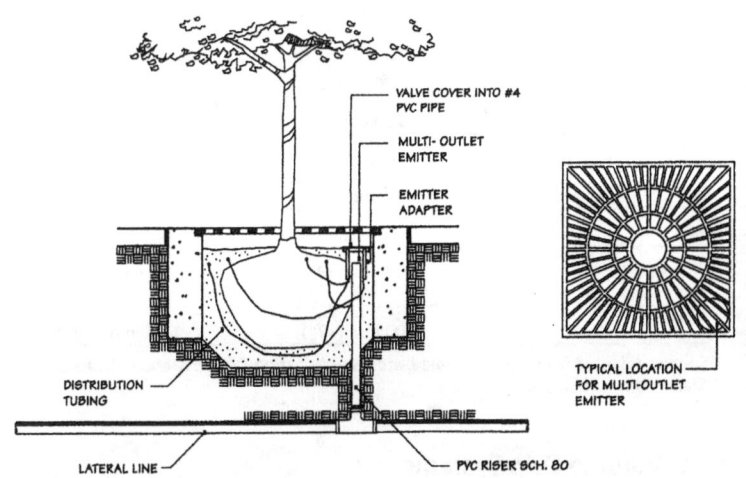

**Figure 19.7. Drip emitter installation for trees with tree grates.**

*Irrigation* ▪ 375

**TABLE 19.12. Maximum emitter spacing.**

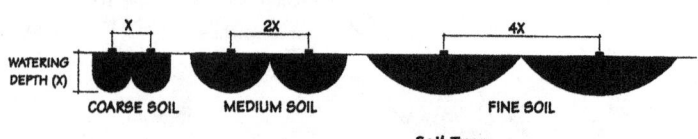

| Emitter Flow | Coarse | Soil Type Medium | Fine |
|---|---|---|---|
| 1.9 LPH (0.5 GPH) | 300 mm (12") | 700 mm (28") | 1000 mm (40") |
| 3.8 LPH (1.0 GPH) | 600 mm (24") | 1000 mm (40") | 1250 mm (50") |
| 7.6 LPH (2.0 GPH) | 1000 mm (40") | 1250 mm (50") | 1650 mm (66") |

Source: Adapted from *Low-Volume Landscape Irrigation Design Manual*, Donald B. Clark (ed.), Rainbird, Inc., 1994.

**TABLE 19.13. Recommended emitter spacing.**

| Soil Type | Minimum Desired Watering Depth | Emitter Spacing |
|---|---|---|
| Coarse | 150 mm (6") | Drip not Recommended |
| | 300 mm (12") | 300 mm (12") |
| | 450 mm (18") | 450 mm (18") |
| | 600 mm (24") | 600 mm (24") |
| Medium | 150 mm (6") | 300 mm (12") |
| | 225 mm (9") | 450 mm (18") |
| | 300 mm (12") | 600 mm (24") |
| | 450 mm (18") | 900 mm (36") |
| Fine | 150 mm (6") | 600 mm (24") |
| | 225 mm (9") | 900 mm (36") |
| | 300 mm (12") | 1200 mm (48") |

Source: Adapted from *Low-Volume Landscape Irrigation Design Manual*, Donald B. Clark (ed.), Rainbird, Inc., 1994.

## Low-Volume Drip Systems

### Emitter Selection and Layout

Manufacturers provide a wide variety of emitters to meet the needs of any particular application, climate, or soil conditions. Consult proprietary data for specific information on the selection and layout of drip emitters. Figures 19.6 and 19.7 illustrate typical emitter installations.

The following should be considered in the layout of low volume systems:

• Lateral lengths of delivery systems should not exceed 60 m (200 ft).

- Flow rates should not exceed 750 L/h (200 GPH).
- Maximum working pressure should not exceed 275 kPa (40 psi).
- 15 mm (½ inch) PVC pipes or polyethylene tubing should be used.

For densely planted areas, soil infiltration rate and desired watering depth are important factors in layout of emitter devices. Table 19.12 illustrates the emitter spacing required to water to the same depth in different types of soil. Table 19.13 lists recommended spacing for watering to varying soil depths.

For individual plants, the minimum area to be wetted should be ½ the area of the plant's mature canopy. The number of emitters required is calculated by the formula:

$$\text{Number of emitters} = \frac{50\% \text{ canopy area in m}^2 \text{ (ft}^2)}{\text{Soil Area Wetted by Emitter in m}^2 \text{ (ft}^2)}$$

Figure 19.8 provides a graphical means to calculate the number of required emitters for individual plants, and the estimated duration of irrigation for various climates.

### Container Plants

Table 19.14 recommends irrigation duration for plants in containers. Table 19.15 lists the frequency for watering container plants.

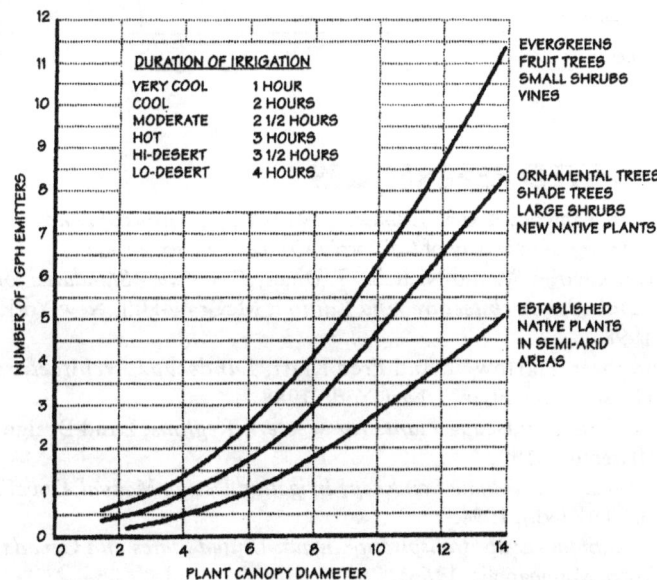

**Figure 19.8. Simplified drip irrigation design chart (U.S. units).**

**TABLE 19.14. Irrigation duration for plants in containers (min).**

| Container size, gal. | Emitter flow size, Gph | Soil Type | | | |
|---|---|---|---|---|---|
| | | Sandy | Medium | Heavy | Potting |
| 1 | 0.5 | 3 | 5 | 11 | 2 |
| 2 | 0.5 | 6 | 10 | 25 | 5 |
| 5 | 1.0 | 8 | 15 | 30 | 6 |
| 15 | 1.0 | 25 | 40 | 90 | 20 |
| 25 | 1.0 | 40 | 75 | 150 | 30 |

**TABLE 19.15. Irrigation frequency for plants in containers (days).**

| Climate | Soil Types | | | |
|---|---|---|---|---|
| | Sandy | Medium | Heavy | Potting |
| Very cool | 2 | 3 | 8 | 2 |
| Cool | 1½ | 2 | 6 | 1 |
| Moderate | 1½ | 2 | 6 | 1 |
| Hot | 1 | 2 | 5 | 1 |
| High — desert | 1 | 1½ | 4 | 1 |
| Low — desert | 1 | 1 | 3 | 1 |

# SUGGESTED REFERENCES

Costello, Laurence R. et al, *Estimating Water Requirements of Landscape Plantings*, University of California Cooperative Extension.

Harris, Charles W. and Nicholas T. Dines, *Time-Saver Standards for Landscape Architecture, 2nd Edition*, McGraw-Hill, New York, 1998.

Landphair, Harlow C. and Fred Klatt, *Landscape Architecture Construction*. Elsevier, New York, 1988.

Perry, Bob, *Landscape Plants for Western Regions*, Land Design, Claremont, 1992.

Rain Bird, *Low-Volume Landscape Irrigation Design Manual*, Donald B. Clark (ed.), 1994.

Toro, *Rainfall-Evapotranspiration Data: United States and Canada*, Toro, Minneapolis, 1966.

STANDARDS

TECHNIQUES

DEVICES

ADMINISTRATION

# ADMINISTRATION

# *Project Management*

# 20

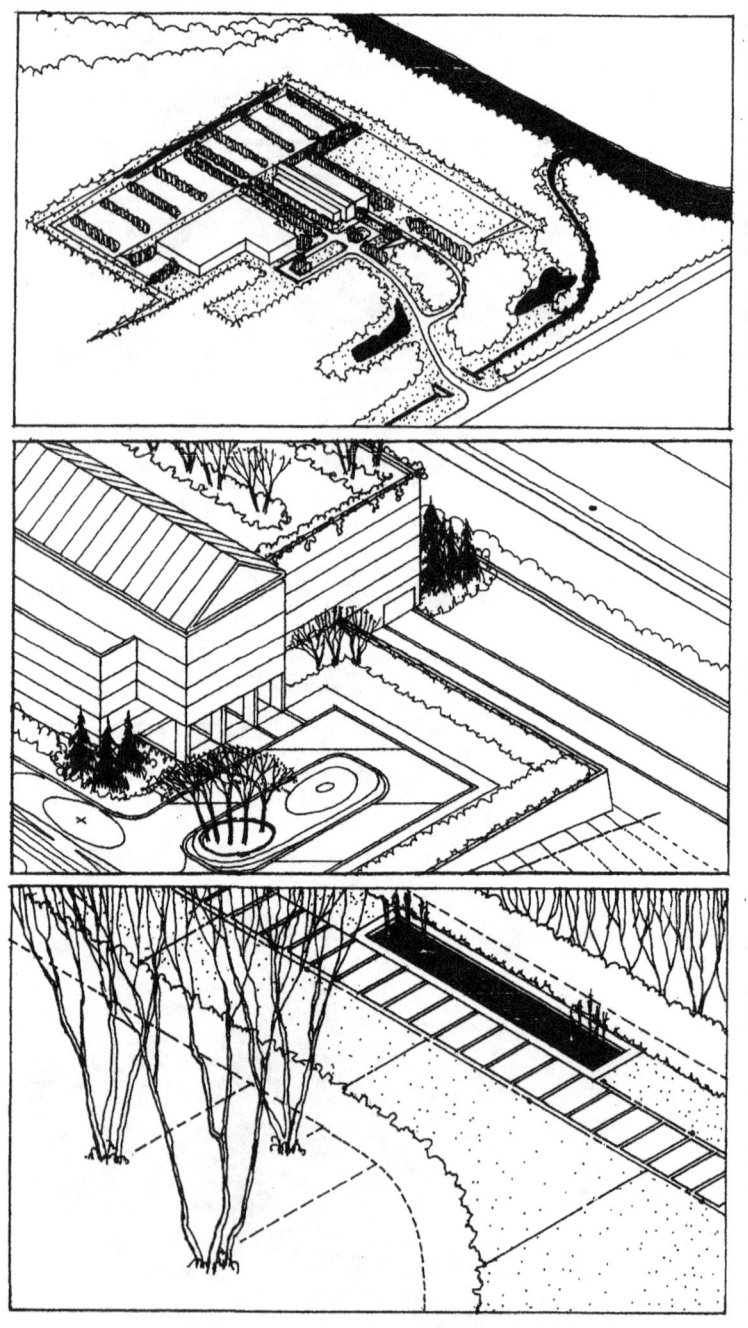

## LARGE SCALE PROJECT MANAGEMENT

Large scale projects, typically relating to public works require collaboration with a broad range of planning, design, and engineering offices and agencies. Emphasis is on managing work flow and coordinating change orders necessitated by project complexity and the higher probability of encountering unknown circumstances. Time management by CPM and budgetary oversight are two prime concerns.

## MEDIUM SCALE PROJECT MANAGEMENT

Housing, business parks, schools, and recreational park projects in both public and private settings typify medium scale projects. Although inter-professional coordination is still an important issue, the work being managed tends to be more predictable and typically falls within commonly understood procedures and contracts. Time and budgets are very critical because there is less economy of scale and fewer margins for error. Client management becomes more prominent at this scale.

## SMALL SCALE PROJECT MANAGEMENT

Small scale projects are by necessity more client oriented, and the work is usually more focused on negotiating the design on-site and staying within budgets. Large operating budgets and profits are the exception rather than the rule at this scale. Emphasis is placed on people management and negotiation skills. There is an expectation of custom or non-standard design and highly personalized service.

ADMINISTRATION

**P**ROJECT MANAGEMENT is a critical part of the execution of professional services. It organizes time and personnel, it manages the execution of contract documents, it monitors changes and field observations, it coordinates schedule updates and closes out final contract provisions. Large scale projects require complex management teams and sub-groups to coordinate inter-professional collaboration. Medium to small scale projects typically require more focus on the primary contract and client interaction. Project management concepts for design offices and agencies are derived from general business management principles and adapted by such professional organizations as ASLA, AIA, and APA.

## DIAGNOSTIC ASSESSMENT

*What are the key components of project management?*

Project Management can be broken down into five basic components: planning and scheduling, personnel and resource allocation, controlling and updating, project closeout, and construction observation.

*How do development scale and scope affect project management strategies?*

Large scale projects typically require more complex coordination of consultants and subcontractors than do small scale and narrow scope projects. Work flow and time management are very critical in larger projects because problems are less transparent and require extra diligence to discover problems as they occur and to identify potential problems before they have a chance to develop.

*How may the project type determine the method for developing a project budget?*

Small scale projects are often conducive to historical precedent models within a firm, and budgets may be derived from key time and scope indicators (multipliers). Large scale projects commonly require a multi-layered unit cost assessment, composed of subcontractor and consultant bids (engineers, architects, planners, etc.).

*What are key considerations for closing out a project?*

The project close out serves to properly archive all instruments of service for legal reference, to update the firm's historical labor costs records, to record and file new details or fabrication specifications, and to calculate the actual project profit and labor multiplier for future reference.

# KEY PROJECT MANAGEMENT COMPONENTS

## Contractual Responsibilities

All participating parties in the land development process must assume their respective responsibilities prior to and during the execution of design and planning services. Project management strategies are aimed at coordinating all participants, administering the requirements of the contract, and delivering the final product within the designated budget and time frame parameters.

### Owner or Client

The owner or client typically determines the initial goal and scope of a project and assumes responsibility for all legal and monetary matters with regard to land acquisition and financing, by working directly with planners, political representatives, lawyers, bankers, realtors, and developers.

### Design Professionals

Design professionals produce physical feasibility studies, final development programs, conceptual studies, design development plans, and construction documents, which anticipate the problems of building in a particular region, locale, or landscape setting. They commonly interact with planning and regulatory agencies, and fellow professionals (sub-consultants) on the development team. A primary task is to study the local building codes and by-laws that pertain to the subject development.

### General Contractor

The general contractor determines the most cost-effective methods for transforming the design plans into the proposed development as indicated on the construction documents. Expertise involves selection of proper methods and equipment, purchasing proper materials, negotiating with sub-contractors and supervising their work, and securing the appropriate permits and utility hook-ups.

## Planning

Before a project may begin, the *scope of work* and *scope of services* must be clearly understood and transformed into work tasks for the purpose of establishing a project budget and a time frame.

### Scope of Work

The scope of work describes the outcome of the project and establishes a mutually agreeable legal framework for defining the professional services, which are required to achieve the desired outcome. An effective scope of work also implies what work and services will be excluded. A final scope of work is developed after preliminary studies and client interviews to determine final program and budgetary parameters.

## Scope of Services

The scope of services outlines and describes the professional services required to achieve the outcome described in the scope of work. Comprehensive descriptions of professional services are available from both AIA and ASLA. Commonly offered landscape architecture services are described as follows:

- *Development Feasibility Planning*: Provides client with a basis to assess alternative methods for determining the general legal, physical, economic, cultural, and environmental factors, which may affect the general feasibility of a proposed project.
- *Development Programming*: Provides alternative programming concepts, which affect the project scope and potential outcomes.
- *Landscape Planning*: Provides advice on land use patterns, visual resource analysis, corridor planning, or conservation and development policy recommendations.
- *Landscape Assessment*: Provides a summary of key features of a development parcel with the aim of identifying suitable development areas, areas requiring conservation and protection, and areas restricted by regulation.
- *Master Planning Services*: Provides an overall strategic plan and a suggested sequence of development for larger scaled institutional, recreational, or commercial projects.
- *Schematic Studies*: Provides initial conceptual planning and design studies to test programming and development assumptions, and to investigate form implications based upon previous assessment and program studies. Schematic designs are typically carried to a level of detail, sufficient to prepare a general cost analysis.
- *Design Development Services*: Provides pre-construction design documents, which reflect final decisions concerning position, form, dimensions, materials, details, and costs. Cost calculations at the end of this process should indicate if the project is within the scope of the contract expectations.
- *Construction Documents Preparation*: Provides bid documents (drawings and specifications) for the purpose of project construction. A final cost estimate is typically made when documents are 90-100% complete and serves as the basis for bid comparisons.
- *Construction Observation Services*: Provides construction observation services to monitor construction progress and compliance with construction documents and contract provisions.

**TABLE 20.1. Time allocation for design services for preliminary budget purposes.**

| Phase | AIA Guidelines |
|---|---|
| Assessment and schematics | 15% |
| Design development | 20% |
| Construction documents | 40% |
| Bidding/ negotiation | 5% |
| Construction administration | 20% |

## Scheduling and Budgeting

### Scheduling

The prime objective of project scheduling is to ensure that specified tasks are completed on time and within the allocated budget. This requires systematic monitoring of work progress and adjustments as required. Table 20.1 indicates the amount of time commonly allocated to specific phases within a project. Modern practice is less likely to neatly divide work in discrete segments as shown in Table 20.1 because the computer allows the designer to extend the design development phase by eliminating redundant iterations required in more linear methods of working. The actual time allocated to the production of CD's has been reduced, but it has been replaced by more extensive global changes in drawings later in the production phases. Close coordination with sub-consultants is very important to avoid errors due to faulty updating of all files across disciplines. Each project requires careful weighing of specific variables, which may affect such time allocations. CPM scheduling (Critical Path Method), is a commonly used method of managing time, events, and the probability of completing tasks as the project unfolds. CPM charts are updated daily on large projects, and periodically on less comprehensive projects. These charts are converted to time/task duration bar charts (See Chapter 9: Construction Operations).

### Budgeting

The general project budget is derived directly from the scope of work and services documents. Firms commonly use historical or industry standards on which to estimate the amount of time required to execute the services as specified in the client agreement. A project must be broken down into segments and each segment assigned a percentage of time available as indicated in Table 20.1. Tasks are assigned to specific personnel or teams, and costs are calculated as part of a project budget summary report as shown in Table 20.2. The summary report indicates total direct labor (actual wages before payroll burden and overhead), the overhead (typically $1.5 - 1.8 \times$ direct labor), reimbursable expenses (costs associated with

ADMINISTRATION

**TABLE 20.2. Typical project budget report summary, showing billable hours, direct labor costs, overhead, reimbursable expenses, and profit calculation.**

| Direct Labor | Hours* | Billings** |
|---|---|---|
| Preliminary design | 40 | $800 |
| Design development | 35 | $700 |
| Etc. (Additional services) | Total direct labor | $20,000 |
| | Overhead (1.8) | $28,000 |
| | Reimbursable expenses † | $8,000 |
| | Total costs | $56,000 |
| | 15% Profit on OH + DL | $7,200 |
| | Project price | $63,200 |

(Derived from Getz, Business Management in the Smaller Firm, PMA, 1986)

* Hours are estimated for each task listed in the scope of services.

** Billings are a product of direct labor hourly wage times the estimated hours per task.

† Reimbursable expenses are external to profit and contain a separate 10% markup as shown.

services outside of regular overhead), and profit (which may range from 15- 20%). Projects with a high degree of uncertainty may require a 5% contingency allowance to account for unforeseen events.

### Overhead Expenditures

- *Indirect labor:* Non-billable work often associated with marketing.
- *Payroll burden:* Payroll charges associated with taxes, health plans, retirement, etc.
- *Space costs:* Rental and associated utility expenses.
- *Liability insurance:* Professional liability protection.
- *Interest:* Debt service on all outstanding business loans and leases.
- *Bad debts:* Uncollectable fees or other losses requiring a write-off.
- *Training and education:* Staff training, seminars, re-tooling, etc.
- *General and administrative expenses:* Support staff, associated supplies, non-billable telecommunications, etc.

### Firm Multiplier

Alternately, a firm with a substantial financial database may use a multiplier to achieve the same project price estimate. A multiplier is a factor, which incorporates the cost of payroll burden, overhead (indirect expenses), and profit. The direct labor cost (DL) times the office multiplier yields the amount, which may be billed to the client for labor (professional services). Conversely, the multiplier for a particular project or a project phase may be determined by dividing the sum of direct labor, overhead, and profit, by

# Annual Overhead Rate

A firm's annual overhead rate is found by dividing the total annual overhead expenditure (OH) by the total annual direct labor expenditure (DL):

$$\frac{OH}{DL} = \text{Direct labor multiplier ratio (typically 1.5 to 1.8)}$$

The overhead ratio will fluctuate within a project from task to task, and may vary from 1.2 to 1.9. Periodic calculations during the project are useful to track the actual value for the whole project.*
   * Note: Overhead includes payroll burden, which typically ranges from 0.3 to 0.4 and when added to other costs in the overhead expenditure list, yields a rate of 1.5 to 1.8 on average. Rates vary regionally.

the direct labor cost (DL) pertaining to that project or phase. Two critical factors affect multiplier rates:

- *Risk:* High risk increases the contingency allowance requirement, and therefore increases total project cost. High risk also requires higher profit goals to justify the risk and uncertainty.
- *High overhead:* High overhead due to high regional labor costs or rental rates increases a firm's multiplier rates. High overhead requires high productivity to stay competitive, and is a prime factor affecting firm profitability.

Efficiency of operation (high productivity and low overhead) allows a firm to provide services at a lower rate without sacrificing profit margin. Poor efficiency (low productivity and high overhead) forces a firm to sacrifice profit to compete with more efficient firms.

## MULTIPLIER EXAMPLE

Assume a firm is bidding on a small housing project with approved zoning in place. The firm estimates $20,000 in direct labor (DL) costs, $8,000 in reimbursable expenses, and a firm multiplier based on previous experience of 2.8. Determine total project cost.

Total project cost = (DL × firm multiplier) + expenses
                              + 10% expense markup
                   = (20,000 × 2.8) + 8,000 + 800
                   = $64,800

Assume the firm is also bidding on a similar housing project with zoning subject to approval and wetland regulation issues. Labor is identical to the previous example, but a firm multiplier of 3.2 is used to account for a 5% contingency and a 20% profit goal due to the risk potential.

Total project cost = (DL × firm multiplier) + expenses
                              + 10% expense markup
                   = (20,000 × 3.2) + 8,000 + 800
                   = $72,800

ADMINISTRATION

# Calculating a Multiplier

A multiplier may be calculated by dividing the revenue earned on labor, by the direct labor (DL).

$$\frac{\text{Revenue earned on firm's labor}}{\text{Direct Labor (hourly wages)}} = \text{Multiplier}$$

Where:
DL = $20,000
OH = $30,000 (1.5 rate)
Profit = $10,000 (20% of $50,000)

$$\frac{\$60,000 \text{ [DL+OH+20\% Profit]}^*}{\$20,000 \text{ [DL]}} = 3.0$$

*$60,000 does not include reimbursable expenses (flow through expenses), which are marked up at 10-12% and added to generate the total project budget.

## Average Hourly Payroll Cost

The average hourly payroll cost on a particular project will vary from month to month due to fluctuations in task types and varying rates of efficiency. The average hourly payroll cost may be calculated as follows:

*Average Hourly Payroll Cost* = $\dfrac{\textit{Gross payroll} + 0.25 \textit{ cost factor}}{\textit{Total hours worked}}$ *

*Where:*

> *Gross payroll = Direct labor for the subject work period.*
> *Total hours worked = Time sheet summaries for the subject work period*

\* Note: The cost factor will vary by region and economic sector. A range of 0.25 – 0.30 is common, and is a factor of regulated and negotiated payroll burden.

## Contract Types

There are a number of contract types, which may serve as a basis for an agreement. The client often determines the type of contract required for a project. Each firm may be familiar with one or two types through favorable experience. Each contract type has advantages and disadvantage and should be chosen to achieve a specific goal. Basic types are summarized below:

- *Cost plus fixed fee:* Allows the recovery of all costs, but limits the fee and profit to a fixed amount, and is often favored by governmental agencies due to appropriation cycles. Governments disallow costs associated with interest, promotion, or other marketing expenses, so such costs must be factored into the negotiated fee.

**TABLE 20.3. Typical design firm multiplier values and associated circumstances.**

| Multiplier factors | Multiplier value* |
|---|---|
| Low risk, routine, highly automated work | 2.5–3.0 |
| Higher risk, unusual work, with new processes | 3.0–3.4 |

\* The typical design firm multiplier ranges from 2.8 to 3.2 and reflects a desired profit goal of 15 - 20 % (Getz, PMA, Inc.)

- *Multiplier times direct labor:* Allows for a simple method for calculating billing amounts and guarantees a fixed profit (multiplier contains profit and overhead costs), but requires a negotiated expenditure cap and disclosure of employee salary rates on the invoice.
- *Percentage of construction costs:* Suitable for highly predictable work, for which a firm has well-established protocols. Billing is simplified to reflect percent of completion at periodic intervals within a fixed negotiated sum.
- *Lump sum fee:* Lump sum fees are effective for maximizing profit for low risk work well within the competency and experience level of the firm. It requires a well-defined scope, but is susceptible to lower profit if unforeseen problems arise during the project.
- *Standard hourly billing rates:* These rates include overhead and profit, and are charged to work tasks, rather than to individual employees on a bill. Similar to a multiplier times direct labor, it runs the risk of loss in an environment of rapidly rising labor costs. It is useful for projects of short duration for this reason.
- *Retainer:* An annual fee typically paid by a client of long-standing, for whom periodic services covering an agreed number of hours are required. It is for special occasions only, since it commonly requires attention upon client request, regardless of firm workflow.

## Personnel and Resource Allocation

Scheduling determines the amount of time, measured in person days or hours that may be allocated to a particular project task or phase. The project manager is required to assign personnel, space, and equipment to a project within the projected time/ task framework. Additionally, the firm must tie performance thresholds to payment schedules to maintain adequate cash flow. The project schedule is therefore linked to the project contract's payment schedule.

### Time Over-runs

If a project requires more time than originally allocated to complete a particular phase, the project manager may consider a number of options.

ADMINISTRATION

Additional time for a particular task may be borrowed from a less important (non-critical) task. The time budget must remain in balance, so an alternative less time consuming method for achieving the non-critical task (donor activity) may be required. For example, a particular task may be eliminated if it can be folded into another, without upsetting the scheduled workflow. If time is not re-allocated within the project budget, the firm will lose the profit calculated on the basis of the original schedule. In any event, the project manager must work to fulfill the requirements of the project contract and the client's expectations.

## Controlling and Updating

Schedules are guides, which require monitoring and updating due to both task accomplishment and unforeseen disruptions as well. Tools to help monitor progress and to allocate remedies are:

### Records and Progress Reports

Project files require daily updates of all construction documents, phone logs, correspondence, change orders, and client meetings. Records must be in written form and all telephonic and electronic exchanges should be noted in attached follow-up memos. All project personnel should prepare periodic summary reports so that the work phase and time schedule may be monitored and adjusted. Updates and reports should be distributed to all project personnel.

### Team and Project Meetings

Written and electronic communications should be augmented with strategically timed team meetings to ensure that progress is being made on all time goals and to clarify any misunderstandings. All meetings should have minutes or summaries, which are distributed to all relevant parties.

### Project Bar Charts

CPM charts, bar charts, and task milestone charts are typically employed to graphically illustrate the project time-line, linked to calendar dates and activities by type and duration. Emphasis is placed on beginning and ending dates for each activity. Professional time management software is readily available for this purpose.

## Construction Project Administration
### Administration and Project Observation

Verbal orders given to the contractor or subcontractor by the landscape architect or the owner should be followed up with written confirmation and added to the project file. Any order, which instructs the contractor to pursue a course of action not contained in the original contract, may result in a request by the contractor for additional compensation. In either case, it is common practice to request a written quote for the additional work before such work is initiated.

## Field Orders and Change Orders

Field orders are directives affecting minor changes in the contractor's work. A change order is typically a written document, which becomes a permanent part of the construction documents. They are typically entered onto sequentially pre-printed forms, and become a part of the contract documents. All verbal orders must be contemporaneously converted to a written form.

## Interpretation, Clarification, and Directives

The designer should contractually retain the right to interpret plans, details, or specifications as questions arise so that design integrity may be maintained. Interpretations must be timely so as not to create costly delays, and entered into the record in written form. If actual revisions are required, they should be provided in advance of actual construction to avoid delays. The contract amount might be affected by such clarifications.

## Request of Estimate or Price Quotation

All changes in scope should be accompanied by a request of the contractor for written price increase or decrease estimate.

## Scheduled Job Meetings and Visits

Meetings are typically weekly, and should be strategic to avoid unneeded disruption of work.

## Materials and Samples Submittals and Reviews

All material samples must be submitted by the contractor well in advance of their scheduled placement so they may be reviewed by the designer for compliance with specifications.

## Substitutions or Equivalents

The designer should retain the contractual authority to allow or disallow substitutions of specified materials. All decisions should be recorded in job meeting minutes and entered into the project record.

## Shop Drawings

The contract may require shop drawings depicting the details of fabrications of specified elements. All reviewed and accepted submittals should be recorded in the project files as part of the "as built" record.

### Time Delays and Extensions

Time delays due to unforeseen events (weather extremes, material shortage due to external factors, etc.) may lead to requests for contract extensions or alterations of procedures. All changes must be entered as amended contract items in the written record.

### Payment Requests and Certificates of Payment

Payments to the contractor are periodic (typically monthly) and are part of the payment schedule in the contract. Payment is tied to completion of specified work. Commonly, 10% of each payment is retained in escrow and not released until all mechanics liens have been cleared.

### Verification of Quality and Quantity

*Preventative observation* by the designer is preferable to corrective observation in the field. Preventative observation occurs as work commences and progresses and aims to spot problems as they arise. *Corrective observation* typically occurs after the contractor has completed all work, and the aim is to examine the work for compliance. Corrective action is therefore disruptive and costly to all parties at this point in the process. It is better to anticipate and negotiate with the contractor.

### Tests

Tests required to establish strength of materials or to certify regulatory compliance should be stated in the contract documents and the results should be entered into the project document record.

### Rejections and Shut-downs

The contract should provide for the rejection of all faulty materials, manufactured components, or on-site fabrications or installations. The designer or designated agent (consultant) must retain the right to reject completed work if it does not comply with the contract document requirements. Shutdowns may be required if the contractor refuses to correct cited work in a timely fashion. Repeated shut-downs and violations may result in the release of the contractor.

### As-built Record Enforcement

To avoid costly post construction development of as-built document records, it is imperative that as-built records be created contemporaneously with execution of work, especially in the case of all infrastructure utilities.

### Project Records

All project records, including change orders, memos, minutes, test results, etc. need to be carefully filed for easy access both during and after the project. They contain the written record of all decisions, which may require review from time to time as disputes arise.

## Unauthorized Contract Changes

Contract changes unsupported by written documentation and prior approval, may constitute an unauthorized contract change and may be deemed in violation of the contract. Numerous minor verbal orders in the field may have an undesirable cumulative effect.

## Project Closeout
### Advance Notices

The contractor must give ample notice (typically seven days) to all affected parties when observation of completed work, or submitted materials is required. All observations and acceptances must be duly documented. Final acceptance should be duly noted and posted as a means of commencing the mechanic's lien period.

### Pre-final Observation and Punch Lists

It is useful practice to conduct a pre-final observation prior to final acceptance observation. This allows the contractor time to take corrective actions. Such a practice may result in a more timely close-out at final acceptance, with regard to final payments.

### Construction Completion Observation

*Conditional acceptance* of completed work is sometimes granted when it is in the best interest of the client to take delivery of the completed work, and the nature of the defective work is minor. *Final acceptance* of completed work should be granted when all of the construction work has been completed in accordance with the contract terms. Date and time of completion should be recorded and parties should be notified.

### Maintenance Period

The maintenance period refers to the contractor's responsibility to maintain plant materials to facilitate proper establishment prior to final acceptance. The length of the maintenance period varies by region and local conditions. Severe weather or other factors may require extension of the period at agreed upon extra compensation.

### Certifications of Compliance

Certifications of compliance provide a written record, which satisfies regulatory and performance requirements set forth in the contract.

### Mechanics Lien Statutes and Releases

Within thirty to ninety days (depending on legal jurisdiction), all claims by subcontractors of non-payment must be received by the client or approved agent. If no such claims materialize after this period, the client authorizes that the contractor be paid the remaining 10% retention escrow as final payment for construction services provided.

ADMINISTRATION

### Withheld Funds

Withheld funds may be retained as part of the 10% retention escrow to ensure mechanics lien compliance, or for such reasons as, unsatisfactory work, damaged property, or failure to perform.

### Bonding Company Responsibility and Rights

The purpose of a bond is to guarantee to the owner that the contract will be performed as specified in the contract. Bond types vary, and it is advisable for the owner or agent to secure aid of legal counsel to prepare a bond that covers faithful performance of labor and materials. Bond forms are typically part of the contract agreement.

### Penalties and Bonuses—Contract Period

The contractor's performance may be penalized for delays and rewarded for completion ahead of schedule. However, it must be clearly shown that delays are not caused by unavoidable externalities.

## Post Completion
### As-built Records

The project should not be accepted as complete until all as-built drawings have been delivered.

### Manuals, Special Tools, and Operating Instruments

The owner may require operating and maintenance manuals and tools for installed equipment. Such requirements should be specified in the contract.

### Guarantees

Guarantees are typically of two types: *Contractor's guarantee* for performance as specified, and *manufacturer's guarantee* for products installed. Required guarantees must be indicated in the contract.

### Replacements

If equipment or products fail, replacements should bear the same guarantee as the original equipment.

### Mechanics Lien Releases

All mechanic lien releases for all labor, materials, suppliers, and subcontractors should be received before final payment is made to complete the contract, and before the bonding company is notified of such completion.

**Follow-ups**

It is wise practice to make periodic follow up visits to the completed project and record observations in a written memorandum for the client's benefit. Observations may include aspects of maintenance, or suggestions of new products. Such visits demonstrate long term interest in the client's project and is a valuable form of marketing for repeat work.

## SUGGESTED REFERENCES

AIA, *The Architect's Handbook of Professional Practice, 12th Edition*, AIA Press, Washington, D. C., 1993.

Burstein, David, and Frank Stasiowski, *Project Management for the Design Professional, 2nd Edition*, Whitney Library of Design, New York, 1991.

Fee, Sylvia Hollman, *Means Landscape Estimating, 2nd Edition*, R. S. Means Company, Inc., Kingston, MA, 1999.

Getz, Lowell, *Business Management in the Smaller Design Firm*, PMA, Inc., Newton, 1986.

Marshall, Lane, *Landscape Architecture: Guidelines to Professional Practice*, 2nd Edition, LAF, Washington, D. C., 1986.

Rogers, Walter, *The Professional Practice of Landscape Architecture*, VNR, New York, 1997.

Sharkey, Bruce G., *Ready, Set, Practice: Elements of Landscape Architecture Professional Practice*, John Wiley & Sons, Inc., 1994.

Stitt, Fred, *Design Office Management Handbook*, Arts and Architecture Press, 1988.

ADMINISTRATION

ADMINISTRATION

*Permitting Processes*

21

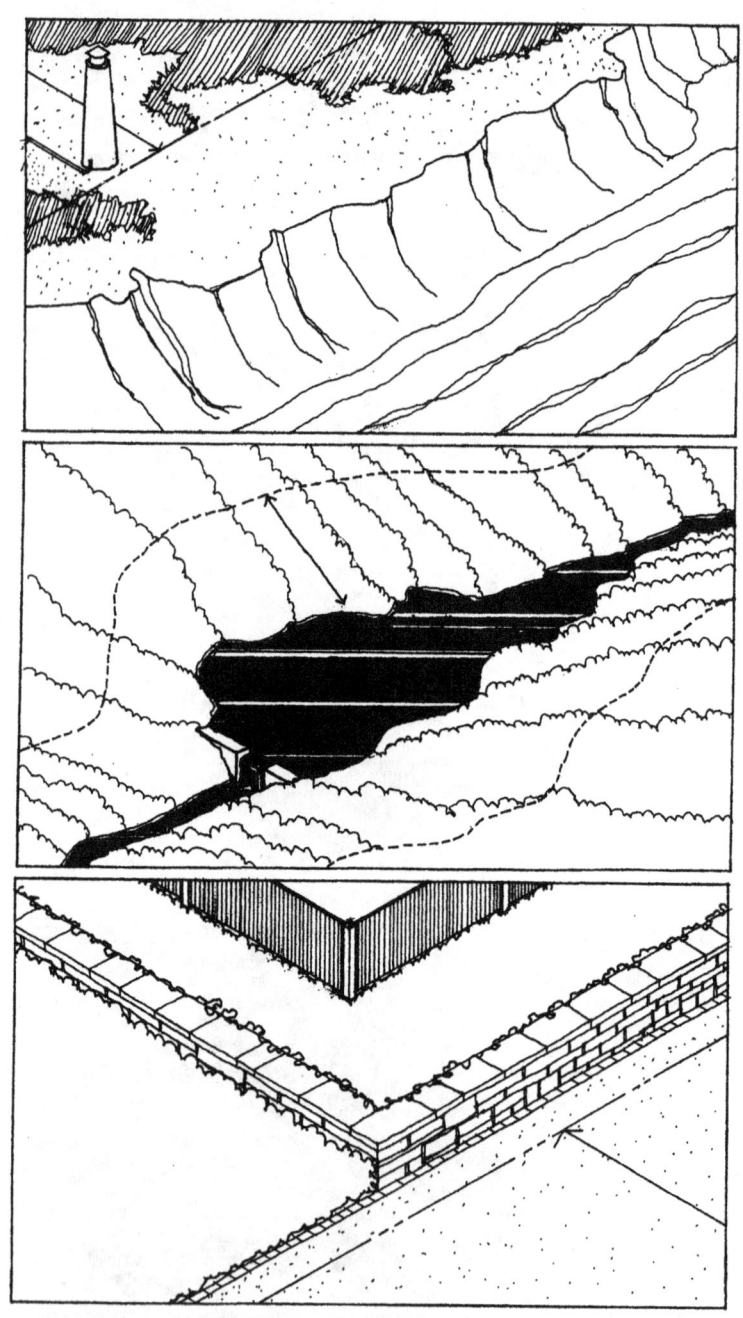

## FEDERAL PERMITTING PROCESSES

In the United States, larger projects entirely or partly financed, assisted, conducted, regulated or approved by federal agencies may require the preparation of an environmental impact statement prior to approval. Projects impacting water resources may require a variety of federal permits, including Section 404 and Section 10 permits from the Army Corp of Engineers for the alteration of wetlands and water bodies, and NPDES permits from the EPA for construction activities.

## STATE PERMITTING PROCESSES

A number of states have adopted broader reaching environmental regulations modeled after federal legislation. Many state environmental policy acts require the preparation of environmental impact reports for projects that exceed a certain size, scope, or significance of impact. Other state regulations may require permits for activities that impact wetlands, water bodies, air quality, energy resources and historic or cultural resources. Specific regulations vary widely from state to state and should always be consulted prior to initiating a project.

## LOCAL PERMITTING PROCESSES

Most local communities have established zoning regulations or other land use controls. Regulations typically dictate allowable uses, densities, sizes and arrangements of structures and lots. Developments consistent with zoning regulations often do not require approval beyond the required construction permits, unless the proposed use is identified as conditional in the ordinance. However, the rezoning of property, subdivision of land, or deviation from established standards often triggers a permit process. Aesthetic controls, historic, open space, or agricultural preservation regulations, and landscape regulations are common in more sophisticated ordinances and may require special review and approval.

ADMINISTRATION

L EGAL PROCEDURES REQUIRED FOR SITE DEVELOPMENT and other landscape architectural activities are a function of federal, state, and local (i.e., county, regional, and/or municipal) law in the United States. Generally, federal and state regulations aim at protecting ecological and cultural resources of significant concern, while local communities provide further regulations for the protection of public health, safety and welfare. Specific regulations, standards, and procedures vary significantly among states and local jurisdictions. This chapter provides a general overview of permitting procedures commonly found in the United States, but does not provide detailed information about all specific laws and requirements. Local, state, and federal codes should always be consulted to stay abreast of changes in legislation, and to ensure all requirements are adequately met by the project.

# DIAGNOSTIC ASSESSMENT

*What federal and state permits are required for the project?*

A number of federal environmental policies require review and approval of most large-scale projects, and most projects impacting critical resources, such as endangered species habitat or wetlands. Many states have adopted further regulations, modeled after federal policies, that place further restrictions and additional review processes for projects impacting resources of significant regional concern. These permits significantly increase the time and resources devoted to project review and approval.

*What are the applicable local regulations that require official review and approval?*

Most local communities have adopted zoning, subdivision, and other regulations that control the type of uses, densities and design standards of development projects. In addition to this review and approval, construction permits are required for most projects.

# FEDERAL AND STATE REGULATIONS

## Environmental Impact Analysis

The National Environmental Policy Act (NEPA) requires the preparation of an environmental impact statement (EIS) to assess the impact of a major federal action on the quality of the environment. The EIS's discussion of environmental impacts forms the scientific and analytic basis for the comparisons of alternatives by decision makers, which are the heart of the EIS process. NEPA applies only to projects and programs entirely or partly financed, assisted, conducted, regulated or approved by federal agencies.

### Determination of Significance

Actions triggering an EIS are defined by statute or determined to be significant by agency officials. While the determination of significance is discretionary, the Council on Environmental Quality (CEQ) provides guidelines that stress analysis of context and intensity. The regulatory definition of context provides that the significance of an action must be analyzed in several contexts such as society as a whole (human, national), the affected region, the affected interests, and the locality. Significance varies with the setting of the proposed action. Intensity is defined as the severity of impact from the proposal. Table 21.1 outlines considerations in evaluating intensity, as defined by CEQ.

### TABLE 21.1. Considerations for evaluating intensity of environmental impacts.

1. Impacts that may be both beneficial and adverse. A significant effect may exist even if the Federal agency believes that on balance the effect will be beneficial.

2. The degree to which the proposed action affects public health or safety.

3. Unique characteristics of the geographic area such as proximity to historic or cultural resources, park lands, prime farmlands, wetlands, wild and scenic rivers, or ecologically critical areas.

4. The degree to which the effects on the quality of the human environment are likely to be highly controversial.

5. The degree to which the possible effects on the human environment are highly uncertain or involve unique or unknown risks.

6. The degree to which the action may establish a precedent for future actions with significant effects or represents a decision in principle about a future consideration.

7. Whether the action is related to other actions with individually insignificant but cumulatively significant impacts. Significance exists if it is reasonable to anticipate a cumulatively significant impact on the environment. Significance cannot be avoided by terming an action temporary or by breaking it down into small component parts.

8. The degree to which the action may adversely affect districts, sites, highways, structures, or objects listed in or eligible for listing in the National Register of Historic Places or may cause loss or destruction of significant scientific, cultural, or historical resources.

9. The degree to which the action may adversely affect an endangered or threatened species or its habitat that has been determined to be critical under the Endangered Species Act of 1973.

10. Whether the action threatens a violation of Federal, State, or local law or requirements imposed for the protection of the environment.

Source: Adapted from *Council on Environmental Quality,* Regulations for Implementing NEPA.

ADMINISTRATION

## Analysis of Impacts

Although NEPA primarily focuses on environmental planning, the statute includes several provisions that encourage agencies to consider the social, economic, cultural and historic impacts of their actions, as well as the environmental and human health impacts. Table 21.2 lists impacts that must be considered in the analysis. The discussion must include both direct and indirect effects of a proposed project. The requisite level of detail for an EIS depends on the nature and scope of the proposed action. The discussion of environmental effects of alternatives need not be exhaustive. What is required is information sufficient to permit a reasoned choice of alternatives as far as environmental aspects are concerned.

### TABLE 21.2. Impacts to be considered in preparation of an environmental impact statement (EIS).

* Ecological (such as the effects on natural resources and on the components, structures, and functioning of affected ecosystems)
* Aesthetic
* Historic
* Cultural
* Economic
* Social
* Health

Note: Impacts should be considered, whether direct, indirect, or cumulative. Effects may also include those resulting from actions that may have both beneficial and detrimental effects, even if on balance the agency believes that the effect will be beneficial.

Source: Adapted from *Council on Environmental Quality, Regulations for Implementing NEPA.*

### Structure of Process

The Development of an EIS consists of three major stages: 1) scoping, 2) preparation of draft EIS, and 3) preparation of final EIS. The scoping process determines issues to be addressed and identifies the significant issues related to a proposed action. The agency must publish a notice of intent to prepare an EIS and solicit input from the public regarding the scope of the issues and alternatives to be considered. Table 21.3 lists key components of the scoping process.

After an agency completes the scoping process for an EIS, the agency prepares a draft EIS in accordance with the scope that was developed through the scoping process. The intent of the draft is to solicit feedback from appropriate federal, state and local agencies, as well as other interested parties. CEQ guidelines require an interdisciplinary approach to authoring an EIS, which insure the integrated use of the natural and social sciences, as well as the environmental design arts, in addressing the impacts outlined in Table 21.2. Reports are encouraged to be less the 150 pages in most circumstances and for proposals of unusual scope or complexity shall normally be less than 300 pages. Table 21.4 lists the EIS format recommended by CEQ.

After the close of the comment period on a draft EIS, the authoring agency will evaluate comments and prepare a final EIS. The agency shall discuss at appropriate points in the final statement any responsible opposing view that was not adequately discussed in the draft statement and shall indicate the agency's response to the issues raised.

### TABLE 21.3. Key components of EIS scoping process.

**AS PART OF THE SCOPING PROCESS THE LEAD AGENCY SHALL:**

1. Invite the participation of affected Federal, State, and local agencies, any affected Indian tribe, the proponent of the action, and other interested persons (including those who might not be in accord with the action on environmental grounds).

2. Determine the scope and the significant issues to be analyzed in depth in the environmental impact statement.

3. Identify and eliminate from detailed study the issues which are not significant or which have been covered by prior environmental review, narrowing the discussion of these issues in the statement to a brief presentation of why they will not have a significant effect on the human environment or providing a reference to their coverage elsewhere.

4. Allocate assignments for preparation of the environmental impact statement among the lead and cooperating agencies, with the lead agency retaining responsibility for the statement.

5. Indicate any public environmental assessments and other environmental impact statements which are being or will be prepared that are related to but are not part of the scope of the impact statement under consideration.

6. Identify other environmental review and consultation requirements so the lead and cooperating agencies may prepare other required analyses and studies concurrently with, and integrated with, the environmental impact statement.

7. Indicate the relationship between the timing of the preparation of environmental analyses and the agency's tentative planning and decision-making schedule.

**AS PART OF THE SCOPING PROCESS
THE LEAD AGENCY MAY ALSO:**

8. Set page limits on environmental documents.

9. Set time limits.

10. Adopt procedures to combine its environmental assessment process with its scoping process.

11. Hold an early scoping meeting or meetings, which may be integrated with any other early planning meeting the agency has. Such a scoping meeting will often be appropriate when the impacts of a particular action are confined to specific sites.

Source: Adapted from Council on Environmental Quality, *Regulations for Implementing NEPA.*

ADMINISTRATION

**TABLE 21.4. Recommended report format for EIS.**

The following standard format for environmental impact statements should be followed unless the agency determines that there is a compelling reason to do otherwise:
  (a) Cover sheet.
  (b) Summary.
  (c) Table of contents.
  (d) Purpose of and need for action.
  (e) Alternatives including proposed action.
  (f) Affected environment.
  (g) Environmental consequences.
  (h) List of preparers.
  (i) List of agencies, organizations, and persons to whom copies of the statement are sent.
  (j) Index.
  (k) Appendices (if any).

Source: *Adapted from Council on Environmental Quality, Regulations for Implementing NEPA.*

## SEPAs

As a result of NEPA, a number of states adopted state environmental policy acts (SEPAs) to evaluate impacts of development for projects requiring state and/or local governmental action. While statutes vary from state to state, many are modeled after NEPA regulations, and require the preparation of an environmental impact report (EIR) for projects that exceed established thresholds related to size, scope, or significance of impact. SEPA regulations typically affect many large projects that are exempt from NEPA regulations because they do not require federal involvement.

## Water Resource Protection

The Clean Water Act and other federal policies require permits for altering or impacting water bodies, wetlands, and water quality resulting from stormwater runoff. These include:

**SECTION 404 PERMIT** — requires a project involving the discharge of dredged or fill material into waters of the United States (including federally defined wetlands) to obtain a permit from the Army Corps of Engineers. The permit may be a programmatic general permit, an individual permit or an official letter of permission. Many states have adopted similar regulations requiring state-issued permits for activities affecting wetlands and water bodies.

**SECTION 10 PERMIT** — requires a federal permit from the Army Corps of Engineers for dredging, filling or obstruction of navigable waters. The application for the Section 10 Permit is often submitted in conjunction with an application for a Section 404 Permit.

**EPA STORMWATER NOTICES OF INTENT AND/OR NPDES PERMITS** — required for stormwater discharges associated with certain industrial activities. Industrial activity was recently redefined to include construction activity including clearing, grading, and excavation activities except operations that result in the disturbance of less than five acres of total land area, which are not part of a larger common plan of development or sale. Many states or local communities have approved NPDES General Permits for stormwater systems that provide coverage for construction projects. The project owner and operator is required to file a Notice of Intent (NOI) and pollution abatement plan with the Environmental Protection Agency to be included under the NPDES general permit.

## Flood Protection

National Flood Insurance Act and Disaster Protection Act Certification prohibits banks from issuing loans secured by improved real estate located in an area having flood hazards, and in which flood insurance is available, unless the building securing the loan is covered by flood insurance. For insurance purposes, special flood hazards are defined as 100-year flood plains. This usually requires review and certification of building plans by the lender. Flood Insurance Rate Maps (FIRMs) are published by FEMA and delineate flood hazards for local communities.

## Historic Preservation

National Historic Preservation Act Section 106 requires that certain federally assisted, permitted and licensed activities that might have an adverse effect on properties listed with, or eligible for listing with, the national Register of Historic Places be reviewed concerning that effect and its consequences. Many states and local communities have adopted similar legislation.


# LOCAL REGULATIONS

## Zoning Regulations

Most local communities in the United States have established zoning regulations as the basic means of land use control. Zoning divides the community into districts and specifies allowable uses within each, as well as the intensity of such uses, and the size and arrangement of building, parking, and other structures on the landscape, including height, setback, and total lot coverage. In addition, aesthetic controls, historic preservation, and landscape regulations are often included within the zoning ordinance. While zoning regulations vary widely across the country, they typically consist of a zoning map that delineates the boundaries of each district within the community, and an ordinance document that outlines the regulations for each district.

### Rezoning

New development often requires the rezoning of land to change allowable uses, densities, or design standards on a given site. Figure 21.1 outlines

ADMINISTRATION

the typical process for rezoning requests. Zoning ordinances may or may not specifically identify the criteria for review and approval of a rezoning request, and these criteria may vary widely. Typically, they include consistency with the community's long-range plan, the ability to provide adequate and cost-effective public services and utilities to the proposed project, and the potential for adverse impacts on adjacent properties, including property values.

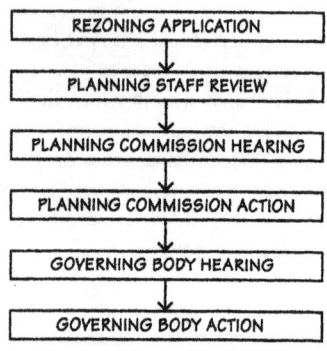

**Figure 21.1. Typical approval process for rezoning requests.**

## Variances

Zoning variances allow for departure from the standard rules outlined in the zoning ordinance. Variances are intended to alleviate "unnecessary hardship," typically associated with the physical characteristics of the land (e.g. unusual lot shape, the presence of flood plains or other hazards in existing lots). Most variances that are granted are for minor exceptions to setbacks or other design standards in existing neighborhoods, such as expansion of patios, decks, or carports, where adverse impacts on neighboring properties are minimal. Variances typically require public hearings, and input from adjacent property owners is often a vital factor in granting or denying such minor variances. Variances in allowable uses are rarely granted, as physical characteristics of a site do not typically represent a use hardship. Rezoning requests are a more common approach to resolving proposals for different uses.

## Subdivision Regulations

Subdivision regulations dictate the division of larger (usually undeveloped) parcels into individual building lots. These regulations typically deal with all aspects of subdivision design, including lot size and shape (consistent with the zoning ordinance), utility extensions, street width and layout. Construction standards are often included in the regulations, as well as parks and open space dedication requirements. Figure 21.2 outlines the typical process for subdivision review and approval. Rezoning requests generally

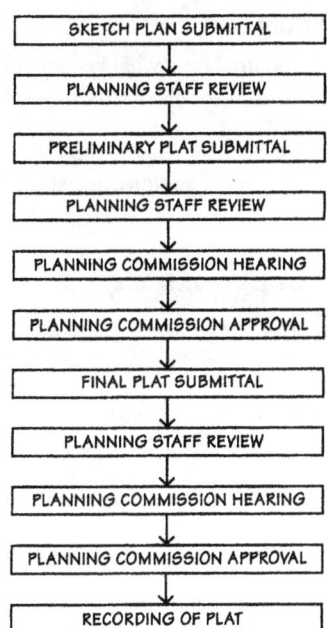

```
┌─────────────────────────────┐
│    SKETCH PLAN SUBMITTAL     │
└─────────────────────────────┘
              ↓
┌─────────────────────────────┐
│    PLANNING STAFF REVIEW     │
└─────────────────────────────┘
              ↓
┌─────────────────────────────┐
│  PRELIMINARY PLAT SUBMITTAL  │
└─────────────────────────────┘
              ↓
┌─────────────────────────────┐
│    PLANNING STAFF REVIEW     │
└─────────────────────────────┘
              ↓
┌─────────────────────────────┐
│ PLANNING COMMISSION HEARING  │
└─────────────────────────────┘
              ↓
┌─────────────────────────────┐
│ PLANNING COMMISSION APPROVAL │
└─────────────────────────────┘
              ↓
┌─────────────────────────────┐
│     FINAL PLAT SUBMITTAL     │
└─────────────────────────────┘
              ↓
┌─────────────────────────────┐
│    PLANNING STAFF REVIEW     │
└─────────────────────────────┘
              ↓
┌─────────────────────────────┐
│ PLANNING COMMISSION HEARING  │
└─────────────────────────────┘
              ↓
┌─────────────────────────────┐
│ PLANNING COMMISSION APPROVAL │
└─────────────────────────────┘
              ↓
┌─────────────────────────────┐
│      RECORDING OF PLAT       │
└─────────────────────────────┘
```

**Figure 21.2. Typical approval process for subdivision requests.**

precede subdivision applications due to the significant expense of site planning, and the potential for controversy in rezoning requests.

## Planned Unit Development Regulations

A planned unit development (PUD) allows for the mixture of residential, commercial, industrial, and institutional uses not typically provided by traditional zoning regulations. PUDs also permit more creative and environmentally responsive design, through flexible design standards. These regulations effectively combine rezoning and subdivision approval processes, often resulting in a more thoughtful design solution. However, PUD proposals may result in longer review and approval times, as the use, density and design standards are not clearly spelled out within regulations and are subject to discretionary approval.

## Aesthetic Controls and Historic Preservation Regulations

Many jurisdictions have established aesthetic controls or historic preservation regulations to preserve and protect the integrity of key neighborhoods or districts within the community. Specific standards vary widely, but typically involve some form of design review by an appointed board to ensure aesthetic quality or historical consistency. These additional controls are typically specified within the local zoning ordinance.

ADMINISTRATION

## Construction Permits

Permits are usually required for a wide variety of construction activities, including clearing, grading, erosion control, structures, utilities, and many site improvements such as patios, decks, fences, retaining walls and water features. Inspection of activities is usually required. Local regulations vary widely with regard to permit exemptions, and should always be consulted.

# SUGGESTED REFERENCES

Council on Environmental Quality, *Regulations for Implementing NEPA*.

Dewberry and Davis, *Land Development Handbook*, McGraw-Hill, New York, 1996.

So, Frank S. and Judith Getzels, *The Practice of Local Government Planning*, ICMA, Washington D.C., 1988.

# Cost Estimating

22

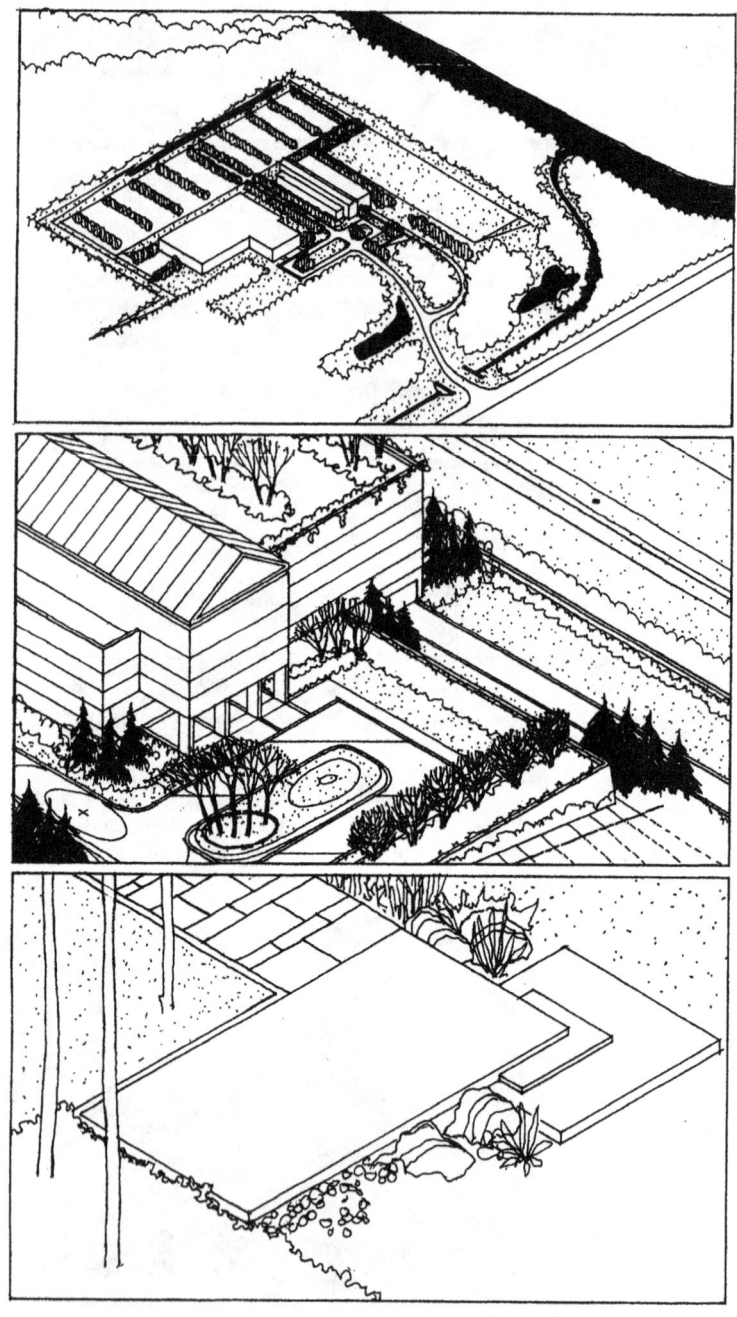

## LARGE SCALE SITE DEVELOPMENT COSTS

Large scale site development often requires heavy duty construction methods and may benefit from large scale economies. As square unit prices decrease due to large areas and volumes, financing costs may increase due to time factors. Critical path planning is essential to maintain financial feasibility. A large portion of the budget is devoted to infrastructure installation. Development is most often phased into intermediate development projects to control both time and design finish quality.

## MEDIUM SCALE SITE DEVELOPMENT COSTS

Medium scale development typically employs more conventional construction methods, and financing periods are less protracted. Unit prices are slightly higher than large scale construction prices, but quantities tend to be smaller. Development typically must conform to local regulations, and often ties into existing infrastructure.

## SMALL SCALE SITE DEVELOPMENT COSTS

Small scale development costs are often governed by custom fabrications and less standard design details. Unit costs tend to be higher due to small quantities of materials employed. Spatially restricted sites may require small equipment and extensive hand labor to execute the work. Such restrictions may also require less than ideal construction sequencing.

ADMINISTRATION

E STIMATING THE COST OF proposed site development projects requires extensive field knowledge and accurate historical records of development costs within the region and the local market. Most design firms rely on experience with similar recent projects to guide cost estimating, and many also subscribe to national and regional cost data base publications to maintain currency with labor and square unit costs. The ultimate cost of any site construction is a reflection of the cost of materials, labor, machine and equipment time, plus the contractor's profit and overhead required to install the design as specified.

## DIAGNOSTIC ASSESSMENT

*What is the type and scale of the proposed construction project?*

The project type refers to the land use typology as well as to the specific array of program elements, such as heavy duty site road, large parking lots, large open athletic fields, clustered buildings and botanical plantings associated with a college or research park. The scale of the project refers to the scope of work and the size of the landscape intervention. These two elements imply the potential human experience of the proposed plan and the type of construction required to build it.

*What are the components of a typical cost estimate for site development?*

The cost estimate typically follows the sections of the CSI (Construction Specifications Institute) MASTERFORMAT. The proposed work is broken down into materials and their quantities, methods of installation, required labor and machinery, profit and business overhead, and all additional charges required to execute the general requirements of the contract.

*What methods of quantity take-off are appropriate for various types of projects?*

Unit cost methods of estimating require the most detailed itemized accounting of volumes of materials, number of fabricated elements, and precise methods of execution as required by the specifications. "Square unit" estimates and "system estimates," require linear and area take-off, volumes within categorical operations such as cut and fill, and enumeration of individual elements such as trees, shrubs, light fixtures, etc.

*What are reliable sources for unit cost data to establish a preliminary cost estimate?*

An established professional design office typically keeps records of past projects and maintains familiarity with local prices and contracting protocols, which may be specific to the region or local culture. Additionally, national and regional cost data books are published annually, and are based on a broad array of recently built projects and trends in labor and material prices. These published works often factor in externalities, which may be missing from purely locally derived cost case studies.

# PROJECT SCALE AND COSTS

Large projects clearly benefit from scale economies not available in medium and small scale development. For example, the cost per square meter of sod for a 100 m² (1,000 ft²) installation may be up to 30% greater than the cost for a 1000 m² (10,000 ft²) installation. Most of the cost difference is attributable to lower material prices for bulk orders (gross amounts) and larger machines used for site preparation and for actually placing the sod (large rolls placed by machine rather than by hand labor). However, the cost of the mechanization is high per day and requires careful planning and supervision to avoid costly down time, which in extreme cases could eliminate the scale economy benefit. Conversely, using large machines on a small scale project may be ill-advised due to the initial mobilization cost required merely to transport the machine to the project site. In certain instances, concentrated use of hand labor may be far more economical.

# PROJECT TYPE AND COSTS

Square unit costs may vary widely from one project to the next even though they are of the same type. Figure 22.1 illustrates the relationship of design complexity and degree of finish to the square unit combined site cost required to construct the project. Sections (a), (b), and (c) illustrate different design alternatives for the proposed office building. Each alternative indicates different degrees of finish and material choices. This variation relates to the scope of the project (See Chapter 9: Construction Operations). Figure 22.1 illustrates the dangers of using a single project case study to determine comparable costs for a similar proposed design. The scope and degree of finish must also be comparable. For example, the documented cost per car stall in a parking structure may range from a low of $9,000 to a high of $15,000. It is important to understand the mean value for preliminary planning.

# COST ESTIMATE COMPONENTS

Accurate cost estimates of site construction projects begin with accurate construction documents which are fully dimensioned, detailed, specified,

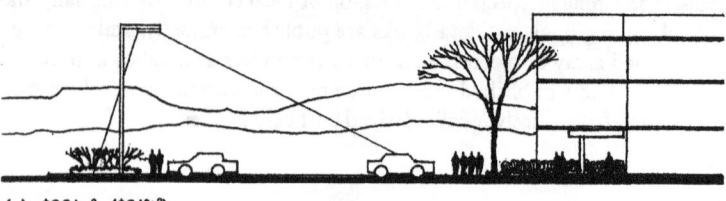

(a) $20/m^2$ ($2/ft^2$)

(b) $60/m^2$ ($6/ft^2$)

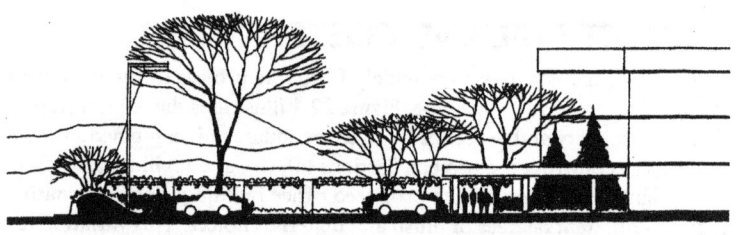

(c) $150/m^2$ ($15/ft^2$)

**Figure 22.1. Illustration of square unit cost differentials for three versions of the same commercial office project. (a) at $20/m² ($2/ft²); (b) at $60/m² ($6/ft²); and (c) at $150/m²($15/ft²). Finishes and design details influence the final cost.**

and based upon accurate and complete existing conditions surveys (See Chapter 9: Construction Operations). The components of a cost estimate are described as follows:

## Material Costs

Material costs represent the sum total required to purchase and deliver the material to the site. It does not include installation. If long delays occur during the design or bidding process, the effects of inflation must be added.

## Labor Costs

Labor costs are derived from regional or local hourly wage rates, and are indicated by trade. Productivity data is used to determine the average output for a particular task and is measured in units installed, or work accomplished per hour.

## Equipment Crew Costs

Productivity data may refer to the crew size required per unit per hour or day. For example, a crew may have the capacity to install 137 m (450 ft) of 150 mm x 450 mm (6 in x18 in) granite curbing per day. That productivity rate is based on a crew of four laborers, one foreman, two equipment operators (operator plus an oiler), and one 2.7 metric ton Gradall. The total daily cost without overhead and profit (O&P) is $1,827.70, which equals a rate of $87.75 per hour. This rate combines the equipment cost per day with the crew rate per day.

## Equipment Costs

Equipment costs refer to the total costs of using the equipment on the site per day. Charges include rental, fuel, oil, and routine maintenance costs. A general rule of thumb is that weekly rental is 3 times daily rental, and that monthly rental is 3 times weekly rental.

## General Requirements Costs

General Requirements cost items refer to the fees charged by various contractors associated with the construction work, and includes architects, engineers, installers, and prime contractors. Charges are typically taken as a percentage of the total cost plus O&P (overhead and profit). For example, an architect's fee may range from 5% to 16%, depending on magnitude of the total cost and other factors. Subcontractors typically charge 10% on average.

## Overhead and Profit

The total cost of any operation equals the sum total of bare material costs, plus profit, the base labor cost plus overhead and profit, and the bare equipment cost plus profit. Labor overhead includes the typical payroll

**TABLE 22.1. Total project item cost calculation model**

| | | | | |
|---|---|---|---|---|
| Bare Material Cost | = | $18.00 | | |
| + 10% Profit | + | $1.80 | = | $19.80 |
| Labor for Crew A = | | | | |
| Labor Hour Cost | = | $40.00 | | |
| × Labor Hours Required | × | 1.5 | = | $60.00* |
| Bare Equipment Cost | | $1.00 | | |
| + 10% Profit | = + | $0.10 | = | $1.10 |
| *Total Cost (Rounded)* | | | = | *$81.00* |

*Labor cost includes overhead and profit (O&P).

burden and all associated business costs and profit. Table 22.1 illustrates a model for calculating an item cost, including overhead and profit.

## Additional Cost Factors

As previously stated, cost factors for the same type of development can vary significantly from place to place and from time to time. The following represents additional factors that affect costs.

- *Design quality:* Variations in material quality and craftsmanship need to be accounted for in cost estimating. Less expensive work may not result in the intended aesthetic or functional results.
- *Overtime:* Contingencies involving delays due to weather, or supply problems may require overtime charges. Shifting of personnel from one task to another in order to achieve a critical path deadline may also incur overtime charges.
- *Productivity:* Most productivity data assumes ideal conditions (output during an eight hour day). Extremely hot or cold temperatures, or excessive precipitation may drastically alter standard productivity expectations. Standards may vary regionally and culturally.
- *Project scale:* Large, medium, and small scale construction operations are significantly different in scope and procedure (See Chapter 9: Construction Operations). Unit costs are significantly higher in small scale construction.
- *Location:* Remote locations may have lower labor costs but transportation costs for hauling materials may be higher than normal. These two factors need to be studied.
- *Unpredictable factors:* Factors such as weather, shifts in the business cycle, or requirements to substitute materials or procedures, may account for unanticipated cost shifts. Understanding the economic and political externalities is important in estimating for large projects.
- *Contingencies:* If construction documents are not complete, or if a preliminary cost estimate is required for general budget purposes, a

5% to 10% contingency allowance is commonly added. As stated earlier, inflation must be factored for projects of long duration.

## Quantity Take-off Methods

Quantity take-off begins with complete drawings drawn to scale. Each drawing indicates the type of work to be done and specifies dimensions and references plan elements to construction details and specific materials. The specifications describe the materials and their properties, attributes, and performance requirements. The plans are used to determine the lengths, square areas, and volumes of all proposed elements. They also identify the number and location of items to be installed, such as trees, shrubs, lights, fences, benches, flagpoles, etc. Construction contractors separate each item as a quantity, which must be furnished and installed. For example, a 100 m² park plaza is converted into a sequential construction operation employing material, equipment, and labor. Quantities represent material costs and labor operations represent payroll costs. All construction categories may be analyzed in this manner, including planting, earthwork, site improvements, and others. These raw costs are added to overhead and profit calculations to arrive at the final price. The plaza may be itemized as follows:

## Park Plaza Take-off

- Clear and strip 110 m² (1,076 ft²) [100 m² + edge extension]. Clear light brush and haul and stockpile 18 m³ (24 yd³) [110 m² x 150 mm = 16.5 m³ + 11% swell)].
- Cut 300 mm (12 in) and haul 37 m³ (48 yd³) [33 m³ + 11% swell = 37 m³].
- Prepare subgrade, 110 m² (1,180 ft²) with 3 passes of vibrating roller.
- Place and compact 250 mm (10 in) of graded aggregate base in two lifts [27.5 m³ + 10% swell = 30 m³ delivered (40 yd³)].
- Install 45 m (148 ft) of aluminum edge restraint with spikes as per specifications.
- Place and vibrate with 2 passes, 25 mm (1 in) of silica sand. Haul 28 m³ of sand from stockpile [25 m³ + 10% swell = 28 m³ (37 yd³)].
- Install, dry grout, and sweep 4900 concrete pavers, [100 m² (1,076 ft²) @ 49 pavers / m² (4.5 / ft²)].

# PRICING

## Plaza Unit Price Cost Calculation

Unit pricing requires broad field experience and results in the most accurate, but time consuming method of cost estimating. Each quantity or item is assigned a time estimate, which is then multiplied by a labor and machine rate to arrive at a raw figure. Overhead and profit, plus all other charges incurred in the general contract are added to create the bid price. This method is used in competitive bidding circumstances. In the quantity take-off described above, the accumulated charges for materials, labor, overhead and profit, and contract administration would equal $6,461.00 in current U.S. dollars in a particular region. This figure would be the bid price based on a unit price bid.

## Square Meter Cost Estimate

If the total plaza cost is calculated to be $6,461.00, then the square meter price for the 100 $m^2$ plaza is $64.61 (rounded up to $65.00). Unit prices are layered composites of discrete operations. For example, the cost of clearing and stripping this modest area may be calculated at $1.60 per square meter ($0.16 per sq ft). The cost of each operation is converted to a series of square meter costs and the layers are added up to achieve the square meter unit price of $65.00 ($6.50 per sq ft). Cost data base publishers compile national and regional costs for all items in the CSI MASTERFORMAT (Construction Specifications Institute). Such data sources are published annually and may be subscribed to online or in book formats.

## Systems Estimates

Systems estimating groups together discrete operations to create an assembly of processes or parts, which may be added to other parts to create a finished estimate. For example, the plaza construction requires that the subgrade must be fine graded, and prepared to receive aggregate by a vibrating roller, and that 300 mm (12 in) of aggregate must be trucked to the site, dumped, spread in two lifts, and vibrated with a heavy roller. This subgrade preparation and aggregate base preparation may be considered as one type of "system" common to all subbase construction. The variables are type of subgrade preparation (equipment and number of passes), the type and depth of aggregate, and number of lifts to be used. A deciduous tree pit is another example of a system or assembly of materials and processes, which may be generalized by soil type, tree size and type. Many cost data publications create standard assemblies of common site elements.

## Material Lifecycle Cost Estimates

Lifecycle costs are a function of the durability of materials, their embodied energy costs, the cost of annual maintenance and repair, the replacement value in discounted currency, and the recycling potential of the materials or products. Additionally, high initial cost must be amortized to distribute the costs over a longer time period to justify the investment. Similarly, materials or assemblies with high embodied energy values must also be long lasting or easily recyclable to justify both energy investment and initial cost (See Chapter 5: Conservation Standards for embodied energy data).

Figure 22.2 diagrams the life-cycle of basic building materials with the aim of illustrating the flow of energy and wastes and how recycling of certain materials reduces the energy demand for new materials by exploiting previously expended embodied energy.

Life-cycle checklist for construction materials

1. Raw material acquisition (mining, harvesting, extraction): Is the resource renewable or sustainable; is the energy required sustainable; and what percent of the waste produced is renewable?
2. Raw material processing and manufacturing: In addition to the above, what toxicity to air, water, or soils is produced by processing?
3. Product packaging: Is packaging recyclable, or does the packaging contain substances harmful to the environment?
4. Product distribution: Is distribution local; and what type and amount of energy is required to transport the material?
5. Installation, use, and maintenance: What energy is required to install and maintain the product; what is its rate of degradation; and is there toxicity associated with installation, use, or maintenance?
6. Final disposal, recycling, and re-use: Is product recyclable or reusable; what energy is consumed during recycling or disposal; and what environmental toxicity results from disposal?

Key characteristics for comparing one material to another are:

1. Regional availability-local extraction/manufacture.
2. Recyclability (how many times the material can be recycled and retain integrity).
3. Reusability.
4. Durability and life span.
5. Toxicity of the product or of the materials used to maintain the product during its life.
6. Efficiency of product's performance as a design component.
7. Savings on other materials not used because this product is used.
8. Savings in energy not consumed over the life span of the installation because this product is used.
9. Any combination of these factors.

Deferred maintenance is another often overlooked cost factor. The cost of replacing a failed design element in the future (5-10 years), may exceed the accrued annual deferred maintenance expenditures by a factor of 10 in the extreme case, and by a factor of 3-4 in the typical case. Deferred maintenance is a false economy in most circumstances.

## Cost Data Sources

A number of national and regional cost data services provide a broad array of prices for standard items found in site construction. R. S. Means Company, Inc., publishes a substantial number of square unit cost data books as well as numerous well illustrated reference books on aspects of cost estimating relevant to both medium to large scale heavy site construction.

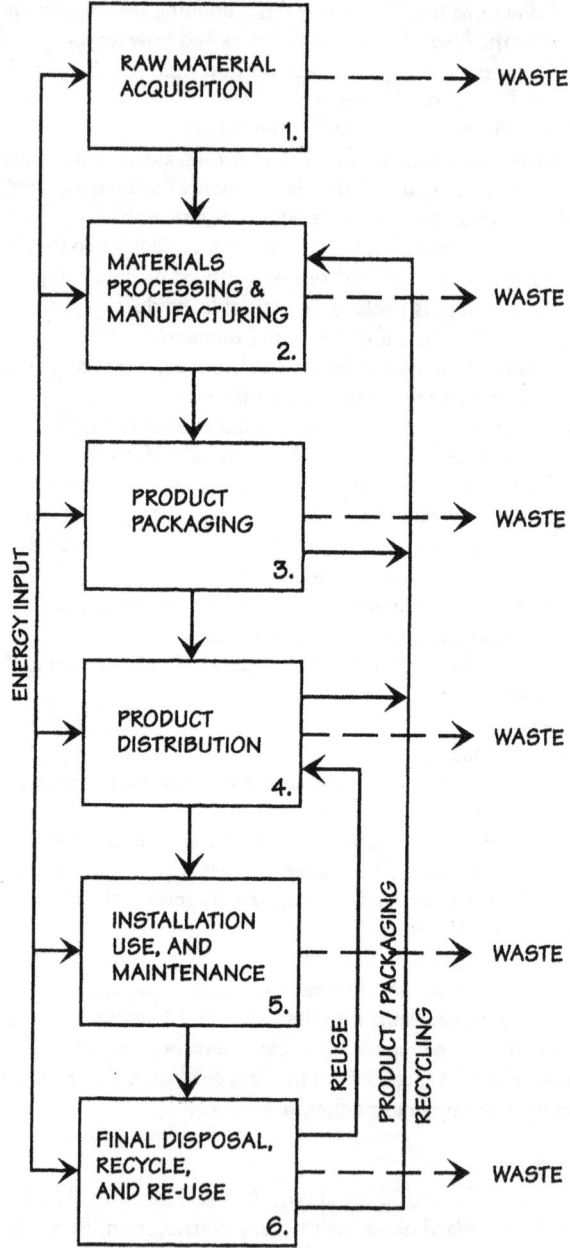

**Figure 22.2. Construction material life-cycle chart.**

Material is updated annually. The W. F. Dodge Company produces significant cost source data for institutional and large scale architecture and related site work.

## SUGGESTED REFERENCES

Dewberry, Sidney O., (Editor), *Land Development Handbook*, McGraw-Hill Book Co., New York, 1996.

Fee, Sylvia Hollman, *Means Landscape Estimating, 3nd Edition*, R. S. Means Co., Inc., Kingston, MA, 1999.

Means, R. S., Company, *Means Building Construction Cost Data:* Metric Edition, R. S. Means Company, Inc., Kingston, MA, 2000.

Means, R. S., Company, *Means Site Work and Landscape Cost Data, 19th Annual Edition*, R. S. Means Company, Inc., Kingston, MA, 2000.

Harris, Charles W. and Nicholas T. Dines, *Time-Saver Standards for Landscape Architecture, 2nd Edition*, McGraw-Hill, New York, 1998.

ADMINISTRATION

# Metric Conversion Guidelines

# RULES FOR WRITING
# METRIC SYMBOLS AND NAMES

- Print unit symbols in upright type and in lower case except for liter (L) or unless the unit name is derived from a proper name.
- Print unit names in lower case, even those derived from a proper name.
- Print decimal prefixes in lower case for magnitudes $10^3$ and lower (that is, k, $\mu$, m, and n) and print the prefixes in upper case for magnitudes $10^6$ and higher (that is, M and G).
- Leave a space between a numeral and a symbol (e.g. 45 kg not 45kg).
- Do not use a degree mark (°) with Kelvin temperature (k).
- Do not leave a space between a unit symbol and its decimal prefix (e.g. kg, not k g).
- Do not use the plural of unit symbols (e.g. 45 kg, not 45 kgs), but do use the plural of written unit names (e.g. several kilograms).
- For technical writing, use symbols in conjunction with numerals (the area is 10 m2); write out unit names if numerals are not used (carpet is measured in square meters). Numerals may be combined with written unit names in non-technical writing (10 meters).
- Indicate the product of two or more units in symbolic form by using a dot positioned above the line (kg·m·s2).
- Do not mix names and symbols (write N·m or newton meter, not N·meter).
- Do not use a period after a symbol except when it occurs at the end of a sentence (e.g. 12 g, not 12g.).
- Always use decimals, not fractions (e.g. 0.75 g, not ¾ g).
- Use a zero before the value marker for values less than one.
- Use spaces instead of commas to separate blocks of three digits for any number over four digits (e.g. 45 138 kg or 0.004 46 kg, or 4371 kg).
- In the United States, the decimal marker is a period; in other countries, a comma is typically used.

# CONVERSION AND ROUNDING

In a "soft" conversion, an exact U.S. unit measurement is converted to its exact (or near exact) metric equivalent. In a "hard" conversion, a new rounded, rationalized metric number is created that is convenient to work with and remember.

- Wherever possible, convert measurements to rounded, rationalized "hard" metric numbers. For instance, if anchor bolts are to be imbedded to a depth of 10 inches, the exact converted length of 254 mm might be rounded to either 250 mm (9.84 inches) or 260 mm (10.24 inches). The less critical the number, the "rounder" it can be, but ensure that allowable tolerances or safety factors are not exceeded. When in doubt, stick with the exact "soft" conversion.
- When converting numbers from U.S. units to metric, round the metric value to the same number of digits. In all cases, use professional rounding to determine the exact value.
- Round to "preferred" metric numbers. While the preferred numbers for the "1 foot 12 inches" system are, in order of preference, those divisible by 12, 6, 4, 3, 2 and 1, preferred metric numbers are, in order of preference, those divisible by 10, 5, 2 and 1 or decimal multiples thereof.

## SPECIFICATIONS

Metric specifications should use "mm" for almost all measurements. The use of mm is consistent with the dimensions specified in major codes. Meters should be used only where large, round metric sizes are specified. Centimeters should not be used in specifications.

## DRAWINGS

- Use only one unit of measure on a drawing. Except for large scale site or cartographic drawings, the unit should be the millimeter (mm).
- Delete unit symbols but provide an explanatory note ("All dimensions are shown in millimeters" or "All dimensions are shown in meters"). Whole numbers always indicate millimeters; decimal numbers taken to three places always indicate meters.
- Where modules are used, the recommended basic module is 100 mm, which is similar to the 4-inch module used in building construction (4 inches = 101.6 mm).

# DRAWING SCALES

All scales are expressed as non-dimensional ratios.

## Comparison of drawing scales.

| Inch-Foot Scales | Inch-Foot Ratio | Metric Scale |
|---|---|---|
| Full Size | 1:1 | 1:1 |
| Half Size | 1:2 | 1:2* |
| 4" = 1'0" | 1:3 | |
| 3" = 1'0" | 1:4 | 1:5 |
| 2" = 1'0" | 1:6 | |
| 1½" = 1'0" | 1:8 | 1:10 |
| 1" = 1'0" | 1:12 | |
| ¾" = 1'0" | 1:16 | 1:20 |
| ½" = 1'0" | 1:24 | 1:25* |
| ¼" = 1'0" | 1:48 | 1:50 |
| 1" = 5'0" | 1:60 | |
| ⅛" = 1'0" | 1:96 | 1:100 |
| 1" = 10'0" | 1:120 | |
| ¹⁄₁₆" = 1'0" | 1:192 | 1:200 |
| 1" = 20'0" | 1:240 | 1:250* |
| 1" = 30'0" | 1:360 | |
| ¹⁄₃₂" = 1'0" | 1:384 | |
| 1" = 40'0" | 1:480 | 1:500 |
| 1" = 50'0" | 1:600 | |
| 1" = 60'0" | 1:720 | |
| 1" = 80'0" | 1:960 | 1:1000 |

* Limited use as metric scales.

# DRAWING SIZES

The ISO "A" series drawing sizes are preferred metric sizes for design drawings. There are five "A' series sizes:

A0 is the base drawing size with an area of one square meter. Smaller sizes are obtained by halving the long dimension of the previous size. All A0 sizes have a height to width ratio of one to the square root of 2.

| Size | Sheet Size |
| --- | --- |
| A0 | 1189 x 841 mm (46.8 x 33.1 inches) |
| Al | 841 x 594 mm (33.1 x 23.4 inches) |
| A2 | 594 x 420 mm (23.4 x 16.5 inches) |
| A3 | 420 x 297 mm (16.5 x 11.7 inches) |
| A4 | 297 x 210 mm (11.7 x 8.3 inches) |

# RULES FOR MEASUREMENT

## Length

- Use only the meter and millimeter in design and construction.
- Use the kilometer for long distances and the micrometer for precision measurements.
- Avoid use of the centimeter.
- For survey measurement, use the meter and the kilometer.

## Rules for Area

- The square meter is preferred.
- Very large areas may be expressed in square kilometers and very small areas, in square millimeters.
- Use the hectare (10 000 square meters) for land and water measurement only.
- Avoid use of the square centimeter.
- Linear dimensions such as 40 × 90 mm may be used; if so, indicate width first and height second.

## Rules for Volume and Fluid Capacity

- Cubic meter is preferred for volumes in construction and for large storage tanks.
- Use liter (L) and milliliter (mL) for fluid capacity (liquid volume).

## Rules for Angles and Slopes

- Plane angles in surveying (cartography) will continue to be measured in degrees (either decimal degrees or degrees, minutes, and seconds) rather than the metric radian.

- Slope is expressed in non-dimensional ratios. The vertical component is shown first and then the horizontal. The units that are compared should be the same (meters to meters, millimeters to millimeters). For slopes less than 45°, the vertical component should be unitary (for example, 1:20). For slopes over 45°, the horizontal component should be unitary (for example, 5:1).

## Rules for Structural Calculations

- There are separate units for mass and force. The kilogram (kg) is the base unit for mass, which is the unit quantity of matter independent of gravity. The newton (N) is the derived unit for force (mass times acceleration, or kg·m/s²). It replaces the unit "kilogram-force" (kgf), which should not be used.
- Do not use the joule to designate torque, which is always designated newton meter (N·m).
- The pascal (Pa) is the unit for pressure and stress (Pa = N/m²) . The term "bar" is not a metric unit and should not be used.
- Structural calculations should be shown in MPa or kPa.

### Conversion factors.

| Quantity | From Inch-Pound Units | To Metric Units | Multiply By: |
|---|---|---|---|
| Length | mile | km | 1.609 344 |
| | yard | m | 0.914 4 |
| | foot | m | 0.304 8 |
| | | mm | 304.8 |
| | inch | mm | 25.4 |
| Area | square mile | km² | 2.590 00 |
| | acre | m² | 4 046.856 |
| | | ha | 0.404 685 6 |
| | square yard | m² | 0.836 127 36 |
| | square foot | m² | 0.092 903 04 |
| | square inch | mm² | 645.16 |
| Volume | acre foot | m³ | 1 233.49 |
| | cubic yard | m³ | 0.764 555 |
| | cubic foot | m³ | 0.028 316 8 |
| | | cm³ | 28 316.85 |
| | | L | 28.316 85 |
| | 100 board feet | m³ | 0.235 974 |
| | gallion | L | 3.785 41 |
| | cubic inch | cm³ | 16.387 064 |
| | | mm³ | 16 387.064 |
| Mass | lb | kg | 0.453 592 |
| | kip (1000 lb) | metric ton | 0.453 592 |
| Mass/unit length | plf | kg/m | 1.488 16 |

# Conversion factors (continued).

| Quantity | From Inch-Pound Units | To Metric Units | Multiply By: |
| --- | --- | --- | --- |
| Mass/unit area | psf | kg/m² | 4.882 43 |
| Mass density | pcf | kg/m³ | 16.018 5 |
| Force | lb | N | 4.448 22 |
| | kip | kN | 4.448 22 |
| Force/unit length | plf | N/m | 14.593 9 |
| | klf | kN/m | 14.593 9 |
| Pressure, stress, | psf | Pa | 47.880 3 |
| modulus of elasticity | ksf | kPa | 47.880 3 |
| | psi | kPa | 6.894 76 |
| | ksi | Mpa | 6.894 76 |
| Bending moment, | ft-lb | N.m | 1.355 82 |
| torque, moment | ft-kip | kN.m | 1.355 82 |
| of force | | | |
| Moment of mass | lb-ft | kg.m | 0.138 255 |
| Moment of inertia | lb-ft² | kg.m² | 0.042 140 1 |
| Second moment of area | in⁴ | mm⁴ | 416 231 |
| Section modulus | in³ | mm³ | 16 387.064 |
| Temperature | °F | K | 5/9(°F-32)+273.15 |
| | | °C | 5/9(°F-32) |
| Energy, work, | kWh | MJ | 3.6 |
| quantity of heat | Btu | J | 1 055.056 |
| | ft-lbf | J | 1.355 82 |
| Power | ton (refrig.) | kW | 3.517 |
| | Btu/s | kW | 1.055 056 |
| | hp (electric) | W | 745.700 |
| | Btu/h | W | 0.293 071 |
| Thermal resistance | ft²-h-°F/Btu | m².K/W | 0.176 110 |
| (R value) | | | |
| Volume rate of flow | ft³/s | m³/s | 1.028 316 8 |
| | cfm | m³/s | 0.000 471 947 4 |
| | | L/s | 0.471 947 4 |
| Velocity, speed | ft/s | m/s | 0.3048 |
| Luminous intensity | cd | cd | 1 (same unit) |
| Luminance | lambert | kcd/m² | 3.183 01 |
| | cd/ft² | cd/m² | 10.763 9 |
| | footlambert | cd/m² | 3.426 26 |
| Luminous flux | lm | lm | 1 (same unit) |
| Illuminance | footcandle | lux | 10.763 9 |

# REFERENCES

The metric units in this appendix are those adopted by the U.S. government (see the Federal Register of December 20, 1990; Federal Standard 376A, *Preferred Metric Units for Use by the Federal Government*; and PB 89-226922, *Metric Handbook for Federal Officials*).

ASTM E 62 1, *Standard Practice for Use of Metric (SI) Units in Design and Construction.*

ANSI/IEEE 268, *American National Standard Metric Practice*

ASTM E 380, *Standard Practice for the Use of the International System of Units (SI).*

American National Metric Council, *Metric Editorial Guide.*

U.S. Metric Association, *Metric Units of Measure and Style Guide.*

# Index

# A

accessibility 31, 40
accessible route 40, 43
advance notice 395
aerial photogrammetry 145
aerobic digesters 114, 116
aesthetic considerations
    brick and concrete block walls 283
    stone walls 289
    wood and metal fences 278
aesthetic controls 409
aggregate base 168, 169, 260, 262, 263, 264, 269, 270
AIA 384, 386, 397
anaerobic digesters 115
APA 384
arterial streets 52
as-built records 394, 396
ASLA 384, 386
athletic facility 261
average walking distance 34
axioms 5, 6-10

# B

backfill 167, 242, 245, 249, 254
backhoe 166
bar charts 387, 392
barrier design 277-278
beams 298, 299-300, 303, 304
bearing capacity 240, 241
benchmarks 141, 143, 148, 153
billing 388, 391
biodiversity 96, 221
bioengineering 220, 229
biomass 85, 86, 96
bioretention ponds 212, 215
boardwalks 295, 296, 297, 303
bonding company 396
bonuses 396
boundary definition 275
boundary survey 141, 144
brownfields 88

bulldozer 163, 164, 165, 166, 168, 169
business development 121, 130-131
business parks 121, 123, 130, 131

# C

cadastral survey 144
camping 77
candlepower 344
cantilevered wall 247, 248, 252-253
cascading waterfalls 318
certificates of payment 394
certifications of compliance 395
cesspools 107, 116
change orders 383, 392, 393, 394
changes, unauthorized 395
channels, stormwater 195, 196, 199, 206, 208
circulation control 275
circulation patterns 123, 124
clay lenses 327
clay soil 167
clean-up 170
clearing and grubbing 163
client 383, 384, 385, 386, 387, 388, 390, 391, 392, 395, 397
climate zones. 89
closeout 384, 395
cluster treatment systems 111
co-ordinates 149, 150
cold 260, 262, 264, 267
collected rainwater 102
collector streets 52
colloidal soil 260, 263, 269
commercial center design 129
communication 4, 5, 10
community commercial 121, 122, 129
community facility standards 132-135
community parks and recreation planning data 63-82
community scale 11, 20, 21

CPSIA information can be obtained
at www.ICGtesting.com
Printed in the USA
FSHW02n0201020818
50992FS

9 780071 344227